MICROECONOMICS
Theory and Applications

EDWIN MANSFIELD

WHARTON SCHOOL
UNIVERSITY OF PENNSYLVANIA

MICROECONOMICS

Theory and Applications

W · W · NORTON & COMPANY · INC ·

NEW YORK

To Dixie

who asked that this dedication
be as short as possible

Contents

Preface   xv

CHAPTER 1 – Introduction to Microeconomics   1

1. Introduction   *2.* Example 1: Optimal Production Deci-
sions   *3.* Example 2: Pricing Policy   *4.* Example 3: Rules
for Optimal Resource Allocation   *5.* Example 4: Public
Policy concerning Market Structure   *6.* Microeconomics:
Problem-Solving and Science   *7.* Human Wants and
Resources   *8.* Technology   *9.* The Tasks Performed by an
Economic System   *10.* Our Mixed Capitalist System
11. The Price System and Microeconomics   *12.* Model-
Building and the Role of Models   *13.* The Evaluation of a
Model   *14.* Summary

CHAPTER 2 – The Tastes and Preferences of the Consumer   20

1. Introduction   *2.* The Nature of the Consumer's Preferences   *3.* Indifference Curves   *4.* Characteristics of Indifference Curves   *5.* The Marginal Rate of Substitution
6. Utility   *7.* Cardinal Utility   *8.* The Rational Consumer
9. The Budget Line   *10.* The Equilibrium of the Consumer
11. Revealed Preference and the Measurement of Indifference Curves   *12.* Determinants of Consumer Tastes and
Preferences   *13.* Exchange between Consumers   *14.* Fissionable Materials: An Application of the Theory of
Exchange   *15.* Solution to the Problem   *16.* Summary

CHAPTER 3 – Consumer Behavior and Individual Demand   **50**

1. Introduction   *2.* The Equilibrium of the Consumer: Review and Another Viewpoint   *3.* Effects of Changes in Consumer Money Income   *4.* Income-Consumption and Engel Curves   *5.* Effects of Changes in Commodity Price *6.* The Individual Demand Curve: Location and Shape *7.* Price Elasticity of Demand   *8.* Price Elasticity, Total Expenditure, and the Price-Consumption Curve   *9.* Substitution and Income Effects   *10.* Normal and Inferior Goods   *11.* The New York Water Crisis: An Application *12.* The RAND Study and Consumer's Surplus   *13.* The RAND Solution   *14.* Indexes of the Cost of Living *15.* The Laspeyres Index, Paasche Index, and Changes in Consumer Welfare   *16.* A Graphical Interpretation *17.* Summary

CHAPTER 4 – Market Demand   **79**

1. The Market   *2.* The Market Demand Curve: Derivation and Elasticity   *3.* Graphical Measurement of the Price Elasticity of Demand   *4.* Price Elasticity and Total Money Expenditure   *5.* Determinants of the Price Elasticity of Demand   *6.* The Income Elasticity of Demand   *7.* Cross Elasticities of Demand   *8.* The Sellers' Side of the Market and Marginal Revenue   *9.* Determination of the Marginal Revenue Curve   *10.* Industry and Firm Demand Curves *11.* Marginal Revenue and the Elasticity of Demand *12.* Measurement of Demand Curves   *13.* Urban Transportation: An Illustration   *14.* A Business Pricing Problem *15.* Summary

CHAPTER 5 – The Firm and Its Technology   **114**

1. The Assumption of Profit Maximization   *2.* Technology and Inputs   *3.* The Short Run and the Long Run   *4.* The Production Function   *5.* The Law of Diminishing Marginal Returns and the Geometry of Average and Marginal Product Curves   *6.* The Three Stages of Production

7. The Production Function: Two Variable Inputs   *8*. Isoquants   *9*. Substitution among Inputs   *10*. The Long Run
and Returns to Scale   *11*. Measurement of Production
Functions   *12*. Summary

Appendix : Organization of the Firm and Alternative
Models of Firm Behavior

CHAPTER 6 – Optimal Input Combinations and Cost Functions   148

1. Introduction   *2*. The Optimal Combination of Inputs
3. Isocost Curves and Isoquants   *4*. The Production of
Corn: An Application   *5*. The Nature of Costs   *6*. Social
v. Private Costs and Explicit v. Implicit Costs   *7*. The
Proper Comparison of Alternatives   *8*. Cost Functions in
the Short Run   *9*. Average and Marginal Costs   *10*. Geometry of Average and Marginal Cost Functions   *11*. The
Break-Even Chart: An Application   *12*. Cost Functions
in the Long Run   *13*. The Shape of the Long-Run Average
Cost Function   *14*. The Measurement of Cost Functions
15. Summary

CHAPTER 7 – Optimal Production Decisions and Linear Programming   186

1. Introduction   *2*. The Output of the Firm in the Short
Run   *3*. Price Equals Marginal Cost   *4*. The Multiproduct
Firm: The Choice of Output Combinations   *5*. Decision-
Making in Defense: An Application   *6*. Linear Program-
ming   *7*. The Firm's Production Decisions as a Linear
Programming Problem   *8*. The Finishing of Cotton Cloth:
An Illustration   *9*. Isoquants   *10*. Isoprofit Curves and a
Graphical Solution   *11*. Minimization of Costs   *12*. The
Production of Automobiles and Trucks: Another Illustra-
tion   *13*. Computational Efficiency and the Comparison of
Solutions at "Extreme Points"   *14*. The Dual Problem and
Shadow Prices   *15*. Application of Linear Programming in
the Petroleum Industry   *16*. Summary

CHAPTER 8 – Price and Output under Perfect Competition   222

1. Market Structure: An Introduction   *2.* Perfect Competition   *3.* Price Determination in the Market Period   *4.* The Supply Curve of the Firm in the Short Run   *5.* Short-Run Supply Curve of the Industry   *6.* Short-Run Equilibrium Price and Output for the Industry   *7.* The Long-Run Adjustment Process   *8.* Long-Run Equilibrium of the Firm   *9.* Constant Cost Industries   *10.* Increasing and Decreasing Cost Industries   *11.* The Allocation Process: Short and Long Run   *12.* The Path to Equilibrium and the Cobweb Theorem   *13.* Estimates of Elasticity of Supply   *14.* The Cotton Textile Industry: A Case Study   *15.* Agricultural Prices and Output: An Application   *16.* Analysis of Government Subsidy Programs   *17.* Summary

CHAPTER 9 – Price and Output under Pure Monopoly   253

1. Pure Monopoly   *2.* Reasons for Monopoly   *3.* The Monopolist's Demand Curve   *4.* The Monopolist's Costs   *5.* Short-Run Equilibrium Price and Output   *6.* Relationship Between Price and Output   *7.* Long-Run Equilibrium Price and Output   *8.* Multiplant Monopoly   *9.* Effects of Changes in Demand and Cost   *10.* Comparison of Monopoly with Perfect Competition   *11.* Bilateral Monopoly   *12.* Price Discrimination   *13.* Other Types of Price Discrimination   *14.* Discrimination and the Existence of the Industry   *15.* Public Regulation of Monopoly   *16.* Alcoa: A Case Study of Unregulated Monopoly   *17.* The Michigan Telephone Industry: A Case Study of Regulation   *18.* Summary

CHAPTER 10 – Price and Output under Monopolistic Competition   285

1. Historical Background   *2.* Product Differentiation, the Group, and Other Assumptions   *3.* Demand Curves under Monopolistic Competition   *4.* Equilibrium Price and Output in the Short Run *5.* Equilibrium Price and Output in the Long Run *6.* Product Variation *7.* Selling Expenses *8.* Excess Capacity in Monopolistic Competition *9.* Comparisons with Perfect Competition and Monopoly *10.* Criticisms of the Theory of Monopolistic Competition *11.* Summary

CHAPTER 11 – Price and Output under Oligopoly **304**

1. Oligopoly: Definition, Causes, and Classification *2.* The Cournot Model *3.* The Edgeworth Model *4.* The Chamberlin Model *5.* The Kinked Demand Curve Model *6.* The Theory of Games *7.* Mixed Strategies *8.* More Complicated Games and Limitations of Game Theory *9.* Collusion and Cartels *10.* The Instability of Cartels *11.* Collusion in the Electrical Equipment Industry *12.* Price Leadership *13.* Cost-Plus Pricing *14.* The Long Run and Barriers to Entry *15.* Nonprice Competition *16.* Effects of Oligopoly *17.* Summary

CHAPTER 12 – Price and Employment of Inputs under Perfect Competition **332**

1. Incomes: Distribution and Inequality *2.* Price and Employment of Inputs *3.* Profit Maximization and Input Employment *4.* The Firm's Demand Curve: The Case of One Variable Input *5.* The Firm's Demand Curve: The Case of Several Variable Inputs *6.* The Market Demand Curve *7.* Determinants of the Elasticity of Demand for an Input *8.* The Market Supply Curve *9.* The Market Supply Curve: The Backward-Bending Case *10.* Determination of Price and Employment of an Input *11.* The Cost of a Volunteer Army: An Application *12.* The Concept of Rent *13.* Quasi-Rents *14.* Qualitative Differences in Input *15.* Wage Differentials among Labor of Similar Quality *16.* The Elasticity of Substitution and the Distribution of Income *17.* Shortages of Scientists and Engineers: Another Application *18.* Summary

CHAPTER 13 − Price and Employment of Inputs under Imperfect Competition   **361**

1. Introduction   *2*. Profit Maximization and Input Employment: Imperfect Competition in the Product Market   *3*. The Firm's Demand Curve: The Case of One Variable Input   *4*. The Firm's Demand Curve: The Case of Several Variable Inputs   *5*. The Market Demand Curve and Input Price   *6*. Monopsony   *7*. Input Supply Curves and Marginal Expenditure Curves   *8*. Price and Employment: A Single Input   *9*. Price and Employment: Several Inputs   *10*. Baseball: A Case Study   *11*. Labor Unions   *12*. Collective Bargaining and Bilateral Monopoly   *13*. The Nature of Union Objectives   *14*. Tactical Considerations in Collective Bargaining   *15*. Economic Effect of Unions   *16*. Summary

CHAPTER 14 − General Equilibrium Analysis and Resource Allocation   **384**

1. Introduction   *2*. Partial Equilibrium Analysis v. General Equilibrium Analysis   *3*. The Nature and Existence of General Equilibrium   *4*. The Conditions for the Existence of General Equilibrium   *5*. A Simple Model of General Equilibrium   *6*. Equations of the Model   *7*. Existence of a Solution   *8*. Input-Output Analysis: An Extension and Application   *9*. A Simple Input-Output Model   *10*. Applicability of Input-Output Analysis   *11*. Resource Allocation and the Edgeworth Box Diagram   *12*. Exchange   *13*. Production   *14*. The Product Transformation Curve   *15*. Production and Exchange   *16*. The Marginal Rate of Product Transformation, the Marginal Rate of Substitution, and Consumer Satisfaction   *17*. Summary

CHAPTER 15 − Welfare Economics   **412**

1. Introduction   *2*. Interpersonal Comparisons of Utility and Income Distribution   *3*. Marginal Conditions for Optimal Resource Allocation   *4*. Agricultural Price Supports: An Application   *5*. The Utility-Possibility Curve and the Social Welfare Function   *6*. Perfect Competition and Economic Efficiency 7. Economic Planning and Marginal Cost Pricing 8. Marginal Cost Pricing: A Case Study 9. External Economies and Diseconomies 10. Public Policy Toward Basic Research: An Application 11. Urban Renewal: A Further Application 12. Increasing Returns and Public Goods 13. When Is a Change an Improvement? 14. Arrow's Impossibility Theorem 15. The Theory of the Second Best 16. Summary

CHAPTER 16 – Technological Change and Economic Progress   440

1. Introduction 2. Technological Change 3. Change in Technique 4. Classifications of Technological Change 5. Productivity Growth and the Measurement of Technological Change 6. Determinants of the Rate of Technological Change 7. Research and Development: A Learning Process 8. Parallel Development Efforts 9. The Costs of Development 10. Innovation 11. The Diffusion of Innovations 12. Static Efficiency and Economic Progress 13. Imperfect Competition and Technological Change 14. The Giant Corporation, Industrial Concentration, and Technological Change 15. The Patent System 16. Summary

Index   469

Preface

This book is designed for students who are taking intermediate courses in microeconomics. It covers the full range of microeconomic theory. The topics included are standard fare in the intermediate course, with one exception: the final chapter is concerned with technological change, a new and fast growing area within microeconomics. I devote somewhat more attention than has been customary to modern theories of the firm: for example, linear programming is integrated with the older theory, and not left dangling as an ill-fitting appendage. In addition, there is a more complete treatment of modern welfare economics and the theory of general equilibrium than is generally given.

Often, microeconomic theory is presented in a vacuum, carefully sealed off from real world problems. I have chosen instead to present this theoretical material in conjunction with applications and real cases. In my own courses, I have found the most effective way to teach microeconomic theory is to demonstrate how microeconomics can be, and has been, used by decision-makers. If one takes the time to show students the relevance and power of microeconomic theory, they are usually motivated to learn it more thoroughly. Their interest in microeconomics is invariably heightened once they discover that it can throw light on policy issues in both the public and private sectors.

Where possible, I have included some material dealing with the measurement of the concepts that are discussed, my feeling being that microeconomic theory is best presented with a healthy jigger or two of empirical material. But the empirical material, as well as the applications, play a small role in terms of space; in all, they occupy only about 15 per cent of the book. This is because the primary emphasis is on the basic theory, not on problem solving. In short, this is a book on microeconomics, reasonably pure and simple.

The discussion throughout is pitched at a level appropriate for most undergraduates. No mathematics beyond basic algebra is required, but mathematical explanations are often provided in the footnotes for students with a knowledge of calculus.

I want to express my appreciation to Mark Daniels of Brown University, Robert Kuenne of Princeton University, and Fred Westfield of Vanderbilt University for their detailed readings of the manuscript. Their comments resulted in a considerable improvement of the book. I also want to thank Richard Nelson of Yale University who read and commented on Chapter 16. His remarks, too, were very helpful. Turning to the editorial and publishing end of the work, I want to thank Donald S. Lamm of W. W. Norton and Company for his customary skill in handling these matters. Finally, I want to thank my wife for the many ways that she has helped me, now and in the past. Of course, I alone am responsible for any errors. As much as I would like to shift the responsibility to others, I'm afraid that it cannot be done.

E.M.

Philadelphia
October, 1969

1

Introduction to Microeconomics

1. Introduction

There are some subjects that are of interest to nearly everyone, because they are of central importance in nearly everyone's life. Economics is such a subject. It helps us to understand the nature and organization of our society, the arguments underlying many of the great public issues of the day, and the operation and behavior of business firms and other economic decision-making units. Everyone needs to know something about economics to function effectively and responsibly as a citizen, an administrator, a worker, or a consumer.

Precisely what does economics deal with? According to one standard definition, economics is concerned with the way in which resources are allocated among alternative uses to satisfy human wants. It is customary to divide economics into two parts: microeconomics and macroeconomics. Microeconomics deals with the economic behavior of individual units like consumers, firms, and resource owners; while macroeconomics deals with the behavior of economic aggregates like gross national product and the level of employment.

This book is concerned with microeconomics. A general definition of microeconomics fraught with vague words like "resources" and "human wants" is unlikely to communicate to the reader the power of micro-economic theory or its usefulness in solving important problems in the real world. After wading through such an introductory discussion, the reader's interest in the subject is often banked, not kindled. To avoid this problem, we begin our discussion by giving four examples of the kinds of problems that microeconomics can help to solve. (Each of these examples is con-sidered in detail in subsequent chapters.) Although these four examples cover only a small sample of the questions to which microeconomics is relevant, they give the student a reasonable first impression of the nature of microeconomics and its relevance to the real world.

2.   Example 1: Optimal Production Decisions

Business firms are constantly faced with the problem of choosing among alternative ways of manufacturing their product. For example, consider a textile mill that, among other things, finishes cotton cloth. Suppose that the output rate in the firm's finishing department is limited by the capacity of its finishing equipment and the amount of skilled labor it has available to carry out the work. The firm is considering the use of three finishing processes: processes 1, 2, and 3. Suppose that the firm knows that the profit per batch of cotton cloth finished with each of the processes is as shown in Table 1.1. For example, each batch of cotton cloth finished with process 1

Table 1.1.   Characteristics of Three Processes
for Finishing Cloth in Cotton Mill.

	PROCESS 1	PROCESS 2	PROCESS 3
Profit per batch of cotton cloth finished	$1.00	$0.90	$1.10
Man-hours of skilled labor required per batch finished	0.40	0.50	0.35
Machine hours of finishing equipment required per batch finished	3.00	2.50	5.25

yields a profit of $1. Suppose that the number of man-hours of skilled labor and the number of machine hours of finishing equipment required to finish a batch of cotton cloth with each process is as shown in Table 1.1. For example, process 1 requires the use of 3 machine hours of finishing equipment and 0.4 man-hours of skilled labor per batch of cotton cloth that is finished.

Under these circumstances, if 6000 machine hours per week is the maximum capacity of the finishing equipment and 600 man-hours per week is the maximum amount of skilled labor that the firm can hire, which processes should the firm use? And how many batches of cloth should be finished using each process? This is an example of one type of problem that microeconomics is designed to solve. It is a problem faced by an individual firm that is trying to maximize its profit or attain some other set of objectives of its owners and managers. Microeconomics serves as the basis for, and is helpful in promoting an understanding of, the powerful modern tools of managerial decision-making that help to solve problems of this sort. These tools are applicable to government as well as business. Thus the techniques introduced in recent years in the Department of Defense and other government agencies to promote better decision-making are fundamentally applications of microeconomics.[1]

3. Example 2: Pricing Policy

Most firms are also faced with the problem of pricing their product. For example, suppose that a firm is the sole producer of a product and that it can sell this product in New Jersey and Pennsylvania, but that the law prohibits the product from being carried from one state to the other. The amount of the product that the firm can sell at various prices in Pennsylvania is shown in Table 1.2. Similarly, the amount of the product that the firm can sell at various prices in New Jersey is also shown in Table 1.2. Since the product cannot be carried from one state to another, the firm is able to set different prices for the product in the two states. If it costs the firm $1.00 to produce each ton of product, what price should the firm charge in each state if it wants to maximize its profits?

---

[1]For the answer to the problem posed in this section, see Chapter 7.

Table 1.2.   Relationship between Price
and Quantity Sold in New Jersey
and Pennsylvania.

NEW JERSEY

PRICE PER TON IN NEW JERSEY	QUANTITY SOLD IN NEW JERSEY
$1.00	1000 tons
1.10	900
1.20	800
1.30	700
1.40	600
1.50	500
1.60	400

PENNSYLVANIA

PRICE PER TON IN PENNSYLVANIA	QUANTITY SOLD IN PENNSYLVANIA
$1.00	1500 tons
1.10	1400
1.20	1300
1.30	1200
1.40	1100
1.50	1000
1.60	900
1.70	800
1.80	700

This kind of problem faces many, many firms. Since many goods and services cannot be resold, it is often possible for the producer of such goods or services to sell them at different prices to different groups of consumers. For example, an operation to cure a particular type of cancer may be $500 for a rich man and $100 for a poor man. In these cases—as well as in the simpler and more straightforward case where a firm's product can be sold only at a single price—it is important that the firm know how to set price to achieve its objectives. Microeconomics provides a basis for analyzing and solving such problems. When a management consultant is hired to help solve a problem of this sort, his recommendations, if sound, will rely heavily on the application of well-established principles of microeconomics.[2]

4. Example 3: Rules for Optimal Resource Allocation

In the previous two sections we were concerned with problems facing business firms (or individual government agencies). Although such problems are important and interesting, they are by no means the only type dealt with by microeconomics. On the contrary, much of microeconomics is concerned with problems that face us all as citizens. Together we must somehow decide how we want to organize the production and marketing of goods and services in our country. We must also decide how these goods and services are to be distributed among the people. Some of the subtlest and most significant applications of microeconomics are in this area.

At the moment, there is a great deal of talk concerning the "restructuring" of various aspects of society. Suppose that we ask the following basic question: If we could "restructure" the entire economic system and if we agreed that the goal was to make anyone better off (in terms of his own tastes) as long as this did not make someone else worse off (in terms of the latter's tastes), what sort of changes would we be justified in making? Students sometimes complain that they are not confronted with "big questions" or "relevant questions." Surely such complaints cannot be lodged legitimately against this question! Having said this, it is important to add that microeconomics has progressed far enough to be able to provide at

---

[2]For a description of the way in which a pricing problem like that described in this section can be solved, see Chapter 9.

As in the case of the previous example, this problem may seem quite simple to solve, at least to some readers, and they may wonder why special techniques are required to solve such easy problems. The reason is that the problems that occur in real life often involve more variables and are more complicated than those presented in these two sections. The examples given here were constructed to illustrate the type of problems with which microeconomics attempts to deal, and for this purpose, it is best to strip the problem to the simplest essentials. But it would be very misleading to conclude that because trial-and-error methods—and patience—can produce a solution to these examples, such methods—and perhaps a little more patience—can also produce a solution to most real problems. Microeconomics attempts to provide techniques to help solve problems of this sort when trial-and-error and other such methods are not adequate.

least partial answers to this kind of question, which is fortunate since the value of a field lies more in its power to answer questions than in the audacity with which it poses them. Nonetheless, the reader should not be encouraged to believe that microeconomics is the key that by itself will unlock the answers to the great social problems of the day. Microeconomics provides a way of thinking about many of these problems that is valuable, as indicated perhaps by the formidable number of economists appointed by both Democratic and Republican Administrations to positions of great responsibility in dealing with these problems. But microeconomics, although valuable, is only one of many disciplines that have important roles to play in this area.[3]

5.   Example 4: Public Policy Concerning Market Structure

Another problem that faces us all as citizens is concerned with the way that industries are structured. Suppose for simplicity that all industries sell to a large number of independent buyers, none of which is in a position to influence the price of the product. Suppose that we have three choices: to allow each industry to be taken over by a single firm, to allow each industry to become dominated by a few firms (but prevent a single firm from taking over), or to make sure that each industry is composed of a large number of independent firms. Which choice should we make?

This is a very important problem—and one that continues to be the center of considerable controversy. In the United States, the antitrust laws are designed to promote competition and to control monopoly. For example, the Sherman Act of 1890, the first major federal legislation directed against monopoly, outlaws conspiracies or combinations in restraint of trade and forbids the monopolizing of trade or commerce. This seems to indicate that we as a nation have decided not to allow industries to be taken over by a single firm. But is this policy justified? To what extent has it been outmoded by developments in the 80 years that have elapsed since the passage of the Sherman Act?

According to some prominent observers, a policy designed to insure that each industry be composed of a large number of independent firms would be a mistake. They claim that very large firms are required in many industries to insure efficiency and promote progress. How can their arguments be evaluated? What criteria can be used to judge the relative advantages of

---

[3]For a discussion of the problem described in this section, see Chapter 15.

alternative ways that industries can be structured? In various discussions, one often hears of the advantages of a competitive system in which industries are composed of many small firms. In what sense can such a system be shown to be optimal? Is it always optimal, or just under certain special conditions?

This problem is of the utmost importance, since it concerns the basic framework within which the nation's business activity is carried out. It is one of the most fundamental questions of public policy. Compared with the problems of the individual firms in Sections 2 and 3, it is—like the problem in Section 4—certainly more difficult to formulate and to solve, if for no other reason than that it is harder to decide what benefits the entire country than it is to decide what benefits a particular firm. By the same token, this problem is much broader than the problems discussed in Sections 2 and 3. Whereas our interest there was to find policies that would benefit a particular firm, our interest here is to find policies that will benefit the nation as a whole.

This is another example of a problem that microeconomics is aimed at helping to solve. Although it is not possible to solve this problem in as neat or as simple a fashion as one might solve a less complicated problem, it is possible to throw considerable light on the issues involved—and microeconomists have labored for generations to see to it that problems of this sort are analyzed as dispassionately and as scientifically as possible. Moreover, the results have been put to use in the world of action as well as in the world of speculation and study. The lawyer who argues an antitrust case, and the judge who decides one, must both rely on and use the principles of microeconomics.[4]

6. Microeconomics: Problem-Solving and Science

Sections 2 through 5 have provided some examples of problems that microeconomics is designed to help solve. These examples are useful in indicating the relevance of microeconomics but they may be misleading if they suggest that microeconomics is wholly a bag of techniques to solve practical problems. On the contrary, *microeconomics, like any branch of science or social science, is concerned with the explanation and prediction of observed phenomena regardless of whether these explanations or predictions have any immediate*

---

[4]For discussion of the problem described in this section, see Chapters 8 to 11, 15, and 16.

applications to practical problems. As indicated in the previous sections, it has turned out that many parts of microeconomics have been relevant and useful in solving practical problems, but this does not mean that all of microeconomics *has* found an application of this sort or that all of microeconomics *should* find an application of this sort.

For example, one of the principal objectives of microeconomics is to answer questions like the following: What determines the price of various commodities? (Why is steak more expensive than hamburger?) What determines the amount that a worker makes? (Why are physicians paid more than carpenters?) What determines the way that a consumer allocates his income among various commodities? (How will an increase in the price of butter affect the amount of margarine purchased by Mrs. Brown?) What determines how much of a particular commodity will be produced? (What accounts for the woeful decrease in the number of cigar-store Indians produced?) What determines the number and size of firms in a particular industry? (Why are there so many producers of wheat and so few producers of automobiles?)

None of these questions is, as it stands, in the form of a practical problem. Yet to understand the world about us and to perform effectively as a citizen, administrator, or worker, it is obvious that one must have at least a minimal understanding of the answers to these questions. The situation is something like that of mathematics. Although pure mathematics is not concerned with the solution of particular problems, it has turned out that various branches of mathematics are of great value in solving practical problems. And a minimal knowledge of mathematics is extremely important as a basis for understanding the world around us and for further professional and technical training.

7. Human Wants and Resources

At the beginning of this chapter, we gave a very brief definition of economics, which must now be expanded and explained. It will be recalled from Section 1 that we said that economics focuses on the way in which resources are allocated among alternative uses to satisfy human wants. This is a perfectly satisfactory definition but it does not mean much unless we define what is meant by human wants and by resources. What do these terms mean?

Human wants are the things, services, goods, and circumstances that people desire. Wants vary greatly among individuals and over time for the same individual. Some people like sports, others like books; some want to travel, others want to putter in the yard. An individual's desire for a particular good during a particular period of time is not infinite but in the aggregate human wants seem to be insatiable. Besides the basic desires for food, shelter, and clothing, which must be fulfilled to some extent if the human organism is to maintain its existence, wants arise from cultural factors. For example, society, often helped along by advertising and other devices to modify tastes, promotes certain images of the "full, rich life," these images frequently entailing the possession and consumption of certain types of automobiles, houses, appliances, and other goods and services.

Resources are the things or services used to produce goods which can be used to satisfy wants. Economic resources are scarce, while free resources, such as air, are so abundant that they can be obtained without charge. The test of whether a resource is an economic resource or a free resource is price: economic resources command a nonzero price but free resources do not. In a world where all resources were free, there would be no economic problem since all wants could be satisfied.

An economic resource that is used in the production of a particular good is called an input. Thus, in the example in Section 2, the inputs in the finishing of cotton cloth were skilled labor and finishing equipment. Economic resources have alternative uses, a particular resource being useful in the production of many types of goods. For example, the skilled labor used by the cotton mill could be used by many other kinds of firms and in many other kinds of work. Of course, as resources become more specialized, there generally are fewer alternative jobs for them—but there are still some. Even the cotton mill's finishing equipment can probably be adapted for somewhat different uses.

Economic resources are of a variety of types. In the nineteenth century, it was customary for economists to classify economic resources into three categories: land, labor, and capital. In recent years this sort of classification has tended to go out of style in part because each category contains such an enormous variety of resources. Nevertheless, it is worthwhile defining each of these general types of resources. Land is a shorthand expression for natural resources. Labor is human effort, both physical and mental. Capital includes equipment, buildings, inventories, raw material, and other non-human producible resources that contribute to the production, marketing, and distribution of goods and services. Note that the economist's definition of capital is different from that of the man in the street who employs the word to mean money. For example, a man with a hot dog stand who has $100 in his pocket may say that he has $100 in capital; but his definition is different from that of the economist who would also include in the man's capital the value of his stand, the value of his equipment, the value of his inventory of hot dogs and mustard, and the value of other nonlabor resources (other than land) that he uses.

8.   Technology

Another term that must be defined at this point is technology. Technology is society's pool of knowledge regarding the industrial arts. Technology consists of knowledge used in industry concerning the principles of physical and social phenomena (such as the laws of motion and the properties of fluids), knowledge regarding the application of these principles to production (such as the application of various aspects of genetic theory to the breeding of new plants), and knowledge regarding the day-to-day operation of production (such as the rules of thumb of the skilled craftsman). Note that technology is different from the techniques in use, since not all that is known is likely to be in use. Also, technology is different from pure science, although the distinction is not very precise: pure science is directed toward understanding, whereas technology is directed toward use.

The important thing about technology is that it sets limits on the amount and types of goods that can be derived from a given amount of resources. Put differently, it sets limits on the extent to which human wants can be satisfied by a given amount of resources. For instance, consider the example of the cotton mill in Section 2. With the existing technology, the only three processes that are available require the input combinations shown in Table 1.1. Given the existing technology, Table 1.1 shows that there is no way to finish a batch of cotton cloth using only 0.10 man-hours of skilled labor and 1.0 machine hours of finishing equipment. This is beyond the current state of the art. Engineers and craftsmen do not yet know how to accomplish this. It is obvious that this limitation of existing knowledge results in a corresponding limitation on how much the firm can produce with its 600 man-hours of skilled labor and its 6000 machine hours of finishing equipment. When, and if, technology advances to the point where it is possible to finish a batch of cotton cloth with 0.10 man-hours of skilled labor and 1.0 machine hours of finishing equipment, the firm will be able to produce more with its existing amount of skilled labor and equipment. More will then be produced with the existing resources.

9.   The Tasks Performed by an Economic System

Economics, of course, deals with the functioning of economic systems— just as, for example, biology deals with the functioning of biological systems.

Perhaps the best way to define the economic system is to describe what it does. A society's economic system must allocate its resources among competing uses, combine and process these resources in such a way as to produce goods and services, determine the amount of various goods and services that will be produced, distribute these goods and services among the society's members, and provide for the future growth of the society's per capita income. Put in a single sentence, these tasks do not seem quite as awesome as in fact they are. To do justice to each of these tasks, a fuller explanation is needed.

First, the economic system must allocate its resources among competing uses and combine and process these resources to produce the desired level and composition of output. Suppose that the desired level and composition of output is known. There usually are many ways of producing a commodity, and it is not easy to decide which way is best. For example, a plant can use different types and quantities of equipment, different amounts and qualities of raw materials, different amounts and qualities of labor, different locations, different means of transporting and distributing its product, and different ways of informing potential customers of the product's existence. Of the many combinations of resources that could be used, which should be used? Or looking at the problem from a somewhat different point of view, there is an enormous quantity and variety of resources in any society: how should each of these resources be used?

Even if some smart Philadelphia lawyer, or some other form of philosopher-king, could tell us which combination of resources is best for the production of each good, this would not be a complete solution to the problem. He would have to find a way to insure that this combination would in fact be used. The difficulty of solving this aspect of the problem should not be underestimated. Even in highly disciplined organizations like armies, it is not unusual for a general's plan of action to be executed improperly, even distorted considerably.

Second, an economic system must determine the level and composition of output. To what extent should society's resources be used to produce weapons systems? To what extent should they be used to rebuild the cities? To what extent should they be used to produce cotton and wool cloth? To what extent should they be used to produce artificial fibers like nylon? To what extent should they be used to produce dresses with miniskirts? To what extent should they be used to produce dresses with ankle-length skirts? What is the proper combination of goods—weapons systems, rebuilt cities, natural fibers, artificial fibers, miniskirts, ankle-length skirts, and so on— that should be produced? The enormous complexity of this question, as well as its importance, should be obvious. If the reader feels a bit overwhelmed by it, he is getting precisely the message we wish to convey.

Third, the economic system must also determine how the goods and services that are produced are distributed among the members of society. How much of each type of good and service is each person to receive? This is a subject that has generated, and continues to generate, heated controversy. Some people are in favor of a relatively egalitarian society where the amount received by one family varies little from that received by another family of the same size. Other people favor a less egalitarian society where the amount that a family or person receives varies a great deal. Few people favor a thoroughly egalitarian society, if for no other reason than that some differences in income are required to stimulate workers to do certain types of work.

Fourth, another important task of an economic system is to maintain and provide for an adequate rate of growth of per capita income. The goal of economic growth is a relatively new one, most past societies having had economies that were unprogressive. Regardless of its newness, however, it has come to be regarded as an extremely important task, particularly in the less developed countries of Africa, Asia, and South America. There is very strong pressure in these countries for changes in technology, the adoption of superior techniques, increases in the stock of capital resources, and better and more extensive education and training of the labor force, these being viewed as some of the major ways to promote the growth of per capita income.

10. Our Mixed Capitalist System

The previous section described the four basic functions that any economic system must perform. How does our economic system in the United States perform each of these functions? Let's begin with the determination of the level and composition of output in the society. How is this decided? In a substantially free enterprise economy, such as ours, consumers choose the amount of each good that they want, and producers act in accord with these decisions. The importance that consumers attach to a good is indicated by the price they are willing to pay for it. However, consumer sovereignty does not extend to all areas of our society. For example, the provision of fire protection, the operation of schools, and the development of weapons systems are political decisions. Moreover, with regard to the consumption of commodities like drugs, society imposes limits on the decisions of individuals.

Going back to the first function described in the previous section, how does our economic system allocate its resources among competing uses and process these resources to obtain the desired level and composition of output? Basically, the price system does the job by indicating the desires of workers and the relative value of various types of materials and equipment as well as the desires of consumers. For example, if bricklayers are scarce relative to the uses for them, their price in the labor market—their wage—will be bid up and they will tend to be used only in the places where they are most productive. The forces that push firms in the direction of actually carrying out the proper decisions take the form principally of profits or losses. Profits are the carrot and losses are the stick which are used to eliminate the less efficient and the less alert firms and to increase the more efficient and the more alert.

Although decentralized decision-making based on the price system is used to organize production in most areas of our economy, there are notable exceptions. For example, in the acquisition of new weapons by the Department of Defense, the price system, in anything like its customary form, has not been applied. Instead, the government has exercised control over sellers through the auditing of costs and through the intimate involvement of its agents in the managerial and operating structure of the sellers. Moreover, there is extensive government ownership of the seller's facilities; the government decides what weapons are to be created through its program decisions; and it often decides how they are to be created and produced.

Turning to the next function, how does our economic system determine how much in the way of goods and services each member of the society is to receive? In general, the income of an individual depends largely on the quantities of resources of various kinds that he owns and the prices he gets for them. For example, if a man both works and rents out houses he owns, his income is the number of hours he works per year multiplied by his hourly wage rate plus the number of houses he owns times the annual rental per house. Thus, the distribution of income depends on the way that resource ownership is distributed. Some individuals own higher-priced labor resources than others, because of greater intelligence or superior training. Some individuals own a much greater amount of capital and land than others. However, this is only part of the story. The government modifies the resulting distribution of income by imposing progressive income taxes and by welfare programs like aid to dependent children. In this way, an attempt is made to reduce income differentials somewhat.

Finally, how does our economic system provide for an adequate rate of growth of per capita income? A nation's rate of growth of per capita income depends on the rate of growth of its resources and the rate of increase of the efficiency with which they are used. In our economy, the rate at which labor and capital resources are increased is motivated, at least in part, through the price system. Higher wages for more highly skilled work are an incentive for an individual to undergo further training and education. Capital accumulation occurs in response to expectations of profit. Increases in efficiency, due in considerable measure to the advance of technology, are also stimulated by the price system, but it must be recognized that the government plays an extremely significant role in supporting research and development. In areas like defense, space, atomic energy, and many aspects of agriculture and medicine, the government plays a dominant role in research and development.

11. The Price System and Microeconomics

From the discussion in the previous section it is clear that the price system plays a major role in the way our economy goes about performing the four principal functions that any economic system must perform. It is not the only means by which our economy goes about performing these tasks, but its role is very important. A person who wants to understand the way in which our economic system functions must therefore have at least a working knowledge of how the price system works. Microeconomics—or at least a major part of it—is often called price theory because so much of it is concerned so directly with the workings of the price system.

At this point, we are in a position to bring together various strands of the preceding discussion in order to describe more fully the nature and purpose of microeconomics. Economics, it will be recalled from Sections 1 and 7, deals with the way in which scarce resources are allocated among alternative uses to satisfy human wants. Microeconomics, it will be recalled from Section 1, is the branch of economics that is concerned with the economic behavior of individual consumers, firms, and resource owners, not with the aggregate changes of the economy. According to the previous paragraph, one of the principal purposes of microeconomics is to provide an under-standing of the workings and effects of the price system, which plays an important role in the way our economy functions.

In the course of providing such an understanding, microeconomics helps to answer questions of the kind discussed in Section 6: What determines the price of various commodities? What determines the amount that a worker makes? What determines the way that a consumer allocates his income among various commodities? What determines how much of a particular commodity will be produced? What determines the number and size of firms in a particular industry? Moreover, in the course of investigating these and related questions, microeconomics has shed considerable light on the kinds of problems discussed in Sections 2 to 5: How should a firm choose among alternative manufacturing processes if it wants to maximize its profits? What sort of pricing policy should it adopt? What kinds of social changes can be made if it is agreed that the goal is to make anyone better off if it does not make someone else worse off? What are the advantages and disadvantages of various ways in which industries might be organized?

12. Model-Building and the Role of Models

Before concluding this introductory chapter, it is important that we describe briefly the basic methodology used in microeconomics to answer the kinds of questions cited above. This methodology is much the same as that used in any other type of scientific analysis, the basic procedure being the formulation of models. A model is composed of a number of assumptions from which conclusions—or predictions—are deduced. For example, suppose that we wanted to formulate a model of the solar system. We might represent each of the planets by a point in space, and we might make the assumption that each would change position in accord with certain mathematical equations. Based on this model, we might predict when an eclipse would occur.[5]

To be useful, a model must in general simplify and abstract from the real situation. Although the assumptions that are made obviously must bear some relationship to the type of situation to which the model is applicable (since randomly chosen assumptions are unlikely, for example, to predict eclipses very well), it is very important to understand that the assumptions need not be exact replicas of reality. Thus, in the example above, the fact that planets are in fact not points makes little or no difference. Moreover, even if the equations representing their movements are somewhat in error, this may make little difference since, despite these errors, the model may predict well enough to be useful. In both the physical and social sciences, models based on simplified and idealized circumstances have found many, many uses. Also, some assumptions may refer to things that are not directly

---

[5]See Irwin Bross, *Design for Decision*, New York: Macmillan, 1953, pp. 161–82.

measurable, like utility in economic theory. The fact that they are not directly measurable does not mean that they are useless: Their usefulness depends on whether or not they result in models that are more powerful and accurate.

There are a number of important reasons why economists, like other scientists, use models. One is that the real world is so complex that it is necessary to simplify and abstract if any progress is to be made. Another is that a simple model may be the cheapest way of obtaining needed information. Of course, although the use of models is well accepted throughout the various branches of the scientific community, this does not mean that all models are good or useful. A model may be so over-simplified and distorted that it is utterly useless. The trick is to construct a model in such a way that irrelevant and unimportant considerations and variables are neglected, but the important factors—those that have an important effect on the phenomena the model is designed to predict—are included.

13. The Evaluation of a Model

The purpose of a model is to make predictions concerning phenomena in the real world, and in many respects the most important test of a model is how well it predicts these phenomena. In this sense, a model that predicts the price of coffee within plus or minus 1 cent a pound is better than a model that predicts the price of coffee within plus or minus 2 cents a pound. Of course, this does not mean that a model is useless if it cannot predict very accurately. Under some circumstances, one does not need a very accurate prediction. For some purposes, it is sufficient that a model's predictions be accurate to within a mile; for other purposes, its predictions must be accurate to within a gnat's whisker. Also, for some purposes, a model's predictions must describe various aspects and dimensions of reality; for other purposes, only one aspect or dimension is important.

A model's predictions are derived by applying the rules of logic to the assumptions. For example, in the model of the solar system described above, we see at what point in time an eclipse will occur according to the model by making computations based on the model's assumptions and employing the rules of logic. One elementary test of a model's predictions is whether or not they really do flow logically from the model's assumptions. Sometimes errors of logic and computation creep in to mar a prediction.

More fundamentally, another test of a model is whether its assumptions are logically consistent, one with another. Sometimes the scientist or social scientist, in building a model, makes assumptions that are not really compatible.

Another important consideration in judging a model is the range of phenomena to which it applies. In any science, there is a great and understandable attempt to formulate models that are as general as possible. A model that can predict the behavior of any consumer in the economy is more valuable than one that can predict only the behavior of John Jones. Hence the economist is much more interested in a model that is relevant to many consumers in the economy than in one that is relevant to only one consumer. However, the more general a model is meant to be, the more difficult it is to attain a given degree of accuracy. It is relatively easy to construct empirically valid models with little or no generality. For example, if one wanted to go to the trouble of studying a particular person's eating habits, it is likely that one could formulate a model that would predict his choice of breakfast food cereals pretty well. But it would be much more difficult to find a model that would be equally accurate in predicting the choice of any type of food by any consumer in the economy. If a theory is to be general, it must ignore many details (and sometimes some variables that are considerably more important than details), the result being that its predictions are likely to fall short—perhaps considerably short—of a high degree of accuracy.[6]

It is important to add another point that is frequently misunderstood: If one is interested in predicting the outcome of a particular event, he will be forced to use the model that predicts best, even if this model does not predict very well. The choice is not between a model and no model; it is between one type of model and another. After all, if one must make a forecast, he will use the most accurate device that he can to make such a forecast. And any such device is a model of some sort. Consequently, when economists make simplifying assumptions and derive conclusions that are only approximately true, it is somewhat beside the point to complain that the assumptions are simpler than reality or that the predictions are not always accurate. All of this may be true, but if the predictions are better than those obtained on the basis of other models, this model must be used until something better comes along. Thus, if a model can predict the price of coffee to within plus or minus 1 cent a pound and no other model can do better, this model will be used even if those interested in predicting the price of coffee bewail the model's limitation and wish it could be improved.

---

[6]An interesting discussion of model-building is contained in K. Cohen and R. Cyert, *Theory of the Firm*, Englewood Cliffs: Prentice-Hall, 1965, Chapter 2.

The basic point can perhaps be illustrated by the story of the man whose weakness was games of chance and whose wife told him one day that the local casino was dishonest and asked him to stop visiting it. He replied "It's a darned shame and I'd like to stop going . . . but it's the only game in town." Similarly, if a model is the best that is available, it will—and should—be used until a better model appears.

At this point, a final word should be added concerning the microeconomic models discussed in subsequent chapters. No claim is made that these models are sufficiently accurate or powerful to solve all—or most—of the problems that face firms, governments, or others. Some of these models have been used to predict reasonably well; others have not been nearly so successful. Still others have not really been tested, and no one knows how well they would predict. Moreover, no claim is made that the models discussed in subsequent chapters are the last word on the subject. Undoubtedly they will be improved. All that we do claim is that, according to a consensus of the economics profession, they are the best models we have. Like the local casino they may have their imperfections (although dishonesty is not among them), but they are the best in town.

14. Summary

Economics deals with the way in which resources are allocated among alternative uses to satisfy human wants. Economic activity is directed toward the satisfaction of human wants, resources being the things and services used to produce goods that can satisfy wants. Economic resources are scarce and have a nonzero price; free resources are not scarce and can be obtained free of charge. Technology is society's pool of knowledge regarding the industrial arts. It sets limits on the amount and types of goods and services that can be derived from a given set of resources.

Any economic system must accomplish four tasks: it must allocate resources, determine the composition of output, distribute the product, and provide for growth. In our society, individual consumers have great power in determining the composition of output; the prices they are willing to pay for a good indicate how much importance they attach to it. The price system also is an important determinant of how resources are allocated and how the product is distributed. However, since our economy is mixed, government also plays a very important role in these tasks. In some areas, the composition of output and the allocation of resources are determined by political decisions. Moreover, the government modifies the distribution of income, and it plays an important role in stimulating and maintaining growth.

The methodology used by economists is much the same as that used in any other type of scientific analysis, the basic procedure being the formulation of models. Economic theory is divided into two parts: microeconomics and macroeconomics. Microeconomics is concerned with the economic behavior of individual economic units like consumers, firms, and resource owners. One of the most important purposes of microeconomics is to provide an understanding of the working and effects of the price system. In the course of providing such an understanding, microeconomics helps to answer many practical problems of businesses and governments and throws important light on many fundamental issues that confront the responsible citizen and his elected representatives. Much of this chapter has been devoted to examples of the kinds of problems microeconomics can help to solve.

SELECTED REFERENCES

Friedman, Milton, "The Methodology of Positive Economics," *Essays in Positive Economics*, Chicago: University of Chicago Press, 1953.

Harrod, Roy, "Scope and Method of Economics," *Economic Journal*, 1938.

Lange, Oscar, "The Scope and Method of Economics," *Readings in the Philosophy of Science*, Herbert Feigl and May Brodbeck, Eds., New York: Appleton-Century-Crofts, 1953.

Marshall, Alfred, *Principles of Economics*, London: Macmillan, 1920.

Robbins, Lionel, *An Essay on the Nature and Significance of Economic Science*, London: Macmillan, 1935.

2

The Tastes and Preferences of the Consumer

1. Introduction

Microeconomics is the branch of economics that deals with the behavior of individual decision-making units. One of the most important of these units in the American economy is the consumer. For many purposes the consumer is not an individual but a household, the decisions regarding the purchase of a house or car, for example, often being household rather than individual decisions. In other cases, however, the individual person is the consumer, as, for example, when he buys himself a meal at a restaurant. Regardless of the precise way in which the consumer is defined, there are millions of consumers in the United States—and they spend a great deal of money. In 1967, the American consumer spent almost $500 billion on goods and services. About 70 percent of the goods and services produced by the American economy go directly to consumers.

In this chapter we present a simple model to represent the consumer's tastes and to help predict how much of various commodities he will buy. Some of the important concepts that are introduced in this model are indifference curves, utility, the marginal rate of substitution, and the budget line. After discussing this model of a single consumer, we present a simple model of exchange between two consumers. Finally, we show how this body of theory has been applied to help solve a very important practical problem involving the allocation of fissionable materials.

2.   The Nature of the Consumer's Preferences

Our purpose in this chapter is to present a simple model of consumer behavior that will enable us to predict how much of a particular commodity— hot dogs, paint, housing—a consumer buys during a particular period of time.   Clearly, one of the most important determinants of a consumer's behavior is his tastes or preferences.   After all, some consumers like Shakespeare while others like comic books; some like Verdi and others like the Beatles.   And it is obvious that these differences in tastes result in quite different decisions by consumers as to what commodities they buy.   In this section we present three basic assumptions that the economist makes about the nature of the consumer's tastes.

To begin with, suppose that the consumer is confronted with any two market baskets, each containing various quantities of commodities.   For example, one market basket might contain 1 ticket to a baseball game and 3 chocolate bars, while the other might contain 4 bottles of soda and a bus ticket.   The first assumption that the economist makes is that the consumer can decide whether he prefers the first market basket to the second, whether he prefers the second to the first, or whether he is indifferent between them.[1] This certainly seems to be a plausible assumption.

Second, we assume that the consumer's preferences are transitive.   For example, if he prefers blondes to brunettes and brunettes to redheads, he must also prefer blondes to redheads.   Otherwise his preferences would not be transitive, which would mean that his preferences would be contradictory or inconsistent.   Similarly, if he is indifferent between mince pie and pumpkin pie and between pumpkin pie and apple pie, he must also be indifferent between mince pie and apple pie.   His tastes may be judged to be shallow or deep, lofty or mean, selfish or generous: this makes no difference to the theory.   But his preferences must be transitive.   Although not all consumers

---

[1]One way of telling whether the consumer prefers one market basket to another is to set equivalent prices for them and ask which one the consumer wants.

may exhibit preferences that are transitive, this assumption certainly seems to be a plausible basis for a model of consumer behavior.

Third, we assume that the consumer always prefers more of a commodity to less. For example, if one market basket (a very big one) contains 15 harmonicas and 2 gallons of gasoline, whereas another market basket (also big) contains 15 harmonicas and 1 gallon of gasoline, we assume that the first market basket, which unambiguously contains more commodities, is preferred. Also, we assume that, by adding a certain amount of harmonicas to the second market basket, we can make it equally desirable in the eyes of the consumer to the first market basket; that is, we can make the consumer indifferent between them. These assumptions, like the previous two, seem quite plausible.

3. Indifference Curves

If the assumptions in the previous section hold, we can represent the consumer's tastes or preferences by a set of indifference curves. For example, suppose that we confine our attention to the 10 market baskets in Table 2.1, the first market basket containing 1 lb of meat and 4 lb of potatoes, the second market basket containing 1 lb of meat and 6 lb of potatoes, and so on. Suppose that the consumer is asked to choose between various pairs of these market baskets and that he is indifferent between some of these market baskets. For example, he may not care whether he consumes 4 lb of meat plus 2 lb of potatoes or 2 lb of meat plus 3 lb of potatoes. Suppose that we

Table 2.1. Alternative Market Baskets.

MARKET BASKET	MEAT (LB)	POTATOES (LB)
	(PER UNIT OF TIME)	
1	1	4
2	1	6
3	2	3
4	2	4
5	3	2
6	3	3
7	4	1
8	4	2
9	5	0
10	5	1

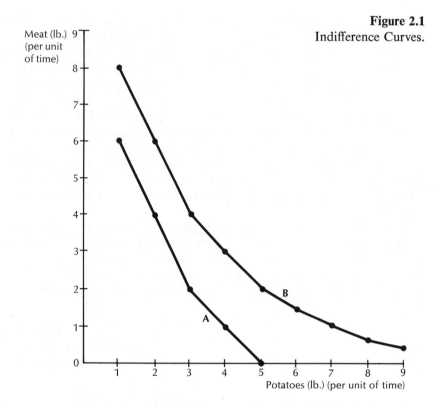

Figure 2.1
Indifference Curves.

Meat (lb.)
(per unit
of time)

Potatoes (lb.) (per unit of time)

enlarge the number of market baskets (containing various quantities of meat and potatoes) under consideration, so that we include all market baskets in which from 1 to 8 lb of meat are combined with from 1 to 8 lb of potatoes. Then suppose that we plot each of the market baskets on a diagram like Figure 2.1 and that curve *A* is the set of points representing market baskets among which the consumer is indifferent. For example, this curve includes all of the market baskets that the consumer regards as being equivalent (in terms of his satisfaction) to 4 lb of meat plus 2 lb of potatoes.

Curve *A* is an indifference curve. Of course there are many such indifference curves, each pertaining to a different level of satisfaction. For example, indifference curve *B* in Figure 2.1 represents a higher level of utility than indifference curve *A*, since it includes market baskets with more of both meat and potatoes than the market baskets represented by indifference curve *A*. One can visualize a series of indifference curves—one showing all market baskets that are equivalent (in the eyes—or belly—of the consumer) to 1 lb of potatoes and 2 lb of meat, one showing all market baskets that are equivalent to 2 lb of potatoes and 1 lb of meat, one showing all market baskets that are equivalent to 2 lb of potatoes and 2 lb of meat, and so on. The resulting series of indifference curves is called an indifference map.

A consumer's indifference map lies at the heart of the theory of consumer behavior, since such a map provides a representation of the consumer's tastes. To illustrate how a consumer's indifference map mirrors his tastes, consider the various indifference maps in Figure 2.2. Consumer A's indifference curves are relatively steep, whereas consumer B's indifference curves are relatively flat. What does this mean? Apparently consumer A needs several extra units of good Y to compensate for the loss of a single unit of good X, whereas consumer B needs less than one extra unit of good Y to compensate for the loss of a single unit of good X. Thus, in this sense, good Y is less important (relative to good X) to consumer A than to consumer B.

What about consumers C and D in Figure 2.2? Apparently consumer C regards good X as useless, since he does not care whether he has more or less of it. Consumer D seems to regard good X as a nuisance, since he is willing to reduce the amount of good Y he consumes in order to get rid of some good X. Situations of this sort are ruled out by the third assumption

Figure 2.2
Indifference Maps of
Various Consumers.

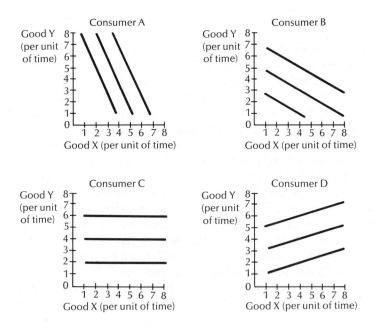

in the previous section. This does not mean that some things are not a nuisance. It means only that in the case of consumer D we would define a commodity as *the lack of good X*, not the consumption of good X. Using this simple, legitimate trick, we no longer violate the third assumption in the previous section, since more of all commodities is now preferred to less.

4. Characteristics of Indifference Curves

All indifference curves have certain characteristics that should be noted. First, given the fact (noted immediately above) that every commodity is defined so that more of it is preferred to less, it follows that indifference curves must have a negative slope. If more of both commodities is desirable, and if one market basket has more of good Y, it must have less of good X than another market basket if the two market baskets are to be equivalent in the eyes of the consumer. If the two market baskets are equivalent, and if one market basket contains more of both commodities—which would be the case if an indifference curve had a positive slope—it would mean that one or the other of the commodities is not defined so that more of it is preferred to less.

Second, given the fact that every commodity is defined so that more of it is preferred to less, it also follows that indifference curves that are higher in graphs like Figure 2.1 represent greater levels of consumer satisfaction than indifference curves that are lower. For example, curve *B* in Figure 2.1 is preferred to curve *A*. Why? Because the higher curve, Curve *B*, includes market baskets with as much of one good and more of the other (or as

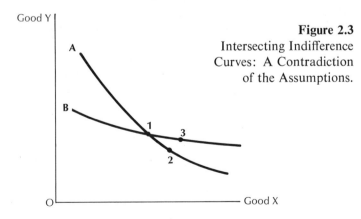

Good Y

A

B

1

3

2

O

Good X

Figure 2.3
Intersecting Indifference
Curves: A Contradiction
of the Assumptions.

much of the second good and more of the first) than the lower curve, Curve *A*. This is what we mean when we say that a curve is "higher" or "lower."

Third, indifference curves cannot intersect. For example, take the case of two intersecting indifference curves in Figure 2.3. On indifference curve *A*, market basket 1 is equivalent to market basket 2. On indifference curve B, market basket 1 is equivalent to market basket 3. Hence, if the indifference curves intersect, market basket 2 must be equivalent to market basket 3. But this cannot be, since market basket 3 contains more of both commodities than market basket 2, and commodities are defined so that more of them is preferred to less. If the consumer's tastes are transitive, as we assumed in the previous section, there cannot be an intersection of indifference curves.

5.   The Marginal Rate of Substitution

We pointed out in Section 3 that consumers differ in the importance that they attach to an extra unit of a particular good. Of course, this is hardly news. For example, it is well known that an alcoholic will sometimes trade a valuable item like a watch for an extra drink of whiskey, whereas the president of the Temperance Union will not give a cent for an extra (presumably the first) dose of Demon Rum. However, news or not, it is useful to have a measure of the relative importance attached by the consumer to the acquisition of another unit of a particular good. The measure that economists have devised is called the *marginal rate of substitution*, a term indicative of the economist's talent for elegant and graceful phrase-making.

The marginal rate of substitution is defined as the number of units of good Y that must be given up if the consumer, after receiving an extra unit of good X, is to maintain a constant level of satisfaction. For example, in Figure 2.4, the consumer can give up $(OY_2 - OY_1)$ units of good Y to receive $(OX_2 - OX_1)$ extra units of good X, and this trade will leave him no better or no worse off. Thus the marginal rate of substitution of good X for good Y is $(OY_2 - OY_1)/(OX_2 - OX_1)$. This is the number of units of good Y that must be given up—per unit of good X received—to maintain a constant level of satisfaction.

More precisely, the marginal rate of substitution is equal to minus one times the slope of the indifference curve.[2] Thus, the marginal rate of sub-

---

[2]See Footnote 4. The definition in the previous paragraph is an approximation that is quite adequate when good X is measured in small units.

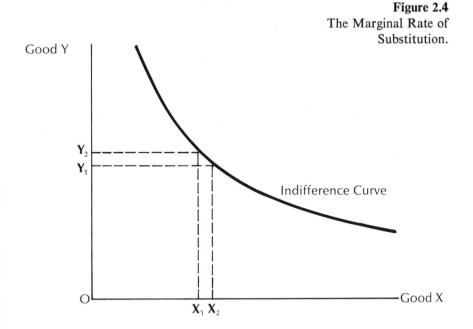

Figure 2.4
The Marginal Rate of
Substitution.

stitution of good X for good Y is higher for consumer A (whose indifference curve on p. 24 is steeper) than for consumer B (whose indifference curve is flatter). In general, the marginal rate of substitution will vary from point to point on a given indifference curve, since the indifference curve's slope will vary from point to point. For example, on indifference curve *A* (or curve *B*) in Figure 2.1, the marginal rate of substitution of potatoes for meat gets smaller as the consumer has more potatoes and less meat.

In the economist's model of consumer behavior it is generally assumed that indifference curves have the sort of shape exhibited by curves *A* and *B* in Figure 2.1. More specifically, it is assumed that they show that the more the consumer has of a particular good, the less will be the marginal rate of substitution of this good for any other good. Put somewhat crudely, this amounts to assuming that the more the consumer has of a particular good, the less important to him (relative to other goods) is an extra unit of this good. In mathematical terms, this assumption means that indifference curves are convex. In other words, an indifference curve lies above its tangent, as illustrated in panel A of Figure 2.5. This contrasts with the case presented in panel B of Figure 2.5 where the indifference curve is not convex.[3]

---

[3]The assumption of convexity may not always hold, but a discussion of cases where it fails belongs in a more advanced book.

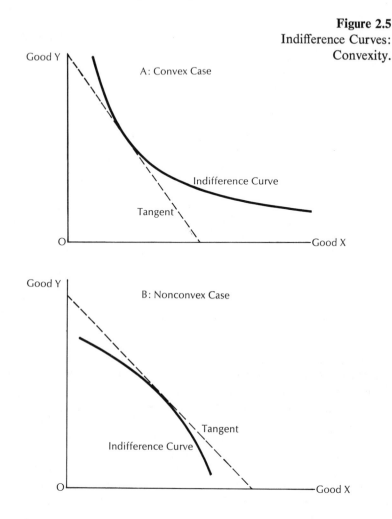

Figure 2.5
Indifference Curves:
Convexity.

6. Utility

In Section 4, we said that the consumer's indifference map is a representation of his tastes. This certainly is true, since the consumer's indifference map shows each and every one of his indifference curves. Thus, if we could start at his lowest indifference curve and number each indifference curve from the lowest to the highest, we could determine which market baskets will be preferred over other market baskets by the consumer. For example,

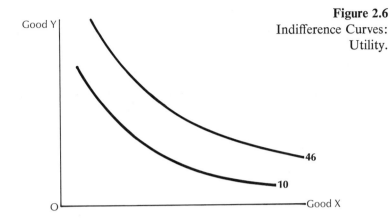

Figure 2.6
Indifference Curves:
Utility.

if the curve labeled 10 in Figure 2.6 is the 10th from the lowest and the curve labeled 46 in Figure 2.6 is the 46th from the lowest, we know that any market basket on curve 46 will be preferred to any market basket on curve 10.

Going a step further, we could simply attach a number, a utility, to each of the market baskets that might confront the consumer. The utility would indicate the level of enjoyment or preference attached to a market basket. Since all market baskets on a given indifference curve yield the same amount of satisfaction, they would have the same utility. Market baskets on higher indifference curves would have higher utilities than market baskets on lower indifference curves.

The purpose of attaching these utilities to market baskets is that we can tell at a glance which market baskets the consumer would prefer over other market baskets. If the utility attached to the first market basket is higher than the second, he will prefer the first over the second market basket. If the utility attached to the first market basket is lower than the second, he will prefer the second over the first market basket. If the utility attached to the first market basket equals the second, he will be indifferent between the two market baskets.

How should we choose these utilities? Any way will do as long as market baskets on the same indifference curve receive the same utility and market baskets on higher indifference curves receive higher utilities than market baskets on lower indifference curves. For example, one set of numbers that will do perfectly well is the set we derived by numbering the indifference curves from lowest to highest. Thus all market baskets on the lowest indifference curve would be given a utility of 1, all market baskets on the second lowest indifference curve would be given a utility of 2, and so on. (What would be the utility attached to the market baskets on the curve labeled 10 in Figure 2.6? Answer: 10.)

But this is by no means the only way to choose these utilities. For example, we could attach a utility of 2 to all of the market baskets on the lowest indifference curve, a utility of 4 to all of the market baskets on the second lowest indifference curve, and so on. This will work too. All that is necessary is that the market baskets on the same indifference curve receive the same utility and that market baskets on higher indifference curves receive higher utilities than market baskets on lower indifference curves.[4]

7. Cardinal Utility

The utilities described in the previous section are *ordinal utilities*. No particular meaning or significance attaches to the scale that is used or to the size of the difference between the utilities attached to two market baskets. The only thing that can be said on the basis of these utilities is that market baskets with higher utilities are preferred by the consumer to market baskets

---

[4]Let U represent the consumer's utility and let the consumer consume x_1 units of good 1, x_2 units of good 2, etc. The utility function is the relationship between U and $x_1, x_2, \cdots, x_n$. It is
$$U = U(x_1, x_2, \cdots, x_n)$$
(In early formulations of utility theory, it was assumed that utility was an additive quality, i.e., that
$$U = U_1(x_1) + U_2(x_2) + \cdots + U_n(x_n)$$
but this assumption was scrapped by modern economists.)

Using this utility function, one can define an indifference curve very simply. An indifference curve is given by the equation
$$U(x_1, x_2, \cdots, x_n) = a$$
where a is a constant.

At this point, recall the fact that the marginal rate of substitution equals minus one times the slope of the indifference curve. Suppose that there are only two commodities and that an indifference curve is
$$U(x_1, x_2) = a$$
Taking the total derivative, we obtain

$$\frac{\partial U}{\partial x_1} dx_1 + \frac{\partial U}{\partial x_2} dx_2 = 0$$

Thus, the slope of the indifference curve is

$$\frac{dx_2}{dx_1} = -\frac{\partial U}{\partial x_1} \div \frac{\partial U}{\partial x_2}$$

which equals minus one times the marginal rate of substitution of the first good for the second good.

Figure 2.7
Total Utility Curve.

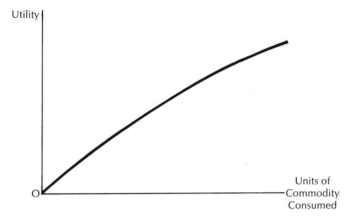

with lower utilities, and that market baskets with equal utilities are equivalent in the eyes of the consumer. This is the nature of modern utility theory as developed by economists like Slutsky, Hicks, Allen, and Hotelling.[5] This type of utility theory should be distinguished from an older type of utility theory which viewed the amount of satisfaction that a consumer derived from a market basket as being measurable.

According to economists in the nineteenth and early twentieth centuries, the satisfaction a consumer derived from the consumption of a particular market basket was measurable—and it was called the utility of the market basket to the consumer. For example, one hot dog for lunch might result in 5 utils[6] of utility for Mr. Jones; two hot dogs for lunch might result in 9 utils of utility. The greater the amount of a commodity that is consumed per unit of time, the greater will be the consumer's total utility, at least up to a certain saturation point. Thus one can draw a curve, like that in Figure 2.7, showing for a given consumer the total utility of various quantities consumed of a particular commodity.

In this older utility theory, marginal utility played an important role. Marginal utility was defined as the change in total utility that results from a one-unit change (per unit of time) in consumption of the commodity. For example, the marginal utility of Mr. Jones's second hot dog was 4 utils, since

---

[5]For example, see J. Hicks, *Value and Capital*, New York: Oxford University Press, 1946; H. Hotelling, "Demand Functions with Limited Budgets," *Econometrica*, 1935; and P. Samuelson, *Foundations of Economic Analysis*, Cambridge: Harvard University Press, 1947.

[6]A util is the unit in which it was supposed that utility could be measured.

this was the extra utility that the second hot dog added. The first hot dog provided him with 5 utils of satisfaction. The first and second hot dogs together provided him with 9 utils of satisfaction. Thus the second hot dog must have provided an extra 4 utils of satisfaction above and beyond what the first hot dog provided. This was the marginal utility derived from the second hot dog.

The utilities visualized by this older theory were cardinal utilities, as distinct from ordinal utilities. In other words, utility was viewed as measurable in the same sense as a man's height is measurable. This, of course, is a very dubious assumption and modern economists seldom resort to it.

8. The Rational Consumer

Returning to our discussion of indifference curves, how can we use these curves to help predict the behavior of the consumer? Given the consumer's tastes, we assume that he is rational, in the sense that he tries to get on the highest possible indifference curve. In other words, he tries to maximize utility. To maximize utility, the consumer must take account of factors other than his own tastes. He must take account of the prices of various commodities and the level of his money income, since both of these factors limit, or constrain, the nature and size of the market basket that he can buy.

The consumer's money income is the amount of money that he can spend per unit of time.[7] If a consumer had an infinite money income, he would not have to worry about certain market baskets' being too expensive for him to purchase. He could simply buy the market basket he liked best—the market basket on his highest indifference curve. But no one has an unlimited money income. Even the Rockefellers and Mellons cannot get on their highest indifference curve, since this would mean the expenditure of more than even they have. For us poorer folk, the problem is much more difficult still, since our incomes are much smaller. What we can buy is much more severely constrained by our incomes.

Besides his money income, the consumer must also take account of the prices of all relevant commodities. The price of a commodity is the amount of money that the consumer must pay for a unit of the commodity. The

---

[7]To the extent that the consumer can borrow, the amount he can borrow can, for some purposes, also be included as income, since it increases the amount the consumer can spend during the period.

higher prices are, the fewer units of a commodity can be bought with a given money income. For example, an income of $5000 went a lot further when movies were 50 cents and soda pop was 5 cents a bottle than it does now when movies are often $2 and soda pop is 10 cents a bottle. Perhaps you cannot trust anyone over thirty on some counts, but you can on this point.

9. The Budget Line

More specifically, how do the consumer's money income and the level of commodity prices influence the nature and size of the market baskets available to the consumer? To answer this, it simplifies matters without distorting the essentials of the situation if we assume that there are only two commodities that the consumer can buy, good X and good Y. Since the consumer must spend all of his money income on one or the other of these two commodities,[8] it is evident that

$$Q_xP_x + Q_yP_y = I \tag{2.1}$$

where Q_x is the amount the consumer buys of good X, Q_y is the amount the consumer buys of good Y, P_x is the price of good X, P_y is the price of good Y and I is the consumer's money income. For example, if the price of good X is $1 a unit and the price of good Y is $2 a unit and the consumer's income is $100, it must be true that $Q_x + 2Q_y = 100$. Note that we assume that the consumer takes prices as given. This, of course, is generally quite realistic.

It is possible to plot the combinations of quantities of goods X and Y that the consumer can buy on the same sort of graph as the indifference map. Solving Equation 2.1 for Q_y, we have

$$Q_y = \frac{1}{P_y}I - \frac{P_x}{P_y}Q_x \tag{2.2}$$

Equation 2.2, which is a straight line, is plotted in Figure 2.8. The first term on the right-hand side of Equation 2.2 is the intercept of the line on the vertical axis: it is the amount of good Y that could be bought by the consumer if he spent all of his income on good Y. The slope of the line is equal to the negative of the price ratio, P_x/P_y.

---

[8]Of course, the consumer can also save some of his income but, from the point of view of this model, "savings" can be viewed as a "commodity" like any other. Thus, with this amendment, Equation 2.1 can easily encompass saving.

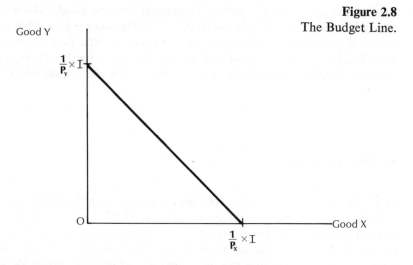

Figure 2.8
The Budget Line.

The straight line in Equation 2.2 is called the *budget line*. It shows all of the combinations of quantities of good X and good Y that the consumer can buy. In subsequent sections, we shall be interested in the effects of changes in product prices and money income on consumer behavior. These changes are reflected by changes in the budget line. Equation 2.2 shows that increases in money income increase the intercept of the budget line, but leave unaffected the slope of the budget line. For example, Figure 2.9 shows the effect of an increase in income, C being the original budget line and D being the budget line after the increase in income. Conversely, de-

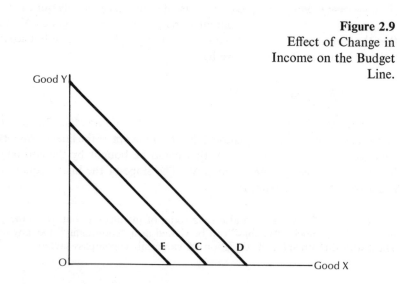

Figure 2.9
Effect of Change in Income on the Budget Line.

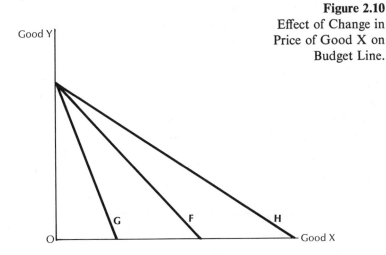

Figure 2.10
Effect of Change in
Price of Good X on
Budget Line.

creases in income lower the intercept of the budget line. In Figure 2.9, E
is the budget line after a decrease in income, C once again being the original
budget line.

Equation 2.2 also shows what happens to the budget line if the price of
good X changes. Increases in P_x increase the absolute value of the slope of
the budget line; decreases in P_x decrease the absolute value of the slope.
The vertical intercept of the line is unaffected. Figure 2.10 shows the effect
of changes in P_x on the budget line. Suppose that the original budget line
is F. If P_x increases, the budget line becomes G. If P_x decreases, the budget
line becomes H. Intuitively, it is easy to see why an increase (decrease) in
the price of good X results in the budget line's cutting the X axis at a point
closer to (farther from) the origin. The point where the budget line cuts the
X axis equals the maximum number of units of good X that the consumer
can buy, and this number obviously is inversely related to the price of good X.

10.   The Equilibrium of the Consumer

Given that the consumer is constrained to purchase one of the market
baskets that lies on the budget line, which one will he choose? To answer
this question, we assume, as noted in Section 8, that the consumer tries to
maximize utility. This assumption is so general and so reasonable that most
people would accept it as a good approximation to reality. Of course, this
is not to deny that some acts are irrational. However, by and large, people's
actions seem to be such that they promote, not frustrate, the achievement

of their goals. Even the ascetic, although his actions may seem irrational at first glance, can be regarded as attempting to maximize utility, if we recognize the very peculiar nature of his tastes.

Going a step further, we note that, although the consumer may attempt to maximize his utility, he may not succeed in doing so because of miscalculation or for other reasons. The problem of maximizing utility may not be as simple as it looks. For example, how many people know how much their cars really cost them? It is not that they do not know how to do the arithmetic, although even the brightest people have been known to have lapses in this regard. More important is the fact that what should or should not be regarded as a cost in a particular situation is not always straightforward. More will be said on this score in subsequent chapters. For the moment, all we want to point out is that consumers may not be able to achieve the maximization of utility, at least right away.

However, if the consumer is allowed some time to adapt and to learn, it seems likely that he will eventually find the market basket that maximizes his utility. Let us define his equilibrium behavior as a course of action by him that will not be changed in favor of some other course of action, if his money income, his tastes, and the prices he faces remain the same. Then his equilibrium behavior will be to choose the market basket that maximizes his utility. And eventually one would expect the consumer to come very close to acting in accord with his equilibrium behavior.

More precisely, what market basket will maximize the consumer's utility? Figure 2.11 brings together the consumer's indifference map and his budget

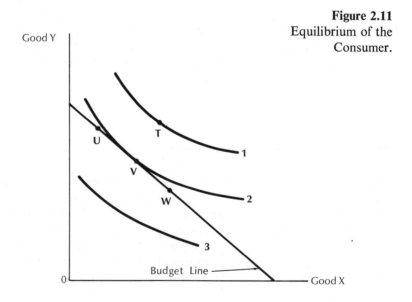

Figure 2.11
Equilibrium of the
Consumer.

line. All of the relevant information needed to answer this question is contained in Figure 2.11. *The indifference map shows what the consumer's preferences are.* For example, any market basket on indifference curve 1 is preferred to any on indifference curve 2; and any market basket on indifference curve 2 is preferred to any on indifference curve 3. The consumer would like to choose a market basket on the highest possible indifference curve. This is the way for him to maximize his utility.

But not all market baskets are available to him. *The budget line shows what the consumer can do.* He can choose any market basket such as U, V, or W on the budget line, but he cannot obtain a market basket like T which is above the budget line. (Of course, he can also buy any market basket below the budget line, but any such market basket lies on a lower indifference curve than a market basket on the budget line.) Since this is the case, the market basket that will maximize the consumer's utility is the one on the budget line that is on his highest indifference curve—which is V in Figure 2.11. It can readily be seen that this market basket is at a point where the budget line is tangent to an indifference curve. This market basket, V, is the one that the rational consumer would, according to our model, be predicted to buy in equilibrium.[9]

---

[9]Mathematically, one can state the conditions for equilibrium as follows: Suppose that the consumer's utility function is
$$U = U(x_1, x_2, \cdots, x_n)$$
Then he maximizes U subject to the constraint that
$$x_1 p_1 + x_2 p_2 + \cdots + x_n p_n = I$$
where p_i is the price of the ith good. To maximize U subject to the constraint, we construct the function
$$L = U(x_1, x_2, \cdots, x_n) - \lambda(x_1 p_1 + x_2 p_2 + \cdots + x_n p_n - I)$$
where λ is a Lagrangian multiplier. The first-order conditions for a maximum are:
$$\frac{\partial L}{\partial x_1} = \frac{\partial U}{\partial x_1} - \lambda p_1 = 0$$
$$\frac{\partial L}{\partial x_2} = \frac{\partial U}{\partial x_2} - \lambda p_2 = 0$$
$$\cdots \cdots \cdots \cdots \cdots \cdots \cdots$$
$$\frac{\partial L}{\partial x_n} = \frac{\partial U}{\partial x_n} - \lambda p_n = 0$$
$$\frac{\partial L}{\partial \lambda} = x_1 p_1 + x_2 p_2 + \cdots + x_n p_n - I = 0$$
From these equations it follows that
$$\frac{\partial U}{\partial x_1} \div p_1 = \frac{\partial U}{\partial x_2} \div p_2 = \cdots = \frac{\partial U}{\partial x_n} \div p_n$$
$$x_1 p_1 + x_2 p_2 + \cdots + x_n p_n - I = 0$$
We ignore the possibility of "corner" solutions where the optimal value of some of the X's is zero. This remains true until Chapter 7 when linear programming is described.

11. Revealed Preference and the Measurement of Indifference Curves

Thus far we have assumed that the consumer's indifference curves were measured by asking him to choose between various market baskets in the way described in Section 3. However, after thinking about this procedure for a short while, one might object that people cannot, or will not, provide trustworthy answers to direct questions concerning their preferences. The man who surreptitiously visits an erotic stage show (and repeatedly buys the best seats in the house) may claim that such shows are sinful and re-pugnant to him. Is there any way to measure a person's indifference curves other than by asking direct questions concerning his tastes? Is there any way to deduce a consumer's indifference curves from his actual behavior rather than from his professed preferences?

The theory of revealed preference, a relatively new part of microeconomics, is an attempt to do just that. We assume what we can vary the consumer's money income and the prices he faces, these factors being changed in accord with the experiment. Then assuming that the consumer's tastes remain fixed during the course of the experiment, we see how he reacts to the various levels of money income and prices. The basic idea behind the formulation and interpretation of the experiments is as follows: The consumer may choose one market basket over a second market basket either because he prefers the first to the second or because the first is cheaper than the second. Thus, if we vary prices so that the first market basket is not cheaper than the second and if the first is still chosen over the second, we can be sure that the first market basket is preferred over the second.

Consider the case of two commodities, good X and good Y. Let A in Figure 2.12 represent the market basket (Oa of good X and Oa' of good Y) that the consumer purchases when his budget line is QQ'. From this it follows that every point (each representing a market basket) on or below QQ' is revealed to be inferior to A in the eyes of this consumer, since all of these points were available to the consumer and he chose A. Moreover, every point in the shaded area above and to the right of A is preferred to A because each such point represents a market basket with at least as much of both commodities as A. Thus, since a commodity is defined so that more of it is preferred to less, each such point must be preferred to A. Therefore the indifference curve running through point A must lie in between the budget line and the shaded area.

Figure 2.12
Revealed Preference.

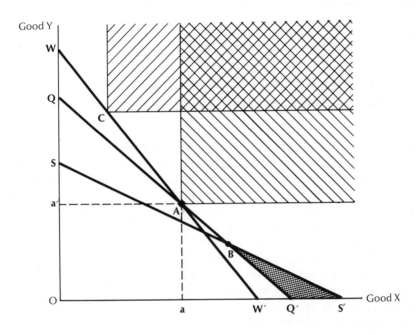

To get a better idea of the location and shape of this indifference curve, consider any other point on *QQ'*—for example, *B*. This point is inferior to *A* but there is some budget line that will make the consumer purchase it. Suppose that this budget line is *SS'*. Then we can deduce that the blackened area is inferior to *A* in the eyes of the consumer, since it is inferior to *B*, and *B* is inferior to *A*. This procedure can be used to narrow the zone of ignorance —the zone where we are unsure whether the included points are inferior or superior to *A*—that is below and to the right of *A*. To narrow the zone of ignorance above and to the left of *A*, we adopt the following procedure. We establish a new budget line, *WW'*, which includes point *A*. Let *C* be the market basket the consumer chooses when he has the new money income and prices represented by this new budget line. Since *C* is no more expensive than *A* under these conditions, *C* is shown to be preferred to *A*. Moreover, all points above and to the right of *C* are also preferred to *A*, since they are preferred to *C*, and *C* is preferred to *A*.

If these procedures were repeated over and over again, one would eventually derive an indifference curve. Obviously, however, this would be a long and laborious process. The theory of revealed preference is more important as a means of demonstrating that indifference curves can, in principle, be derived in this way, than as a means of actually deriving indifference curves.[10]

12.   Determinants of Consumer Tastes and Preferences

In previous sections of this chapter, we have discussed how the consumer's tastes can be represented and the way his tastes influence the market basket he chooses. But we have said nothing about the factors that determine his tastes. Clearly, his tastes can be changed by various forms of experience. The child whose widest grins of satisfaction are reserved for candy and other sweets grows into the man who politely declines a sweet drink in favor of a dry martini. The boy who regards the ballet as sissy stuff grows to be the man who pays $10 for a ticket to the Royal Ballet and gives away complimentary ring-side tickets to the fights. Age has a great effect on a person's tastes: so does education. Indeed, one of the benefits of education is that it allows people to appreciate and enjoy various forms of experience more keenly than they otherwise would.

Another factor influencing a consumer's tastes is his observation of what other consumers have. These effects are sometimes called demonstration effects. For example, if the Joneses have a Cadillac, their neighbors, the Smiths, may feel that they should have one, too. Or if the Jones's daughter can buy expensive clothes, Mrs. Smith may feel that her daughter should have them, too. (Whether Mr. Smith feels this way is another matter—which indicates the importance of asking in a particular case what individuals are regarded as the "consumer," and how decisions are made.) Sometimes an opposite kind of effect is at work: If many consumers have a certain commodity, others may not want it. For example, the snobbish Whites may take pride in having tastes that are different from the common herd of mankind.

---

[10]The theory of revealed preferences assumes the following: First, if a market basket is purchased when this market basket is more expensive than another market basket, it must also be purchased when it is no more expensive. This rules out snob effects, where preferences are affected by prices. Second, if one market basket is chosen over a second and a second is chosen over a third, the first must be chosen over the third. This is the assumption of transitivity. Third, given any market basket, it is assumed that there exists some budget line that will lead the consumer to buy it.

Another important determinant of a consumer's tastes is the advertising and selling expenses incurred by manufacturers and sellers of various goods and services. There can be no doubt that advertising influences consumers, although the extent of its influence varies greatly from one product to another, and from one consumer to another. For goods where quality is hard for the consumer to measure, and where the relative advantages of a particular good or brand are not very great, advertising may play a very important role. Of course, advertising also plays a significant role merely by informing the consumer of the existence and characteristics of new products. Much more will be said about the effects of advertising in subsequent chapters.

Finally, we have assumed in previous sections that a consumer's tastes (i.e., his indifference map) are independent of the structure of prices. For example, changes in the prices of meat and potatoes are not supposed to affect the indifference map in Figure 2.1. This rules out cases in which goods are consumed because they are expensive—conspicuous consumption— and cases in which quality is judged by price. This assumption is a reasonable first approximation but it obviously does not hold for all cases. It is possible to extend our model to allow for violations of this assumption, but a discussion of such extensions properly belongs in a more advanced text.

13. Exchange between Consumers

Up to this point, our discussion has focused entirely on a single consumer, his tastes, and his behavior. In this section we extend the analysis to include more than one consumer, our object being to explain the exchange that can fruitfully take place between consumers. The essential elements of our theory can be presented if we assume that there are only two consumers, Bill and Joe, and only two commodities good X and good Y. We assume that Bill has a certain amount of each of the goods and that Joe has a certain amount of each of the goods. Moreover, we assume that they meet and discuss the possibility of trading. The question is: What sort of trading or exchange will occur?

To answer this question, we construct a special diagram, called an *Edgeworth box diagram*. This diagram is shown in Figure 2.13. It is constructed in the following way: The width of the box, which is equal to *OK*, is the total amount of good X that Bill and Joe together have. The height of the box, which is equal to *OC*, is the total amount of good Y that Bill and Joe together have. The amount of good X that Bill has is measured horizontally from the origin at 0. The amount of good Y that Bill has is measured

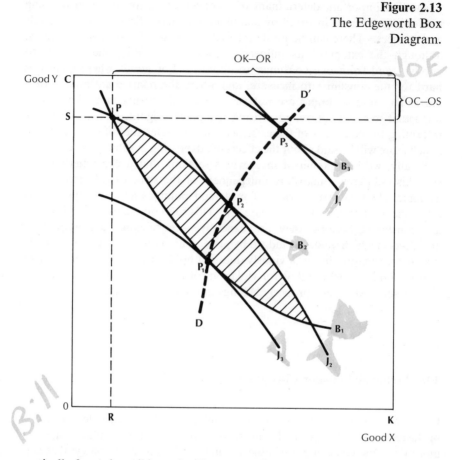

Figure 2.13
The Edgeworth Box
Diagram.

vertically from the origin at 0. Thus any point in the box diagram indicates a certain amount of good X and a certain amount of good Y that Bill has. For example, the point, P, indicates that Bill has OR units of good X and OS units of good Y.

The amount of good X that Joe has is measured by the horizontal distance to the left of the upper right-hand corner of the box diagram. And the amount of good Y that Joe has is measured by the vertical distance downward from the upper right-hand corner of the box diagram. Thus, every point in the diagram represents an amount of good X and an amount of Y that Joe has. For example, the point P indicates that Joe has (OK − OR) units of X and (OC − OS) units of good Y.

Suppose that, when Bill and Joe meet, the amounts of good X and good

Y that they have is such that point P represents the allocation of goods between them. That is, Bill has OR units of good X and OS units of good Y, and Joe has $(OK - OR)$ units of good X and $(OC - OS)$ units of good Y. In this situation, what sort of trading will take place between them? What can be said about the optimal allocation of the goods between them? To find out, we must insert the indifference curves of Bill and Joe into the Edgeworth box diagram in Figure 2.13. Three of Bill's indifference curves are B_1, B_2, B_3, the highest indifference curve being B_3 and the lowest indifference curve being B_1. Three of Joe's indifference curves are J_1, J_2, and J_3, the highest indifference curve being J_3 and the lowest indifference curve being J_1. In general, Bill's satisfaction increases as we move from points close to the origin to points closer to the upper right-hand corner of the box. Conversely, Joe's satisfaction increases as we move from points close to the upper right-hand corner to points closer to the origin.

Given the initial allocation of good X and good Y, Bill is on indifference curve B_1, and Joe is on indifference curve J_2. If both men are free to trade, it would obviously be in the interest of both parties for Bill to trade some good Y in exchange for some good X. Unless there is coercion, the point where they will finally end up is somewhere in the shaded area in Figure 2.13, this area including all points where both men are no worse off than at P. The exact point to which they will move cannot be predicted, however. If Joe is the more astute bargainer, he may get Bill to accept the allocation at point P_1, where Bill is no better off than before (since he is still on indifference curve B_1) but Joe is much better off (since he moves on to indifference curve J_3). If Bill is the more astute bargainer, he may get Joe to accept the allocation at P_2, where Joe is no better off than before (since he is still on indifference curve J_2) but Bill is much better off (since he moves to indifference curve B_2). The ultimate outcome is likely to be a point between P_1 and P_2.

If after some exchange occurs, a point is reached where Bill's indifference curve is tangent to Joe's indifference curve, then there is no opportunity for further mutually advantageous exchange. One man can be made better off only by making the other man worse off—and surely such a situation would not result in further exchange. The locus of points, DD', where such a tangency occurs is called the *contract curve*. Some points on the contract curve are points P_1, P_2, and P_3 in Figure 2.13. Because of obstinacy or ineptness, exchange may cease at a point off the contract curve, but this would not be optimal in the following sense: The contract curve is an optimal set of points in the sense that, if the consumers are at a point *off* the contract curve, it is always preferable for them to move to a point *on* the contract curve, since one or both can gain from the move while neither incurs a loss. Clearly, such a move results in a net gain.

14. Fissionable Materials: An Application of the Theory of Exchange

In Chapter 1, we said that microeconomic theory has turned out to be useful in helping to solve many important practical problems; yet in this chapter we have provided no evidence so far to support that statement. The material provided in previous sections of the present chapter must be understood if the reader is to understand the theory of consumer behavior. But it is by no means obvious how it would enable anyone to solve any kind of a practical problem. Appearances, however, can be deceiving. The kind of analysis discussed in this chapter can be useful in many contexts. The purpose of this section is to describe a very important problem that confronted American defense planners in the early 1950s. In the following section, we show how some of the models described in previous sections were used to help solve this problem.

About 1950, one of the key problems in the defense establishment was the allocation of fissionable material—U258 and Pu239. In particular, how much of our supply of fissionable material should be used for strategic purposes, and how much should be used for tactical purposes? The strategic forces, principally long-range bombers at that time, were the foundation of our capability to strike back at an enemy's cities and bases. The tactical forces were concerned with more limited engagements with enemy forces. At that time, the strategic mission had exclusive claim on the national stockpile of fissionable materials, and an urgent question was whether some tactical air squadrons should be equipped with small-yield atomic weapons. This very important question occupied and concerned the minds of some of the nation's highest officials.

Both for the strategic and tactical mission, the two most important determinants of the effectiveness of the mission were (1) the amount of fissionable material used, and (2) the number of aircraft used. Within limits, it was possible to substitute airplanes for fissionable material and vice versa. For example, if the object of an Air Force operation was the expected destruction of a certain number of targets, fewer aircraft would be required to destroy these targets if atomic weapons, rather than conventional weapons, were used. Also, one way of increasing the probability that a bomb would get to the target was to have several empty decoy bombers accompanying each aircraft with an atomic bomb, which clearly was a way of substituting aircraft for fissionable materials.

In the very short run, it was sensible to view the total number of aircraft available for either strategic or tactical missions as fixed. It was also sensible to view the total amount of fissionable material available for either strategic or tactical missions as fixed. However, this was appropriate only in analyzing the problem in the short run; in the long run, it was possible to add to our supplies of aircraft and fissionable materials. Also, it is important to note that there was no way to establish the relative importance of strategic and tactical targets. For example, no one was willing to say that the destruction of a strategic target was worth the destruction of two tactical targets. Instead, strategic and tactical targets were regarded as incommensurable.[11]

15.　Solution to the Problem

The reader can be forgiven if he asks in a somewhat bewildered tone, "What in the world has this problem got to do with the theory of consumer preferences we discussed in previous parts of this chapter?" The answer is that, strange as it may seem, economists used the theory of exchange described in Section 13 to help solve this question. The way in which they solved the problem is instructive in many respects, one being that it illustrates how simple models can be adapted to throw light on very complicated problems.

In effect, the economists said, "Let's view the strategic mission as one consumer and the tactical mission as another consumer. Let's regard airplanes and fissionable material as two goods to be allocated between these two consumers, the total amount of these two goods being fixed in the very short run. Let's use as an indifference curve for the strategic mission the combinations of aircraft and fissionable material that will result in the expected destruction of a particular number of strategic targets. Let's use as an indifference curve for the tactical mission the combinations of aircraft and fissionable material that will result in the expected destruction of a particular number of tactical targets. Then let's use the Edgeworth box diagram to indicate which allocations of aircraft and fissionable materials between strategic and tactical missions are on the contract curve. This will tell us whether the existing allocation is on the contract curve. If it isn't, the allocation can be improved."

---

[11]Consequently, it was not possible to combine the expected number of strategic and tactical targets destroyed into a single measure of destructive impact and solve the problem by finding the allocation of aircraft and fissionable material that maximized this over-all measure of destructive impact.

To actually attack the problem in this way, the first step, of course, was to construct the appropriate Edgeworth box diagram. Figure 2.14 shows what the resulting box diagram looked like. As in Figure 2.13, any point in the diagram represented a possible allocation of the two goods, airplanes and fissionable material, between the two "consumers," the strategic mission and the tactical mission. For example, point P in Figure 2.14 represents a case where the strategic mission gets OU units of aircraft and OV units of fissionable material, and the tactical mission gets $(OA - OU)$ units of aircraft and $(OM - OV)$ units of fissionable material.

The two "consumers" are not ordinary consumers. They are military missions. What do indifference curves mean in such a situation? Consider the tactical mission's indifference curve, T_1. Each point on T_1 represents a combination of aircraft and fissionable material that results in the same number of *tactical* targets expected to be destroyed. The fictitious consumer, "the tactical mission," is viewed as being interested in maximizing the expected number of tactical targets that can be destroyed. In other words,

Figure 2.14
Allocation of Fissionable
Materials and Airplanes
between Strategic and
Tactical Missions.

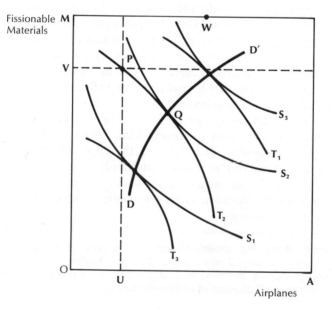

the expected number of tactical targets that can be destroyed is a measure of this consumer's "utility." Thus he is indifferent among all of the points on T_1. And he clearly prefers indifference curve T_2 to indifference curve T_1. Similarly, consider the strategic mission's indifference curve, S_1. Each point on S_1 represents a combination of aircraft and fissionable material that results in the same number of *strategic* targets expected to be destroyed. The fictitious consumer, "the strategic mission," is viewed as being interested in maximizing the expected number of strategic targets that can be destroyed. In other words, the expected number of strategic targets that can be destroyed is a measure of the consumer's utility. Thus he is indifferent among all of the points on S_1, and he prefers S_2 to S_1.

From the discussion in Section 13, we know that any allocation of aircraft and fissionable materials that is represented by a point that is not a point of tangency between an indifference curve of the tactical mission and an indifference curve of the strategic mission is not an optimal allocation. For example, P in Figure 2.14 is not an optimal allocation, since it is not a point of tangency between an indifference curve of the tactical mission and an indifference curve of the strategic mission. Why isn't P an optimal allocation? Because if we hold constant the expected number of tactical targets that can be destroyed (the "utility" of the tactical mission), we can increase the expected number of strategic targets that can be destroyed (the "utility" of the strategic mission) by moving to point Q. The locus of optimal points—the contract curve—is shown by DD' in Figure 2.14.

Having constructed the contract curve, what did the economists conclude? Recall that the existing allocation assigned all of the nation's stockpile of fissionable material to the strategic mission and none to the tactical mission. Thus, the existing allocation was at point W in Figure 2.14. However, according to the economist's calculations, this point was not on the contract curve, DD'. Consequently, the existing allocation was shown to be sub-optimal, a movement to the contract curve being called for. Specifically, the stockpile of fissionable material needed to be reallocated, some atomic weapons being reserved for the tactical mission. However, this analysis could not indicate which particular point on the contract curve should be chosen, since this decision hinged on whether we wanted to increase our strategic capability at the expense of our tactical capability, or vice versa. On the basis of the information given here, no judgment on this score could be made.[12]

---

[12]For further discussion of this problem, see S. Enke, "Using Costs to Select Weapons," *American Economic Review*, May 1965, and "Some Economic Aspects of Fissionable Materials," *Quarterly Journal of Economics*, May 1954. This example is taken largely from these papers.

This is an important and interesting example of the application of the theory described in previous sections. In addition, it illustrates the fact that most aspects of microeconomics are concerned with means to achieve specified ends, not with the choice of ends. Thus economists in the case discussed here were able to increase the destructive power of given supplies of aircraft and fissionable material. But they took as given the hypothesis that it was a good thing to increase their destructive power. In other words, they took as given the fact that the "utility" of the "consumers" should be increased. In certain circumstances, this hypothesis could be quite wrong. For example, there might be circumstances where an increase in destructive power might increase the chances of war. Of course, this does not mean that it is not valuable to have techniques like those discussed here: They are obviously of great value. What it does mean is that one cannot expect them to do more than they are designed to do.

16. Summary

The consumer is, of course, one of the most important types of decision-making units in the economy. Clearly, among the most important determinants of a consumer's behavior are his tastes or preferences. We assume that, when confronted with two market baskets, a consumer can say which one he prefers, or whether he is indifferent between them. Also, we assume that his tastes are transitive and that a commodity is defined in such a way that "more" is preferred to "less." If these assumptions hold, we can represent a consumer's tastes by a set of indifference curves. An indifference curve must have a negative slope, and two indifference curves cannot intersect. The slope of an indifference curve (multiplied by minus one) is called the marginal rate of substitution. The marginal rate of substitution shows approximately how many units of one good must be given up if the consumer, after receiving an extra unit of another good, is to maintain a constant level of satisfaction.

We can attach a number called a utility to each market basket that might confront a consumer, this utility being higher for preferred market baskets. Since all market baskets on a given indifference curve yield the same amount of satisfaction, they have the same utility. Market baskets on higher indifference curves have higher utilities than those on lower indifference curves. Any system of assigning utilities will do as long as market baskets on higher indifference curves receive higher utilities than market baskets on lower indifference curves and market baskets on the same indifference curve receive the same utility. These utilities are ordinal utilities, not the cardinal utilities used in older versions of utility theory.

Given the consumer's tastes, we assume that he is rational, in the sense that he tries to get on the highest indifference curve. In other words, he tries to maximize utility. The budget line indicates all of the combinations of quantities of goods—all of the market baskets—that the consumers can buy, given his money income and the level of each price. In equilibrium, we would expect the consumer to attain the highest level of satisfaction that is compatible with the budget line. This means that in equilibrium the consumer will choose the market basket on the budget line that is on the highest indifference curve. This market basket is at a point where the budget line is tangent to an indifference curve.

The theory of revealed preference shows how one could measure an indifference curve by watching the consumer's behavior rather than recording his professed preferences. A consumer's tastes are affected by age and education, the behavior and purchases of others, and by advertising and other selling expenses. The theory of exchange uses the Edgeworth box diagram to analyze the sort of trading or exchange that will take place between two consumers. The contract curve, which includes points of tangency between indifference curves of the two consumers, is an optimal set of points in the sense that, if the consumers are at a point off the contract curve, it is always preferable for them to move to a point on the contract curve. In the fifties, the theory of exchange was used to help solve a very important practical problem concerning the allocation of fissionable material. The nature of the problem and its solution illustrate the way in which this body of theory has been used.

SELECTED REFERENCES

Hicks, John, *Value and Capital*, Oxford: Oxford University Press, 1946.

Henderson, James, and Richard Quandt, *Microeconomic Theory*, New York: McGraw-Hill, 1958.

Marshall, Alfred, *Principles of Economics*, London: Macmillan, 1920.

Stigler, George, "The Development of Utility Theory," *Journal of Political Economy*, August 1950.

———, *The Theory of Price*, New York: Macmillan, 1966.

Samuelson, Paul, *Foundations of Economic Analysis*, Cambridge, Mass.: Harvard University Press, 1947. (Advanced)

Leibenstein, Harvey, "Bandwagon, Snob, and Veblen Effects in the Theory of Consumers' Demand," *Quarterly Journal of Economics*, May 1950.

3

Consumer Behavior and Individual Demand

1. Introduction

In the previous chapter, we looked in some detail at the nature of consumer tastes and preferences, and we presented a model of consumer behavior. In this chapter, we develop this model further, our primary purpose being to show how the consumer responds to changes in his money income or to changes in the prices of commodities. Some of the important concepts that are introduced in this chapter are individual demand curves, the elasticity of demand, Engel curves, substitution effects, income effects, and inferior goods. These concepts are central to the microeconomic theory of consumer behavior and individual demand. In addition, we present some illustrations of how this theory has been applied to help solve important problems of public policy.

2. The Equilibrium of the Consumer: Review and Another Viewpoint

To begin with, it is useful to review briefly the conditions under which the consumer is in equilibrium. However, rather than merely parrot what has already been said in the previous chapter, we look at these conditions from a somewhat different point of view. We said in Section 10 of the previous chapter that the consumer's equilibrium market basket is at a point where the budget line is tangent to an indifference curve: This is the market basket that maximizes the consumer's utility. Since the slope of the indifference curve equals minus one times the marginal rate of substitution of good X for good Y (see Section 5, Chapter 2) and since the slope of the budget line is $-P_x/P_y$ (see Section 9, Chapter 2), it follows that the rational consumer will choose in equilibrium to allocate his income between good X and good Y in such a way that the marginal rate of substitution of good X for good Y equals P_x/P_y.

This is a famous result—and a very useful one that should be understood fully. It is easier to agree that it is true than it is to see what it really means and why it is true. Perhaps the best way to understand this result is to define once again the marginal rate of substitution: The marginal rate of substitution is the rate at which the consumer is *willing* to substitute good X for good Y, holding his total level of satisfaction constant. Thus, if the marginal rate of substitution is three, the consumer is willing to give up three units of good Y in order to get one more unit of good X.

On the other hand, the price ratio, P_x/P_y, is the rate at which the consumer is *able* to substitute good X for good Y. Thus, if P_x/P_y is two, he *must* give up two units of good Y to get one more unit of good X. What the result described in this section is really saying is: The rate at which the consumer is willing to substitute good X for good Y (holding satisfaction constant) must equal the rate at which he is able to substitute good X for good Y. Otherwise it is always possible to find another market basket that will increase the consumer's satisfaction. And this means, of course, that the present market basket is not the equilibrium one that maximizes consumer satisfaction.

To see that this must be the case, suppose that the consumer has chosen a market basket in which the marginal rate of substitution of good X for good Y is three. Suppose that the price ratio, P_x/P_y, is two. If this is the case, the consumer can trade two units of his good Y for an extra unit of good X in the market, since the price ratio is two. But this extra unit of good X is worth three units of good Y to the consumer, since the marginal rate of substitution is three. Consequently, he can increase his satisfaction by trading good Y for good X—and this will continue to be the case as long as the marginal rate of substitution exceeds the price ratio. Conversely, if the marginal rate of substitution is less than the price ratio, the consumer can increase his satisfaction by trading good X for good Y. Only when the marginal rate of substitution equals the price ratio does the consumer's market basket maximize his utility.

3.   Effects of Changes in Consumer Money Income

Having done some useful reviewing, let us turn to new territory and consider the effect of changes in money income on the amount of good X and
good Y purchased by the consumer. For example, suppose that the consumer is a student and that the amount of money he earns and receives
from home increases from $2000 to $3000 a year. What effect will this have
on his purchases? How much of the extra money will he spend on books?
On reconnaisance missions to nearby girls' schools? On clothes? On food?

In the previous chapter, we saw that an increase in money income results
in an increase in the intercept of the budget line, but leaves unaffected the
slope of the budget line (as long as the prices of commodities remain constant). Similarly, a decrease in money income results in a decrease in the
intercept of the budget line, but leaves unaffected the slope of the budget line
(as long as the prices of commodities remain constant). To determine the
effect of a change in money income on the market basket chosen by the consumer, one can compare the equilibrium position based on the budget line
corresponding to the old level of money income with the equilibrium position
based on the budget line corresponding to the new level of money
income.

For example, suppose that the budget line corresponding to the old level
of income—$2000 in the case of the student—is A in Figure 3.1. Given the
consumer's indifference map, the market basket that maximizes his utility
is comprised of Oa units of good X and Ob units of good Y, if his income
is at the old level. Now suppose that his income rises—to $3000 in the case
of the student—and that the new budget line is B in Figure 3.1. With these
new conditions, the market basket that maximizes his utility is comprised
of Oc units of good X and Od units of good Y.

Clearly, the way in which an increase in money income influences a consumer's purchases depends on his tastes. In other words, the nature of the
market basket chosen at the old income, the nature of the market basket
chosen at the new income, and consequently the nature of the difference
between these two market baskets is influenced by the shape of the consumer's indifference curves. Also, the way in which an increase in money
income influences a consumer's purchases depends on the price ratio, P_x/P_y.
Of course, this price ratio is held constant when we analyze the effects of
changes in money income on consumer behavior, but the level at which the
price ratio is held constant will influence the results.

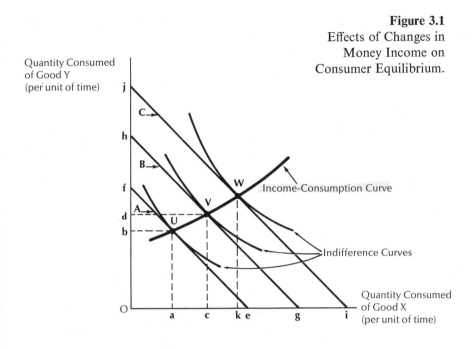

Figure 3.1
Effects of Changes in
Money Income on
Consumer Equilibrium.

4.   Income-Consumption and Engel Curves

Holding commodity prices constant, we find that each level of money income results in an equilibrium market basket for the consumer. That is, corresponding to each level of money income is an equilibrium market basket for a particular consumer. For example, the equilibrium market baskets corresponding to three income levels are represented by points *U*, *V*, and *W* in Figure 3.1. If we connect all of the points representing equilibrium market baskets corresponding to all possible levels of money income, the resulting curve is called the income-consumption curve. Figure 3.1 shows such a curve.

The income-consumption curve can be used to derive Engel curves, which are important for studies of family expenditure patterns. An Engel curve is the relationship between the equilibrium quantity purchased of a good and the level of income.[1]   Christian Engel was a nineteenth-century German statistician who did pioneering work related to such curves; economists have named them after him.

It is easy to see how an Engel curve can be derived from the income-consumption curve. Take the case in Figure 3.1 as an example. When money income equals P_x times Oe (or P_y times Of, since they are equal), the income-consumption curve shows that the consumer buys Oa units of good X. When money income equals P_x times Og (or P_y times Oh), the income-consumption curve shows that the consumer buys Oc units of good X. When money

Figure 3.2
The Engel Curve
for Good X.

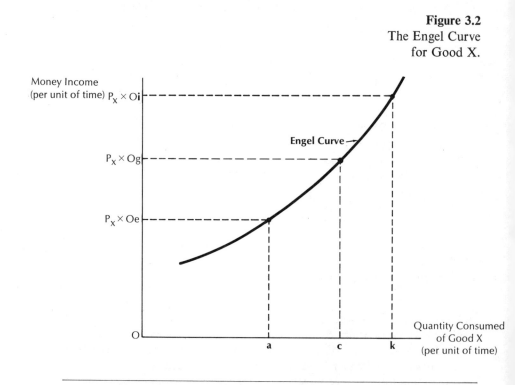

<hr>

[1]Often an Engel curve is defined to be the relationship between the consumer's *expenditure* on a commodity and his money income. But since commodity prices are held constant, his expenditure on the product is proportional to the number of units of the commodity that he consumes. So it makes no real difference for present purposes whether we use expenditure or quantity demanded of the commodity as the relevant variable.

income is P_x times *Oi* (or P_y times *Oj*), the income-consumption curve shows that the consumer buys *Ok* units of good X. These are three points on the Engel curve for good X for this consumer, each of these points showing the equilibrium amount of good X that he purchases at a certain level of money income. As more and more points are included, all of the points on the Engel curve for good X for this consumer are traced out, the result being that shown in Figure 3.2.

Figure 3.3
Engel Curves:
Various Shapes.

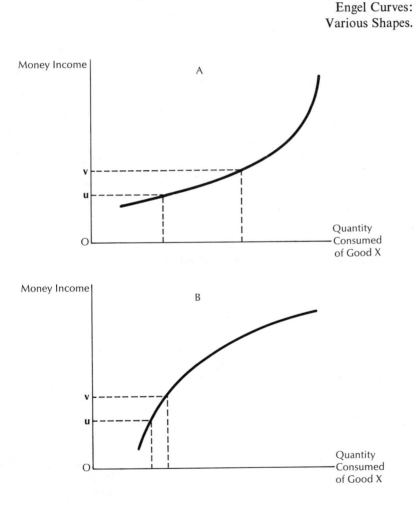

Of course, the shape of a consumer's Engel curve for a particular good will depend on the nature of the good, the nature of the consumer's tastes, and the level at which commodity prices are held constant. For example, Engel curves with quite different shapes are shown in panels A and B of Figure 3.3. According to the Engel curve in panel A, the quantity consumed of the good increases with income, but at a *decreasing* rate. According to the Engel curve in panel B the quantity consumed of the good increases with income, but at an *increasing* rate. A comparison of panel A with panel B shows that a change in income from Ou to Ov does not have as great an effect on consumption of the good in panel B as on consumption of the good in panel A.

In general, one would expect that Engel curves for goods like salt and shoe laces would show that the consumption of these commodities does not change very much in response to changes in income. For example, only a rather unusual type of person would respond to a large increase in income by gorging himself with salt and shoe laces—singly or in combination. On the other hand, goods like caviar and filet mignon might be expected to have Engel curves showing that their consumption increases considerably with increases in income. In general, this is probably so. But one should be careful about such generalizations. For example, if the consumer were a vegetarian, this would not hold true for filet mignon.

5. Effects of Changes in Commodity Price

In the previous two sections we have been concerned with the effect of changes in money income on the market basket that, in equilibrium, will be chosen by the consumer. Another important question is: Holding the consumer's money income constant, what will be the effect of a change in the price of a certain commodity on the amount of this commodity that the consumer will purchase? For example, take the case of the college student mentioned in Section 3. Suppose that his income remains constant at $2000 and that the prices of all commodities other than food are held constant. Suppose that the price of food is allowed to vary and that we watch how the quantity of food that he consumes (per unit of time) varies in response to changes in the price of food. What sort of relationship exists between the price of food and the quantity of food that he consumes (per unit of time)?

This case is unnecessarily specific. Let's pose the question more generally. Let's assume that there are only two commodities, good X and good Y.

Suppose that the price of good Y and the money income of the consumer is held constant, but the price of good X is allowed to vary from one level to another. Suppose that the budget line corresponding to the original price of good X is *B* in Figure 3.4. If the price of good X is increased and the new budget line is *C*, the new equilibrium market basket for the consumer will be *T*, rather than the original equilibrium market basket of *S*. (In the previous chapter, we saw that an increase in the price of good X increases the absolute value of the slope of the budget line but does not affect the vertical intercept of the line.) Thus, the increase in the price of good X will result in the consumer's buying *Ou* units of good X and *Ov* units of good Y, rather than the original market basket composed of *Or* units of good X and *Os* units of good Y.

Figure 3.4
Effects of Changes in
Price of Good X on
Consumer Equilibrium.

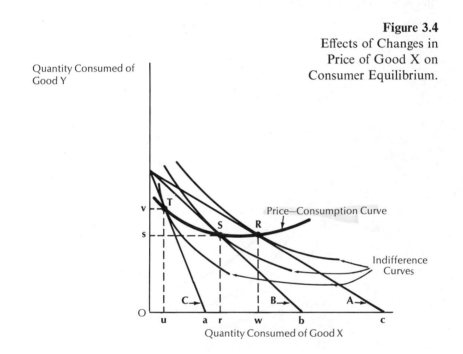

Corresponding to each price of good X is an equilibrium market basket that can be determined in this way. The curve that connects the various equilibrium points is called the *price-consumption curve*. Figure 3.4 shows the price-consumption curve for this consumer, given the level of his money income and the price of good Y. One reason why the price-consumption curve is of interest is that it can be used to derive the consumer's individual demand curve for the commodity in question. The individual demand curve shows how much of a given commodity the consumer would purchase (per unit of time) at various prices of the commodity, holding constant the consumer's money income, his tastes, and the prices of other commodities. The individual demand curve is one of the central concepts in the theory of consumer behavior.

How can the individual demand curve be derived from the price-consumption curve? To illustrate the procedure, consider the case in Figure 3.4. When the price of good X is I/Oa (where I is the money income of the consumer), the price-consumption curve shows that the consumer buys Ou units of good X.[2] When the price of good X is I/Ob, the price-consumption curve shows that the consumer buys Or units of good X. When the price of good X is I/Oc, the price-consumption curve shows that the consumer buys Ow units of good X. These are three points on the individual demand curve. By deriving more and more points in this way, one can obtain the entire individual demand curve for good X. The result, DD', is shown in Figure 3.5.

Figure 3.5
Individual Demand
Curve for Good X.

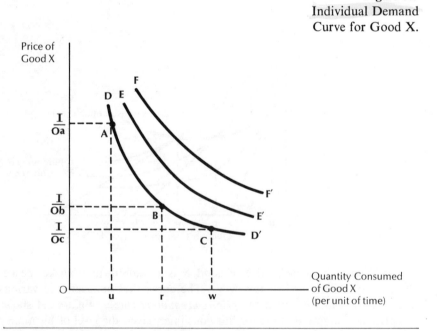

[2]From Figure 3.4, we know that the price of good X must be I/Oa when the budget line is C because, if the consumer devotes all of his money income, I, to good X, he can get Oa units of good X.

6.   The Individual Demand Curve: Location and Shape

The location and shape of an individual demand curve will depend on the level of money income and the level at which the prices of other goods are held constant, as well as on the nature of the commodity and the tastes of the consumer. For example, suppose that we consider the demand curve for good X of the consumer represented in Figure 3.5. If his income were to be held constant at a level higher than *I*, a different demand curve would result. Rather than *DD'* it might be *EE'* in Figure 3.5. Also, if the price of good Y were higher than that assumed in Figure 3.4, a different demand curve would result. Rather than *DD'*, it might be *FF'* in Figure 3.5. An important point to remember about a demand curve is that it is always drawn with certain assumptions about the level of the consumer's money income and the level of other prices in mind. In general it is only valid if these assumptions are correct.

It is important to differentiate between shifts in a consumer's demand curve for a particular commodity and changes in the amount of the commodity that he consumes. As we have seen, a consumer's demand curve may shift because of changes in his income or changes in the prices of other goods. It may also shift because of changes in his tastes. Such shifts in his demand curve are likely to result in changes in the amount of the commodity that he consumes. But they are not the only reason why changes may occur in the amount of the commodity that he consumes. In addition, changes in the price of the good will result in changes in the amount of the commodity that he consumes. We must be careful to distinguish between cases where the demand curve remains the same and changes in the consumption of the commodity occur because of changes in the commodity's price, and those cases where the demand curve shifts. The movement from point *A* to point *B* in Figure 3.5 is an example of the former; the shift of the demand curve from *DD'* to *EE'* is an example of the latter.

7.   Price Elasticity of Demand

Individual demand curves differ greatly in shape. In the case of some commodities a consumer's consumption of the commodity is quite sensitive to its price, small changes in price resulting in considerable changes in the amount he consumes. On the other hand, in the case of other commodities, the consumer's consumption of the commodity is not at all sensitive to its price, large changes in price resulting in only small changes in the amount that he consumes. To gauge the sensitiveness, or responsiveness, of the quantity demanded to changes in price, economists use a measure called the price elasticity of demand. The price elasticity of demand is defined to be the percentage change in quantity resulting from a 1-percent change in price.[3]

For example, suppose that a 1-percent reduction in the price of thumb tacks results in a 2-percent increase in the quantity demanded by young Billy Jones, who delights in putting them on dimly lit park benches. For this budding juvenile delinquent, the price elasticity of demand for thumb tacks is two. Convention dictates that we give the elasticity a positive sign despite the fact that the change in price is negative and the change in quantity demanded is positive. Clearly, the price elasticity of demand will generally vary from one point to another on an individual demand curve. For example, in the case of Master Jones, the price elasticity of demand may be higher when thumb tacks are a penny a piece than when they are two for a penny. Similarly, the price elasticity of demand will vary from consumer to consumer. For example, Mary Jones, Billy's sister, may have a much lower price elasticity of demand for thumb tacks than he does.

Alfred Marshall, the great English economist of about 70 years ago, was one of the first economists to give a clear formulation of the concept of the price elasticity of demand. It is a very important concept and one that will be used repeatedly throughout this book. One thing to note at the outset is that the price elasticity of demand is expressed in terms of *relative* changes in price and quantity demanded, not *absolute* changes in price and quantity demanded. This is because absolute changes are difficult to interpret. For example, suppose that a price goes up by a dime. This is a lot for a subway ride but little for a house. Similarly, it is a lot for a bottle of beer but little for a 50-gallon keg. A frequent error is to confuse the price elasticity of demand with the slope of the individual demand curve. They are by no means the same thing.[4]

---

[3]More accurately, if q is the quantity demanded and p is the price, the price elasticity of demand is

$$\eta = \frac{-dq}{dp}\frac{p}{q}$$

More will be said about the measurement of the price elasticity of demand in Chapter 4.

[4]The slope of the demand curve is dq/dp. A glance at Footnote 3 above will show that this is quite different from the price elasticity of demand.

· 8. Price Elasticity, Total Expenditure, and the Price-Consumption Curve

The demand for a commodity is said to be *price elastic* if the elasticity of demand exceeds one. The demand for a commodity is said to be *price inelastic* if the elasticity of demand is less than one. And the demand for a commodity is said to be of *unitary elasticity* if the price elasticity of demand is equal to one.

Suppose that a consumer's demand for a commodity is elastic, i.e., the price elasticity of demand exceeds one. In this situation, if the price is reduced, the percentage increase in the quantity consumed is greater than the percentage reduction in price. (That this is the case follows from the definition of the price elasticity of demand.) Consequently, a price reduction must lead to an increase in the consumer's expenditure on the product, and a price increase must lead to a decrease in the consumer's expenditure on the product. On the other hand, suppose that the consumer's demand for a commodity is inelastic, i.e., the price elasticity of demand is less than one. In this situation, if the price is reduced, the percentage increase in the quantity consumed is less than the percentage reduction in price. Thus, a price reduction must lead to a decrease in the consumer's expenditure on the product, and a price increase must lead to an increase in the consumer's expenditure on the product. Finally, if the demand for a product is of unitary elasticity, price increases or decreases do not affect the consumer's expenditure on the product.

Whether the demand for a commodity is price elastic, price inelastic, or of unitary elasticity can be determined from the slope of the price-consumption curve if we construct the price-consumption curve in the following way: Suppose that the commodity in question is good X. Suppose that we define as good Y the money spent by the consumer on goods other than good X. Admittedly, good Y is a peculiar sort of commodity but there is nothing to prevent us from defining a commodity in this way. In weighing every purchase, the consumer must decide whether he is willing to give up money he can spend on other goods—that is, good Y—for good X. Since good Y is money, its price is always one. For example, it takes a quarter to buy a quarter. The introduction of this kind of good Y is a useful trick that we will adopt elsewhere in this chapter.

Figure 3.6 shows the price-consumption curve, which is constructed in the way described in Section 5, for three different consumers. In panel A,

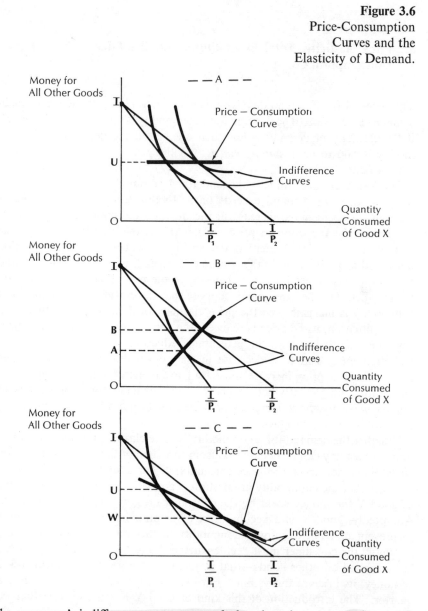

Figure 3.6
Price-Consumption
Curves and the
Elasticity of Demand.

the consumer's indifference curves are such that the price-consumption curve has zero slope. Thus, the amount of the consumer's income *not spent* on good X (this being the amount of good Y) remains constant at *OU*, when the price is decreased from P_1 to P_2. Consequently, the amount spent on good X must have remained constant, which means that the demand for good X is of unitary elasticity. In panel B, the upward sloping price-consumption curve indicates that this consumer's demand for good X is price inelastic. Why? Because a decrease in price from P_1 to P_2 results in an increase (from OA to OB) in the amount not spent on good X, which means that the consumer's expenditure on good X must have declined with a decrease in price.

In panel C, the downward sloping price-consumption curve indicates that the third consumer's demand for good X is price elastic. Why? Because a decrease in price from P_1 to P_2 results in a decrease (from OU to OW) in the amount not spent on good X, which means that the consumer's expenditure on good X must have increased with a decrease in its price. Thus, to summarize, a horizontal price-consumption curve implies that demand is of unitary elasticity; an upward sloping price-consumption curve implies that demand is price inelastic; and a downward sloping price-consumption curve implies that demand is price elastic.

9. Substitution and Income Effects

When the price of a good changes, the consumer is affected in two ways: first, he has a different real income, and second, he is likely to substitute now cheaper goods for more expensive goods. The total effect of a price change is illustrated in Figure 3.7. The original price ratio is given by the slope of the budget line A. Given this price ratio, the consumer chooses point U on indifference curve 1, and consumes Ox_1 units of good X. Now suppose that the price of good X is increased and B is the new budget line. Given the new price ratio, the consumer chooses point V on indifference curve 2, and consumes Ox_2 units of good X. The total effect of the price change on the quantity demanded of good X is a reduction of $Ox_1 - Ox_2$ units.

The total effect of this—or any—price change can be divided into two parts: the substitution effect and the income effect. First, consider the substitution effect. In Figure 3.7, when the price of good X increases, it is clear that a decrease occurs in the consumer's level of satisfaction, or real income: he winds up on indifference curve 2 rather than indifference curve 1. Suppose that, when the price goes up, we could increase the consumer's money income by an amount sufficient to keep him on his old indifference curve. If this could be done, it would mean that the budget line would be parallel to the budget line B, but that it would be tangent to indifference

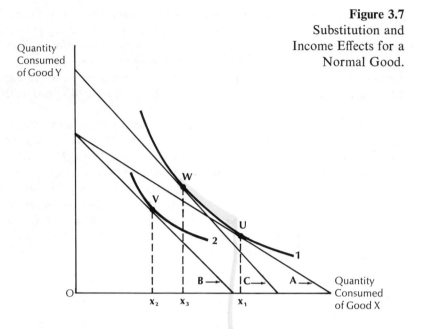

Figure 3.7
Substitution and
Income Effects for a
Normal Good.

curve 1. This hypothetical budget line is labeled *C* in Figure 3.7. The substitution effect is defined to be the movement from the original equilibrium point *U* to the imaginary equilibrium point *W*, which corresponds to the hypothetical budget line *C*. In terms of quantity the substitution effect is the reduction from Ox_1 to Ox_3 units of good X. Put differently, it is the change in quantity demanded of good X resulting from a price change when the level of satisfaction, or real income, is held constant.

Next, consider the income effect. The movement from the imaginary equilibrium point *W* to the actual new equilibrium point *V* is the income effect. This movement does not involve any change in prices, the price ratio being the same in budget line *C* as in budget line *B*. It is due to a change in total satisfaction, or *real income*, such a change being a movement from one indifference curve to another. In general, the income effect is defined to be the change in quantity demanded of good X due entirely to a change in real income, *all prices being held constant*. In Figure 3.7, it is the reduction from Ox_3 to Ox_2 units. The total effect of a change in price is obviously the sum of the income effect and the substitution effect.[5]

---

[5]For an explanation of substitution and income effects in elementary mathematical terms, see J. Henderson and R. Quandt, *Microeconomic Theory*, New York: McGraw-Hill, 1958.

10. Normal and Inferior Goods

The substitution effect is always negative. That is, if the price of good X increases and real income is held constant, there will always be a decrease in the consumption of good X; and if the price of good X decreases and real income is held constant, there will always be an increase in the consumption of good X. This result follows from the fact that indifference curves have a negative slope (see Chapter 2). However, the income effect is not predictable from the theory alone. In most cases, one would expect that increases in real income will result in increases in consumption of a good and that decreases in real income will result in decreases in consumption of a good. This is the case for so-called *normal goods*. But not all goods are normal. Some goods are called inferior goods because the income effect is the opposite (of that of a normal good) for them. An illustration of an inferior good is given in Figure 3.8, where real income is assumed to increase from indifference curve 1 to indifference curve 2. Prices are assumed to be the same before and after the increase in real income, the original budget line being *A* and the subsequent budget line being *B*. Figure 3.8 shows that, because of the

Figure 3.8
An Inferior Good.

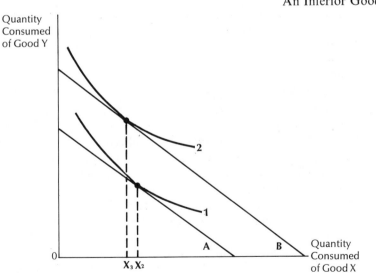

shapes of the indifference curves, the consumer purchases (OX_2-OX_3) fewer units of good X after the increase in real income than he originally did.

Ordinarily, the substitution effect of a price change is strong enough to offset an inferior good's income effect, the consequence being that the quantity demanded of a good is inversely related to its price. However, it is possible for an inferior good to have an income effect that is so strong that it offsets the substitution effect, with the result that the quantity demanded is directly related to the price, at least over some range of variation of price. A case of this sort is known as *Giffen's paradox*. For Giffen's paradox to occur, a good must be an inferior good, but not all inferior goods exhibit Giffen's paradox.

Oleomargarine is likely to be an inferior good for many consumers. Increases in real income are likely to lead to a substitution of butter for oleomargarine. Many other examples of inferior goods could be put forth, although, as stated above, inferior goods are in the minority. Giffen's paradox is a much, much rarer phenomenon. In the rest of this book, we shall assume that goods do not exhibit Giffen's paradox. That is, all demand curves are assumed to have a negative slope.

11.   The New York Water Crisis: An Application

Previous sections have presented a model of how consumers respond to changes in price and money income. But no attempt has been made to indicate how this model can be used to help solve practical problems. In the balance of this chapter, we discuss some applications of this model. To begin with, we describe a major problem that confronted New York City in 1949 and 1950.[6] At that time New York City experienced a water crisis, the average rate at which water was used being in excess of the yield of the water system. Various solutions to the problem were proposed. For example, the Board of Water Supply requested approval of the construction of a new dam and reservoir. In response to the crisis, the Mayor asked his Committee on Management Survey to examine the question and make recommendations. After looking into the problem, the Committee recommended that no new dam be built. Instead they recommended the use of universal metering, together with the elimination of leakage and waste from street mains.

---

[6]Many of the studies discussed in this book go back a number of years because it is easier to obtain permission to publish the results of such studies, because of publication lags, and so forth.

The idea behind metering was quite simple. Many consumers paid only a flat fee for water and were not metered. With metering, consumers would be charged about 15 cents per 100 cu ft of water. Obviously, since metering would increase the price of using an extra 100 cu ft of water from zero to 15 cents, it would result in the consumer's decreasing his use of water. According to the Mayor's Committee on Management Survey, universal metering would save about 200 million gallons of water per day.

The problem facing the city of New York, however, was whether or not metering was the best way of meeting the crisis. Another possible way to meet the crisis was to build the new dam proposed by the Board of Water Supply. Which solution was the best? After some deliberation it was decided to build the new dam. Was this the right decision?

12.   The RAND Study and Consumer's Surplus

A few years after it was decided to build the dam, a group of economists at the RAND Corporation studied this decision, their purpose being to show how microeconomic techniques could help to solve such problems.[7] Although the RAND study could not affect the decision in New York, it was hoped that it would affect such decisions at other times and places. In this section, we describe the way that the RAND economists attacked the problem. To begin with, one of the most important considerations in deciding whether New York should have adopted more extensive metering or built the new dam was the cost of meeting the crisis in each way. Which would be less costly?

According to various estimates the cost of providing water with the new dam would be about $1000 per million gallons per day. According to the Committee on Management Survey, the cost of metering would be about $50 per million gallons per day. But this was only part of the cost of metering, since it did not include the loss to consumers arising from the fact that they would be led to consume less water. To make a fair comparison of the cost of metering with the cost of a new dam, one should include such losses. But how can one make estimates of the monetary value of these losses? This is a very difficult question, more difficult than one may recognize at first glance.

---

[7]See J. Hirshleifer, J. Milliman, and J. De Haven, *Water Supply*, Chicago: University of Chicago Press, 1960, Chapter X. This application is also cited, but in somewhat less detail in G. Stigler, *The Theory of Price*, New York: Macmillan, 1967, pp. 78–81.

The RAND economists attempted to answer this question by using some results based on the sort of model we have discussed in this and the previous chapter. Suppose that a consumer is obliged to consume Q gallons of water per day rather than $Q + \Delta$ gallons of water per day. To measure the monetary value of the loss of Δ gallons of water per day, the RAND economists, following earlier economists like Jules Dupuit and Alfred Marshall,[8] used the maximum amount that the consumer would be willing to pay for the Δ gallons of water per day. Thus, if John Jones were willing to pay up to 10 cents a day to avoid losing 100 gallons of water per day, this would be the monetary value to him of the loss of this much water.

It is important to note that the monetary value to the consumer of the Δ gallons of water—that is, the maximum amount that he would pay for the Δ gallons of water—may be considerably more than the consumer actually pays for the Δ gallons of water. This is true for other commodities as well. For example, a man may be willing to pay up to $200 to avoid spending a week-end with his in-laws, but a merciful Providence may enable him to pay only $10 to avoid such a week-end. The difference between the maximum amount that the consumer would pay and the amount he actually pays is called *consumer's surplus*. For example, the consumer's surplus of the man who avoids his in-laws at a cost of $10 is $190.

Is there any way to tell from a consumer's demand curve for water how much—at the most—he is willing to pay to avoid the loss of Δ gallons of water per day? Under certain very special assumptions, there is a way. Suppose that we plot the consumer's indifference curves in Figure 3.9, the amount of water consumed per day being one good and the amount of money that the consumer can spend on all goods other than water being the other good. Suppose that the indifference curves (I, II, and III, as well as others not shown) are parallel, the vertical distance between any two indifference curves being the same regardless of where along the horizontal axis one measures this distance. This is a very restrictive assumption, but according to some economists it may be a reasonable approximation for commodities, like water, on which the consumer spends only a small amount of his income.[9]

What does it mean when we assume that the indifference curves in Figure 3.9 are parallel? If they are parallel, their slopes must be equal at a

---

[8]J. Dupuit, *Annales des Ponts et Chaussées*, 1844; and A. Marshall, *Principles of Economics*, London: Macmillan, 8th Ed., p. 842.

[9]Basically, the assumption underlying the analysis is that the marginal utility of income is constant. If this is the case, the indifference curves in Figure 3.9 will be parallel. This assumption is stringent indeed. See P. Samuelson, *Foundations of Economic Analysis*, Cambridge, Mass.: Harvard University Press, 1947, pp. 189–202; and J. Hicks, *Value and Capital*, London: Oxford University Press, 1946, pp. 38–41.

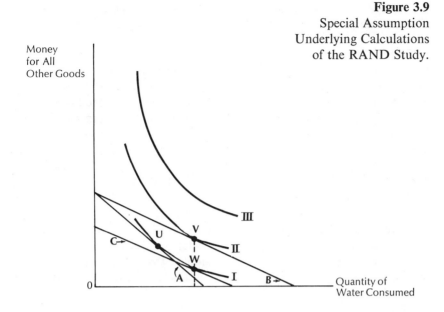

Figure 3.9
Special Assumption
Underlying Calculations
of the RAND Study.

given point along the horizontal axis. This means that, if a change occurs in the price of water, the income effect (on the consumption of water) of the price change is zero. To see this, suppose that the price of water decreases so that the consumer's equilibrium point shifts from U to V. The income effect of this price decrease can be measured by inserting a budget line, C, which has the slope of the new budget line, B, but which is parallel to the old indifference curve, I. If this fictitious budget line were the real one, the equilibrium point would be W. The income effect is the movement along the horizontal axis from W to V, which is clearly equal to zero.

13. The RAND Solution

The RAND economists' analysis rested on the assumption that the indifference curves in Figure 3.9 are parallel. Given this assumption, one can calculate from a consumer's demand curve for water how much—at the most —he is willing to pay to avoid having to consume Q gallons of water per day rather than $Q + \Delta$ gallons of water per day. The calculation is simple: *One simply computes the area under his demand curve for water between Q*

and $Q + \Delta$. The first objective of this section is to prove that this is so. Then we show how the RAND economists used this result to help solve the problem.

To prove that the maximum amount that the consumer will pay for the extra Δ gallons of water per day is the area under his demand curve between Q and $Q + \Delta$, we begin by constructing Figure 3.10, another graph in which the amount of water consumed is on the x axis and the amount of money spent on goods other than water is on the y axis. Suppose that A is the point at which the consumer is consuming Q gallons of water per day and spending the rest of his income, M, on other goods. If I_1 is the consumer's indifference curve that goes through A, it is obvious from Figure 3.10 that δ_1 is the amount of money income that the consumer would be willing to pay for an extra gallon of water per day. Suppose, however, that the consumer only has to pay z dollars to get the extra gallon of water per day. Then if I_2 is the consumer's indifference curve that goes through the point at which the consumer consumes $Q + 1$ gallons of water per day and spends $(M - z)$ dollars on other goods, the maximum amount that the consumer would be willing to pay to get a second extra gallon of water per day is δ_2. However,

Figure 3.10
The Maximum Amount
the Consumer Will Pay
to Consume $Q + \Delta$
Rather Than Q Gallons
of Water per Day.

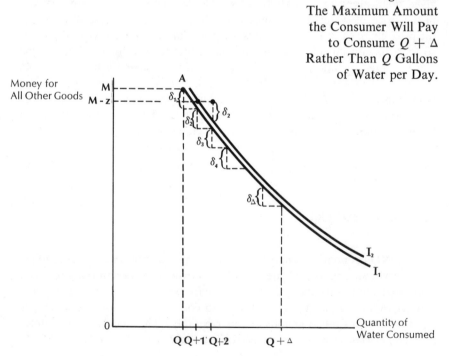

because of the assumption that the indifference curves are parallel, δ_2 is also the difference that would compensate for a second extra gallon of water per day if the consumer were still on I_1.

Adding one extra gallon after another per day, we find by repeated use of this same reasoning that the maximum amount that the consumer is willing to pay can be determined by reference to I_1 alone. For example, the maximum amount that the consumer would pay for the third extra gallon per day is δ_3. Consequently, the maximum total amount that the consumer would pay to consume $Q + \Delta$ gallons per day of water rather than Q gallons per day is $L(= \delta_1 + \delta_2 + \delta_3 + \cdots + \delta_\Delta)$. Moreover, since the maximum prices for the $(Q + 1)$th gallon, the $(Q + 2)$th gallon, ... and the $(Q + \Delta)$th gallon are clearly the prices corresponding to these numbers of gallons on the consumer's demand curve, L must equal the area under the consumer's demand curve between Q and $Q + \Delta$.

Returning to New York's problem, the RAND study also assumed, in effect, that the demand curve was approximately linear. Under this assumption, the area under the demand curve for each consumer would be about 7.5 cents per hundred cu ft times the number of cubic feet that was saved. This fact is shown in Figure 3.11. This amounts to about $100 per million

Figure 3.11
Area under the
Consumer's Demand
Curve for Water.

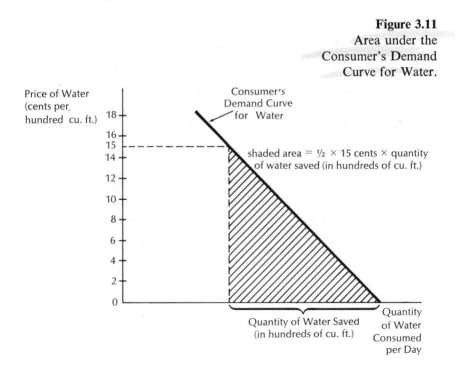

gallons. Thus the total cost of saving water through metering, including the costs cited in Section 12—was estimated by the RAND study to be about $150 per million gallons. This seemed to be lower than the cost of providing water with the new dam. Thus the RAND study seemed to suggest that metering might have been cheaper than building the dam.

This is an interesting example of the use of the theory of consumer demand. However, it should be recognized that this kind of analysis is fraught with many difficulties. For one thing, the assumption of parallel indifference curves may not be a good approximation. For another, there are problems, described in Chapter 15, involved in comparing and combining the results for different consumers.[10]   Still further, the proper decision depends on forecasts of rainfall as well as on growth in water usage. Subsequent studies have shown that the RAND study seriously overestimated the level of rainfall in the mid-sixties.[11]

14.   Indexes of the Cost of Living

Another type of problem in which the theory described in previous sections has proved useful is in the construction of index numbers of the cost of living. The phrase *cost of living* means the cost of living at a constant level of satisfaction. Cost-of-living indexes have always been closely associated with inflation, its measurement, and its problems. Labor unions want to know whether wages are keeping pace with the cost of living. Government officials must keep track of the extent to which inflationary pressures are in evidence.

How can indexes of the cost of living be constructed? To what extent can we infer from these indexes that increases or decreases have occurred in consumer welfare? For example, if a family earned $7000 in 1965 and $8400 in 1970, was it really better off in 1970, or were prices so much higher in 1970 that it really was worse off then? Ideally, a cost-of-living index is constructed so that the consumer's real income can be determined by dividing his money income by the index. Thus, if the ideal index went up by less than

---

[10]For example, who will receive the benefits? Who will pay the costs? How can we tell whether one set of citizens should reap benefits at the expense of some other set of citizens?

[11]See J. Hirshleifer and J. Milliman, "Urban Water Supply: A Second Look," *American Economic Review*, May 1967. I am indebted to E. Burmeister and R. Pollak for helpful discussions of these topics.

20 percent between 1965 and 1970, the family in question was better off in 1970; otherwise it was not.

In practice, cost-of-living indexes, like most things in life, are not ideal. The two basic types of indexes that can be used are the Laspeyres index and the Paasche index. To illustrate how these indexes are constructed, suppose that the family in the previous paragraph buys only two commodities. (We can easily show that the results are true for any number.) Suppose that it buys x_1 units of good X and y_1 units of good Y in 1970 and x_0 units of good X and y_0 units of good Y in 1965. Suppose that the price of good X is P_{x1} in 1970 and P_{x0} in 1965 and that the price of good Y is P_{y1} in 1970 and P_{y0} in 1965.

The Laspeyres index measures the change in the cost of the market basket purchased by the consumer in the original year, in this case 1965. Thus it equals

$$L = \frac{x_0 P_{x1} + y_0 P_{y1}}{x_0 P_{x0} + y_0 P_{y0}}$$

On the other hand, the Paasche index measures the change in the cost of the market basket purchased in the later year, in this case 1970. Thus it equals

$$P = \frac{x_1 P_{x1} + y_1 P_{y1}}{x_1 P_{x0} + y_1 P_{y0}}$$

15. The Laspeyres Index, Paasche Index, and Changes in Consumer Welfare

Given the prices paid by the family $(P_{x0}, P_{x1}, P_{y0}, P_{y1})$ and the quantities consumed (x_0, x_1, y_0, y_1), suppose that we computed these two indexes. What could we conclude from them? Recall that the family's money income went up by 20 percent between 1965 and 1970. If the Laspeyres index, L, is greater than 1.20, can we be sure that the consumer, i.e., the family, was worse off in 1970 than in 1965? If the Laspeyres index is less than 1.20, can we be sure that the consumer was better off in 1970 than in 1965? What about the Paasche index? If P is greater than 1.20, can we be sure that the consumer was worse off in 1970 than in 1965? If P is less than 1.20, can we be sure that the consumer was better off in 1970 than in 1965?

The first thing to note is that the cost of the market basket actually chosen in 1965 equaled

$$x_0 P_{x1} + y_0 P_{y1}$$

in 1970. Thus, if the family's income in 1970 exceeds this amount, it must be better off in 1970 than in 1965, since it can buy the old market basket—and more—in 1970. But the family's income in 1970 will exceed this amount if

$$x_0 P_{x1} + y_0 P_{y1} < x_1 P_{x1} + y_1 P_{y1}$$

since the quantity on the right-hand side must equal the family's income in 1970. If we divide both sides of the inequality by $(x_0 P_{x0} + y_0 P_{y0})$, it follows that the family must be better off in 1970 than in 1965 if the Laspeyres index, L, is less than the ratio of 1970 to 1965 income—1.20 in this case.

The next thing to note is that the family must have been better off in the earlier year if it could have bought the 1970 market basket in 1965 but did not do so. Thus it must have been better off in 1965 if

$$x_0 P_{x0} + y_0 P_{y0} > x_1 P_{x0} + y_1 P_{y0}$$

since the quantity on the left-hand side must equal the family's income in 1965. Dividing both sides of this inequality by $(x_1 P_{x1} + y_1 P_{y1})$, we find that the family must have been better off in 1965 than in 1970 if the ratio of the family's 1965 to 1970 money income exceeded $1/P$, or if the ratio of 1970 to 1965 money income is less than the Paasche index.

Thus we can be sure that the consumer's welfare has increased if the ratio of his later money income to his earlier money income is greater than the Laspeyres index. And we can be sure that his welfare has decreased if the ratio of his later money income to his earlier money income is less than the Paasche index. If neither of these conditions holds, we cannot tell whether an increase or a decrease has occurred in the consumer's welfare. Of course, these results are based on the assumption that the consumer's tastes and the quality of the goods remain constant during the relevant time interval. Otherwise the problem is completely intractable if not meaningless.

16. A Graphical Interpretation

The results of the previous section throw considerable light on an important and difficult problem. Basically, these results are nothing more than simple applications of the theory of consumer behavior. To see this, consider Figure 3.12(a), which shows the family's indifference curves, I_1 and I_2, the budget line in 1965, A, and the family's 1965 market basket, Q_{65}. Suppose that we calculate how much the family's 1965 market basket would have cost in 1970 and that we see how well off the family would have been in 1970

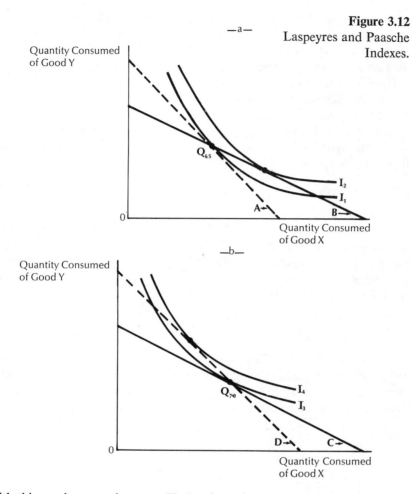

Figure 3.12
Laspeyres and Paasche
Indexes.

with this much money income. Under these circumstances, the 1970 budget
line would have been

$$x_1 P_{x1} + y_1 P_{y1} = I'$$

where $I' = x_0 P_{x1} + y_0 P_{y1}$. This budget line is shown as B in Figure 3.12(a).

It is obvious from Figure 3.12(a) that, if its 1970 income is I', the family
was at least as well off in 1970 as it was in 1965. It can certainly attain the
indifference curve, I_1, that it attained in 1965. Moreover, in general, it can
attain a higher indifference curve, I_2. Thus the ratio of the 1970 cost of attaining the 1965 indifference curve to the 1965 cost of attaining it is at most

$$\frac{I'}{x_0 P_{x0} + y_0 P_{y0}} = \frac{x_0 P_{x1} + y_0 P_{y1}}{x_0 P_{x0} + y_0 P_{y0}} = L$$

since the family's 1965 income was $x_0 P_{x0} + y_0 P_{y0}$. This, of course, is pre-cisely the result we obtained in the previous section: If the ratio of the consumer's money income in 1970 to his money income in 1965 is greater than the Laspeyres index, we can be sure that his welfare has increased.

Turning to the Paasche index, consider Figure 3.12(b), which shows the family's indifference curves, I_3 and I_4, the budget line in 1970, C, and the fam-ily's 1970 market basket, Q_{70}. Suppose that we calculate how much the 1970 market basket would have cost in 1965 and that we see how well off the family would have been in 1965 with this much money income. Under these circumstances, the 1965 budget line would have been

$$x_0 P_{x0} + y_0 P_{y0} = I''$$

where $I'' = x_1 P_{x0} + y_1 P_{y0}$. This budget line is shown as D in Figure 3.12(b).

It is obvious from Figure 3.12(b) that, if its 1965 income was I'', the family was at least as well off as in 1970. It can certainly attain the indifference curve, I_3, that it attained in 1970. Moreover, in general, it can attain a higher indifference curve, I_4. Thus the ratio of the 1970 cost of attaining the 1970 indifference curve to the 1965 cost of attaining it is at least

$$\frac{x_1 P_{x1} + y_1 P_{y1}}{I''} = \frac{x_1 P_{x1} + y_1 P_{y1}}{x_1 P_{x0} + y_1 P_{y0}} = P$$

since the family's 1970 income was $x_1 P_{x1} + y_1 P_{y1}$. This, too, is precisely the result we obtained in the previous section: If the ratio of the consumer's money income in 1970 to his money income in 1965 is less than the Paasche index, we can be sure that his welfare has decreased.[12]

17. Summary

Another way of expressing the conditions for consumer equilibrium is as follows: The rational consumer will choose in equilibrium to allocate his income between good X and good Y in such a way that the marginal rate

---

[12]This discussion of index numbers has benefited from the lucid presentation in G. Stigler, *op. cit.*, pp. 74–78. For further discussion, see P. Samuelson, *Foundations of Economic Analysis*, Cambridge, Mass.: Harvard University Press, pp. 146–163. Also, note that index numbers are often expressed as 100 times L or 100 times P, rather than L or P. Which is used should be clear from the context in which they appear.

of substitution of good X for good Y equals the ratio of the price of good X to the price of good Y. If we hold commodity prices constant, each level of money income results in an equilibrium market basket for the consumer, the curve that connects the points representing all of these equilibrium market baskets being called the income-consumption curve. The income-consumption curve can be used to derive the Engel curve, which is the relationship between the equilibrium amount of a good purchased by a consumer and the level of the consumer's money income. Engel curves play an important role in family expenditure studies.

Holding constant the consumer's money income as well as the prices of other goods, we can determine the relationship between the price of a good and the amount of this good that a consumer will consume. This relationship is called the consumer's individual demand curve for the good in question. The individual demand curve, one of the central concepts in the theory of consumer behavior, can be derived from the price-consumption curve, which includes all of the equilibrium market baskets corresponding to various prices of the good.

The location and shape of an individual demand curve will depend on the level of money income and the level at which the prices of other goods are held constant, as well as on the nature of the good and the tastes of the consumer. It is important to differentiate between shifts in a consumer's demand curve for a particular commodity and changes in the amount of the commodity that he consumes. Individual demand curves differ greatly in shape. In some cases, small changes in a good's price result in large changes in the amount of it that is consumed by the consumer; in other cases, large changes in a good's price result in small changes in the amount of it that is consumed by the consumer. To gauge the sensitiveness or responsiveness of the quantity demanded to changes in price, economists use a measure called the price elasticity of demand. The price elasticity of demand is defined to be the percentage change in quantity resulting from a 1-percent change in price.

The demand for a commodity is price elastic if the elasticity is greater than one, price inelastic if the elasticity is less than one, and of unitary elasticity if the elasticity equals one. A price reduction increases the consumer's total expenditure on the commodity if the demand is price elastic, decreases the consumer's total expenditure on the commodity if the demand is price inelastic, and does not affect the consumer's total expenditure on the commodity if the demand is of unitary elasticity. Using this fact, the price-consumption curve can be used to indicate whether the demand for a commodity is price elastic, price inelastic, or of unitary elasticity. Of course, the price elasticity of demand varies in general from point to point on the individual demand curve.

The total effect of a price change on the quantity demanded can be divided into two parts: the substitution effect and the income effect. The substitution effect is the change in quantity demanded of a good resulting from a price change when the level of satisfaction, or real income, is held constant. The income effect shows the effect of the change in real income that is due to the price change. The substitution effect is always negative. The income effect is not predictable from the theory alone: its sign is different for normal goods than for inferior goods.

An illustration of how this model of consumer behavior has been used to help solve practical problems is provided by the RAND Corporation's study of solutions to New York City's water crisis in the early fifties. An important question in this case was: How can one make estimates of the monetary value of the loss to consumers arising from the fact that, if metering were adopted, they would be led to consume less water? If certain restrictive assumptions are made, this question can be answered, at least approximately. Another type of problem where this sort of model has proved useful is in the construction of index numbers of the cost of living. The two basic types of indexes that can be used are the Laspeyres index and the Paasche index. Using these indexes, it is often possible to determine whether a consumer's welfare has increased or decreased during a particular period.

SELECTED REFERENCES

Hicks, John, *A Revision of Demand Theory*, Oxford: Oxford University Press, 1956.

Henderson, James and Richard Quandt, *Microeconomic Theory*, New York: McGraw-Hill, 1958.

Marshall, Alfred, *Principles of Economics*, London: Macmillan, 1920.

Stigler, George, *The Theory of Price*, New York: Macmillan, 1966.

Samuelson, Paul, *Foundations of Economic Analysis*, Cambridge, Mass.: Harvard University Press, 1947. (Advanced)

4

Market Demand

1. The Market

The previous chapter was concerned with the determinants of the quantity of a good demanded by an individual consumer. For many purposes, it is not so much the quantity demanded by a particular consumer that counts; instead it is the quantity demanded by all the consumers in a market. For example, the auto industry is much more concerned with the quantity of cars that will be demanded by the entire national market than with the quantity of cars that you or I will purchase next year. Economists, too, when confronted with many problems, are much more interested in the quantity of a good demanded in a market than in the quantity of a good demanded by a particular individual.

In this chapter we are concerned with market demand. After showing how the market demand curve is related to the demand curves of the individual consumers in the market, we define the price elasticity of market demand, show how it can be estimated, and discuss its importance and its determinants. Then we take up the effects of two other factors, beside the good's price, on the quantity of the good that is demanded in the market— aggregate money income and the prices of other commodities. Next, we look at market demand from the seller's side of the market, emphasis being placed on the concept of marginal revenue and the differences between the

79

demand curve for the industry and the demand curve for the firm. Finally, we discuss the measurement of market demand curves, and we describe two cases where such measurements were used to help guide public and private decision-makers.

At the outset, we must describe what we mean by a market. This is not quite as straightforward as it may seem, since most markets are not well defined in a geographical or physical sense. (For example, the New York Stock Exchange is an atypical market in the sense that it is located principally in a particular building.) What is a market? A good working definition is a group of firms and individuals that are in touch with each other in order to buy or sell some good. Of course, not every person in a market has to be in contact with every other person in the market; a person or firm is part of a market even if it is in contact with only a subset of the other persons or firms in the market.

Markets vary enormously in their size, arrangements, and procedures. For some household goods, all of the housewives west of the Rockies may be members of the same market. For other goods like Rembrandt paintings, only a few collectors, dealers, and museums scattered around the world are members of the market. Basically, however, all markets consist primarily of buyers and sellers, although third parties like brokers and agents may be present as well. In most markets, the sellers suggest the price, but this is not always the case. In this chapter, we assume that the consumers act independently and accept prices as given.

2. The Market Demand Curve: Derivation and Elasticity

In Section 5 of Chapter 3, we showed how an individual demand curve can be derived from a consumer's indifference map. This demand curve is of course the relationship between the quantity of the good demanded by the consumer (per unit of time) and the good's price, the money income of the consumer and the prices of other goods being held constant. The shape and level of the individual demand curve obviously depend on the consumer's tastes, as reflected in his indifference map. They also depend on the level of the consumer's money income and the level of the prices of other goods.

The market demand curve for a commodity is simply the *horizontal* summation of the individual demand curves of all the consumers in the market. Put differently, to find the market quantity demanded at each price, we add up the individual quantities demanded at that price. For example, Table 4.1

Table 4.1. Individual and Market Demand Schedules.

PRICE (CENTS PER UNIT OF THE COMMODITY)	QUANTITY DEMANDED (PER UNIT OF TIME)				QUANTITY DEMANDED IN MARKET (PER UNIT OF TIME)
	INDIVIDUAL A	INDIVIDUAL B	INDIVIDUAL C	INDIVIDUAL D	
	(UNITS OF THE COMMODITY)				
1	50	40	30	20	140
2	40	30	25	19	114
3	30	20	18	18	86
4	25	15	13	17	70
5	20	14	13	16	63
6	15	13	11	15	54
7	10	12	9	14	45
8	8	11	7	13	39
9	6	10	5	12	33
10	5	9	3	11	28

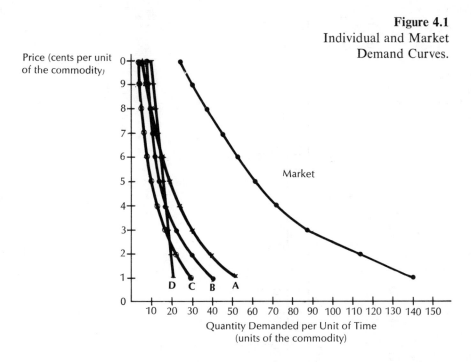

Figure 4.1
Individual and Market
Demand Curves.

Price (cents per unit of the commodity)

Quantity Demanded per Unit of Time
(units of the commodity)

shows the individual demand schedules[1] for four consumers. If these four consumers comprise the entire market, the market demand schedule is given in the last column of Table 4.1. Figure 4.1 shows the individual demand curves based on these same data, as well as the resulting market demand curve.

The market demand curve for a commodity is one of the most important concepts in microeconomics. The market demand curve shows how much of the commodity will be purchased (per unit of time) by the consumers in the market at each possible price (given that the level of money income of the consumers and the prices of other commodities are held constant). Information regarding the market demand curve is of the utmost importance to producers of the commodity: Obviously, they need to know how much can be sold at various prices. The market demand curve is also of great importance to economists because, as we shall see in subsequent chapters, it plays an important role in determining the price of the commodity.

The shape of a commodity's market demand curve varies from one commodity to another and from one market to another. Since individual demand curves almost always slope downward to the right, it follows that market

---

[1] A demand schedule is a table showing the quantity demanded at various prices.

demand curves will do so, too. But market demand curves, like individual demand curves, vary in the sensitivity of quantity demanded to price. In some markets a small change in price results in a large change in quantity demanded; in other markets, a large change in price results in a small change in quantity demanded. As in the case of individual demand curves, the elasticity of demand is used to measure the responsiveness of the quantity demanded in the market to changes in price.

It will be recalled from Chapter 3 that the price elasticity of demand is defined as the percentage change in quantity that results from a 1-percent change in price (the sign of the elasticity being made positive). For example, if a 1-percent reduction in the price of jelly beans results in a 3-percent increase in the amount of jelly beans sold in the Canadian market, the elasticity of market demand for jelly beans in Canada is three.[2]

Suppose that we have a table showing the quantity of a commodity demanded in the market at various prices. How can we estimate the price elasticity of market demand? Let ΔP be a change in the price of the good and ΔQ be the resulting change in its quantity. If ΔP is very small, we can compute the *point elasticity of demand:*

$$\eta = -\frac{\Delta Q}{Q} \div \frac{\Delta P}{P} \tag{4.1}$$

For example, consider Table 4.2 where data are given for very small increments in the price of the commodity. If we want to estimate the price elastic-

Table 4.2. Quantity Demanded at Various Prices for Small Increments in Price.

PRICE (CENTS PER UNIT OF COMMODITY)	QUANTITY DEMANDED PER UNIT OF TIME (UNITS OF COMMODITY)
99.95	40,002
100.00	40,000
100.05	39,998

---

[2]More precisely, the price elasticity of demand is

$$-\frac{dQ}{dP} \div \frac{Q}{P}$$

where Q is the quantity demanded of the commodity and P is its price. The definitions in the text are the same, except that finite differences are substituted for the derivatives.

ity of demand when the price is between 99.95 cents and $1, we have

$$\eta = - \frac{40{,}002 - 40{,}000}{40{,}000} \div \frac{99.95 - 100}{100} = .1$$

Note that we used $1 as P and 40,000 as Q. We could have used 99.95 cents as P and 40,002 as Q, but it would have made no real difference to the answer. (Try it and see.)

However, if we have data concerning only large changes in price (i.e., if ΔP and ΔQ are large), the answer may vary considerably depending on which value of P and Q is used in Equation 4.1. For example, take the case in Table 4.3. Suppose that we want to estimate the price elasticity of demand in the price range between $4 and $5. Then, depending on which value of P and Q is used, the answer will be

$$\eta = - \frac{20 - 3}{3} \div \frac{4 - 5}{5} = 28.33$$

$$\eta = - \frac{3 - 20}{20} \div \frac{5 - 4}{4} = 3.40$$

The difference between these two results is enormous. In a case of this sort, it is advisable to compute the *arc elasticity of demand*, which uses the average value of P and Q:

$$\eta = \frac{-\Delta Q}{(Q_1 + Q_2)/2} \div \frac{\Delta P}{(P_1 + P_2)/2} = \frac{\Delta Q(P_1 + P_2)}{\Delta P(Q_1 + Q_2)} \qquad (4.2)$$

where P_1 and Q_1 are the first values of price and quantity demanded, and P_2 and Q_2 are the second set. Thus, in Table 4.3,

$$\eta = - \frac{20 - 3}{11.5} \div \frac{4 - 5}{4.5} = 6.65$$

This is as good a way as any to get around this difficulty.

Table 4.3. Quantity Demanded at Various Prices for Large Changes in Price.

PRICE ($ PER UNIT OF COMMODITY)	QUANTITY DEMANDED PER UNIT OF TIME (UNITS OF COMMODITY)
3	40
4	20
5	3

3. Graphical Measurement of the Price Elasticity of Demand

The previous section has provided us with a way of computing the price elasticity of demand from a table like Tables 4.2 or 4.3. But suppose that we are given a demand curve. Is there any way to make a rough estimate of the price elasticity at a given point on this demand curve by means of visual inspection of the demand curve? The answer is yes, the following method being applicable to problems of this sort.

Suppose that the problem is to estimate the price elasticity of demand at point A on the demand curve, BB', in Figure 4.2. The first step is to

Figure 4.2
Graphical Measurement
of Price Elasticity.

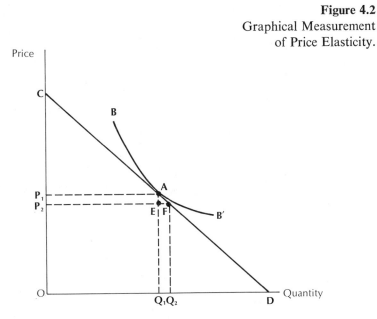

construct the tangent to BB' at point A, this tangent being labeled CAD. If the price falls from OP_1 to OP_2, the resulting change in the quantity demanded can be approximated by Q_1Q_2. This approximation should be reasonably good if the change in price is small or if the demand curve is close to linear. Thus the elasticity at point A can be approximated by

$$\frac{Q_1Q_2}{OQ_1} \div \frac{P_2P_1}{OP_1} = \frac{Q_1Q_2}{P_2P_1} \cdot \frac{OP_1}{OQ_1}$$

It is obvious that $Q_1Q_2 \div P_2P_1 = EF \div EA$. Also, since AEF and AQ_1D are similar right triangles, $EF \div EA = Q_1D \div Q_1A = Q_1D \div OP_1$. Thus,

$$\eta = \frac{Q_1D}{OP_1} \cdot \frac{OP_1}{OQ_1} = \frac{Q_1D}{OQ_1}$$

and since $Q_1D \div OQ_1 = AD \div CA$,

$$\eta = AD \div CA \qquad (4.3)$$

This result, which is easy to interpret and apply, is exact if the demand curve is linear. If the price change is small, it is a good approximation even if the demand curve is not linear.

Let us apply this result to the case of a linear demand curve, such as BA in Figure 4.3. It is obvious from inspection of this figure that the elasticity

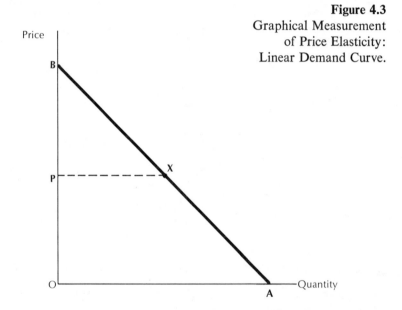

Figure 4.3
Graphical Measurement
of Price Elasticity:
Linear Demand Curve.

of demand exceeds one at prices exceeding OP, that the elasticity of demand is less than one at prices under OP, and that there is unitary elasticity of demand at a price of OP. To prove that there is unitary elasticity of demand at a price of OP, we need only note that $XA = BX$. To prove that the elasticity of demand is greater than one at prices above OP, choose any price above OP and find the point corresponding to this price on the demand curve; it is clear that the distance from this point to A is greater than the distance from this point to *B*. To prove that the elasticity of demand is less than one at prices under *OP*, choose any price below *OP* and find the point corresponding to this price on the demand curve; it is clear that the distance from this point to *A* is less than the distance from this point to *B*.

4. Price Elasticity and Total Money Expenditure

The price elasticity of demand is of interest to economists because it is a useful way to describe an important aspect of the market for a commodity. Whether they know it or not, the producers of a commodity should also be interested in the price elasticity of demand. Why? Because they are interested in questions like: Will an increase in price result in an increase in the total amount spent by consumers on the product? Or will an increase in price result in a decrease in the total amount spent by consumers on the product? The answers to these questions depend on the price elasticity of demand, as we shall show in this section.

Suppose that the demand for the product is price elastic, i.e., the price elasticity of demand exceeds one. The total amount of money spent by consumers on the product equals the quantity demanded times the price per unit. In this situation, if the price is reduced, the percentage increase in quantity demanded is greater than the percentage reduction in price (since this follows from the definition of the price elasticity of demand). It then follows that a price reduction must lead to an increase in the total amount spent by consumers on the commodity.

The reasoning used here is, of course, just the same as that used in Section 8 of Chapter 3 where we showed that the same kind of result holds at the level of the individual consumer. If we apply this reasoning to other possible cases as well, we find that, if the demand is price elastic, a price increase leads to a reduction in the amount of money spent on the commodity. If the demand is price inelastic, a price decrease leads to a reduction in the total amount spent on the commodity, and a price increase leads to an increase in the amount spent on the commodity. If the demand is of unitary elasticity, an increase or decrease in price has no effect on the amount spent on the commodity.

These results can be illustrated with the linear demand curve in Figure 4.3. As we move down the demand curve from *B* to *X*, the elasticity of demand gets smaller, but it always exceeds one. Thus the total amount spent on the good increases continually as we move from *B* to *X*. At point *X*, since there is unitary elasticity, there is no change in the total amount spent on the good.

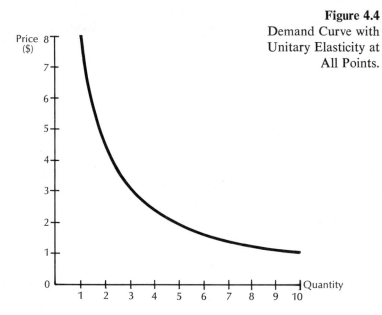

Figure 4.4
Demand Curve with
Unitary Elasticity at
All Points.

Moving from X to A, the elasticity of demand is always less than one. Thus the total amount spent on the good decreases continually as we move from X to A.

Another interesting case is shown in Figure 4.4. The demand curve shown there is a rectangular hyperbola, which means that

$$q = \frac{a}{p} \qquad (4.4)$$

where q is the quantity demanded of the good, p is its price, and a is some constant. It can be shown that this kind of demand curve is of unitary elasticity at all points. Thus changes in price have no effect on the total amount spent on the product. It is evident from Equation 4.4 that, regardless of the price, the total amount spent on the product will be a ($10 in Figure 4.4).

5. Determinants of the Price Elasticity of Demand

In previous sections we have stressed the importance of the price elasticity of demand, but nothing has been said about the determinants of the price elasticity of demand. What determines whether the demand for a commodity is price elastic or price inelastic in a certain price range? Why does the price elasticity of demand for one commodity equal 3.0 and the price elasticity of demand for another commodity equal 1.5? This is a very important question, and the one to which we turn our attention in this section.

First, and foremost, the price elasticity of demand for a commodity depends on the number and closeness of the substitutes that are available. If a commodity has many close substitutes, its demand is likely to be price elastic. If increases occur in the price of the product, a large proportion of its buyers will turn to the close substitutes that are available; if decreases occur in its price, a great many buyers of substitutes will switch to this product.

Of course, the extent to which a commodity has close substitutes depends on how narrowly it is defined. In general, one would expect that, as the definition of the product becomes narrower and more specific, the product has more close substitutes and its demand becomes more price elastic. Thus the demand for a particular brand of cigarettes is likely to be more price elastic than the over-all demand for cigarettes and the demand for cigarettes is likely to be more price elastic than the demand for tobacco products as a whole. If a commodity is defined so that it has perfect substitutes, its price elasticity of demand is infinite. Thus, if the cotton produced by Farmer Jones is exactly the same as the cotton produced by other farmers and if he increases his price slightly (to a point above the market level), his sales would be reduced to nothing.

Second, it is often asserted that the price elasticity of demand for a commodity is likely to depend on the importance of the commodity in consumers' budgets. For example, the demand for commodities like thumb tacks, pepper, and salt may be quite inelastic. The typical consumer spends only a very small fraction of his income on such goods. On the other hand, for commodities that bulk larger in the typical consumer's budget, like major appliances, the elasticity of demand may tend to be higher. Consumers are likely to "shop around" to a greater extent in the case of goods that require larger outlays. Third, it is often asserted that the price elasticity of demand for a commodity depends on the range of uses for it. If a commodity has a wide range of uses, it is often felt that its demand will be more elastic than if it can be used in only one area.

Finally, the price elasticity of demand for a commodity is likely to depend on the length of the period to which the demand curve pertains. (Every market demand curve—like every individual demand curve—pertains, of course, to a certain time interval.) In general, demand is likely to be more elastic, or less inelastic, over a long period of time than over a short period of time. The longer the period of time, the easier it is for consumers and business firms to substitute one good for another. If, for example, the price of natural gas should decline relative to other fuels, the consumption of natural gas in the week after the price decline would probably increase very little. But over a period of several years, people would have an opportunity to take account of the price decline in choosing the type of fuel to be used in new houses and renovated old houses. In the longer period of several years, the price decline would have a greater effect on the consumption of natural gas than in the shorter period of one week.

6. The Income Elasticity of Demand

Up to this point, we have been concerned solely with the effect of price on the quantity of the commodity demanded in the market. Yet price is not the only factor that influences the quantity demanded in the market. Another important factor is the level of money income among the consumers in the market. For example, if housewives have plenty of money to spend, the quantity demanded of beef is likely to be greater than if they are poverty-stricken. Of if incomes in a particular community are high, the quantity demanded of caviar is likely to be greater than if incomes are low.

For an individual consumer, we saw in Chapter 3 that the relationship between money income (per period of time) and the amount consumed of a particular commodity (per period of time) can be represented by an Engel curve. Recall that this curve is based on the condition that the prices of all commodities remain constant. At any point on the Engel curve, one can characterize the sensitivity of the amount consumed to changes in the consumer's money income by the *income elasticity of demand*, which is defined as

$$\eta_I = \frac{\Delta Q}{Q} \div \frac{\Delta I}{I} \tag{4.5}$$

where ΔQ is the change in quantity consumed that results from a small change in the consumer's money income ΔI, Q is the original quantity consumed, and I is the original money income of the consumer.[3]

Some goods have positive income elasticities, indicating that increases in the consumer's money income result in increases in the amount of the good

---

[3]More precisely, the income elasticity of demand is

$$\frac{dQ}{dI} \div \frac{Q}{I}$$

The definition in the text is the same except that finite differences are substituted for derivatives.

consumed. For example, one would generally expect steak and caviar to have positive income elasticities. Other goods have negative income elasticities, indicating that increases in the consumer's money income result in decreases in the amount of the good consumed. For example, margarine and poor grades of vegetables and other types of food might have negative income elasticities.[4] However, one must be careful to point out that the income elasticity of demand for a good is likely to vary considerably, depending on the level of the consumer's money income. Thus, in some ranges of income, the income elasticity may be positive; in other ranges of income, it may be negative.

The concept of income elasticity of demand can be applied to an entire market as well as to a single consumer, the only change in Equation 4.5 being that we must interpret Q as the total quantity demanded in the market, I as the aggregate money income of all consumers in the market, and ΔQ and ΔI as the changes in total quantity demanded and in aggregate money income. As in the case of the individual consumer, it is assumed that the prices of all commodities are held constant. Figure 4.5 shows a variety of possible relationships between the total quantity demanded in the market and the aggregate money income of the consumers. Curve A shows a case in which the income elasticity is greater than one, which means that a 1-percent increase in money income results in more than a 1-percent increase in the total quantity demanded. Curve B shows a case in which the income elasticity is less than one, which means that a 1-percent increase in money income results in less than a 1-percent increase in the total quantity demanded. Case C shows a case in which the income elasticity is negative, indicating that increases in aggregate money income result in decreases in the total quantity demanded.[5]

There are, of course, enormous differences among goods with respect to their income elasticity of demand. No refined statistical surveys are needed to tell us that the income elasticity of demand for high-quality food and clothes is generally higher than the income elasticity of demand for salt and Kleenex. Luxury items are generally assumed to have high income elasticities of demand. Indeed, one way to define luxuries and necessities is to say that luxuries are goods with high income elasticities of demand, and necessities are goods with low income elasticities of demand.

An empirical law of consumption, *Engel's law,* was developed in the nineteenth century by Christian Engel, introduced in Chapter 3. Based on data

---

[4]The similarity between goods with a negative income elasticity and inferior goods should be obvious.

[5]Of course, the quantity demanded may be influenced by the distribution of money income among consumers as well as the aggregate money income. We assume that the income distribution is held constant.

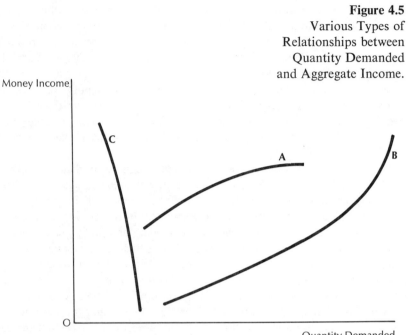

Figure 4.5
Various Types of
Relationships between
Quantity Demanded
and Aggregate Income.

concerning the budgets and expenditures of a large number of families, Engel found that the income elasticity of demand for food was quite low. He concluded from this result that the proportion of its income spent on food by a nation (or a family) was a good index of its welfare, the better-off nations spending a smaller proportion on food than the poorer ones. This generalization is crude, but still serviceable within limits.[6]

7. Cross Elasticities of Demand

In previous sections we have discussed the effects of two factors—the price of the commodity and the level of aggregate money income—on the quantity of the commodity demanded in the market. These two factors are not the only important ones, another important factor being the prices of other

---

[6]For an excellent recent study of Engel's law, see H. Houthakker, "An International Comparison of Household Expenditures Patterns," *Econometrica*, Oct. 1957.

commodities. Holding constant the commodity's own price (as well as the level of money incomes) and allowing the price of another commodity to vary, there may be important effects on the quantity demanded in the market for the commodity in question. By observing these effects, we can classify pairs of commodities as *substitutes* or *complements*, and we can measure how close the relationship (either substitute or complementary) is.

Consider two commodities, good X and good Y. Suppose that good Y's price goes up. What is the effect on the quantity of good X that is bought (per unit of time)? The *cross elasticity of demand* is defined as

$$\eta_{xy} = \frac{\Delta Q x}{Q x} \div \frac{\Delta P y}{P y} \tag{4.6}$$

where $\Delta P y$ is the change in the price of good Y, $P y$ is the original price of good Y, $\Delta Q x$ is the resulting change in the quantity demanded of good X, and $Q x$ is the original quantity demanded of good X. Thus the cross elasticity of demand is the relative change in the quantity of good X resulting from a 1-percent change in the price of good Y.[7]

Whether goods X and Y are classified as substitutes or complements depends on whether the cross elasticity of demand is positive or negative. For example, an increase in the price of lamb, the price of pork remaining constant, will tend to increase the quantity of pork demanded; thus η_{xy} is positive, and lamb and pork are classified as substitutes. On the other hand, an increase in the price of fishing licenses may tend to decrease the purchase of fishing poles, the price of fishing poles remaining constant; thus η_{xy} is negative, and fishing licenses and fishing poles are classified as complements. Figure 4.6 shows the relationship between the consumption of good X and the price of good Y, given that they are substitutes of complements.

The cross elasticity of demand looks at the change in quantity demanded that results from a change in price *without* compensating for the change in the level of real income. This is the only feasible procedure because we seldom have data concerning the indifference maps of individual consumers.

---

[7]More precisely the cross elasticity of demand is

$$\frac{d\,Qx}{d\,Py} \div \frac{Qx}{Py}$$

The definition in the text is the same except that finite differences are substituted for derivatives.

In subsequent discussions of marginal revenue, marginal product, marginal cost, and other such terms, we shall use finite differences and not bother to repeat each time the alternate definition based on the use of derivatives (the alternative definition being obvious in each case).

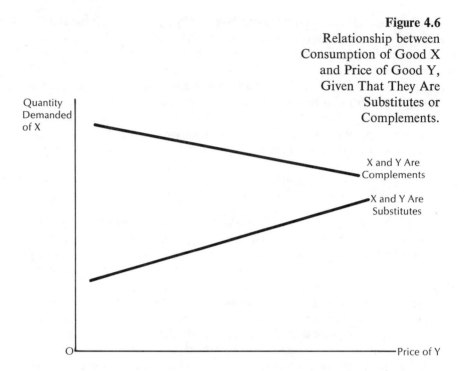

Figure 4.6
Relationship between
Consumption of Good X
and Price of Good Y,
Given That They Are
Substitutes or
Complements.

Moreover, we are generally interested in the relationship between commodities in the whole market rather than the relationship for a particular consumer.[8]

Finally, one other point should be noted. Whether goods X and Y are substitutes or complements can be determined by looking at the relative change in the quantity demanded of good X divided by the relative change in the price of good Y, i.e., η_{xy}. It can also be determined by looking at the relative change in the quantity of good Y divided by the relative change in the price of good X, i.e., η_{yx}. However, it should not be expected that the two elasticities will have the same numerical value. For example, goods X and Y may be substitutes, but the consumption of good X may be more sensitive to changes in the price of good Y than the consumption of good Y is to changes in the price of good X.

---

[8]For a single individual, goods can be classified as substitutes or complements more accurately on the basis of his utility function. Good Y is a substitute (complement) for good X if the marginal rate of substitution of good Y for money is reduced (increased) when good X is substituted for money in such a way as to leave the consumer no better or worse off than before. See J. Hicks, *Value and Capital*, New York: Oxford University Press, 1946, p. 44.

8.   The Sellers' Side of the Market and Marginal Revenue

Up to this point, we have looked at the subject of demand chiefly from the point of view of consumers. But, as we have already noted, the expenditures of the consumers are the receipts of the sellers. In the next three sections, we look at demand from the other side of the market—the seller's side. We begin by defining marginal revenue. Then, in the following section we show how marginal revenue can be estimated from the demand curve. Next, in Section 10, we discuss the differences between the demand curve for the industry and the demand curve for the firm. Finally, in Section 11, we discuss the relationship between marginal revenue and the price elasticity of demand. These results are of great importance and they form a bridge to the theory of the firm, which is presented in succeeding chapters.

The sellers of a commodity are interested, of course, in the total amount of money spent by consumers on the commodity. This amount is called *total revenue* by economists. From the market demand curve, one can easily determine the total revenue of the sellers at each price, since total revenue is, by definition, price times quantity. Thus, in Table 4.4, total revenue is $36 at a price of $9. The value of total revenue at various prices is shown in the third column of Table 4.4.

Table 4.4.   Quantity Demanded, Total Revenue, and Marginal Revenue.

PRICE ($ PER UNIT OF THE COMMODITY)	QUANTITY DEMANDED (UNITS OF THE COMMODITY)	TOTAL REVENUE ($)	MARGINAL REVENUE ($ PER UNIT OF THE COMMODITY)
13	0	0	
			12
12	1	12	
			10
11	2	22	
			8
10	3	30	
			6
9	4	36	
			4
8	5	40	
			2
7	6	42	
			0
6	7	42	
			−2
5	8	40	
			−4
4	9	36	
			−6
3	10	30	

Economists and firms are also concerned with *marginal revenue*, which is defined as the addition to total revenue attributable to the addition of one unit to sales. Thus if $R(q)$ is total revenue when q units are sold and $R(q-1)$ is total revenue when $(q-1)$ units are sold, the marginal revenue between q units and $(q-1)$ units is $R(q) - R(q-1)$. This is illustrated in Table 4.4. For example, when only one unit is sold, it is possible to charge a price of $12 and the total revenue is $12. The marginal revenue between one unit of output and zero units of output is total revenue at one unit of output minus total revenue at zero units of output. Since the latter is zero, the marginal revenue between one unit of output and zero units of output is $12.

It is evident from Table 4.4 that total revenue from a given number of units of output—say n units—is equal to the sum of marginal revenue between 0 and 1 units of output, marginal revenue between 1 and 2 units of output, marginal revenue between 2 and 3 units of output, and so on up to marginal revenue between $(n-1)$ and n units of output. For example, total revenue for 2 units of output is $22, which equals the sum of marginal revenue between 0 and 1 units of output ($12) and marginal revenue between

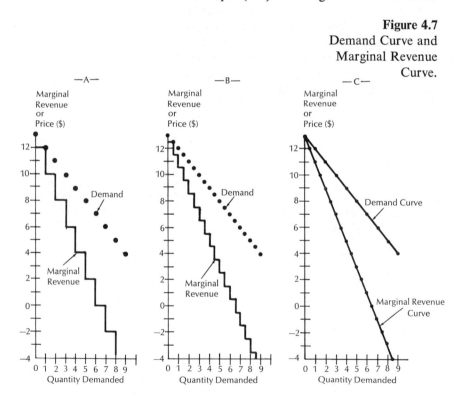

Figure 4.7
Demand Curve and
Marginal Revenue
Curve.

1 and 2 units of output ($10). It is easy to prove that this will always be true. By the definition of marginal revenue, the sum of the marginal revenue between 0 and 1 units of output, 1 and 2 units of output, and so on up to $(n - 1)$ and n units of output is

$$[R(1) - R(0)] + [R(2) - R(1)]$$
$$+ [R(3) - R(2)] + \cdots + [R(n) - R(n - 1)]$$

Since $R(1), R(2), \ldots, R(n - 1)$ appear with both positive and negative signs, they cancel out; and since $R(0) = 0$, this sum must equal $R(n)$.

The *marginal revenue curve* shows marginal revenue at various levels of output of a commodity. For example, panel A of Figure 4.7 shows the marginal revenue curve for the situation in Table 4.4. Note that the marginal revenue curve lies above zero when total revenue is increasing, that it lies below zero when total revenue is decreasing, and that it equals zero when total revenue is at a maximum. For example, in panel A of Figure 4.7, the marginal revenue curve is zero between 6 and 7 units of output, and inspection of Table 4.4 confirms that they are the output levels where total revenue is maximized. Also, marginal revenue is shown to be positive for output levels of less than 6 units and negative for output levels of greater than 7 units; inspection of Table 4.4 confirms that total revenue is increasing up to 6 units of output and is decreasing beyond 7 units of output.

The marginal revenue curve consists of a number of "steps" when the demand curve is defined for only a relatively few points. For example, this is the case in panel A of Figure 4.7. However, as the demand curve is defined for more and more points, the "teeth" of the saw-toothed marginal revenue curve become finer and finer. For example, they are finer in panel B than in panel A. Finally, when the demand curve is continuous, as in panel C, the marginal revenue curve becomes continuous, too.

9. Determination of the Marginal Revenue Curve

Presented with a table like Table 4.4, it is no problem to calculate marginal revenue. But often one is given a demand curve, like DD' in Figure 4.8. How does one go about determining the marginal revenue curve in this case? To begin with, we assume that the demand curve is linear. The results in panel C of Figure 4.7 suggest quite correctly that, if the demand curve is a straight line, the marginal revenue curve will be a straight line, too. Also,

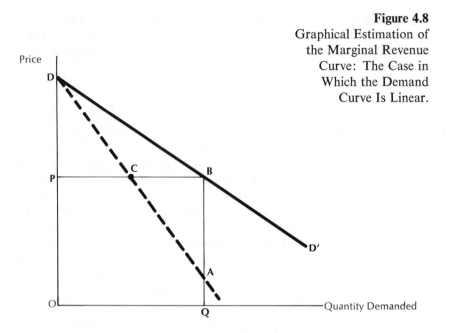

Figure 4.8
Graphical Estimation of the Marginal Revenue Curve: The Case in Which the Demand Curve Is Linear.

they suggest that the marginal revenue curve and the demand curve start out at the same point on the vertical axis.[9] Since the marginal revenue curve is a straight line that intersects the vertical axis at *D*, we need to determine only one additional point on this curve to identify the entire curve, since two points determine a straight line.

Consider any output level, *OQ*, in Figure 4.8. What is the marginal revenue at this point? The total revenue at this point is *OP* times *OQ*, which is the area of the quadrangle, *OPBQ*. The total revenue at this point must also equal the sum of all the marginal revenues up to this point, which is the area *ODAQ*. Thus the unknown *A* (which is what we are trying to determine) must be such that the area of *OPBQ* equals the area of *ODAQ*.

---

[9]Of course, this does not prove that the marginal revenue curve will have these characteristics. To prove that this is the case, let the demand curve be
$$P = a - bQ$$
Then the total revenue curve is
$$R = PQ = aQ - bQ^2$$
and the marginal revenue curve is
$$\frac{dR}{dQ} = \frac{d(PQ)}{dQ} = a - 2bQ$$
Thus the marginal revenue curve is a straight line and it has the same intercept on the y axis (i.e., a) as the demand curve. (P is price, and Q is quantity demanded.)

These two areas have in common the area $OPCAQ$. Deducting this common area, it follows that A must be such that the triangle CBA equals the area of the triangle DPC. But these two triangles are similar, since angle PCD equals angle BCA, and angle DPC equals angle CBA (both being 90°). Thus, if they have the same area, these triangles must be congruent, and PD must equal AB. Consequently, one can find the unknown point A on the marginal revenue curve by dropping a perpendicular from B to the x axis and a perpendicular from B to the y axis, and by marking off a distance of PD from B on the perpendicular QB. Given the determination of A, the entire marginal revenue curve can be constructed by drawing a straight line through D and A.

Another method that is sometimes used is as follows. First, drop a perpendicular from B to the x axis and from B to the y axis. Second, find the midpoint of the perpendicular to the y axis. Call this midpoint C. (In fact, in Figure 4.8, it will accord with C.) Finally, draw a line through D and C. This line is also the marginal revenue curve. Naturally, this method amounts to the same thing as the method described in the previous paragraph, and the results are precisely the same.[10]

Thus far, we have assumed that the demand curve is linear. Fortunately, our procedure needs to be changed only slightly, even if the demand curve is not linear. To illustrate, consider the demand curve, DD', in Figure 4.9. To derive the marginal revenue curve, we begin by finding the marginal revenue at quantity OQ_1. First, drop perpendiculars from B_1 to both axes. Second, form the tangent to the demand curve at B_1 and extend it to intersect the y axis at G_1. Third, to find marginal revenue at OQ_1, deduct an amount equal to P_1G_1 from Q_1B_1 the result being Q_1A_1 which indicates that point A_1 is on the marginal revenue curve. Having found the point on the marginal revenue curve at quantity OQ_1, we can do the same for OQ_2 (the resulting point on the marginal revenue curve being A_2), and so forth. Connecting the resulting points, we can approximate the true marginal revenue curve.

10. Industry and Firm Demand Curves

Throughout this chapter we have been concerned with the market demand curve for a commodity. It is important to distinguish between the market demand curve for a commodity and the market demand curve for the output

---

[10]The results of Footnote 9 show that this is the case.

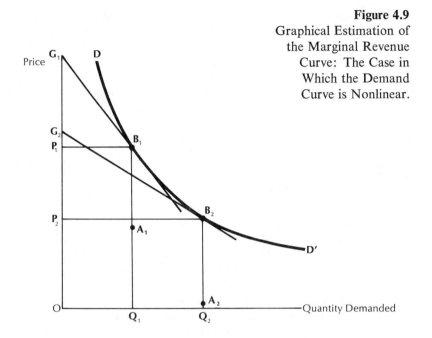

Figure 4.9
Graphical Estimation of
the Marginal Revenue
Curve: The Case in
Which the Demand
Curve is Nonlinear.

of a single firm producing the commodity. Of course, if only one firm produces the commodity, the relevant industry being a *monopoly*, there is no difference between these demand curves. But if there is more than one firm producing the commodity, as is usually the case, the demand curve for the output of each firm will generally be quite different from the demand curve for the commodity. In particular, the firm's demand curve will generally be more price elastic than that facing the industry as a whole, since the products of other firms are close substitutes for the products of any one firm.

Suppose that there are a great many sellers of the product in question, say 50,000 sellers of the same size, and that the conditions in the industry are close to *perfectly competitive*. (In perfect competition, the number of firms is large and their products are homogeneous, and for simplicity it is assumed that the firms have full knowledge of the market. Much more will be said about perfect competition in subsequent chapters.) In a case of this sort, if any one firm were to triple its output and sales, the total industry output would increase by only .004 percent. Since this change in total output is too small to have any noticeable effect on the price of the commodity, each seller can act as if variations in its own output will have no real effect on market price. Put differently, it appears to each firm that it can sell all it wants—within the range that is within its capabilities—without influencing the price. Thus the demand curve facing the individual firm in perfect competition is *horizontal*.

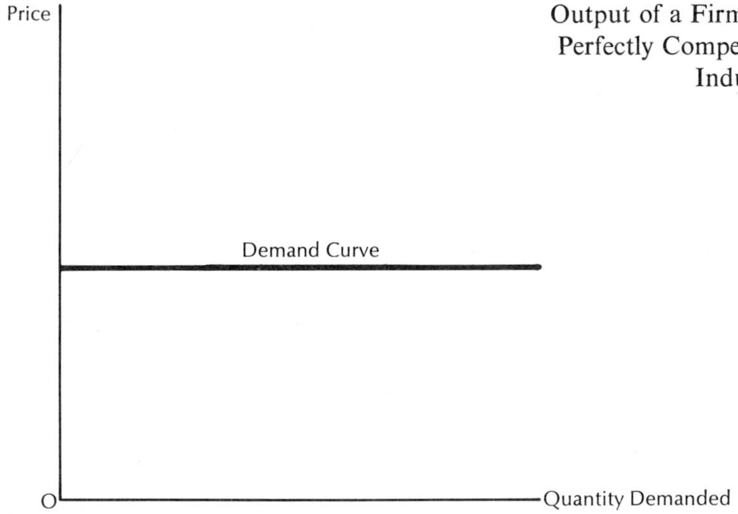

Figure 4.10
Demand Curve for the
Output of a Firm in a
Perfectly Competitive
Industry.

The firm in a perfectly competitive market can increase its sales rate without shading its price to get the extra business. Its demand curve, shown in Figure 4.10, is infinitely elastic: A very small decrease in price would result in an indefinitely large increase in the quantity it could sell, and a very small increase in price would result in its selling nothing. Moreover, since price remains constant, each additional unit sold increases total revenue by the amount of the price, the consequence being that price and marginal revenue are always equal. Thus, in the case of perfect competition, the demand curve facing a particular firm and the marginal revenue curve facing that firm are one and the same.

In a situation where the industry is not perfectly competitive, the demand curve for the output of a particular firm will not be horizontal, but it is likely to be more elastic than the demand curve for the commodity. If competition is not perfect, marginal revenue will not equal price, as it does in perfect competition. Instead, it will be less than price because demand is less than infinitely elastic.[11] (As we shall see in the next section, there is a simple relationship between marginal revenue and the price elasticity of demand.)

---

[11] Let p be price and q be quantity demanded. If the demand curve is $p = f(q)$, marginal revenue is

$$\frac{d(pq)}{dq} = f(q) + q\frac{df(q)}{dq} = p + q\frac{dp}{dq}$$

Thus marginal revenue must be less than price as long as $dp/dq < 0$.

11.   Marginal Revenue and the Elasticity of Demand

Before turning to the measurement of market demand curves, one additional theoretical result should be presented, since it is of widespread use. This result states that there is the following relationship between the elasticity of demand at a certain output level and marginal revenue at that output level:

$$MR = P\left[1 - \frac{1}{\eta}\right] \tag{4.7}$$

where MR is marginal revenue, P is price, and η is the price elasticity of demand. To prove that this is true, consider Figure 4.11. For simplicity, we assume that the demand curve, DD', is linear, but the result holds for

Figure 4.11
Relationship between
Marginal Revenue and
Elasticity of Demand.

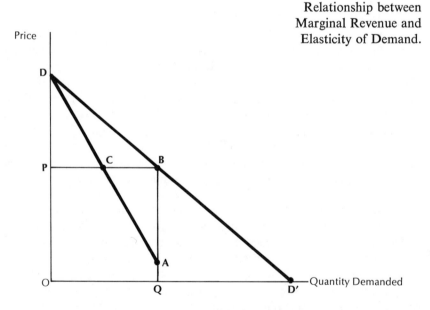

any shape of demand curve. Consider point B on DD'. Using the method described in Section 9, we find that QA is the marginal revenue at B. Using the method described in Section 3, the elasticity of demand at B is $BD' \div DB$. Since $PD \div PB = QB \div QD'$ and $AB = PD$, we know that

$$AB = PB\left[\frac{QB}{QD'}\right] = QB\left[\frac{PB}{QD'}\right]$$

Since $QA = QB - AB$,

$$QA = QB - QB\left[\frac{PB}{QD'}\right]$$

$$= QB\left[1 - \frac{PB}{QD'}\right]$$

Since QA is marginal revenue, QB is price, and $PB \div QD' = OQ \div QD' = DB \div BD' = 1/\eta$, Equation 4.7 follows.[12]

12. Measurement of Demand Curves

The market demand curve plays a very important role in microeconomics, and there have been literally hundreds of published studies—and many more unpublished ones—that attempt to measure the market demand curves for particular commodities. This section describes briefly various ways in which such empirical studies have been carried out. The following two sections provide examples of the ways in which the results of such studies have been used to help solve important practical problems.

One technique that is frequently used to estimate the demand curve for a particular commodity is the direct market experiment. The idea is to vary the price of the product while attempting to keep other market conditions fairly stable (or to take changes in other market conditions into account). For example, the Parker Pen Co. conducted an experiment some years ago to determine the price elasticity of demand of Quink. They raised the price from 15 cents to 25 cents in four cities and found that demand was quite inelastic. Also, in some stores, the old package selling at 15 cents was put next to a package marked "New Quink, 25 cents," the results also indicating that demand was quite inelastic. Attempts were also made to estimate the cross-elasticity of demand with other brands.

---

[12]Of course, it is easy to derive the result of this section from the result of Footnote 11, which is

$$MR = p + q\frac{dp}{dq}$$

It follows from this equation that

$$MR = p\left(1 + \frac{q}{p}\frac{dp}{dq}\right)$$

$$= p\left(1 - \frac{1}{\eta}\right)$$

Another technique that is sometimes employed is to interview consumers and administer questionnaires concerning their buying habits, motives, and intentions. Unfortunately, the direct approach of simply asking people how much they would buy of a particular commodity at particular prices does not seem to work very well in most cases. The snap judgments of consumers in response to such a hypothetical question do not seem to be very accurate. However, more subtle approaches can be of value. For example, interviews indicated that most buyers of a certain baby food selected it on their doctor's recommendation, and that most of them knew very little about prices or substitutes. This information, together with other data, led the manufacturer to the conclusion that the price elasticity of demand was quite low.[13]

Still another very popular technique is the use of statistical methods to extract information from data regarding sales, prices, incomes, and other variables in the past. Basically, what is involved is a comparison of various points in time or various sectors of the market, the point of this comparison being to see what effect the observed variation in price, income, etc., had on the quantity demanded. For example, to estimate the price elasticity of demand, one might plot the quantity demanded in 1968 vs. the 1968 price, the quantity demanded in 1967 vs. the 1967 price, and so on. If the results were as shown by the points in Figure 4.12, one might construct a curve like DD' as an estimate of the demand curve.

Although this example provides some understanding of the type of analysis that is involved, it makes the naive assumption that the demand curve has remained constant over the period. Suppose that the 1968 demand curve was $88'$, that the 1967 demand curve was $77'$, etc. Then the estimated demand curve DD' is a hybrid that resembles none of the true demand curves. Sophisticated econometric techniques have been developed for dealing with this so-called *identification problem*. Econometric techniques have also been devised to measure at the same time the effect of money income and the prices of other commodities on the quantity demanded; thus estimates can be made of the relationship between a commodity's price and the quantity demanded, these other factors being held constant. However, even an elementary description of these econometric techniques lies outside the scope of this book.[14]

Each of the approaches to the measurement of demand curves has its disadvantages. Direct experimentation can be expensive or risky because customers may be lost and profits cut by the experiment. Also, since they

---

[13]J. Dean, "Estimating the Price Elasticity of Demand" in E. Mansfield, *Managerial Economics and Operations Research*, New York: W. W. Norton, 2nd ed., 1970.
[14]For a good description of these techniques, see L. Klein, *An Introduction to Econometrics*, Englewood Cliffs, N.J.: Prentice-Hall, 1962.

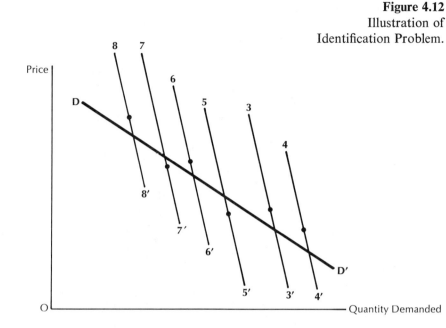

Figure 4.12
Illustration of
Identification Problem.

are seldom really controlled experiments and since they are often of relatively brief duration and the number of observations is small, experiments often cannot produce all of the information that is needed. Interviews and questionnaires suffer from a great many disadvantages, some of which are noted above. So do consumer clinics where consumers are placed in simulated market conditions and changes in their behavior are observed as the conditions of the experiment are changed; consumer clinics are expensive and they cannot avoid the distortion due to the consumers' realizing that they are in an experimental situation.[15]

The difficulties involved in the application of statistical and econometric techniques are also very considerable. Unreliable and biased results can be obtained if important variables are unwittingly (or wittingly) omitted from the analysis. If some of the variables influencing the quantity demanded are highly correlated among themselves, it may not be possible to obtain reliable estimates of the separate effects of each of them. Also, the demand function is likely to be only one of a number of equations that connect the relevant variables, and it may be difficult to unscramble these equations adequately from the available statistics.

There are no easy remedies for these problems. Nevertheless, these

---

[15]W. Baumol, *Economic Theory and Operations Analysis*, Englewood Cliffs, N.J.: Prentice-Hall, 1965, pp. 211–214.

problems, although sometimes formidable, are not insolvable. Many interesting and important studies have been made of the demand curves for particular commodities. And many interesting estimates have been made of the price elasticity, the income elasticity, and the cross elasticity of demand of various commodities. For example, Table 4.5 shows the results of Henry

Table 4.5. Estimated Price Elasticity of Demand for Selected Commodities, United States.

COMMODITY	PRICE ELASTICITY
Beef	0.92
Millinery	3.00
Gasoline	0.52
Sugar	0.31
Corn	0.49
Cotton	0.12
Hay	0.43
Wheat	0.08
Potatoes	0.31
Oats	0.56
Barley	0.39
Buckwheat	0.99

Source: H. Schultz, *Theory and Measurement of Demand*, Chicago: University of Chicago Press, 1938; and M. Spencer and L. Siegelman, *Managerial Economics*, Homewood, Ill.: Richard D. Irwin, 1959.

Schultz's pioneering study of the price elasticity of various farm products, as well as selected results from other studies. Table 4.6 shows various cross-

Table 4.6. Estimated Cross-Elasticities of Demand for Selected Commodities.

COMMODITY	CROSS-ELASTICITY WITH RESPECT TO PRICE OF:	CROSS-ELASTICITY
Beef	Pork	+0.28
Butter	Margarine	+0.67
Margarine	Butter	+0.81
Pork	Beef	+0.14

Source: H. Wold, *Demand Analysis*, New York: John Wiley & Sons, 1953.

elasticities of demand estimated by Herman Wold, in his well-known study. Table 4.7 shows the income elasticity of demand for selected commodities, as estimated by Wold. The reader should study these tables carefully.

Table 4.7. Estimated Income Elasticity of Demand for Selected Commodities.

COMMODITY	INCOME ELASTICITY
Butter	0.42
Cheesc	0.34
Cream	0.56
Eggs	0.37
Fruits and berries	0.70
Flour	−0.36
Liquor	1.00
Margarine	−0.20
Meat	0.35
Milk and cream	0.07
Restaurant consumption	1.48
Tobacco	1.02

Source: H. Wold, *Demand Analysis*, New York: John Wiley & Sons, 1953, p. 265.

13. Urban Transportation: An Illustration

The concepts presented in this chapter are of great importance in helping to solve problems of public and private policy. To illustrate how they can be used, consider the following problem of the New York subways. In the early fifties it was felt by many responsible citizens that the burden on the city budget due to the subway deficit was perhaps the most important single factor in New York City's financial problem. The increased operating cost resulting from the adoption of the 40-hour week, together with higher prices of materials, were expected to cause an operating deficit for 1951–1952 of almost $30 million for the city's transit system.

In response to this problem, the question was raised of whether or not subway fares should be increased. William Vickrey of Columbia University was asked by the Mayor's Committee on Management Survey of the City of New York to make a study of this question and to recommend ways in which the fare structure should be revised. One of the points that Vickrey made in his report was that the answer depended heavily on the price elasticity of demand for subway travel. If demand were price elastic, an increase in subway fares would result in a decrease in total revenues from the subway system. On the other hand, if demand were price inelastic, an increase in subway fares would result in an increase in total revenues from the subway system.

The elasticity of demand for subway travel is likely to differ among various types of riders. Long-haul, rush-hour riders are likely to exhibit the most inelastic demand, since the trip is often a necessity if they are to keep their jobs and there are few alternative means of transportation available. Short-haul traffic is likely to exhibit more elastic demand, since riders can shift to buses or walk. Also, since a good deal of non-rush-hour traffic is nonessential, the price elasticity of demand may be greater than at the rush hours. Vickrey attempted to test these hypotheses, using data on the experience when the fare was increased from 5 cents to 10 cents. In general, his results, although admittedly tenuous, seemed to be quite consistent with them.

If we consider the market as a whole, how price elastic was the demand for subway travel in New York? Vickrey made four estimates of the demand curve, each based on a different assumption regarding its form. In Case A, he assumed that equal *absolute* changes in fare result in equal *absolute* changes in traffic. In Case B, he assumed that equal *absolute* changes in fare result in equal *percentage* changes in traffic. In Case C, he assumed that equal *percentage* changes in fare result in equal *absolute* changes in traffic. And in Case D, he assumed that equal *percentage* changes in fare result in equal *percentage* changes in traffic. His results are shown in Table 4.8. For present purposes, the important point is the relevance and importance of the information provided in Table 4.8 to decisions and policies that had to be made by New York City; we do not need to describe how these estimates were obtained.

What do the results in Table 4.8 indicate? The big thing to note is that, regardless of which case one chooses, the demand for subway travel is shown by Table 4.8 to be price inelastic at the then-prevailing fare of 10 cents. What does this mean? It means that increases in the fare would increase total revenues, since the percentage reduction in passengers would be less than the percentage increase in the fare. To the New York Transit Authority, this was a very important fact. Although price increases for some items (like the records discussed in the following section) may cut total revenue and profits, this was not the case here: A fare increase would increase total revenue and reduce the deficit.[16]

---

[16]This very brief sketch cannot do justice to Vickrey's study, which was concerned with many other important aspects of the problem. See W. Vickrey, *The Revision of the Rapid Transit Fare Structure of the City of New York*, Mayor's Committee on Management Survey, 1952.

Table 4.8. Alternative Estimates of Demand Schedule for Subway Travel, New York, 1952.

FARE (CENTS)	CASE A		CASE B		CASE C		CASE D	
	PASSENGERS	TOTAL REVENUE	PASSENGERS	TOTAL REVENUE	PASSENGERS	TOTAL REVENUE	PASSENGERS	TOTAL REVENUE
	(PASSENGERS AND REVENUES IN MILLIONS PER YEAR)							
5	1945	$ 97.2	1945	$ 97.2	1945	$ 97.2	1945	$ 97.2
10	1683	168.3	1683	168.3	1683	168.3	1683	168.3
15	1421	213.2	1458	218.7	1530	229.5	1547	232.0
20	1159	231.8	1262	252.4	1421	284.2	1457	291.5
25	897	224.2	1092	273.0	1347	336.8	1390	348.2
30	635	190.5	945	283.5	1278	383.4	1340	402.0

Source: W. S. Vickrey, *The Revision of the Rapid Transit Fare Structure of the City of New York,* Technical Monograph No. 3, Finance Project, Mayor's Committee on Management Survey of the City of New York, p. 87.

14. A Business Pricing Problem

The concepts discussed in this chapter are obviously of fundamental importance in the formulation of business policy, as well as public policy. An
interesting case that illustrates the use of the concept of price elasticity by
business is that of Columbia Records in the early forties. In 1938, the
Columbia Broadcasting Company purchased the American Record Company
and changed its name to Columbia Records. When the new company began
operations, classical records were sold by the industry at about $1.50, semi-
classical and well-established popular records were sold at $0.75, and popular
records were sold at $0.35. Among classical records, a sale of 5000 was
considered good; although extremely popular releases might reach a sales
volume of 50,000, some records might not sell more than 200.

In November 1938, a New York newspaper began a promotion scheme
whereby it offered classical albums to its readers at prices averaging about
$0.50 a record. The results were very impressive, more than 50,000 records
of a single symphony being sold in a few weeks. Observing this fact, and the
enthusiastic reception of the radio broadcasts of symphonic and operatic
performances, the executives of the Columbia Broadcasting System concluded that there was a very good opportunity to increase the market for
classical records by price reductions. However, during the first couple of
years, the new company maintained the high level of prices on classical
records while it improved the mechanical quality of its records and the skill
and reputation of the artists it recorded.

Before instituting a price reduction, Columbia obviously had to estimate
more precisely what the effect of a price reduction would be on its revenues
and costs. The answers to these questions clearly depended upon the elasticity of demand for classical records, as well as on the way in which the
firm's costs varied with the quantity of records it produced (a subject that
is discussed at length in Chapter 6). Edward Wallerstein, president of
Columbia Records, began by trying to estimate the public's reaction to lower
prices. He asked a number of dealers to keep detailed records of their
customary sales and then for one month to offer all people who entered their
stores regular classical and semiclassical records at two-thirds of list price.
These dealers found that the unannounced price reduction of 33 1/3 percent
more than doubled the number of records sold. Thus the apparent price
elasticity of demand, judging from this crude experiment, was about six.
This evidence, in addition to the other indications, convinced Wallerstein
that Columbia should go further in analyzing the pros and cons of a price
reduction of substantial magnitude.

Based on the estimated price elasticity of demand, it was possible to estimate the effect of a price cut on the firm's total revenue. In addition, a close examination was made of the firm's cost structure to determine the effect of a price cut on the firm's total costs. Since many costs were fixed, total costs would not increase in proportion to the increased volume resulting from the price cut. After considerable study, it was decided to reduce the price of 10-inch classical records from about \$1.25 to \$0.75 and to reduce the price of 12-inch classical records from about \$1.75 to \$1.00. Presumably a price reduction of this extent was chosen because it was felt to be the most profitable one. The response was overwhelming. Other firms followed Columbia's lead. To the surprise of much of the industry, total expenditure on classical records rose greatly.[17]

This is a good illustration of how the price elasticity of demand must be taken into account in pricing strategy. It also illustrates the claim, frequently made by critics, that firms tend to underestimate the price elasticity of demand. There have been many Congressional investigations of pricing in key industries like steel and autos, and it is frequently alleged in these hearings that the firms in question should, in their own interest as well as the public's, lower their prices. It is difficult to generalize concerning the accuracy of this allegation. In some instances, like the record industry, there seems to have been an underestimation of the elasticity of demand. Whether there are many other cases of this sort is difficult to say.[18]

15. Summary

The market demand curve for a commodity is simply the horizontal summation of the individual demand curves of all the consumers in the market. Since individual demand curves almost always slope downward to the right, it follows that market demand curves will do so, too. For market demand curves, as well as individual demand curves, the price elasticity of demand is a measure of the responsiveness of quantity demanded to changes in price. The price elasticity of demand is defined as the percentage change in quantity resulting from a 1-percent change in price. The price elasticity of demand

[17]For further details concerning this case, see M. McNair and H. Hansen, *Problems in Marketing*, New York: McGraw-Hill, 1949, pp. 596–603.

[18]For some discussion of whether or not this is true in the automobile industry, see *Administered Prices: Automobiles*, Subcommittee on Antitrust and Monopoly, United States Senate, 1958.

will generally vary from one point to another on a demand curve. Estimated price elasticities are of two types: point elasticities and arc elasticities. Graphical techniques are available to estimate the elasticity at a given point.

The price elasticity of demand for a commodity depends on the number and closeness of substitutes that are available. If a commodity has many close substitutes, its demand is likely to be elastic. Of course, the extent to which a commodity has close substitutes depends on how narrowly it is defined. The elasticity of demand may also depend on the importance of the commodity in consumers' budgets, the length of the period to which the demand curve pertains, and the ranges of uses for the commodity. The sellers of a product are particularly interested in the relationship between price changes and changes in the amount of money spent on the product. If the price elasticity of demand is greater (less) than one, reductions in price lead to an increase (decrease) in the total expenditure on the commodity.

The income elasticity of demand is the percentage change in quantity demanded resulting from a 1-percent change in money income. Commodities differ greatly in their income elasticities. Goods that people regard as luxuries are generally assumed to have high income elasticities of demand. Indeed, one way to define luxuries and necessities is to say that luxuries are goods with high income elasticities of demand, and necessities are goods with low income elasticities of demand. The cross elasticity of demand is the relative change in the quantity demanded of good X divided by the relative change in the price of good Y. Whether commodities are classified as substitutes or complements depends on whether the cross elasticity is positive or negative.

Marginal revenue is the addition to total revenue attributable to the addition of the last unit to sales. Obviously, total revenue from n units of output is equal to the sum of marginal revenue in the intervals between 0 and 1 unit of output, 1 and 2 units of output, and so on up to $(n - 1)$ to n units of output. The marginal revenue curve shows marginal revenue at various levels of output of the commodity. Graphical techniques are available to estimate the marginal revenue curve from the demand curve. There is a very simple relation between the elasticity of demand at a certain output level and marginal revenue at the output level. It is important to distinguish between the market demand curve for a commodity and the market demand curve for the output of a single firm producing the commodity. In a perfectly competitive industry, the firm's demand curve will be horizontal. If the industry contains more than one firm but is not perfectly competitive, the firm's demand curve will not be horizontal, but it is likely to be more price elastic than the demand curve for the commodity.

The market demand curve plays a very important role in microeconomics, and there have been many studies that have attempted to measure the demand curve for particular commodities. One technique used to estimate the demand curve is direct market experimentation. Another technique is to interview consumers and administer questionnaires concerning their habits, motives, and intentions. Still another technique is the use of statistical and econometric techniques to extract information from data regarding sales, prices, incomes, and other variables in the past. Each of these approaches has its disadvantages, there being no easy remedy to the estimation problem. Nevertheless, the difficulties generally are not insurmountable. Many interesting and important estimates have been made of the demand curves for various goods.

One case that illustrates the use of these concepts in important practical problems is that of the New York subways in the early fifties. Confronted with the prospect of a large deficit, the subways had to consider the question of a fare increase. Clearly, the desirability of a fare increase depended on the elasticity of demand for subway travel. The available estimates seemed to indicate that demand was inelastic and that an increase in fares would increase total revenues and reduce the deficit. Another illustration is the case of Columbia records in the early forties. After conducting small-scale experiments, Columbia became convinced that the demand for classical records was quite elastic and that profits would be increased by a drastic cut in price. Columbia cut the price in 1940 and the response was in keeping with Columbia's expectations.

SELECTED REFERENCES

Hicks, John, *Value and Capital*, Oxford: Oxford University Press, 1946.

Schultz, Henry, *The Theory and Measurement of Demand*, Chicago: University of Chicago Press, 1938.

Dean, Joel, *Managerial Economics*, Englewood Cliffs, N.J.: Prentice Hall, 1951.

Marshall, Alfred, *Principles of Economics*, London: Macmillan, 1920.

Stigler, George, "The Limitations of Statistical Demand Curves," *Journal of the American Statistical Association*, 1939.

5

The Firm and Its Technology

1. The Assumption of Profit Maximization

In this chapter, we turn from the consumer to the firm, our principal objective being to provide a simple model of the firm and its technology. A firm is a unit that produces a good or service for sale. In contrast to not-for-profit institutions like universities or hospitals, firms attempt to make a profit. There are literally millions of firms in the United States, some being proprietorships, some partnerships, and some corporations. About nine-tenths of the goods and services produced in the United States are produced by firms, the rest being provided by government and not-for-profit institutions. It is obvious that an economy like ours is centered around the activities of firms.

As a first approximation, economists generally assume that firms attempt to maximize profits. However, the economist's definition of profits does not coincide with the accountant's. The economist does not assume that the firm attempts to maximize the current, short-run profits measured by the accountant. Instead he assumes that the firm will attempt to maximize the sum of profits over a long period of time, these profits being properly dis-

114

counted to the present. Also, when the economist speaks of profits, he means profit after taking account of the capital and labor provided by the owners. More will be said on this score in the next chapter.

Although the assumption of profit maximization serves as a reasonable first approximation, it has obvious limitations. For one thing, the making of profits generally requires time and energy, and if the owners of the firm are the managers as well, they may decide that it is preferable to sacrifice profits for leisure. (Profit-maximizers in Miami Beach and the Virgin Islands encourage this type of thinking.) In a case of this sort, it is more accurate to assume that the owner-manager, like the consumer, is maximizing utility, his utility being a function of his profits and the amount of leisure he enjoys. Using the kind of analysis described in Chapter 2, we can determine how much money the owner-manager willl give up for leisure.

It should also be noted that, in an uncertain world, the concept of maximum profit is not clearly defined. Since any particular course of action will not result in a unique, certain level of profit, but in a variety of possible levels of profit, each with a certain probability of occurrence, it makes no sense to speak about the maximization of profits. However, if the firm is able, explicitly or implicitly, to attach a probability to each level of profit that could result from each course of action, it is meaningful to assume that the firm attempts to maximize expected profits.[1] For simplicity, we shall assume in the following pages that the firm has full knowledge of the relevant variables, and that there is no uncertainty.

Observers of the modern corporation often state that profits are not the sole objective of these firms. For example, industry spokesmen often claim that the following objectives are also of importance: achieving better social conditions in the firm's community, increasing (or at least maintaining) its market share, creating an "image" as a good employer and a useful part of the community, and so forth. Beside the question of how seriously one should take such self-proclaimed goals, the important question is how distinct these goals are from the goal of profit maximization. To the extent that many of these goals are simply means to achieve profits *in the long run,* there may be less inaccuracy in the profit maximization assumption than might appear at first glance.

In recent years economists have begun to experiment with models of the firm that do not assume profit maximization. A brief introduction to such

---

[1]Expected profit is defined as the long-term average value of profit—the sum of the various possible levels of profit, each level being weighted by the probability of its occurrence. The firm may be interested in the variance, as well as the expected value of profits, in which case it will maximize some function of both the expected value and the variance.

models is contained in the Appendix to this chapter. Although these models are useful for certain purposes, profit maximization remains the standard assumption in microeconomics. In large part, this is because it is a close enough approximation for many of the most important purposes of microeconomics. For example, even some of the proponents of alternative models admit that profit maximization may be a suitable assumption in models designed to show how the price system functions.

In addition economists are interested in the theory of the profit-maximizing firm because it provides rules of behavior for firms that do want to maximize profits. The theory of the profit-maximizing firm suggests how a firm should operate if it wants to make as such money as possible. Even if a firm does not want to maximize profit, the theory can be useful. For example, it can show how much the firm is losing by taking certain courses of action. In recent years the theory of the profit-maximizing firm has been studied more and more for the sake of determining rules of business behavior.[2]

2. Technology and Inputs

One of the fundamental determinants of a firm's behavior is the state of technology. Whether a firm produces textiles or locomotives, whether a firm is big or small, whether a firm is run by a genius or a moron (or even your brother-in-law), the firm cannot do more than is permitted by existing technology. Technology, as we defined it in Chapter 1, is the sum total of society's pool of knowledge concerning the industrial arts. Although this definition is accurate, it is not very useful in indicating how we can represent the state of technology in a model of the firm. The purpose of the rest of this chapter is to show how economists represent the state of technology.

To begin with, we must define an input. Production processes usually require a wide variety of inputs, an input being anything that the firm uses in its production process. For example, some of the inputs in the iron and steel industry are iron ore, coal, oxygen; skilled labor of various types; the services of blast furnaces, open hearths, electric furnaces, and rolling mills; as well as the services of the people managing the companies. To give a more humble example, the inputs in the production and sale of hot dog

---

[2]For example, see W. Baumol, *Economic Theory and Operations Analysis*, Englewood Cliffs, N.J.: Prentice-Hall, 1965.

sandwiches by a street vendor are the hot dogs, the rolls, the stove, the truck, and the services of the vendor.

In representing and analyzing production processes, we assume that all inputs can be divided into two categories: fixed inputs and variable inputs. A *fixed input* is an input whose quantity cannot be changed during the period of time under consideration. This period will vary from problem to problem. Of course, the amount of most inputs can be varied to some extent, no matter how brief the time interval. But for some inputs, the cost of quick variation in their amount is so large as to make such variation impractical. For simplicity, we regard these inputs as being fixed. The firm's plant and equipment are examples of inputs that often are included in this category.

On the other hand, a *variable input* is an input whose quantity can be changed during the relevant period. For example, the number of workers hired to perform a job like construction can often be increased or decreased on short notice. The amount of raw material used in the production of a commodity like ladies' dresses can often be increased or decreased by using up or building up the firm's inventories. The amount of water used in the production of a service like a car wash can sometimes be varied within limits simply by turning the relevant knobs.

3. The Short Run and the Long Run

Whether or not an input is regarded as variable or fixed depends on the length of the period under consideration. The longer the period, the more inputs are variable, not fixed. Although the length of the relevant period varies from problem to problem, economists have found it useful to focus special attention on two time periods: the short run and the long run. The *short run* is defined to be that period of time in which some of the firm's inputs are fixed. More specifically, since the firm's plant and equipment are among the most difficult inputs to change quickly, the short run is generally understood to mean the length of time during which the firm's plant and equipment are fixed. On the other hand, the *long run* is that period of time in which all inputs are variable. In the long run, the firm can make a complete adjustment to any change in its environment.

In both the short run and the long run, a firm's productive processes ordinarily permit substantial variation in the proportions in which inputs are used. In the long run, there can be no question but that input proportions can be varied considerably. For example, an automobile die can be made on conventional machine tools with more labor and less expensive equipment, or it can be made on numerically controlled machine tools with less labor and more expensive equipment. Similarly, an airplane can be almost handmade or it can be made using much equipment and relatively little labor. In the short run, there are also considerable opportunities for changes in input proportions. For one thing, the ratio between fixed and variable inputs can vary greatly.

Production processes with fixed, not variable, proportions are ones where there is one, and only one, ratio of inputs that can be used. For example, to produce a certain product, 2 hours of labor must be combined with a certain amount of capital. Consequently, if output is increased or decreased, the quantity of all inputs must be varied in proportion to output. There seem to be very few cases where all inputs must be combined in fixed proportions. However, there are cases where the amount of a *certain* input can be varied only within narrow limits. For example, a particular drug may have to contain a certain amount of aspirin per ounce of the drug. Thus it is not unusual for some inputs to be required in relatively fixed proportions but it is very unusual for this to be the case for all, or most, inputs.

4.   The Production Function

For any commodity, the *production function* is the relationship between the quantities of various inputs used per period of time and the maximum quantity of the commodity that can be produced per period of time. More specifically, the production function is a table, a graph, or an equation showing the maximum output rate that can be achieved from any specified set of usage rates of inputs. The production function summarizes the characteristics of existing technology at a given point in time; it shows the technological constraints that the firm must reckon with. In most of this book, we assume that the firm takes the production function as given; in Chapter 16, when we analyze the process of technological change, we study the firm's attempts to change the production function.

To illustrate the production function, consider the simplest case—when there is one fixed input and one variable input. Suppose that the fixed input is the service of an acre of land, the variable input is labor (in man-years), and the output is corn (in bushels). Suppose that a scientifically inclined farmer decides to find out what the effect on annual output will be if he applies various numbers of man-years of labor during the year to the acre of land. (He can vary the number of man-years of labor by hiring fewer or more laborers.) If he obtains the results in Table 5.1, then these results might

Table 5.1. Output of Corn When Various Amounts
of Labor Are Applied to an Acre of Land.

AMOUNT OF LABOR (ANNUAL NUMBER OF MAN-YEARS)	OUTPUT OF CORN (BUSHELS PER YEAR)
1	6
2	13.5
3	21
4	28
5	34
6	38
7	38
8	37

be regarded as the production function in this situation. Alternatively, the curve in Figure 5.1, which presents exactly the same results, might be regarded as the production function.

The production function is an important starting point for the analysis of the firm's technology: It gives us the maximum *total output* that can be realized by using each combination of quantities of inputs. But there is more that we need to know about the production process. In particular, two other important concepts are the average product and the marginal product of an input. The *average product* of an input is total product (i.e., total output) divided by the amount of the input used to produce this amount of output. The *marginal product* of an input is the addition to total output due to the addition of the last unit of the input, the amount of other inputs used being held constant.

To illustrate these concepts, let us go back to the farmer in Table 5.1. On the basis of the production function shown in this table, we can compute the average product and marginal product of labor. Both the average product and the marginal product of labor will vary, of course, depending on how much labor is used. If $Q(L)$ is the total output rate when L man-years of labor are used per year, the average product of labor when L man-years of labor are used per year is $Q(L)/L$. And the marginal product of labor when between L and $(L - 1)$ man-years of labor are used per year is

$$[Q(L) - Q(L - 1)].$$

Thus the average product of labor is 6 bushels of corn per man-year of labor when 1 man-year of labor is used, and the marginal product of labor is 7.5 bushels of corn per man-year of labor when between 1 and 2 man-years

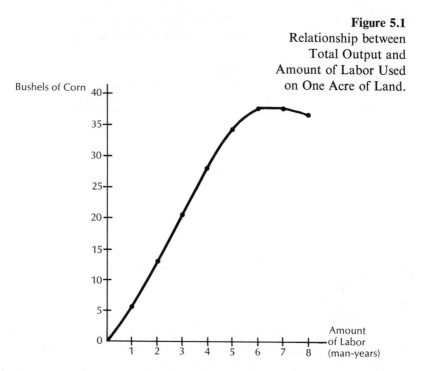

Figure 5.1
Relationship between
Total Output and
Amount of Labor Used
on One Acre of Land.

of labor are used. The results for other levels of utilization of labor are shown in Table 5.2.

Table 5.2.   Average and Marginal Products of Labor.

AMOUNT OF LABOR	TOTAL OUTPUT	AVERAGE PRODUCT OF LABOR	MARGINAL PRODUCT OF LABOR*
0	0	—	—
1	6.0	6.00	6.0
2	13.5	6.75	7.5
3	21.0	7.00	7.5
4	28.0	7.00	7.0
5	34.0	6.80	6.0
6	38.0	6.30	4.0
7	38.0	5.40	0.0
8	37.0	4.60	−1.0

*These figures pertain to the interval between the indicated amount of labor and one unit less than the indicated amount of labor.

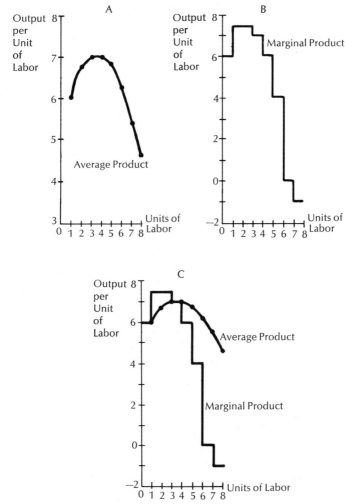

Figure 5.2
Average and Marginal
Product Curves for
Labor.

Panel A of Figure 5.2 shows the average product curve for labor, the numbers having been taken from Table 5.2. As is typically the case for production processes, the average product of labor (which is the only variable input in this case) rises, reaches a maximum, and then falls. Panel B of Figure 5.2 shows the marginal product curve for labor, these numbers also having been taken from Table 5.2. The marginal product of labor also rises, reaches a maximum, and then falls: this too is typical of many production processes.[3]   Finally, panel C of Figure 5.2 shows both the average product curve and the marginal product curve for labor. As is always the case, marginal product exceeds average product when the latter is increasing, equals average product when the latter reaches a maximum, and is less than average product when the latter is decreasing. This is simply a matter of arithmetic: If the addition to a total is greater (less) than the average, the average is bound to increase (decrease).[4]

Tables 5.1 and 5.2 are constructed on the assumption that land, the fixed input, is equal to one acre. Suppose that we could increase the amount of land to two acres. What effect would this have on the total, average, and marginal products of labor? Generally, over the relevant range of production, an increase in the fixed input will result in an increase in all of them. For example, the result might be like that shown in Figure 5.3.

5.   The Law of Diminishing Marginal Returns and the Geometry of Average and Marginal Product Curves

Previous sections have defined the production function and the average and marginal products of an input. We are now in a position to discuss one of the most famous laws of microeconomics—the law of diminishing marginal returns. The law of diminishing marginal returns, like the Scriptures, is

---

[3]Sometimes, however, an input's marginal product decreases throughout the entire range of its utilization.

[4]If x is the amount of the variable input that is used and

$$Q = f(x)$$

where Q is the output rate, then the average product of the variable input is $Q \div x = f(x) \div x$, and the marginal product of the variable input is $dQ/dx = df(x)/dx$. Thus average product is a maximum when

$$\frac{d(Q/x)}{dx} = \left(\frac{dQ}{dx} - \frac{Q}{x}\right)\frac{1}{x} = 0$$

which means that dQ/dx must equal Q/x when the average product is a maximum. But since dQ/dx is the marginal product and Q/x is the average product, this proves the proposition in the text: When the average product is a maximum, the average product equals the marginal product.

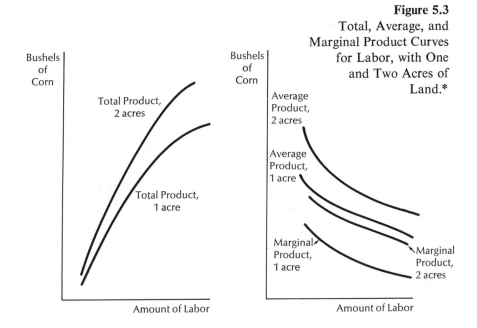

Figure 5.3
Total, Average, and
Marginal Product Curves
for Labor, with One
and Two Acres of
Land.*

*Note that only part of each of these curves is shown, the region where average or marginal product is increasing being omitted.

often quoted and frequently misinterpreted. Put very briefly, this law states that if equal increments of an input are added, the quantities of other inputs held constant, the resulting increments of product will decrease beyond some point; that is, the marginal product of the input will diminish. This law is illustrated by Table 5.2; beyond 3 man-years of labor, the marginal product of labor decreases.

Several things should be noted concerning this law of diminishing returns. First, the law of diminishing returns is meant to be an empirical generalization, not a deduction from physical or biological laws: In fact, it seems to hold for most production functions in the real world. Second, it is assumed that technology remains fixed. The law of diminishing returns cannot predict the effect of an additional unit of input when technology is allowed to change. Third, it is assumed that there is at least one input whose quantity is being held constant. The law of diminishing returns does not apply to cases where there is a proportional increase in all inputs. Fourth, it must be possible, of course, to vary the proportions in which the various inputs are used.

If there is a fixed input and only one variable input, the typical form of the relationship between the amount of the variable input and the total output is given by *OT* in Figure 5.4.[5] Given such a graph, how can we determine the average product and the marginal product of the variable input?

Figure 5.4
Measurement of the
Average Product.

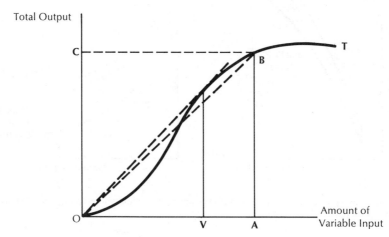

To make the analysis more concrete, suppose that Figure 5.4 refers to another farm like the one in Table 5.1, that the output is corn, and that the variable input is labor. First, consider the average product of the variable input, labor. Since average product equals total product divided by the amount of variable input, the average product of any amount of variable input, *OA*, equals *AB*(=*OC*) divided by *OA*. And *AB/OA* is obviously the slope of the line, *OB*, which joins the origin and the point on the total product curve corresponding to this amount of variable input. Thus the slope of the line joining the origin and the relevant point on the total product curve is equal to the average product of the variable input, labor.

Second, consider the marginal product of the variable input, labor. Given the total product curve in Figure 5.5 (which is the same as that in Figure 5.4), how can we determine the marginal product? If the amount of variable input increases from *OE* to *OF*, total output increases from *OH* to

---

[5]In Figure 5.4, we assume that the amount of the variable output is varied continuously, the result being that the total product, the average product, and the marginal product curves are continuous.

Figure 5.5
Measurement of
Marginal Product.

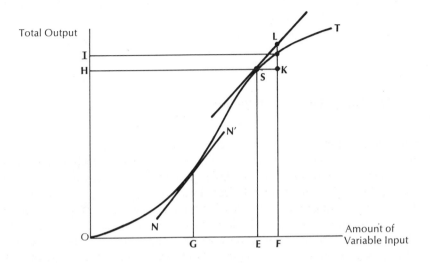

OI. Clearly, as the increment in the amount of variable input becomes smaller and smaller, the extra product divided by the extra variable input, *HI/EF*, approaches the slope of the total product curve at *S*. (Even if the increment is *EF*, the approximation is not too bad: the slope of the total product curve is *KL/SK* = *KL/EF*, which is fairly close to *HI/EF*.) Thus since the slope of a curve at any point equals the slope of its tangent at that point, we can determine the marginal product of any amount of variable input by drawing the tangent to the total product curve at that amount of variable input and measuring its slope. For example, the slope of *NN'* is the marginal product of variable input when *OG* units of variable input are used.

Using these results, it is possible to prove a number of interesting results concerning the average product curve (the curve showing the relationship between average product and the amount of variable input used) and the marginal product curve (the curve showing the relationship between marginal product and the amount of variable input used). To begin with, in Figure 5.4, since a line joining the origin and a point on the total product curve is bound to be steepest (i.e., has the maximum slope) when the line is tangent to the total product curve, it follows that the average product must be a maximum if *OV* units of variable input are used. Moreover, since the tangent to the total product curve is exactly the same as the line joining the origin and the total product curve when *OV* units of the variable input are used, the slope of the tangent must equal the slope of this line, and marginal product must equal average product. Thus *marginal product must equal average product when the latter is a maximum.*[6] Also, since the marginal product is a maximum at *OG* (Figure 5.5), where the slope of the tangent to the total product curve is greatest, and since *OG* is less than *OV*, it follows that *the maximum marginal product occurs at a lower level of variable input than the maximum average product.*

6. The Three Stages of Production

The relationships between total, average, and marginal products can be used to define three stages of production, an understanding of which is very useful in showing that many types of input combinations are clearly inefficient. We begin by defining stage III. As shown in Figure 5.6, stage III covers that range of utilization of the variable input where the marginal product of variable input is negative. The important point to note about stage III is that a rational producer will never operate in this range, because fewer units of the variable input will actually result in more output. Even if the variable input is free, the firm would be foolish to operate in this stage, since the use of fewer units of variable input would increase the firm's output, but not its costs. Certainly, if the variable input is not free, the argument against operation in this stage is even more persuasive. In stage III, the variable input is combined with the fixed input in too large a proportion to be economical. In terms of our agricultural example, land is cultivated more intensively than it should be.

Next, we turn to stage I. As shown in Figure 5.6, stage I covers that range of utilization of variable input where the average product of variable input is increasing. This stage includes the very small levels of utilization of variable input, where increases in variable input result in larger and larger increases in total output. It also includes the point where the marginal product of the variable input reaches a maximum and it stops only at the point where the marginal and average products of the variable input are equal, since this is the point at which the average product of the variable input is a maximum.

What is the significance of stage I? The important point to note about stage I is that the marginal product of the fixed input is negative in this range. Thus, as we shall see, there is a basic symmetry between stage I and stage III. To demonstrate that the marginal product of fixed input is negative

---

[6]Of course, this is precisely the same result as that stated at the end of Section 4.

Figure 5.6
Stages of Production.

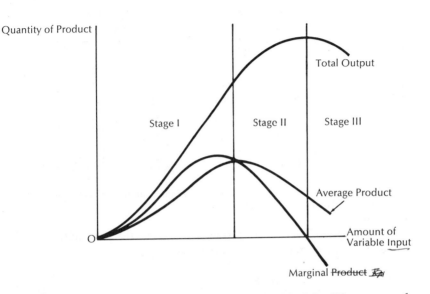

in stage I, consider the agricultural example in Table 5.2. We can use the data shown there to derive the marginal product of the fixed input, land, if we are willing to assume constant returns to scale. (Constant returns to scale mean that, if the quantity of all inputs is changed by X percent, output will change by X percent.) For example, since the third row of Table 5.2 shows that 13.5 bushels result if 1 acre of land and 2 man-years of labor are used, it follows that 6.75 bushels would result if 1/2 acres and 1 man-year were used. Similarly, since the fourth row shows that 21 bushels result if 1 acre and 3 man-years are used, it follows that 7 bushels would result if 1/3 acres and 1 man-year were used. Table 5.3 shows the results for various amounts of land and one man-year of labor.

Based on this information, it is a simple matter to determine the marginal product per acre of land. For example, when the amount of land changes from 1/8 acres to 1/7 acres, the total output increases from 37/8 to 38/7 bushels; thus, the marginal product of land is

$$(\tfrac{38}{7} - \tfrac{37}{8}) \div (\tfrac{1}{7} - \tfrac{1}{8}) = 45 \text{ bushels per acre}$$

Proceeding in this way, one can compute the marginal product of land at each of the levels of utilization of land shown in Table 5.3, the results being shown in Figure 5.7. Similarly, the average product of land can be computed at each of the levels of utilization of land shown in Table 5.3. For

Table 5.3. The Marginal Product of Land.

ACRES OF LAND	AMOUNT OF LABOR	TOTAL PRODUCT	MARGINAL PRODUCT*
1/8	1	$4.60 (= \frac{1}{8} \times 37)$	——
1/7	1	$5.40 (= \frac{1}{7} \times 38)$	$45\{= (\frac{38}{7} - \frac{37}{8}) \div (\frac{1}{7} - \frac{1}{8})\}$
1/6	1	$6.30 (= \frac{1}{6} \times 38)$	$38\{= (\frac{38}{6} - \frac{38}{7}) \div (\frac{1}{6} - \frac{1}{7})\}$
1/5	1	$6.80 (= \frac{1}{5} \times 34)$	$14\{= (\frac{34}{5} - \frac{38}{6}) \div (\frac{1}{5} - \frac{1}{6})\}$
1/4	1	$7.00 (= \frac{1}{4} \times 28)$	$4\{= (\frac{28}{4} - \frac{34}{5}) \div (\frac{1}{4} - \frac{1}{5})\}$
1/3	1	$7.00 (= \frac{1}{3} \times 21)$	$0\{= (\frac{21}{3} - \frac{28}{4}) \div (\frac{1}{3} - \frac{1}{4})\}$
1/2	1	$6.75 (= \frac{1}{2} \times 13.5)$	$-1.5\{= (\frac{13.5}{2} - \frac{21}{3}) \div (\frac{1}{2} - \frac{1}{3})\}$
1	1	6.00	$-1.5\{= (6 - \frac{13.5}{2}) \div (1 - \frac{1}{2})\}$

*These figures pertain to the interval between the indicated amount of land and the amount of land in the row immediately above.

example, when the level of utilization is 1/8 acres, the total output is 37/8 bushels; thus the average product of land is

$$\frac{37}{8} \div \frac{1}{8} = 37 \text{ bushels}$$

The average product curve is also shown in Figure 5.7. Note that the ratio of labor to land inputs is plotted along the horizontal axis in Figure 5.7, and that the marginal product curve and average product curve for labor are also included.

The results demonstrate that the marginal product of land is negative in stage I. They also demonstrate the inherent symmetry of stages I and III. In stage I, the ratio of land to labor is high, labor's average product is rising as the ratio decreases, and the marginal product of land is negative. In stage III, the situation is exactly the reverse: the ratio of labor to land is high, land's average product is rising as the ratio decreases, and the marginal product of labor is negative. The moral is that whenever so little of any input is employed that its average product increases when more of it is employed, some other input is being subjected to such intensive use that its marginal product is negative.

If the firm takes the prices of inputs and the price of its product as given and if it can buy or sell all it wants at these prices, it will try not to operate in stage I, since in stage I it could increase its output level by decreasing the amount of the fixed input that it uses. (But since the fixed input is fixed, at least for the period under consideration, the firm may not be able to vary its utilization for some time.) Also, as we have already seen, the firm will not operate in stage III, since in stage III it can increase its output level by

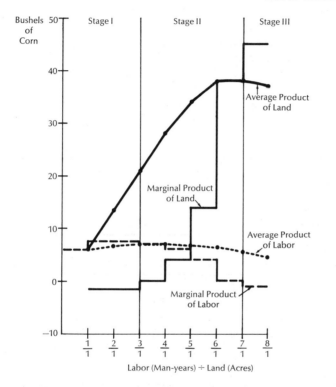

Figure 5.7
Marginal and Average
Product of Land and
Labor at Various
Labor-Land Ratios.

decreasing the amount of the variable input that it uses. Thus the firm will try to operate in stage II, which is defined to include the range of variable input from the point at which the average product of the variable input is a maximum to the point at which the marginal product is zero. In stage II, the marginal product of both inputs is positive.

7. The Production Function: Two Variable Inputs

In the previous sections, we were concerned with the case in which there is only one variable input. In the next three sections, we take up the more general case in which there are two variable inputs. These variable inputs can be thought of as working with one or more fixed inputs, or they may be thought of as the only two inputs (in which case the situation is the long run). In either case, it is easy to extend the results to as many inputs as one likes. This section takes up the production function, Section 8 is concerned with its representation through a system of geometric constructs called isoquants, and Section 9 deals with substitution among inputs.

If we increase the number of variable inputs from one to two, the production function becomes slightly more complicated, but it is still the relationship between various combinations of inputs and the maximum amount of output that can be obtained from them. Really, the only change is that the output is a function of two variables rather than one. For example, suppose in our agricultural example that we allow both land and labor to vary; the results might be given by Table 5.4. This is the production function in

Table 5.4. Hypothetical Production Function for Corn, Two Variable Inputs.

AMOUNT OF LABOR (MAN-YEARS)	NUMBER OF ACRES			
	1	2	3	4
	(BUSHELS OF CORN PRODUCED PER YEAR)			
1	5	11	18	24
2	14	30	50	72
3	22	60	80	99
4	29	80	115	125
5	34	48	140	145

tabular form. Note that we can obtain the marginal product of each input by holding the other input constant. For example, the marginal product of land when 4 man-years are used and when between 1 and 2 acres of land are used is 51 bushels per acre; the marginal product of labor when 2 acres are used and when between 3 and 4 man-years of labor are used is 20 bushels per man-year. Similarly, the average product of either land or labor can be computed simply by dividing the total output by the amount of either land or labor that is used.[7]

---

[7] If x_1 is the amount of the first input and x_2 is the amount of the second input, the production function is
$$Q = f(x_1, x_2)$$
where Q is the output rate. The marginal product of the first input is $\partial Q/\partial x_1$; the marginal product of the second input is $\partial Q/\partial x_2$.

Another way to present the production function is by a surface, like that in Figure 5.8. The production surface is $OAQB$,[8] the height of a point on this surface denoting the quantity of output. Dropping a perpendicular down from a point on the production surface to the "floor" and seeing how far the resulting point is from the labor and land axes indicates how much of each input is required to produce this much output. For example, to produce $U'U$ units of output requires OB_1 $(= A_1U')$ man-years of labor and $OA_1(= B_1U')$ acres of land. Conversely, one can take any amounts of land and labor, say OA_2 units of land and OB_2 units of labor, and find out how much output they will produce by measuring the height of the production surface at D', the point where labor input is OB_2 and land input is OA_2. According to Figure 5.8, the answer equals $D'D$.

Figure 5.8
Production Function,
Two Variable Inputs.

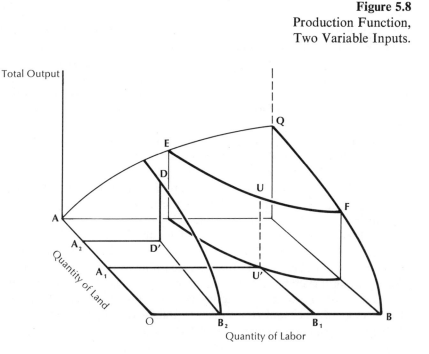

Note that this hypothetical production function illustrates the fact that a given amount of output can be produced in quite different ways. For ex-

---

[8]Note that this surface is not meant to represent the numerical values in Table 5.4 but is a general representation of how a production surface of this sort is likely to appear.

ample, in Table 5.4, 80 bushels of corn can be produced with either 4 man-years of labor and 2 acres of land or with 3 man-years of labor and 3 acres of land. (Moreover, the production function does not include many of the different ways in which a given output can be produced because it includes only efficient combinations of inputs.[9]) Generally there is a variety of ways to produce a given output and a variety of efficient input combinations; thus it is possible for the firm to substitute one input for another in producing a specified amount of output.

8. Isoquants

An isoquant is a curve showing all possible (efficient) combinations of inputs that are capable of producing a certain quantity of output. Given the production function, one can readily derive the isoquant pertaining to any level of output. For example, in Figure 5.8, suppose that we want to find the isoquant corresponding to an output of $U'U$. All that we need to do is to cut the production surface at the height of $U'U$ parallel to the base plane, the result being EUF, and to drop perpendiculars from EUF to the base. Clearly, this results in a curve that includes all efficient combinations of land and labor that can produce $U'U$ bushels of corn.[10]

A number of isoquants, each pertaining to a different output rate, are shown in Figure 5.9. The two axes measure the quantities of inputs that are used. In contrast to the previous diagrams, we assume that labor and capital—not labor and land—are the relevant inputs in this case. The curves show the various combinations of inputs that can produce 50, 100, and 150 units of output. For example, consider the isoquant pertaining to 50 units of output per period of time. According to this isoquant, it is possible to attain this output rate if OL_0 units of labor and OC_0 units of capital are used per period of time. Alternatively, this output rate can be attained if OL_1 units of labor and OC_1 units of capital—or OL_2 units of labor and OC_2 units of capital—are used per period of time.

---

[9]For example, if 2 units of labor and 3 units of capital can produce 1 unit of output, this combination of inputs and output will not be included in the production function if it is also possible to produce 1 unit of output with 2 units of labor and 2 units of capital. The former input combination is clearly inefficient, since it is possible to obtain the result with the same amount of labor and less capital.

[10]Using the notation in Footnote 7, an isoquant shows all combinations of x_1 and x_2 such that $f(x_1, x_2)$ equals a certain output rate.

Figure 5.9
Isoquants.

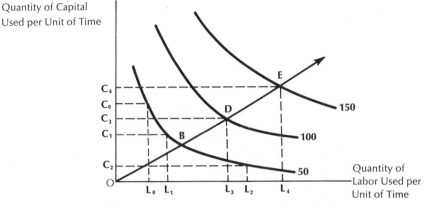

A ray is a line that starts from some point and goes off into space. A ray from the origin, such as $OBDE$, describes all input combinations where the capital-labor ratio is constant, the slope of the ray being equal to the constant capital-labor ratio. For example, at points D and E, 100 and 150 units of output are produced with a capital-labor ratio of $OC_3/OL_3 = OC_4/OL_4$. Moving out from the origin along any ray, such as $OBDE$, we see that various output levels can be produced with the same ratio of one input to another. Of course, the absolute amount of each input increases as we move out to higher and higher output levels, but the ratio of one input to the other remains constant. It is important to understand the difference between such a ray and an isoquant; an isoquant pertains to a fixed, not a changing, output rate and a changing, not a fixed, ratio of inputs.

An isoquant plays much the same kind of role in production theory that an indifference curve plays in demand theory. An indifference curve shows the various combinations of two commodities that provide equal satisfaction to the consumer; an isoquant shows the various combinations of two inputs that result in an equal output for the firm. It is obvious that, like indifference curves, two isoquants cannot intersect. If an intersection were to occur, it would mean that two different output rates are the maximum obtainable from a given combination of resources; this is obviously absurd.

Isoquants can be used to illustrate the case in which inputs must be used in fixed proportions. Figure 5.10 shows a case of this sort, the necessary ratio of capital to labor being the slope of the ray OP. The isoquants are right angles, indicating that, if one input is changed while the other input is held constant, there is no increase in the output rate. In other words, the marginal product of either input is zero if the other input is held constant.

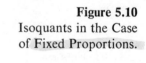

Figure 5.10
Isoquants in the Case
of Fixed Proportions.

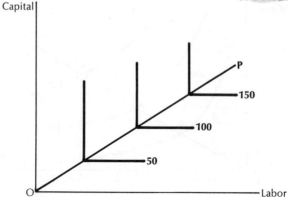

Sometimes there are a number of processes that can be used to produce a given commodity, each utilizing the inputs in fixed proportions (but with the proportions fixed at different levels). This case is discussed at length in Chapter 7, where we take up linear programming.

In some cases, isoquants may have positively sloped segments, or bend back upon themselves, as shown in Figure 5.11. Above *OA* and below *OB*, the slope of the isoquants is positive, which implies that increases in both

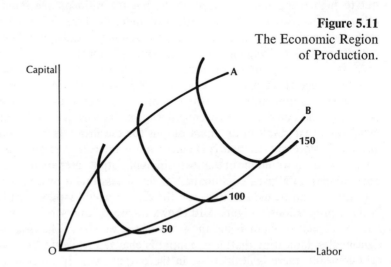

Figure 5.11
The Economic Region
of Production.

capital and labor are required to maintain a certain output rate. Clearly, a profit-maximizing firm will not operate in either of these regions, since it can produce the same output with less of both inputs, which must be cheaper. For this reason, the zone between *OA* and *OB* is often called the *economic region of production.* This region contains the points that correspond to stage II, in the terminology of Section 6 above. Above *OA*, the marginal product of capital is negative; below *OB*, the marginal product of labor is negative.

9. Substitution Among Inputs

From both a practical and a theoretical point of view, it is important to study the rate at which one input must be substituted for another to maintain a constant output rate. Consider the isoquant, ZZ', in Figure 5.12. The relevant output rate can be produced with OL_0 units of labor and OC_0 units of capital. However, if the amount of labor is increased to OL_1, the same output rate can be attained with less capital: OC_1 units rather than OC_0. Thus, in the relevant range, the rate at which labor can be substituted for capital is $-(OC_0 - OC_1)/(OL_0 - OL_1) = BA/BC$, the minus sign being added to make the result a positive number. If we consider a very

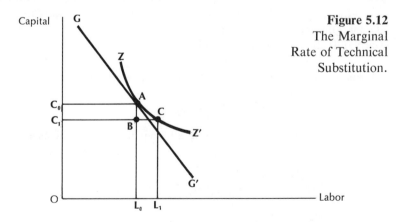

Figure 5.12
The Marginal
Rate of Technical
Substitution.

small increase in labor (OL_1 being very close to OL_0), BA/BC equals minus one times the slope of the tangent, GG', to the isoquant at A, which is called the *marginal rate of technical substitution*. It measures, for small changes in labor, the change in capital required per unit change in labor. The reader will note that, as its name indicates, it is analogous to the marginal rate of substitution in demand theory. (Economists, having found an elegant and felicitous phrase like the marginal rate of substitution, did not want to abandon it for anything cumbersome.)

Using the diagram in Figure 5.12, it is easy to demonstrate that the marginal rate of technical substitution of labor for capital is equal to the ratio of the marginal product of labor to the marginal product of capital. Suppose that labor input is held at the OL_0 level, while capital is increased from OC_1 to OC_0. Output would increase from the level (say Q_1) corresponding to labor of OL_0 and capital of OC_1, to the level corresponding to the isoquant (say Q_0). The marginal product of capital is $(Q_0 - Q_1) \div (OC_0 - OC_1) = (Q_0 - Q_1) \div BA$. On the other hand, suppose that capital is held at OC_1, while labor is increased from OL_0 to OL_1. The marginal product of labor is $(Q_0 - Q_1) \div (OL_1 - OL_0) = (Q_0 - Q_1) \div BC$. Thus the ratio of marginal product of labor to marginal product of capital equals $BA \div BC$, which (in the limit for small changes in the amount of labor) equals the marginal rate of technical substitution.[11]

It is also easy to show that the marginal rate of technical substitution of labor for capital tends to decrease as an increasing amount of labor is substituted for capital. As labor is substituted for capital, the marginal product of labor tends to fall. Increases in labor, holding capital constant, result in a decrease in the marginal product of labor in the economic region of production. When capital is decreased, even more of a decrease occurs in the marginal product of labor, since a decrease in capital results in a downward shift in the marginal product curve for labor. At the same time, the

---

[11]Using the notation in Footnote 7, the total differential of the production function is

$$dQ = \frac{\partial f}{\partial x_1} dx_1 + \frac{\partial f}{\partial x_2} dx_2$$

Since output remains constant along an isoquant, $dQ = 0$ along an isoquant. Thus

$$\frac{\partial f}{\partial x_1} dx_1 + \frac{\partial f}{\partial x_2} dx_2 = 0$$

and the marginal rate of technical substitution, defined as $-dx_2/dx_1$, is

$$\frac{\partial f}{\partial x_1} \div \frac{\partial f}{\partial x_2}$$

which is the ratio of the marginal products. This is another proof of the proposition in the text.

marginal product of capital rises (for the same kinds of reasons) as more labor is substituted for capital. Thus, since the marginal rate of technical substitution equals the marginal product of labor (which is falling) divided by the marginal product of capital (which is rising), it must be falling as labor is substituted for capital.

Since the marginal rate of technical substitution falls as labor is substituted for capital, it follows that isoquants must be convex. (See Chapter 2, Section 5.) Because the marginal rate of technical substitution equals -1 times the slope of the isoquant and because the marginal rate of technical substitution falls as we move to the right along an isoquant, the absolute value of the slope of the isoquant must be getting smaller as we move to the right along an isoquant. But if the absolute value of the slope is getting smaller as we move to the right, the isoquant must be convex.

10. The Long Run and Returns to Scale

Previous sections have shown how a firm's technology can be represented by a production function and have described the characteristics of production functions (and of related concepts like the marginal and average product) that seem to hold in general for production processes. However, one important characteristic of production functions has not been described: how output responds in the long run to changes in the *scale* of the firm. In other words, suppose that we consider a long-run situation in which all inputs are variable, and suppose that the firm increases the amount of all inputs by the same proportion. What will happen to output? This is an important question, the answer to which (as we shall see in subsequent chapters) helps to determine whether firms of certain sizes can survive in the industry.

To repeat, what will happen to output under the assumed conditions? Clearly, there are three possibilities: First, output may increase by a larger proportion than each of the inputs. For example, a doubling of all inputs might lead to more than a doubling of output. This is the case of *increasing returns to scale*. Second, output may increase by a smaller proportion than each of the inputs. For example, a doubling of all inputs might lead to less than a doubling of output. This is the case of *decreasing returns to scale*. Third, output may increase by exactly the same proportion as the inputs. For example, a doubling of all inputs might lead to a doubling of output. This is the case of *constant returns to scale*.

At first glance it may seem that production functions must necessarily exhibit constant returns to scale. After all, if two factories are built with the same plant and the same types of workers, it would seem obvious that twice as much output will result. Unfortunately, it is not as simple as that. For instance, if a firm doubles its scale, it may be able to use techniques that could not be used at the smaller scale. Some inputs are not available in small units; for example, we cannot install half an open hearth furnace. Because of indivisibilities of this sort, increasing returns to scale may occur. Thus, although one could double a firm's size by simply building two small factories, this may be inefficient. One large factory may be more efficient than two smaller factories of the same total capacity because it is large enough to use certain techniques and inputs that the smaller factories cannot use.

Another reason for increasing returns to scale stems from certain geometrical relations. For example, since the volume of a box that is $4 \times 4 \times 4$ ft is 64 times as great as the volume of a box that is $1 \times 1 \times 1$ ft, the former box can carry 64 times as much as the latter box. But since the area of the six sides of the $4 \times 4 \times 4$-ft box is 96 sq ft and the area of the six sides of the $1 \times 1 \times 1$-ft box is 6 sq ft, the former box only requires 16 times as much wood as the latter. Greater specialization also can result in increasing returns to scale: As more men and machines are used, it is possible to subdivide tasks and allow various inputs to specialize. Also, economies of scale may arise because of probabilistic considerations: for example, because the aggregate behavior of a bigger number of customers tends to be more stable, a firm's inventory may not have to increase in proportion to its sales.

Decreasing returns to scale can also occur, the most frequently cited reason being the difficulty of coordinating a large enterprise. It can be difficult even in a small firm to obtain the information required to make important decisions; in a large firm, the difficulties tend to be greater. It can be difficult even in a small firm to be certain that management's wishes are being carried out; in a larger firm these difficulties too tend to be greater. Although the advantages of a large organization seem to have captured the public fancy, there are often very great disadvantages. For example, in certain kinds of research and development, there is evidence that large engineering teams tend to be less effective than smaller ones and that large firms tend to be less effective than small ones.

Diagrams like those in Figure 5.13 can be used to analyze and describe the situation in a particular firm. Panel A describes a case in which there are constant returns to scale. Examination of the isoquants for outputs of 50, 100, and 150 units shows that they intersect any ray from the origin,

Figure 5.13
Constant, Increasing,
and Decreasing Returns
to Scale.

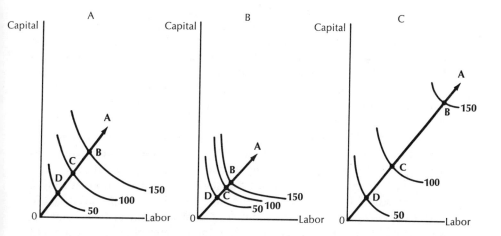

like *OA*, at equal distances. (That is, *OD* = *DC* = *CB*.) In other words, twice as much of both inputs are needed to produce 100 units of output than to produce 50 units of output, and three times as much of both inputs are needed to produce 150 units of output than to produce 50 units of output. Panel B describes a case in which there are increasing returns to scale. In this case, successive isoquants, as one moves out from the origin, become closer and closer together. For example, *OD* > *DC* > *CB*. Panel C describes a case in which there are decreasing returns to scale. In this case, successive isoquants become farther and farther apart as we move out from the origin. For example, *OD* < *DC* < *CB*.

Whether or not there are constant, increasing, or decreasing returns to scale in a particular situation is an empirical question that must be settled case by case. There is no simple, all-encompassing answer.[12] In some industries the available evidence may indicate that increasing returns are present over a certain range of output. In other industries, decreasing or constant returns may be present. In the next section, we turn to a discussion of empirical studies.

---

[12]Also, it is important to note that the answer is likely to depend on the level of output that is considered. There may be increasing returns to scale at small output levels and constant or decreasing returns to scale at larger output levels.

11.   Measurement of Production Functions

Economists and statisticians have devoted a great deal of time and effort, particularly in the postwar period, to the measurement of production functions. Three methods have been used in most of these studies. The first method is based on the statistical analysis of time-series data concerning the amount of various inputs used in various periods in the past and the amount of output produced in each period. For example, one might obtain data concerning the amount of labor, the amount of capital, and the amount of various raw materials used in the steel industry during each year from 1948 to 1970. On the basis of such data and information concerning the annual output of steel during 1948 to 1970, one might estimate the relationship between the amounts of the inputs and the resulting output.

The second method is based on the statistical analysis of cross-section data concerning the amount of various inputs used and output produced in various firms or sectors of the industry at a given point in time. For example, one might obtain data concerning the amount of labor, the amount of capital, and the amount of various raw materials used in various firms in the steel industry in 1970. On the basis of such data and information concerning the 1970 output of each firm, one might estimate the relationship between the amounts of the inputs and the resulting output.

The third method is based on technical information supplied by the engineer or the agricultural scientist. This information is collected by experiment or from experience with the day-to-day workings of the technical process. There are considerable advantages to be gained from approaching the measurement of the production function from this angle because the range of applicability of the data is known, and, unlike time-series and cross-section studies, we are not restricted to the narrow range of actual observations. However, there are also some difficult problems in this approach, which are discussed in the following paragraphs.

All three approaches are handicapped by the fact that the data may not always represent technically efficient combinations of inputs and output. For example, because of errors or constraints, the amount of inputs used by the steel industry in 1970 may not have been the minimum required to produce the 1970 output of the steel industry. Since the production function theoretically includes only efficient input combinations, a case of this sort should be excluded, if our measurements are to be pristine pure. In practice, however, such cases are not always excluded (or recognized) and the resulting production function is in error for this reason.

Another important problem is the measurement of capital input. The principal difficulty stems from the fact that the stock of capital is composed of various types and ages of machines, buildings, and inventories. Combining them into a single measure—or a few measures—is a formidable problem. In addition, errors can arise in the first two techniques because various data points, which are assumed to be on the same production function, are in fact on different ones. Moreover, biases can occur because of identification problems somewhat similar to those discussed in Chapter 4, Section 12.[13]

With regard to the third method, it is difficult to combine the results for the processes for which engineers have data into an over-all plant or firm production function. Since engineering data generally pertain to only a part of the firm's activities, this is often a very hard job. For example, engineering data tell us little or nothing about the firm's marketing or financial activities. Moreover, engineering data are generally available for only parts of the firm's fabricating activities.

Despite these difficulties, estimates of production functions have proved of considerable interest and value. Many of these estimates have been based on the assumption that the production function is a so-called Cobb-Douglas function, which is

$$Q = A\, I_1^{\alpha_1} I_2^{\alpha_2} I_3^{\alpha_3} \tag{5.1}$$

where Q is the output rate; I_1 is the quantity of labor, I_2 is the quantity of capital, and I_3 is the quantity of raw materials; and A, α_1, α_2, and α_3 are parameters that vary from case to case. Ordinarily it is assumed that the α's are less than one, which assures that the marginal product of an input (which equals its α times its average product) decreases with increases in its utilization. Increasing returns to scale occur if $\alpha_1 + \alpha_2 + \alpha_3 > 1$; decreasing returns to scale occur if $\alpha_1 + \alpha_2 + \alpha_3 < 1$.

Table 5.5 shows the estimates of α_1, α_2, and α_3 for a number of industries in the United States and abroad. They provide interesting information concerning production relations in these industries. To see more clearly the implications of these results, note that α_1 is the percentage increase in output resulting from a 1-percent increase in labor, holding the quantities of the other inputs constant. For example, in the French gas industry in 1945, a 1-percent increase in labor would have resulted in a 0.83-percent increase in output. Similarly, α_2 is the percentage increase in output resulting from a 1-percent increase in capital, holding the quantities of other inputs constant.

---

[13]For an excellent review of empirical studies of the production function, see A. A. Walters, "Production and Cost Functions," *Econometrica*, Jan. 1963. This section has benefited considerably from Walters' paper.

Table 5.5.   Estimates of α_1, α_2, and α_3 for Selected Industries.

INDUSTRY	COUNTRY	YEAR	α_1	α_2	α_3	$\alpha_1 + \alpha_2 + \alpha_3$
Gas	France	1945	.83	.10	—	0.93
Railroads	United States	1936	.89	.12	.28	1.29
Coal	United Kingdom	1950	.79	.29	—	1.08
Food	United States	1909	.72	.35	—	1.07
Metals and machinery	United States	1909	.71	.26	—	0.97
Cotton	India	1951	.92	.12	—	1.04
Jute	India	1951	.84	.14	—	0.98
Sugar	India	1951	.59	.33	—	0.92
Coal	India	1951	.71	.44	—	1.15
Paper	India	1951	.64	.45	—	1.09
Chemicals	India	1951	.80	.37	—	1.17
Electricity	India	1951	.20	.67	—	0.87

Source: A. A. Walters, "Production and Cost Functions," *Econometrica*, Jan. 1963.

The results also cast light on returns to scale: in five of the 12 cases, there seem to be decreasing returns; in seven of the 12 cases there seem to be increasing returns to scale. Finally, it is possible to construct isoquants from the results in Table 5.5. For example, Figure 5.14 shows some isoquants for the French gas industry.[14] Note that these isoquants (*A*, *B*, and *C*) are similar in shape to the hypothetical isoquants introduced earlier in this chapter.

12. Summary

As a first approximation, economists generally assume that firms attempt to maximize profits. In recent years, there have been a number of attempts to experiment with alternative assumptions concerning the goals of the firm, most of these alternative assumptions stemming from a more detailed view of the firm's organization. Although these theories are useful for some purposes, profit maximization remains the standard assumption in eco-

[14]See M. Verhulst, "Pure Theory of Production Applied to the French Gas Industry," *Econometrica*, 1948.

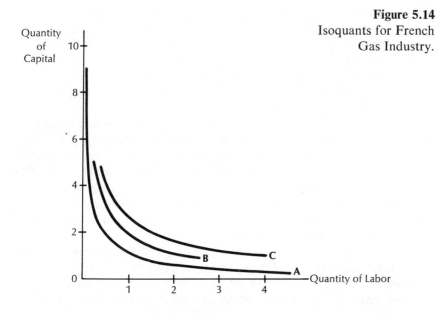

Figure 5.14
Isoquants for French
Gas Industry.

(*Source:* M. Verhulst, "Pure Theory of Production Applied to the French Gas Industry," *Econometrica*, 1948.) Of course, these isoquants are merely illustrative. The mathematical expression for an isoquant is $L = H \div K^{\frac{10}{83}}$, where L is the quantity of labor, K is the quantity of capital, and H is a constant that differs from one isoquant to another.

nomics, because it is a close enough approximation for many important purposes and because it provides rules of behavior for firms that do want to make as much money as possible.

The production function is used by economists to represent the technology available to the firm. For any commodity the production function is the relationship between the quantities of various inputs used per period of time and the maximum quantity of the commodity produced per period of time. In analyzing production processes, we generally assume that all inputs can be divided into two categories: fixed and variable. Corresponding to the idea of fixed and variable inputs is the idea of the short and the long run. Both in the short run and in the long run, a firm's productive processes ordinarily permit substantial variation in input proportions. An isoquant is a curve that shows all possible combinations of inputs that are capable of producing a certain quantity of output.

The law of diminishing marginal returns states that, as equal increments of one input are added, the quantities of other inputs held constant, the resulting increments of product will decrease beyond some point; that is, the marginal product of the input will diminish.   The relationships between total, average, and marginal products can be used to define three stages of production.   Stage I covers the range of variable input over which the average product is increasing, stage III covers that range of variable input over which the marginal product is negative, and stage II covers the rest. If a firm maximizes profits, it will not operate in stage III; a firm in a perfectly competitive industry will try not to operate in stage I.

If the firm increases all inputs by the same proportion and output increases by more (less) than this proportion, there are increasing (decreasing) returns to scale.   Increasing returns to scale may occur because of indivisibility of inputs, various geometrical relations, or specialization.   Decreasing returns to scale can also occur, the most frequently cited reason being the difficulty of managing a huge enterprise.   Whether or not there are constant, increasing, or decreasing returns to scale is an empirical question that must be settled case by case.

Economists and statisticians have devoted a great deal of time and effort in the postwar period to the measurement of production functions.   Three methods have been used in most of these studies: statistical analysis based on time series of inputs and output, statistical analysis based on cross-section data, and analysis based on engineering data.   Many of these estimates have been based on the assumption that the production function is of Cobb-Douglas form.   Although there are a great many difficulties in existing measurement techniques, estimates of production functions have proved of considerable interest and value.

APPENDIX

Organization of the Firm and Alternative
Models of Firm Behavior

In recent years, there have been a number of attempts to experiment with models of the firm based on assumptions other than profit maximization. Most of these alternative models are tied to a more detailed look at the organization of the firm and its divisions.   Until recently, economists have proceeded on the basis of extremely simple assumptions regarding the organization of the firm. Traditionally, they have posited the existence in each firm of an entrepreneur who exercises control over the firm's activities. The entrepreneur decides whether the firm should continue its existence (or be founded in the first place); he sets the price or decides what price to accept; and he decides whether output and capacity should be increased or decreased. He is the locus of decision-making in the firm. This concept of the organization of the firm is not unrealistic in many cases. In the United States, millions of small businessmen satisfy, more or less, the definition of the entrepreneur. For example, in a small tool-and-die shop, there is typically a single owner-manager who makes practically all of the major decisions.

However, in large corporations, the concept of the entrepreneur seems strained, since in most cases there is no single entrepreneur and it is difficult to know exactly where, how, and by whom decisions are made. Rather than a single entrepreneur, there are large numbers of people in middle management, as well as the top brass occupying key management positions, all of whom participate in varying degrees in the formulation of company policy. Various groups within the firm develop their own party lines, and intra-firm politics is an important part of the process determining company policy. For example, if a firm is composed of two divisions (each making a different product), each division may fight to maintain and expand its share of the firm's budget, and each may try to put the other in a subordinate position. Whereas in a small firm it may be fairly accurate to regard the goals of the firm as being the goals of the entrepreneur, in the large corporation the decision on the goals of the firm is in a real sense a matter of politics.

It has been suggested by Herbert Simon[15] and others that the firm "satisfices" rather than maximizes profit. That is, business firms aim at a "satisfactory" rate of profit rather than the maximum figure. A firm's aspiration level is the boundary between "unsatisfactory" and "satisfactory" outcomes. The firm abandons the attempt to maximize profits because the calculations required are too complicated and the available data are too poor. Instead the firm tries to attain certain minimal standards of performance.

This theory would, of course, be incomplete if it did not specify how the firm's aspiration level will change, the aspiration level being a certain goal like "our profit for this year should be $2,000,000." According to some economists, if the environment facing the firm is relatively constant, the aspiration level will tend to be slightly higher than the firm's performance. If performance is improving, the aspiration level will tend to lag behind actual performance; and if performance is decreasing, the aspiration level will tend

---

[15]For example, see H. Simon, *Models of Man*, New York: John Wiley & Sons, 1957.

to be above actual performance. Of course, if the aspiration level is close to the maximum profit, there is little difference between the results obtained by assuming profit maximization and those obtained using "satisficing."

An interesting feature of this theory is that it focuses attention on internal slack in the firm, a concept that has no place in traditional theory. One implication of the traditional assumption that firms maximize profits is that they produce whatever volumes of output they choose at minimum cost. Although this may be a reasonable first approximation, it seems likely that there is a certain amount of slack in most firms, in the sense that costs are not pushed down to the minimum. This slack acts as a cushion when the firm is submitted to pressures from the outside and from within. For example, if profits are reduced by a fall in demand, the firm is sometimes able to recoup part of the losses by eliminating slack, that is, by lowering its costs. However, this slack is usually not created to provide stability; instead it arises from the bargaining process within the firm.[16]

Simon's "satisficing" model is not the only alternative to the assumption of profit maximization. It has also been suggested that, when differences arise between profit maximization and the interests of the management group, executives are likely to follow policies favoring their own interests[17] Important in this regard is the separation of ownership from control in the large corporation in the United States. The owners of the firm—the stock-holders—usually have little detailed knowledge of the firm's operations. Even if the board of directors is made up largely of people other than top management, top management usually has a great deal of freedom as long as it seems to be performing reasonably well. Under these circumstances, one might suppose that the behavior of the firm often will be dictated in part by the interests of the management group, the result being larger salaries, more perquisites, and a bigger staff than otherwise would be the case.

Still another alternative to the assumption of profit maximization has been proposed by William Baumol,[18] who suggests that firms attempt to maximize total sales, rather than profits. However, profits are not ignored;

---

[16]See R. Cyert and J. March, *A Behavioral Theory of the Firm*, Englewood Cliffs, N.J.: Prentice-Hall, 1963, and other works of these authors for a discussion of the topics included in the last few paragraphs.

[17]See R. Marris, *The Economic Theory of "Managerial" Capitalism*, New York: Free Press, 1964; and O. Williamson, *Economics of Discretionary Behavior*, Englewood Cliffs, N.J.: Prentice-Hall, 1964. Of course, middle managers may also act at variance with the policies of top management. See E. Mansfield and H. Wein, "A Study of Decision-Making within the Firm," *Quarterly Journal of Economics*, Nov., 1958.

[18]See W. Baumol, *Business Behavior, Value and Growth*, New York: Macmillan, 2nd ed., 1959.

it is assumed that there is a certain minimum level of profits that the firm attempts to attain. Thus the firm can wind up in one of two types of equilibrium: one where the profit constraint bars the firm from maximizing sales, and one where it does not. According to Baumol, sales represent a measure of management's success, especially since many observers focus attention on a firm's share of the market as an indicator of its performance. Also, according to Baumol, there is a closer correlation between the salaries of the executives and the company's sales than between their salaries and profits.

Although each of these theories is useful for certain purposes and under certain conditions, profit maximization remains the standard assumption in microeconomics. In part, this is because it is a close enough approximation for many important purposes; in part, it is because some of these alternative theories require more in the way of data than does the simpler theory of profit maximization. Even some of the proponents of these alternative theories admit that profit maximization is an adequate assumption for a wide range of important purposes. Also as we have noted before, the theory of the profit-maximizing firm is of great interest because it provides rules of rational behavior for firms that do want to maximize profits.

SELECTED REFERENCES

Carlson, Sune, *A Study on the Pure Theory of Production*, London: P. S. King, 1939.

Cassells, John, "On the Law of Variable Proportions," *Explorations in Economics*, New York: McGraw-Hill, 1936.

Machlup, Fritz, "On the Meaning of the Marginal Product," *Explorations in Economics*, New York: McGraw-Hill, 1936.

Douglas, Paul, "Are There Laws of Production?," *American Economic Review*, March 1948.

Walters, A. A., "Production and Cost Functions," *Econometrica*, 1963.

6

Optimal Input Combinations and Cost Functions

1. Introduction

In the previous chapter we were concerned with the motivation of the firm and the way in which the technology available to the firm can be represented. We decided to assume, as a first approximation, that firms attempt to maximize profit. We also decided that the technology available to the firm can be represented by a production function, which conforms to certain rules like the law of diminishing marginal returns. These decisions take us part way—but only part way—toward a model of the firm. The next step is to determine how a profit-maximizing firm will combine inputs to produce a given quantity of output. That is the purpose of this chapter.

To be specific, suppose that a producer of corn, perhaps the one who so generously provided the basic data used in the previous chapter, decides for some reason to produce 1000 bushels of corn next year. Suppose that, in accord with the conclusions of the previous chapter, we assume that he is an out-and-out profit-maximizer, and that we are given his production

148

function, derived largely through his experiments. On the basis of this information, can we predict what combination of inputs he will use to produce 1000 bushels of corn next year and how much it will cost him to produce this amount? Or putting the problem somewhat differently, suppose that we are hired by the farmer to help him. Can we tell him what combination of inputs he *should* use and how much it *should* cost him to produce this amount?

In this chapter, we begin by determining which combination of inputs a firm will choose if it minimizes the cost of producing a given amount of output. Then we discuss the nature of costs: what is meant by a cost and how various concepts of cost differ from one another. Finally, we show how the short-run and long-run cost functions of the firm can be derived theoretically, and we provide a brief discussion of the measurement of cost functions.

2. The Optimal Combination of Inputs

We begin by considering a firm of any sort, rather than focusing attention on any particular sort of firm, like the farm noted previously. If the firm maximizes profit, it will minimize the cost of producing a given output or maximize the output derived from a given level of cost.[1] This seems obvious. Suppose that the firm is a perfect competitor in the input markets, which means that it takes input prices as given. (The case in which the firm can influence input prices is taken up in Chapter 13.) Suppose that there are two inputs, capital and labor, that are variable in the relevant time period. Also, suppose that the firm decides to spend $200 on these inputs and that the price of labor is $10 per unit and the price of capital is $20 per unit. Table 6.1 shows the marginal product of each input when various combinations of inputs (the total cost of each combination being $200) are used. What combination of capital and labor should the firm choose, if it wants to maximize the quantity of output derived from the given level of cost?

The answer is as follows: The firm will maximize output by distributing its expenditures among various inputs in such a way that the marginal product of a dollar's worth of any one input is equal to the marginal product

---

[1] The conditions for minimizing the cost of producing a given output are the same as those for maximizing the output from a given cost. This is shown in Section 3. Thus we can view the firm's problem in either way.

Table 6.1. Marginal Products of Capital and Labor.

AMOUNT OF INPUT USED		MARGINAL PRODUCT*	
LABOR	CAPITAL	LABOR	CAPITAL
2	9	20	4
4	8	18	6
6	7	16	8
8	6	14	10
10	5	12	12
12	4	10	14
14	3	8	16
16	2	6	18
18	1	4	20

*The marginal products are defined for the interval between the indi-
cated amount of labor or capital and one unit (capital) or two units
(labor) less than this amount.

of a dollar's worth of any other input used. Thus the firm will choose an
input combination such that

$$\frac{MP_a}{P_a} = \frac{MP_b}{P_b} = \cdots = \frac{MP_m}{P_m} \tag{6.1}$$

where $MP_a, MP_b, \ldots, MP_m$ are the marginal products of inputs $a, b, \ldots, m$,
and $P_a, P_b, \ldots, P_m$ are the prices of inputs $a, b, \ldots, m$. In the case in
point, the marginal product of capital should be set at twice the marginal
product of labor, since the price of capital is twice the price of labor. This
occurs at 14 units of labor and 3 units of capital; thus this is the optimal
combination.

To prove that this allocation of cost ($140 to labor and $60 to capital)
is optimal, suppose that we shift $20 from labor to capital (the result being
$120 devoted to labor and $80 to capital). Since the marginal product of
the extra unit of capital that is gained is 14 units of output and the marginal
product of the two units of labor given up is 2 times 8 units of product,[2]
this change will reduce output by 2 units. Similarly, the transfer of $20 from
capital to labor will reduce output.

---

[2]The marginal product of labor between 12 and 14 units of labor is 8 units of output per unit of labor. The marginal product of capital between 3 and 4 units of
capital is 14 units of output per unit of capital.

3.   Isocost Curves and Isoquants

In the previous section, we indicated how a firm will allocate a given expenditure to maximize the output it obtains. In this section, after showing graphically that this solution is correct, we show how a firm will combine inputs to minimize the cost of producing a given volume of output. We begin by determining the various combinations of inputs that the firm can obtain for a given expenditure. For example, if capital and labor are the inputs and the price of labor is P_L per unit and the price of capital is P_C per unit, the input combinations that can be obtained for a total outlay of R are such that

$$P_L L + P_C C = R \tag{6.2}$$

where L is the amount of the labor input and C is the amount of the capital input. Given P_L, P_C, and R, it follows that

$$C = \frac{R}{P_C} - \frac{P_L}{P_C} L \tag{6.3}$$

Thus, the various combinations of capital and labor that can be purchased, given P_L, P_C, and R, can be represented by a straight line like that shown in Figure 6.1, capital being plotted on the vertical axis, labor being plotted on the horizontal. This line, which has an intercept on the y axis equal to R/P_C and a slope of $-P_L/P_C$, is called an *isocost curve.*

Figure 6.1
Isocost Curve.

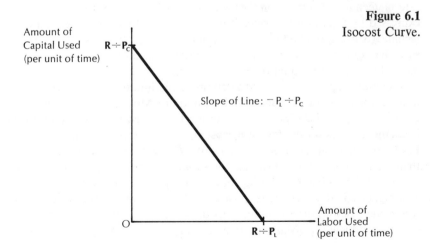

Amount of Capital Used (per unit of time) $R \div P_C$

Slope of Line: $-P_L \div P_C$

O

$R \div P_L$

Amount of Labor Used (per unit of time)

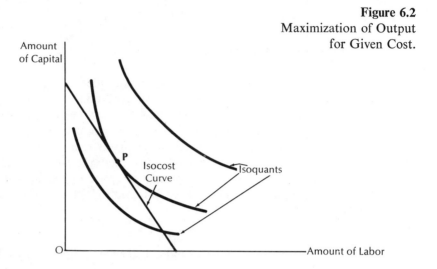

Figure 6.2
Maximization of Output
for Given Cost.

If we superimpose the relevant isocost curve on the firm's isoquant map, we can readily determine graphically which combination of inputs will maximize the output for the given expenditure. Obviously, the firm should pick that point on the isocost curve that is on the highest isoquant, for example, P in Figure 6.2. This clearly is a point where the isocost curve is tangent to the isoquant. Thus, since the slope of the isocost curve is the negative of P_L/P_C and the slope of the isoquant is the negative of the marginal rate of technical substitution, it follows that the optimal combination of inputs must be such that the ratio of input prices, P_L/P_C, equals the marginal rate of technical substitution. This condition is precisely the same as that expressed by Equation 6.1, since it will be recalled that the marginal rate of technical substitution of labor for capital is MP_L/MP_C. Thus we can be sure that our graphical results are precisely the same as those we would have obtained using Equation 6.1.

A similar graph can be used to determine the input combination that will minimize the cost of producing a given output. Moving along the isoquant corresponding to the stipulated output level, we must find that point on the isoquant that lies on the lowest isocost curve, for example, U in Figure 6.3. Input combinations on isocost curves like C_0 that lie below U are cheaper than U, but they cannot produce the desired output. Input combinations on isocost curves like C_2 that lie above U will produce the desired output but at a higher cost than U. It is obvious that the optimal point, U, is a point where the isocost curve is tangent to the isoquant. Thus, to minimize the cost of producing a given output or to maximize the output from a given

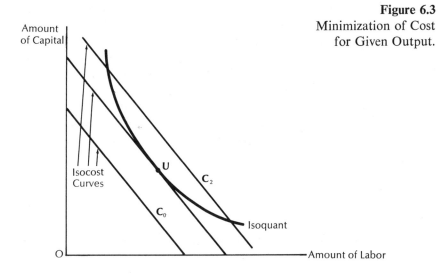

Figure 6.3
Minimization of Cost
for Given Output.

cost outlay, the firm must equate the marginal rate of technical substitution and the input-price ratio.[3]

---

[3]Suppose that Q is the output rate and that the production function is $Q = f(x_1, x_2)$, where x_1 and x_2 are the amounts of the two inputs used. If we want to find the values of x_1 and x_2 that maximize Q for the given cost, C_0, we set up the Lagrangian function:

$$L = f(x_1, x_2) - \lambda(P_1x_1 + P_2x_2 - C_0)$$

where P_1 is the price of the first input, P_2 is the price of the second input, and λ is the Lagrange multiplier. Some first-order conditions are

$$\frac{\partial L}{\partial x_1} = \frac{\partial f}{\partial x_1} - \lambda P_1 = 0 \quad : \quad \frac{\partial L}{\partial x_2} = \frac{\partial f}{\partial x_2} - \lambda P_2 = 0$$

which imply that $\partial f/\partial x_1 \div P_1 = \partial f/\partial x_2 \div P_2 = \lambda$, the condition in Equation 6.1.

If we want to minimize the cost for the given output, Q_0, we set up the Lagrangian function:

$$P_1x_1 + P_2x_2 - M[f(x_1, x_2) - Q_0]$$

where M is the Lagrange multiplier. Some first-order conditions are

$$P_1 - \frac{M\partial f}{\partial x_1} = 0 \quad : \quad P_2 - \frac{M\partial f}{\partial x_2} = 0$$

which imply that $\partial f/\partial x_1 \div P_1 = \partial f/\partial x_2 \div P_2 = 1/M$, the condition in Equation 6.1. If the output level is the same, the values of x_1 and x_2 that are chosen must be the same, regardless of whether the output is maximized for the given cost or the cost is minimized for the given output.

Note that this tells us how to solve the problem posed at the beginning of the chapter—the problem of the farmer who decides for some reason to produce 1000 bushels of corn next year and wants to know what combination of inputs to use. All that we need to do is to estimate the isoquant that pertains to an output by the farm of 1000 bushels of corn per year. (If we are given the farm's production function, this is simple enough.) Then using data concerning the prices of the inputs, we can draw isocost curves, as in Figure 6.3, and determine the point, like U, where the isoquant is tangent to an isocost curve. This point represents the optimal combination of inputs.

4. The Production of Corn: An Application

To show how the theory presented in previous sections can be applied to help improve decision-making, this section describes how Earl Heady, a prominent agricultural economist, helped to determine the optimal combination of fertilizers in the production of Iowa corn.[4] In 1953 he carried out experiments to determine the effect of various quantities of nitrogen (N) and phosphate (P) on corn yield per acre (Y), and found that

$$Y = -5.682 - .316N - .417P$$
$$+ 6.3512\sqrt{N} + 8.5155\sqrt{P} + .3410\sqrt{PN} \qquad (6.4)$$

where P and N are measured in lb per acre and Y is measured in bushels per acre. This equation is, of course, a production function: It shows the amount of output (Y) that can be derived from various amounts of the inputs (N and P). Various isoquants are shown in Figure 6.4.

What is the least-cost combination of nitrogen and phosphate fertilizers? This is an important question, both to farm managers and to the general public. Corn is a very large and valuable crop, and it is important that it be produced as economically as possible. To solve this problem, Heady used the result we derived in Section 2; he said that the optimal N and P must be such that the ratio of the marginal product of nitrogen to its price must equal the ratio of the marginal product of phosphate to its price. At the time of the experiment, the price of nitrogen was 18 cents per lb and the price of phosphate was 12 cents per lb. From Equation 6.4 it follows that

---

[4]See E. Heady, "An Econometric Investigation of the Technology of Agricultural Production Functions," *Econometrica*, Apr. 1957.

Figure 6.4
Corn Isoquants from
Equation 6.4.

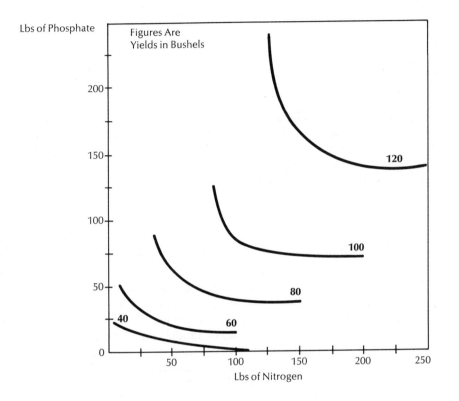

Source: E. Heady, "An Econometric Investigation of the Technology of Agricultural Production Functions," *Econometrica*, Apr. 1957.

$$MP_N = -.316 + 3.1756 \sqrt{\frac{1}{N}} + .1705 \sqrt{\frac{P}{N}} \qquad (6.5)$$

$$MP_P = -.417 + 4.2578 \sqrt{\frac{1}{P}} + .1705 \sqrt{\frac{N}{P}} \qquad (6.6)$$

where MP_N is the marginal product of nitrogen and MP_P is the marginal product of phosphate.

Suppose that a farm manager is thinking of spending $30 per acre on fertilizers and that he wants to know how this expenditure should be allocated between nitrogen and phosphate. Following Equation 6.1, the optimal N and P must be such that

$$\frac{1}{18}\left\{-.316 + 3.1756 \sqrt{\frac{1}{N}} + .1705 \sqrt{\frac{P}{N}}\right\}$$

$$= \frac{1}{12}\left\{-.417 + 4.2578 \sqrt{\frac{1}{P}} + .1705 \sqrt{\frac{N}{P}}\right\},$$

and since he is going to spend $30

$$18N + 12P = 3000.$$

Solving these two equations simultaneously, Heady's results indicate that the optimal input combination is about 91 lb of nitrogen per acre and about 113.5 lb of phosphate per acre. Of course, the figure of $30 was chosen arbitrarily but regardless of the total expenditure that is chosen, this method will provide the optimal allocation.

5. The Nature of Costs

The costs incurred by a firm are often thought to include only the money outlays the firm must make to obtain the use of resources. However, the firm's money outlays are only part of the cost picture. In many cases, economists are interested in the social costs of production, the costs to society when its resources are employed to make a given commodity. Since economic resources are, by definition, limited, when resources are used to produce a certain product, less can be produced of some other product that can be made with those resources. For example, aluminum can be used to produce airplanes, cooking utensils, outdoor furniture, and cans, among other things. Thus, when aluminum is used in the making of airplanes, some value of alternative products is given up.

According to the economist's definition, the cost of producing a certain product is the value of the other products that the resources used in its production could have produced instead. For example, the cost of producing airplanes is the value of the goods and services that could be obtained from the manpower, equipment, and materials used currently in aircraft production. The costs of inputs to a firm are their values in their most valuable alternative uses. These costs, together with the firm's production function (which indicates how much of each input is required to produce various amounts of the product) determine the cost of producing the product. This is called the *alternative cost* doctrine or the *opportunity cost* doctrine.

It is important to note that the alternative cost of an input may not equal its historical cost, which is defined to be the amount the firm actually paid for it. For example, if some gullible Dubuque contractor buys the Brooklyn Bridge for $1000, this does not mean that its value, either to the contractor or to society, is $1000. Similarly, if a firm invests $1 million in a piece of equipment that is quickly out-moded and is too inefficient relative to new equipment to be worth operating, its value is clearly not $1 million. Although conventional accounting rules place great emphasis on historical costs, the economist—and the sophisticated accountant and businessman—stress that historical costs should not be accepted uncritically.

Of course, the alternative cost of an input depends on the use for which the cost is being determined. For example, the cost of a pound of aluminum to transportation uses is the amount the aluminum is worth in non-transportation uses; the cost of a pound of aluminum to the aircraft industry is the amount the aluminum is worth to other transportation industries as well as in non-transportation uses; and the cost of a pound of aluminum to Boeing is the amount the aluminum is worth to other aircraft manufacturers as well as in all non-aircraft uses. If all aluminum were homogeneous in all relevant respects, all three of these alternative costs would tend to be the same, because aluminum would be transfered from low-value uses to high-value uses until the yields in all uses were the same. However, if aluminum is not homogeneous, it is not necessary that these alternative costs be equal.[5]

The alternative uses of a resource will often be different in the long run than in the short run. For example, a plumber has as alternative occupations only those fields that need his skills or less skilled occupations; but given time he can acquire other skills and become a programmer or a machinist. In the long run, alternatives tend to be greater and more varied than in the short run. Frequently, the alternative cost of an input is underestimated because people look only at its alternative uses in the short run.

6. Social vs. Private Costs and Explicit vs. Implicit Costs

The social costs of producing a given commodity do not always equal the private costs, which are defined to be the costs to the individual producer. For example, a steel plant may discharge waste products into a river located near the plant. To the plant, the cost of disposing of the wastes is simply

---

[5]See G. Stigler, *The Theory of Price*, New York: Macmillan, 1966, Chapter 6.

the amount paid to pump the wastes to the river. However, if the river becomes polluted and if its recreational uses are destroyed and the water becomes unfit for drinking, additional costs are incurred by other people. Differences of this sort between private and social costs occur frequently; in Chapter 15 we shall see that such differences may call for remedial public policy measures.

Turning to the private costs of production, it is important to recognize that there are two types of costs, both of which are generally important. The first type is explicit costs, which are the ordinary expenses that accountants include as the firm's expenses. They are the firm's payroll, payments for raw materials, and so on. The second type is implicit costs, which include the costs of resources owned and used by the firm's owner. The second type of costs is often omitted in calculating the costs of the firm.

Implicit costs arise because the alternative cost doctrine must be applied to the firm as well as to society as a whole. When the proprietor of a firm invests his own labor and capital in the business, these inputs should be valued at the amount he would have received if he had used these inputs in another way. For example, if he could have received a salary of $10,000 if he worked for someone else, and if he could have received dividends of $5000 if he invested his money in someone else's firm, he should value his labor and his capital at these rates. It is important that these implicit costs be included in a firm's total costs. Their exclusion can result in serious error.

7. The Proper Comparison of Alternatives

It is also important to note that, in making decisions, costs incurred in the past often are irrelevant. Suppose that you are going to make a trip and that you want to determine whether it will be cheaper to drive your car or to go by bus. What costs should be included if you drive your car? Since the only *extra* costs that will be incurred will be the gas and oil (and a certain amount of wear-and-tear on tires, engine, etc.), they are the only costs that should be included. Costs incurred in the past, such as the original price of the car, and costs that will be the same regardless of whether you make the trip by car or bus, such as your auto insurance, should not be included. On the other hand, if you are thinking about buying a car to make this and many other trips, these costs should be included.[6]

---

[6]This example is worked out in more detail in the paper by E. Grant and W. Ireson in E. Mansfield, *Managerial Economics and Operations Research*, New York: W. W. Norton, second edition, 1970.

As an illustration, consider the case of Continental Air Lines, which deliberately runs extra flights that do no more than return a little more than their out-of-pocket-costs. Suppose that Continental is faced with the decision of whether or not to run an extra flight between City X and City Y. Suppose that the fully allocated costs—the out-of-pocket costs plus a certain percent of overhead, depreciation, insurance, and other such costs—is $4500 for the flight. Suppose that the out-of-pocket costs—the actual sum that Continental has to disburse to run the flight—are $2000 and the expected revenue from the flight is $3100. In a case of this sort, Continental will run the flight. This is the correct decision, since the flight will add $1100 to profit. It will increase revenue by $3100 and costs by $2000. Overhead, depreciation, and insurance would be the same whether the flight is run or not. In this decision, the correct concept of cost is out-of-pocket, not fully allocated costs. Fully allocated costs are irrelevant and misleading here. The importance of this way of looking at costs cannot be overemphasized.[7]

8. Cost Functions in the Short Run

In Sections 2 to 4, we showed how the profit-maximizing firm will choose the combination of inputs to produce any given level of output, this input combination being the one that minimizes the firm's cost of producing this level of output. Given this optimal input combination, it is a simple matter to determine the profit-maximizing firm's cost of producing any level of output, since this cost is the sum of the amount of each input used by the firm multiplied by the price of the input. Given the firm's cost of producing each level of output, we can define the firm's *cost functions*, which play a very important role in the theory of the firm. A firm's cost functions show various relationships between its costs and its output rate. The firm's production function and the prices it pays for inputs determine the firm's cost functions. Since the production function can pertain to the short run or the long run, it follows that the cost functions can also pertain to the short run or the long run. In Sections 8 to 11, we discuss the short-run cost functions; in Sections 12 and 13, the long-run cost functions.

---

[7]See "Airline Takes the Marginal Route," *Business Week*, Apr. 20, 1963. This article is reprinted in E. Mansfield, *ibid.*, as well as D. Watson, *Price Theory in Action*, Boston: Houghton Mifflin, 1965.

It is very important in applied work to recognize what are the relevant alternatives and their effects. In this connection, it may be worthwhile to cite the case of Maurice Chevalier, who, when asked how it felt to have reached his advanced age, is said to have replied: "Fine, relative to the alternative."

The short run is a time period so brief that the firm cannot change the quantity of some of its inputs. As the length of the time period increases, the quantities of more and more inputs become variable. Any time interval between one where the quantity of no inputs is variable and one where the quantity of all inputs is variable could reasonably be called the short run. However, as we pointed out in Chapter 5, we use a more restrictive definition: we say that the short run is the time period so brief that the firm cannot vary the quantities of plant and equipment. These are the firm's *fixed inputs*, and they determine the firm's *scale of plant*. Inputs like labor, which the firm can vary in quantity in the short run, are the firm's *variable inputs*.

The amount of calendar time corresponding to the short run will be longer in some industries than in others. In industries where the amount of fixed inputs are small and relatively easily modified, the short run may be very short. For example, this may be the case in cotton textiles and bituminous coal. On the other hand, in other industries the short run may be measured in years. For example, in the steel industry, it takes a long time to expand a firm's basic productive capacity.

Three concepts of total cost in the short run are important: total fixed cost, total variable cost, and total cost. *Total fixed costs* are the total obligations per period of time incurred by the firm for fixed inputs. Since the quantity of the fixed inputs is fixed (by definition), the total fixed cost will

Table 6.2.   Fixed, Variable, and Total Costs.

UNITS OF OUTPUT	TOTAL FIXED COST	TOTAL VARIABLE COST	TOTAL COST
0	$1000	$ 0	$1000
1	1000	50	1050
2	1000	90	1090
3	1000	140	1140
4	1000	196	1196
5	1000	255	1255
6	1000	325	1325
7	1000	400	1400
8	1000	480	1480
9	1000	570	1570
10	1000	670	1670
11	1000	780	1780
12	1000	1080	2080

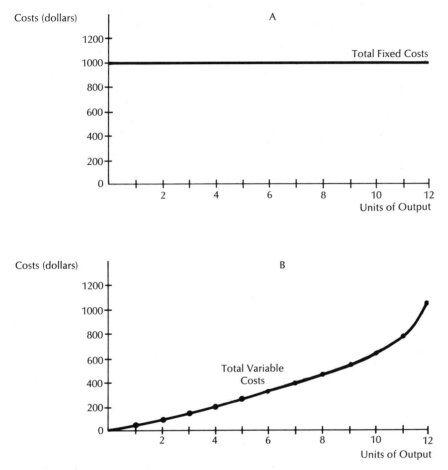

Figure 6.5
Total Fixed and Total
Variable Costs.

be the same regardless of the firm's output rate. Examples of fixed costs are depreciation of buildings and equipment and property taxes. In Table 6.2, the firm's total fixed costs are assumed to be $1000; the firm's total fixed cost function is shown graphically in Figure 6.5.

Total variable costs are the total costs incurred by the firm for variable inputs. They increase as the firm's output rate increases, since larger output rates require larger variable input rates, which mean higher variable costs.

For example, the larger the production of a cotton mill, the larger the quantity of cotton that must be used, and the higher the total cost of the cotton. A hypothetical total variable cost schedule is shown in Table 6.2; Figure 6.5 shows the corresponding total variable cost function. Up to a certain output rate (2 units of output), total variable costs are shown to increase at a decreasing rate; beyond that output level, total variable costs increase at an increasing rate. *This characteristic of the total variable cost function follows from the law of diminishing marginal returns.* At small levels of output, increases in the variable inputs may result in increases in their productivity, the result being that total variable costs increase with output, but at a decreasing rate. Beyond a point, however, there are diminishing marginal returns from the variable input, and total variable costs increase at an increasing rate. More will be said on this score in the next section.

Finally, *total costs* are the sum of total fixed costs and total variable costs. To derive the total cost column in Table 6.2, add total fixed cost and total variable cost at each output. The corresponding total cost function is shown in Figure 6.6. The total cost function and the total variable cost function

Figure 6.6
Total Costs.

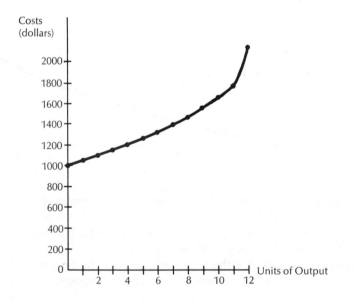

have the same shape, since they differ by only a constant amount.   All of the total cost functions are shown together in Figure 6.7.

Figure 6.7
Fixed, Variable, and
Total Costs.

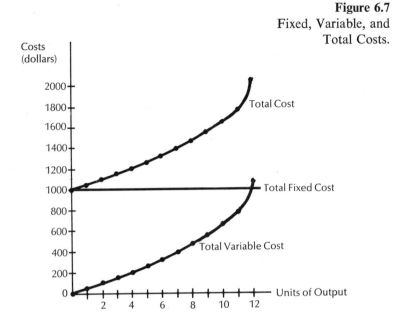

9.   Average and Marginal Costs

The total cost functions are of great importance, but it is possible to get a better understanding of the behavior of cost by looking at the average cost functions and the marginal cost function as well.   There are three average cost functions, corresponding to the three total cost functions.   The *average fixed cost* is total fixed cost divided by output.   Table 6.3 and Figure 6.8 show the average fixed cost function in the example given in Section 8.   The average fixed cost declines with increases in output; mathematically, the average fixed cost function is a rectangular hyperbola.

Table 6.3. Average and Marginal Costs.

UNITS OF OUTPUT	AVERAGE FIXED COST	AVERAGE VARIABLE COST	AVERAGE TOTAL COST	MARGINAL COST*
1	$1000.00 (= 1000 ÷ 1)	$50.00 (= 50 ÷ 1)	$1050.00 (= 1050 ÷ 1)	$50 (= 1050 − 1000)
2	500.00 (= 1000 ÷ 2)	45.00 (= 90 ÷ 2)	545.00 (= 1090 ÷ 2)	40 (= 1090 − 1050)
3	333.33 (= 1000 ÷ 3)	46.67 (= 140 ÷ 3)	380.00 (= 1140 ÷ 3)	50 (= 1140 − 1090)
4	250.00 (= 1000 ÷ 4)	49.00 (= 196 ÷ 4)	299.00 (= 1196 ÷ 4)	56 (= 1196 − 1140)
5	200.00 (= 1000 ÷ 5)	51.00 (= 255 ÷ 5)	251.00 (= 1255 ÷ 5)	59 (= 1255 − 1196)
6	166.67 (= 1000 ÷ 6)	54.17 (= 325 ÷ 6)	220.83 (= 1325 ÷ 6)	70 (= 1325 − 1255)
7	142.86 (= 1000 ÷ 7)	57.14 (= 400 ÷ 7)	200.00 (= 1400 ÷ 7)	75 (= 1400 − 1325)
8	125.00 (= 1000 ÷ 8)	60.00 (= 480 ÷ 8)	185.00 (= 1480 ÷ 8)	80 (= 1480 − 1400)
9	111.11 (= 1000 ÷ 9)	63.33 (= 570 ÷ 9)	174.44 (= 1570 ÷ 9)	90 (= 1570 − 1480)
10	100.00 (= 1000 ÷ 10)	67.00 (= 670 ÷ 10)	167.00 (= 1670 ÷ 10)	100 (= 1670 − 1570)
11	90.91 (= 1000 ÷ 11)	70.91 (= 780 ÷ 11)	161.82 (= 1780 ÷ 11)	110 (= 1780 − 1670)
12	83.33 (= 1000 ÷ 12)	90.00 (= 1080 ÷ 12)	173.33 (= 2080 ÷ 12)	300 (= 2080 − 1780)

*Note that marginal cost pertains to the interval between the indicated output level and one unit less than this output level.

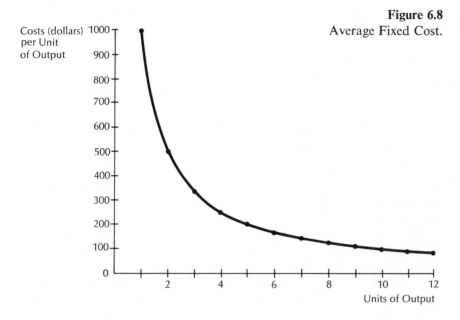

Figure 6.8
Average Fixed Cost.

The *average variable cost* is total variable cost divided by output. For the example in the previous section, the average variable cost function is shown in Table 6.3 and Figure 6.9. At first, increases in output result in decreases in average variable cost, but beyond a point, they result in higher average variable cost. The results of the theory of production in Chapter 5 lead us to expect this curvature of the average variable cost function. If *AVC* is the average variable cost, *TVC* is the total variable cost, *Q* is the quantity of

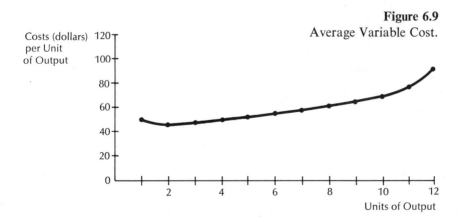

Figure 6.9
Average Variable Cost.

output, V is the quantity of the variable input and P is the price of the variable input, it is obvious that

$$AVC = \frac{TVC}{Q} = P\left(\frac{V}{Q}\right)$$

Thus, since Q/V is the average product of the variable input (AVP),

$$AVC = P\frac{1}{AVP} \tag{6.7}$$

Consequently, since AVP generally rises and then falls with increases in output (see Figure 5.2 on p. 121) and since P is constant, AVC must decrease and then rise with increases in output. The fact that the shape of the average variable cost curve follows in this way from the characteristics of the production function is important and should be fully understood.

The *average total cost* is total cost divided by output. For the example in the previous section, the average total cost function is shown in Table 6.3 and Figure 6.10. The average total cost equals the sum of average fixed cost and average variable cost, which helps to explain the shape of the average total cost function. For those levels of output where both average fixed cost and average variable cost decrease, average total cost must decrease too. However, average total cost achieves its minimum after average variable cost, because the increases in average variable cost are for a time more than offset by decreases in average fixed cost. (All of the average cost curves are shown in Figure 6.12 on page 168.)

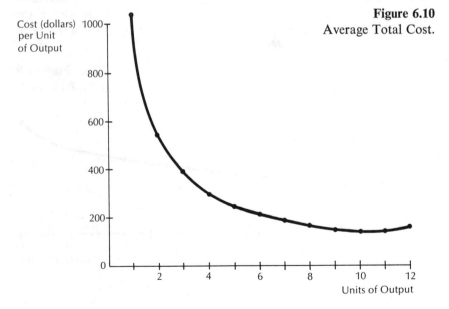

Figure 6.10
Average Total Cost.

The *marginal cost* is the addition to total cost resulting from the addition of the last unit of output. That is, if $C(Q)$ is the total cost of producing Q units of output, the marginal cost between Q and $(Q - 1)$ units of output is $C(Q) - C(Q - 1)$. For the example in the previous section, the marginal cost function is shown in Table 6.3 and Figure 6.11. At low output levels, marginal cost may decrease (as it does in Figure 6.11) with increases in output, but after reaching a minimum, it increases with further increases in output. The reason for this behavior is found in the law of diminishing marginal returns. If ΔTVC is the change in total variable costs resulting from a change in output of ΔQ and if ΔTFC is the change in total fixed costs resulting from a change in output of ΔQ, marginal cost equals

$$\frac{\Delta TVC + \Delta TFC}{\Delta Q}$$

But since ΔTFC is zero (fixed costs being fixed), marginal cost equals

$$\frac{\Delta TVC}{\Delta Q}$$

Moreover, if the price of the variable input is taken as given by the firm, $\Delta TVC = P(\Delta I)$, where ΔI is the change in the quantity of the variable input resulting from the increase of ΔQ in output. Thus the marginal cost equals

$$MC = P\frac{\Delta I}{\Delta Q} = P\frac{1}{MP} \tag{6.8}$$

where MP is the marginal product of the variable input. Since MP generally increases, attains a maximum, and declines with increases in output (see

Figure 6.11
Marginal Cost.

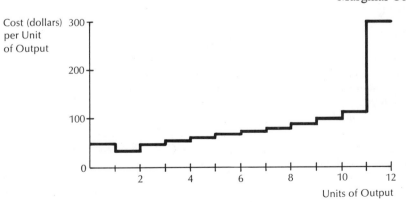

Cost (dollars) per Unit of Output

Units of Output

Figure 5.2 on p. 121), marginal cost normally decreases, attains a minimum, and then increases.[8] The fact that the shape of the marginal cost function depends in this way on the law of diminishing marginal returns is important and should be fully understood.

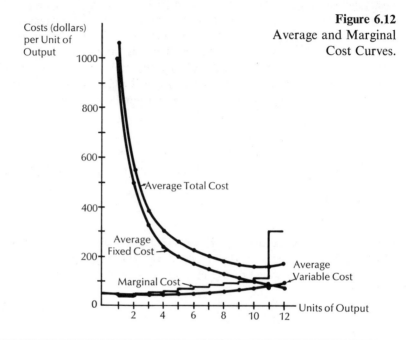

Figure 6.12
Average and Marginal
Cost Curves.

---

[8]If C is total cost, $C = F + V(Q)$, where F is total fixed costs and $V(Q)$ is total variable costs. Thus average fixed costs is F/Q, average variable costs is $V(Q)/Q$, and average total costs is $F/Q + V(Q)/Q$. The marginal cost equals $dC/dQ = dV(Q)/dQ$.

It is easy to show that marginal cost equals average variable cost when average variable cost is a minimum. If average variable cost is a minimum,

$$\frac{d[V(Q)/Q]}{dQ} = \left[\frac{dV(Q)}{dQ} - \frac{V(Q)}{Q}\right]\frac{1}{Q} = 0$$

which means that $dV(Q)/dQ = V(Q)/Q$, which means that marginal cost equals average variable cost. It is also easy to show that marginal cost equals average total cost when average total cost is a minimum. When average total cost is a minimum,

$$\frac{d[F/Q + V(Q)/Q]}{dQ} = \left\{\frac{dV(Q)}{dQ} - \left[\frac{F}{Q} + \frac{V(Q)}{Q}\right]\right\}\frac{1}{Q} = 0$$

which means that $dV(Q)/dQ = F/Q + V(Q)/Q$, which means that marginal cost equals average total cost.

10. Geometry of Average and Marginal Cost Functions

Given the total cost function, we frequently want to derive the average and marginal cost functions. The purpose of this section is to show how this can be done graphically, the procedures being quite similar to those used in Chapter 5, Section 5, to derive average and marginal product curves. Figure 6.13 shows how the average cost function can be derived from the total cost function, OTT', which is shown in panel A. The average cost at any output level is given by the slope of the ray from the origin to the relevant point on the total cost function. For example, the average cost at an output of OQ_0 is the slope of OR. We plot this slope, which equals OU, against OQ_0 in panel B. For each output, we plot in panel B the slope of the ray (from the origin to the relevant point on the total cost function) against the output, the result being AA', the average cost function. Beginning with a very small output, it is clear from Figure 6.13 that increases in output result in decreases in average cost, since the slope of such rays decreases with increases in output. However, it is also clear that average cost reaches a minimum at OQ_1, since beyond OQ_1 the slope of these rays increases with increases in output.

Figure 6.13
Construction of the
Average Cost Function.

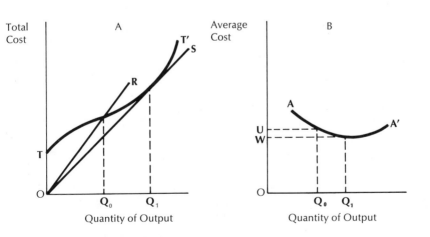

Total Cost

Average Cost

Quantity of Output

Quantity of Output

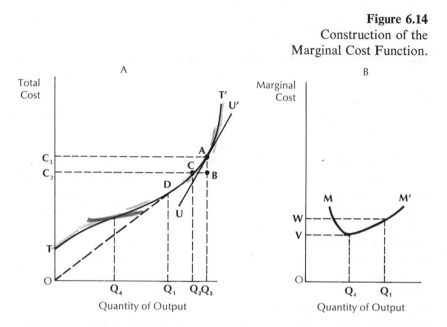

Figure 6.14
Construction of the
Marginal Cost Function.

Figure 6.14 illustrates the derivation of the marginal cost function. As output increases from OQ_2 to OQ_3, total cost (OTT' in panel A) increases from OC_2 to OC_3. Thus the extra cost per unit of output is

$$\frac{OC_3 - OC_2}{OQ_3 - OQ_2} = \frac{BA}{CB}$$

If we increase OQ_2 until the distance between OQ_2 and OQ_3 is extremely small, the slope of the tangent (UU') at A becomes a very good estimate of BA/CB. In the limit, for changes in output in a very small neighborhood around OQ_3, the slope of the tangent to the total cost function at OQ_3 is marginal cost. In panel B, MM' shows the slope of the tangent to the total cost curve at each output; this is the marginal cost curve. It is evident from Figure 6.14 that, at small output rates, marginal cost decreases with increases in output, since the slope of the tangent to the total cost function decreases with increases in output. However, it is also evident that marginal cost reaches a minimum, OV, at OQ_4 and increases thereafter, since the slope of the tangent to the total cost function is a minimum at OQ_4 and increases thereafter.

It should also be noted that when average cost is a minimum (at output OQ_1), the slope of the ray OD equals the slope of the tangent to the total cost function, since OD *is* the tangent to the total cost function. Thus, since average cost equals the slope of the ray OD and marginal cost equals the slope of the tangent to the total cost function, it follows that *average cost must equal marginal cost at the output level where average cost is a minimum.* In Figures 6.13 and 6.14, both equal *OW*.

11. The Break-Even Chart: An Application

A standard tool used by economists to help solve certain kinds of managerial problems is the break-even chart, which is an important practical application of cost functions. Typically, a break-even chart assumes that the firm's average variable costs are constant in the relevant output range. Thus the firm's total cost function is assumed to be a straight line, as shown in Figure 6.15. In Figure 6.15, we assume that the firm's fixed costs are $300 per month and that its variable costs are $1 per unit of output per month. Since average variable cost is constant, the extra cost of an extra unit—marginal cost—must be constant, too, and equal to average variable cost.

To construct a break-even chart, the firm's total revenue curve must be plotted on the same chart with the total cost function. It is generally assumed that the price the firm receives for its product will not be affected by the amount it sells, the result being that total revenue is proportional to output and the total revenue curve is a straight line through the origin. Figure 6.15 shows the total revenue curve, assuming that the price of the product will be $1.50 per unit. The break-even chart, which combines the total cost function and the total revenue curve, shows the monthly profit or loss resulting from each sales level. For example, Figure 6.15 shows that, if the firm sells 300 units per month, it will make a loss of $150 per month. The chart also shows the *break-even point*, the output level that must be reached if the firm is to avoid losses; in Figure 6.15, the break-even point is 600 units of output per month.

In recent years, break-even charts have been used extensively by company executives, government agencies, and other groups. Under the proper circumstances, break-even charts can produce useful projections of the effect of the output rate on costs, receipts, and profits. For example, a firm may use a break-even chart to determine the effect of a projected decline in sales on profits. Or it may use it to determine how many units of a particular product it must sell in order to break even. However, break-even charts must be used with caution, since the assumptions underlying them may be inappropriate. If the product price is highly variable or costs are difficult

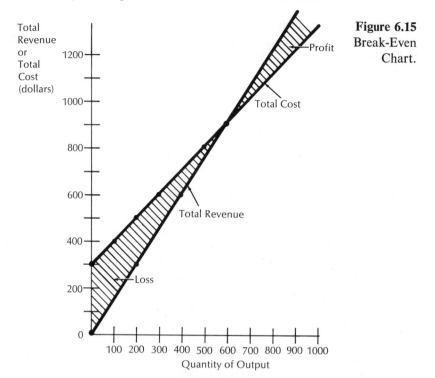

Figure 6.15 Break-Even Chart.

to predict, the estimated total cost function and the estimated total revenue curve may be subject to considerable error.

Although the total cost function generally is assumed to be a straight line in break-even charts, this assumption can easily be dropped and a curvilinear total cost function can be used instead. However, for fairly small changes in output, a linear approximation is probably good enough in many cases. As we shall see in Section 14, empirical studies suggest that the total cost function is often close to linear, as long as the firm is not operating at capacity.[9]

12. Cost Functions in the Long Run

In the long run, the firm can build any scale or type of plant that it wants. All inputs are variable; the firm can alter the amounts of land, buildings, equipment, and other inputs per period of time. There are no fixed cost

---

[9]Note, however, that the results of some of these studies have been subjected to criticism of various sorts. See Section 14.

curves (total or average) in the long run, since no inputs are fixed. A useful way to look at the long run is to consider it a *planning horizon.* While operating in the short run, the firm must continually be planning ahead and deciding its strategy in the long run. Its decisions concerning the long run determine the sort of short-run position the firm will occupy in the future. For example, before a firm makes the decision to add a new type of product to its line, the firm is in a long-run situation, since it can choose among a wide variety of types and sizes of equipment to produce the new product. But once the investment is made, the firm is confronted with a short-run situation, since the type and size of equipment is, to a considerable extent, frozen.

Suppose that it is possible for a firm to construct only three alternative scales of plant, the short-run average cost curve for each scale of plant being represented by S_1S_1', S_2S_2', and S_3S_3' in Figure 6.16. In the long run, the firm can build (or convert to) any one of these possible scales of plant. Which scale is most profitable? Obviously, the answer depends on the long-run output rate to be produced, since the firm will want to produce this output at a minimum average cost. For example, if the anticipated output rate is OQ, the firm should choose the smallest plant, since it will produce OQ units of output per period of time at a cost per unit, OC, which is smaller than what the medium-sized plant (its cost per unit being OB) or the large plant (its cost per unit being OA) can do. However, if the anticipated output rate is OR, the firm should choose the largest plant.

The *long-run average cost curve* shows the minimum cost per unit of producing each output level when any desired scale of plant can be built. In Figure 6.16, the long-run average cost curve is the solid portion of the short-

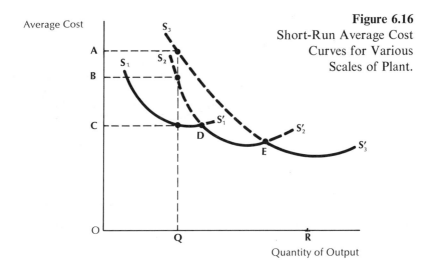

Figure 6.16
Short-Run Average Cost
Curves for Various
Scales of Plant.

run average cost curves, S_1DES_3'. The broken-line segments of the short-run curves are not included because they are not the lowest average costs, as is evident from the figure.

At this point, we must abandon the simplifying assumption that there are only three alternative scales of plant. In fact, there are a great many alternative scales, the result being that the firm is confronted with a host of short-run average cost curves, as shown in Figure 6.17. The minimum cost per unit of producing each output level is given by the long-run average cost curve, LL'. The long-run average cost curve is tangent to each of the short-run average cost curves at the output where the plant corresponding to the short-run average cost curve is optimal. Mathematically, the long-run average cost curve is the "envelope" of the short-run curves.

Note, however, that the long-run average cost (LL') curve is not tangent to the short-run curves at their minimum points, unless the LL' curve is horizontal. When the LL' curve is decreasing, it is tangent to the short-run curves to the left of their minimum points. When the LL' curve is increasing, it is tangent to the short-run curves to the right of their minimum points. A famous mistake was made by the well-known Princeton economist, Jacob Viner, in his pathbreaking 1931 article regarding cost curves. He tried to get the LL' curve to be tangent to the short-run curves at their minimum points. As noted above, this in general cannot be done.

Figure 6.17
Long-Run Average
Cost Curve.

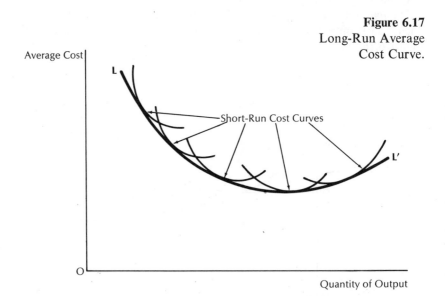

In terms of least-cost input combinations, the long-run average cost curve can be interpreted in the following way: For any specified output, the total cost—and the average cost—is the smallest in the long run when all inputs (not just those that were variable in the short run) are combined in such a way that the marginal product of a dollar's worth of one input equals the marginal product of a dollar's worth of any other input. Only if the firm uses the least-cost combination of all inputs to produce each level of output can the levels of cost shown by the long-run average cost curve be reached.

Given the long-run average cost of producing a given output, it is easy to derive the long-run total cost of the output, since the latter is simply the product of long-run average cost and output. Figure 6.18 shows the relationship between long-run total cost and output, this relationship being called the *long-run total cost function*. Given the long-run total cost function, it is easy to derive the *long-run marginal cost function*, which shows the relationship between output and the cost resulting from the production of the last unit of output, if the firm has plenty of time to make the optimal changes in the quantities of all inputs used. Of course, long-run marginal cost must be less than long-run average cost when the latter is decreasing, equal to long-run average cost when the latter is a minimum, and greater than long-run average cost when the latter is increasing. It can also be shown that, when the firm has built the optimal scale of plant for producing a given level of output, long-run marginal cost and short-run marginal cost will be equal at that output.[10]

---

[10]Suppose that the long-run average cost of producing an output rate of Q is $L(Q)$ and that the short-run average cost of producing this output with the ith scale of plant is $A_i(Q)$. Let $M(Q)$ be the long-run marginal cost and $R_i(Q)$ be the short-run marginal cost with the ith scale of plant. If the firm is maximizing profit, it is operating where short-run and long-run average costs are equal; in other words, $L(Q) = A_i(Q)$. Also, the long-run average cost curve is tangent to the short-run average cost curve, which means that

$$\frac{dL(Q)}{dQ} = \frac{dA_i(Q)}{dQ} \quad \text{and} \quad Q\frac{dL(Q)}{dQ} = Q\frac{dA_i(Q)}{dQ}$$

From these conditions, it is easy to prove that the long-run marginal cost, $M(Q)$, equals the short-run marginal cost, $R_i(Q)$.

$$M(Q) = \frac{d[QL(Q)]}{dQ} = L(Q) + \frac{Q\,dL(Q)}{dQ}$$

$$R_i(Q) = \frac{d[QA_i(Q)]}{dQ} = A_i(Q) + \frac{Q\,dA_i(Q)}{dQ}$$

Since we know from the previous paragraph that $L(Q) = A_i(Q)$ and $Q\,dL(Q)/dQ = Q\,dA_i(Q)/dQ$, it follows that $R_i(Q)$ must equal $M(Q)$.

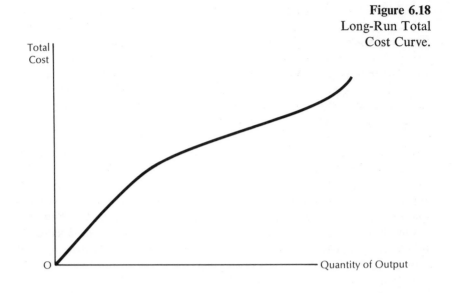

Figure 6.18
Long-Run Total
Cost Curve.

13. The Shape of the Long-Run Average Cost Function

The long-run average cost function in Figure 6.17 is drawn with much the same sort of shape as the short-run average cost function. Both decrease with increases in output up to a certain point, reach a minimum, and increase with further increases in output. However, the factors responsible for this shape are not the same in the two cases. In the case of the short-run average cost function, the theory of diminishing marginal returns is operating behind the scenes. The short-run average cost function turns upward because decreases in average fixed costs are eventually counter-balanced by increases in average variable costs due to decreases in the average product of the variable input. However, the law of diminishing marginal returns is not responsible for the shape of the long-run average cost function, since there are no fixed inputs in the long run.

The determinants of the shape of the long-run average cost function are economies and diseconomies of scale. As pointed out in Chapter 5, increases in scale often result in important economies, at least up to some point. Because larger scale permits the introduction of different kinds of techniques, because larger productive units are more efficient, and because larger plants permit greater specialization and division of labor, the long-run average cost function declines, up to some point, with increases in output. Of course, the range of output over which the average cost function declines varies from industry to industry. (Moreover, in a given industry, this range varies over a period of time, particularly in response to changes in technology.)

Why does the long-run average cost function turn upward? The answer that is generally given is that, beyond a point, increases in scale result in inefficiencies in management. More and more responsibility and power must be given by top management to lower level employees. Coordination becomes more difficult, red tape increases, and flexibility is reduced. It is not easy to determine just when these diseconomies of scale begin to offset the economies of scale already cited. In many industries, the available empirical studies seem to indicate that, after an initial decline, long-run average cost is constant over a considerable range of output. The situation is like that shown in Figure 6.19. Eventually, however, one would expect the long-run average cost to rise.

It is important to note that the shape of the long-run average cost function is of great significance from the viewpoint of public policy. If the long-run average cost function decreases markedly up to a level of output that corresponds to all, or practically all, that the market demands of the commodity, it makes little sense to force competition in this industry, since costs would be higher if the output were divided among a number of firms than if it were

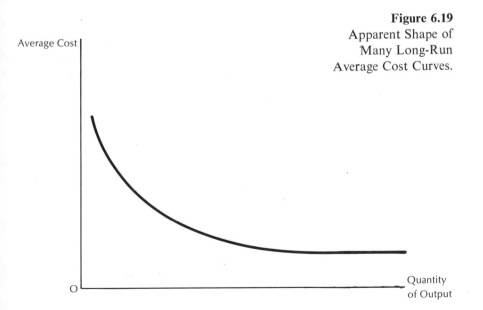

Figure 6.19
Apparent Shape of
Many Long-Run
Average Cost Curves.

produced by only one firm. In this case, the industry is a natural monopoly, and government agencies like the Federal Power Commission and the Federal Communications Commission, rather than competition, are relied on to regulate the industry's performance. (This will be discussed further in Chapter 9.)

14.   Measurement of Cost Functions

Economists have made a great many studies to estimate cost functions in particular firms and industries. Typically, these studies have been based on the statistical analysis of historical data regarding cost and output. Some studies have relied primarily on time-series data, the output level of a firm being related to its costs. For example, Figure 6.20 plots the output level of a hypothetical firm against its costs in various years in the past. Other studies have relied primarily on cross-section data, the output levels of various firms at a given point in time being related to their costs. For example, Figure 6.21 plots the 1969 output of eight firms in a given industry against

Figure 6.20
Relationship between
Total Cost and Output:
Time Series for a
Given Firm.

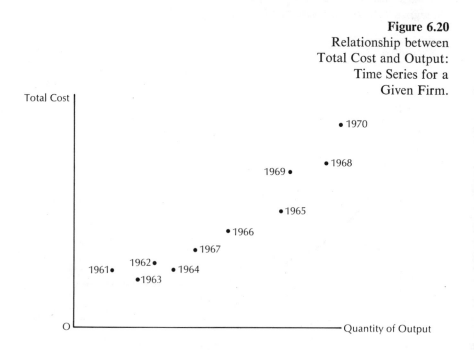

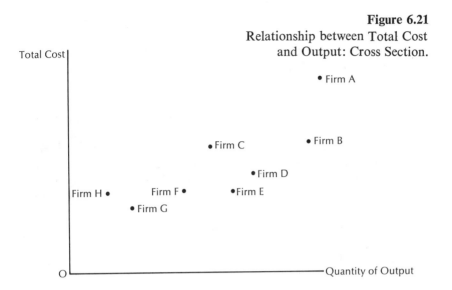

Figure 6.21
Relationship between Total Cost
and Output: Cross Section.

their 1969 costs. Using data of this sort, as well as engineering data, economists have attempted to estimate the relationship between cost and output.

There are a number of important difficulties in estimating cost functions in this way. First, accounting data, which are generally the only cost data available, suffer from a number of deficiencies, when used for this purpose. The time period used for accounting purposes generally is longer than the economist's short run. The depreciation of an asset over a period of time is determined by the tax laws rather than economic criteria. Many inputs are valued at historical, rather than alternative, cost. Moreover, accountants often use arbitrary allocations of overhead and joint costs.

Second, engineering data also suffer from important limitations. Engineering data, like cost accounting data, relate to processes within the firm. One difficulty in using them to estimate cost functions for an entire firm is that the costs of various processes may affect one another and may not be additive. Also, there is the inevitable arbitrariness involved in allocating costs that are jointly attached to the production of more than one commodity in multiproduct firms.

Third, an important criticism of cross-section studies is that they are subject to the so-called "regression fallacy." It is often argued that the output produced and sold by the firm is only partly under the control of the firm and that actual and expected output will differ. When firms are classified by actual output, firms with very high output levels are likely to be producing at an unusually high level, and firms with very low output levels are likely to be producing at an unusually low level. Since firms producing at an unusually high level of output are likely to be producing at lower unit costs than firms producing at an unusually low level of output, cross-section studies are likely to be biased, the observed cost of producing various output levels being different from the minimum cost of producing these output levels.

Despite these and other problems, estimates of cost functions have proved of considerable use, both to economists interested in promoting better managerial decisions and to economists interested in testing and extending economic theory. From the latter point of view, one of the most interesting conclusions of the empirical studies is that the long-run average cost curve in most industries seems to be L-shaped (as in Figure 6.19), not U-shaped. That is, there is no evidence that it turns upward, rather than remains horizontal, at high output levels (in the range of observed data). A summary of the results of the major studies carried out to date is presented in Tables 6.4 and 6.5. The reader should study these tables carefully, since they summarize the results of a great many important studies in this area.

Table 6.4. Results of Studies of Cost Curves: General Industry Studies.*

NAME	INDUSTRY	TYPE	PERIOD	RESULT
Bain (1956)	Manufacturing	Q	L	Small economies of scale of multiplant firms.
Eiteman and Guthrie (1952)	Manufacturing	Q	S	MC below AC at all outputs below "capacity."
Hall and Hitch (1939)	Manufacturing	Q	S	Majority have MC decreasing.
Lester (1946)	Manufacturing	Q	S	Decreasing average variable cost to capacity.
Moore (1959)	Manufacturing	E	L	Economies of scale generally.
T.N.E.C. Monograph 13	Various industries	CS	L	Small- or medium-size plants usually have lowest costs. Blair (1942) draws different conclusions.
Alpert (1959)	Metal	E	L	Economies of scale to 80,000 lb/month; then constant returns.
Johnston (1960)	Multiple product	TS	S	"Direct" cost is linearly related to output. MC is constant.

Dean (1936)	Furniture	TS	S	MC constant. SRAC "failed to rise."
Dean (1941)	Leather belts	TS	S	Significantly increasing MC rejected by Dean.
Dean (1941)	Hosiery	TS	S	MC constant. SRAC "failed to rise."
Dean (1942)	Department store	TS	S	MC declining or constant.
Dean and James (1942)	Shoe stores	CS	L	LRAC is U-shaped (interpreted as not due to diseconomies of scale).
Holton (1956)	Retailing (Puerto Rico)	E	L	LRAC is L-shaped. But Holton argues that inputs of management may be undervalued at high outputs.
Ezekiel and Wylie (1941)	Steel	TS	S	MC declining but large standard errors.
Yntema (1940)	Steel	TS	S	MC constant.
Ehrke (1933)	Cement	TS	S	Ehrke interprets as constant MC. Apel (1948) argues that MC is increasing.
Nordin (1947)	Light plant	TS	S	MC is increasing.

*The following abbreviations are used: MC = marginal cost, AC = average cost, SRAC = short-run average cost, LRAC = long-run average cost, S = short run, and L = long run, Q = questionnaire, E = engineering data, CS = cross section, and TS = time series.

Source: A. A. Walters, "Production and Cost Functions," *Econometrica*, Jan. 1963.

Another interesting conclusion of the empirical studies is that marginal cost in the short run tends to be constant in the relevant output range. As shown in Tables 6.4 and 6.5, this is a frequent result of these studies. This result seems to be at variance with the theory presented in Section 9, which says that marginal cost curves should be U-shaped. To explain this variance, critics have asserted that the empirical studies are biased toward constant marginal cost by the nature of accounting data and the statistical methods used. Another reason why marginal costs appear constant is that the data used in these studies often do not cover periods when the firm was operating at the peak of its capacity. Although marginal costs may well be relatively constant over a wide range, it is inconceivable that they do not eventually increase with increases in output.

Table 6.5.   Results of Studies of Cost Curves:
Public Utilities.

NAME	INDUSTRY	TYPE*	RESULT**
Lomax (1951)	Gas (U.K.)	CS	LRAC of production declines (no analysis of distribution)
Gribbin (1953)	Gas (U.K.)	CS	LRAC of production declines (no analysis of distribution)
Lomax (1952)	Electricity (U.K.)	CS	LRAC of production declines (no analysis of distribution)
Johnston (1960)	Electricity (U.K.)	CS	LRAC of production declines (no analysis of distribution)
Johnston (1960)	Electricity (U.K.)	TS	SRAC falls, then flattens tending towards constant MC up to capacity.
McNulty (1955)	Electricity (U.S.A.)	CS	Average costs of administration are constant.
Nerlove (1961)	Electricity (U.S.A.)	CS	LRAC excluding transmission costs declines, then shows signs of increasing.
Johnston (1960)	Coal (U.K.)	CS	Wide dispersion of costs per ton.
Johnston (1960)	Road passenger transport (U.K.)	CS	LRAC either falling or constant.
Johnston (1960)	Road passenger transport (U.K.)	TS	SRAC decreases.
Johnston (1960)	Life assurance	CS	LRAC declines.

RAILWAYS			
Borts (1960)	U.S.A.	CS	LRAC increasing in East, decreasing in South and West.
Broster (1938)	U.K.	TS	Operating cost per unit of output falls.
Mansfield and Wein (1958)	U.S.A.	TS	MC is constant.

*CS means cross section; TS means time series.
**LRAC means long-run average cost; SRAC means short-run average cost; MC means marginal cost.
Source: A. A. Walters, "Production and Cost Functions," *Econometrica*, Jan. 1963.

Figure 6.22
Total Cost Curve,
Hosiery Mill
(monthly costs).

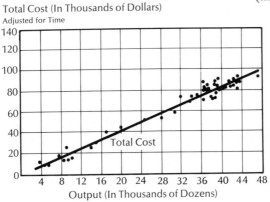

Total Cost (In Thousands of Dollars)
Adjusted for Time

An illustration of the sort of empirical work that has been done in this area is Joel Dean's pioneering study of the short-run cost functions in a hosiery mill. This study, published in 1941, was one of the first attempts by an economist to measure a firm's cost function. Dean found that the total

Figure 6.23
Average and Marginal
Cost Curves,
Hosiery Mill.

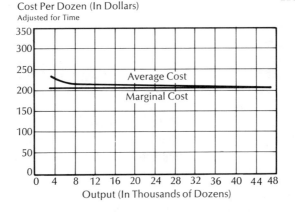

Cost Per Dozen (In Dollars)
Adjusted for Time

Source for Charts 6.22 and 6.23: J. Dean, "Statistical Cost Functions of a Hosiery Mill," University of Chicago Press, supplement to *Journal of Business*, 1941.

cost function was linear within the range of observation, marginal cost being constant. His estimate of the total cost function is shown in Figure 6.22; his estimates of the average and marginal cost functions are shown in Figure 6.23.[11]

15. Summary

To minimize the cost of producing a given output, a firm must combine inputs so that the marginal product of a dollar's worth of any one input is equal to the marginal product of a dollar's worth of any other input. The optimal combination of inputs can be determined graphically by superimposing the relevant isocost curves on the firm's isoquant map, and by determining the point at which the relevant isoquant touches the lowest isocost curve. To illustrate the use of this theory, we described how it was used to derive the optimal combination of fertilizers in the production of Iowa corn.

The cost of producing a certain product is the value of the products that the resources used in its production could have produced instead. This is the alternative cost doctrine. The alternative cost of an input may not be equal to its historical cost, and it is likely to be smaller in the short run than in the long run. The social costs of producing a given commodity do not always equal the private costs, the case of the steel mill that discharges wastes into a river being an example. In making decisions, costs incurred in the past and costs that are the same for all alternative courses of action are irrelevant.

A cost function is a relation between a firm's costs and its output rate. The firm's production function and the prices it pays for inputs determine a firm's cost function. Three concepts of total cost are important in the short run: total fixed costs, total variable costs, and total costs. The average fixed costs, average variable costs, average costs, and marginal costs are also important. The short-run average cost function decreases at first, but eventually it turns up because of the law of diminishing marginal returns. Similarly, the marginal cost curve eventually turns up for the same reason.

A useful way to look at the long run is to view it as a planning horizon.

---

[11]See J. Dean, "Statistical Cost Functions of a Hosiery Mill," University of Chicago Press, supplement to *Journal of Business*, 1941. See also A. A. Walters, "Production and Cost Functions," *Econometrica*, Jan., 1963. This section relies heavily on Walters's excellent survey article.

The determinants of the shape of the long-run average cost function are economies and diseconomies of scale. Because of economies of scale, the long-run average cost curve is likely to decrease, up to some point, with increases in output. As output becomes greater and greater, it is often stated that diseconomies of scale will result, with the consequence that the long-run average cost curve will turn upward. The shape of the long-run average cost curve in a particular industry is of great importance from the viewpoint of public policy.

Economists have made a great many studies to estimate the cost functions of particular firms and industries. Typically, these studies have been based on historical data regarding cost and output, although accounting data, which are generally the only cost data available, suffer from a number of deficiencies when used for this purpose. One of the most interesting conclusions of these studies is that the long-run average cost curve seems to be L-shaped. However, the evidence is limited. Another interesting conclusion is that short-run marginal cost often seems to be constant, not U-shaped. But this may be due in considerable part to the limited range of the observations.

SELECTED REFERENCES

Clark, J. M., *The Economics of Overhead Costs*, Chicago: University of Chicago Press, 1923.

Viner, Jacob, "Cost Curves and Supply Curves," *Zeitschrift Fur National-oekonomie*, 1931, reprinted in American Economic Association, *Readings in Price Theory*, Homewood, Ill.: Richard D. Irwin, 1952.

Stigler, G., *The Theory of Price*, New York, Macmillan, 1966.

National Bureau of Economic Research, *Cost Behavior and Price Policy*, New York, National Bureau of Economic Research, 1943.

Staehle, Hans, "The Measurement of Statistical Cost Functions," *Readings in Price Theory*, Homewood, Ill.: Richard D. Irwin, 1952.

J. Johnston, *Statistical Cost Analysis*, New York: McGraw-Hill, 1960.

7

Optimal Production Decisions and Linear Programming

1. Introduction

The previous chapter showed how a profit-maximizing firm will combine inputs to produce a given amount of output, and indicated how one can determine the relationship between a firm's costs and its output from a knowledge of input prices and the firm's production function. These results are extremely useful but they fall short of providing us with a complete model of the firm. All that they tell us is how the profit maximizing firm will—or should—produce a given amount of output: They do not tell us how much output the firm will choose to produce. The purpose of this chapter is to answer that question for the short run, assuming that the firm takes the price of its product (as well as the price of each input) as given.

186

In addition, we consider a situation where the firm produces more than one product. This, of course, is frequently the case, some of the nation's large corporations being engaged in the production of literally thousands of products. In a case of this sort, how does the firm decide how much of each good to produce? This is a very important question. Again, we assume that the firm takes as given the price of each of the commodities it produces.

These results, together with those in Chapters 5 and 6, provide a reasonably complete model of the firm in the short run, assuming that it takes all prices as given. Having gotten this far, we could go on to the theory of price and output in perfectly competitive markets, which is presented in Chapter 8. However, there are advantages at that point in describing linear programming, a very important tool of microeconomics, and reexamining the theory of the firm from the point of view of linear programming. The advantage of this is that, when looked at from the point of view of linear programming, the theory of the firm gains in realism and becomes much more powerful in handling actual production problems.

2.   The Output of the Firm in the Short Run

The first question we take up in this chapter is: How much output will the firm produce in the short run? In the short run, the firm can expand or contract its output rate by increasing or decreasing the rate at which it employs variable inputs. For simplicity assume that the firm cannot affect the price of its product and that it can sell any amount of its product that it wants at this price (i.e., it is a perfectly competitive firm). Also, assume, as in previous chapters, that the firm maximizes its profits. To illustrate the firm's situation, consider the example in Table 7.1. The market price is $10 a unit, and the firm can produce as much as it chooses. Thus the firm's total revenue at various output rates is given in column 3 of Table 7.1. The firm's total fixed cost, total variable cost, and total cost are given in columns 4, 5, and 6 of Table 7.1. Finally, the last column shows the firm's total profit, the difference between total revenue and total cost, at various output rates.

Figure 7.1 provides a graphical description of the relationship between total revenue and total cost, on the one hand, and output, on the other. Of course, the vertical distance between the total revenue curve and the total cost curve is the profit at the corresponding output rate. Below 2 units of output and above 7 units of output, this distance is negative. Since the firm

Table 7.1. Cost and Revenue of a Firm, Prices Taken as Given by the Firm.

OUTPUT PER PERIOD	PRICE	TOTAL REVENUE	TOTAL FIXED COST	TOTAL VARIABLE COST	TOTAL COST	TOTAL PROFIT
0	$10	$ 0	$12	$ 0	$12	$−12
1	10	10	12	2	14	−4
2	10	20	12	3	15	5
3	10	30	12	5	17	13
4	10	40	12	8	20	20
5	10	50	12	13	25	25
6	10	60	12	23	35	25
7	10	70	12	38	50	20
8	10	80	12	69	81	−1

can sell either large or small volumes of output at the same price per unit, the total revenue curve will be a straight line through the origin. This is always the case when the firm takes the price as given. The total cost curve has the kind of shape we would expect, on the basis of Chapter 6, of a short-run total cost curve.

Based on an examination of either Table 7.1 or Figure 7.1, the output rate that will maximize the firm's profits is either 5 or 6 units per time period. These are the output rates where the profit figure in the last column of Table 7.1 is the largest and where the vertical distance between the total revenue and total cost curves in Figure 7.1 is the greatest.

Table 7.2. Marginal Revenue and Marginal Cost: Prices Taken as Given by the Firm.

OUTPUT PER PERIOD	MARGINAL REVENUE	MARGINAL COST*
1	$10	$ 2
2	10	1
3	10	2
4	10	3
5	10	5
6	10	10
7	10	15
8	10	31

*This is the marginal cost between the indicated output level and one unit less than this output level.

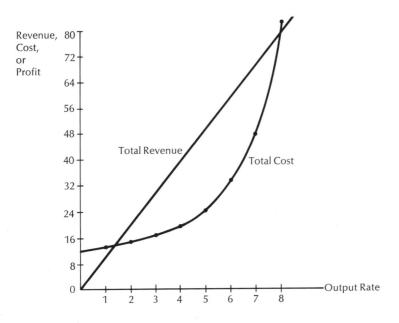

For many purposes it is convenient to present the marginal revenue and marginal cost curves, as well as the total revenue and total cost curves. Table 7.2 shows marginal revenue and marginal cost at each output rate, these figures having been derived in the way shown in Chapters 4 and 6. Figure 7.2 shows the resulting marginal revenue and marginal cost curves. Since the firm takes the price as given, marginal revenue equals price, since the change in total revenue resulting from a one-unit change in sales necessarily equals the price.

The important thing to note is that the maximum profit is achieved at the output rate where price (= marginal revenue) equals marginal cost. Both the figures in Table 7.2 and the curves in Figure 7.2 indicate that price equals marginal cost at an output rate between 5 and 6 units, which we know from Table 7.1 or Figure 7.1 to be the profit-maximizing output. Is this merely a chance occurrence, or will it usually be true that price will equal marginal cost at the profit-maximizing output rate?

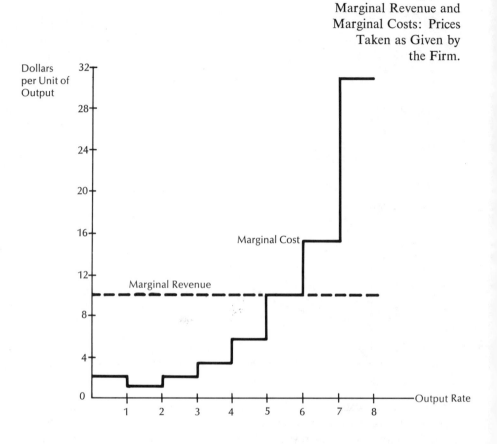

Figure 7.2
Marginal Revenue and
Marginal Costs: Prices
Taken as Given by
the Firm.

3. Price Equals Marginal Cost

The fact that price equals marginal cost at the optimal output rate is not merely a chance occurrence; it will usually be true if the firm takes as given the price of the product. To prove that this is the case, consider Figure 7.3, which shows a typical short-run marginal cost curve, MC. Suppose that the price is OP_0. At any output rate (after perhaps an irrelevant range in which marginal cost is falling) less than OX, price exceeds marginal cost:

thus increases in output will increase profit since they will add more to total revenues than to total costs. At any output rate above *OX*, price is less than marginal cost; thus decreases in output will increase profits, since they will reduce total cost more than total revenue. Since increases in output up to *OX* result in increases in profit and further increases in output result in decreases in profit, *OX* must be the profit-maximizing output.

Even if the firm is doing the best it can, it may not be able to earn a profit. For example, if the price is OP_2 in Figure 7.3, short-run average costs, *AC'*, exceed the price at all possible outputs. Since the short run is too short to allow the firm to alter the scale of its plant, it cannot liquidate its plant in the short run. All that the firm can do is to produce at a loss or discontinue production. The firm's decision will depend on whether the price of the product will cover average variable costs. If there exists an output rate where price exceeds average variable costs, it will pay the firm to produce, even though price does not cover average total costs. If there does not exist an output rate where price exceeds average variable costs, the firm is better off to produce nothing at all. Thus, in Figure 7.3, if the average variable cost curve is *VC''*, the firm will produce if the price is OP_2, but not if it is OP_1.

The reasoning behind this conclusion is as follows: If the firm produces nothing, it must still pay its fixed costs. Consequently, if the loss resulting from production is less than the firm's fixed costs, it is more profitable (in the sense that losses are smaller) to produce than not to produce. On a per unit basis, this means that it is better to produce than to discontinue pro-

Figure 7.3
Short-Run Average and
Marginal Cost Curves.

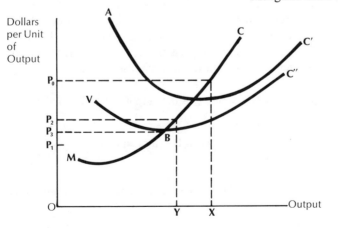

duction if the loss per unit of production is less than average fixed costs, that is, if $ATC - P < AFC$, where ATC is average total costs, P is price, and AFC is average fixed cost. But this will be so if $ATC < AFC + P$, since P has merely been added to both sides of the inequality. Subtracting AFC from both sides, this will be so if $ATC - AFC < P$. But $ATC - AFC$ is average variable costs, which means that we have proved what we set out to prove: that it is better to produce than to discontinue production if price exceeds average variable costs.

Thus if the firm maximizes profit or minimizes losses, it sets its output rate so that short-run marginal cost equals price. But this rule, like most others, has an exception: If the market price is too low to cover the firm's average variable costs at any conceivable output rate, the firm will minimize losses by discontinuing production.[1]

4. The Multiproduct Firm: The Choice of Output Combinations

In previous sections, we assumed that the firm produced only one product. Clearly this is not the case for all firms: some companies like General Motors or General Electric are engaged in the production of many, many types of products. To keep things simple, suppose that we are concerned with a firm that produces only two products, windshield wipers and hearing aids. (From the point of view of sheer glamor, the firm's product line is, of course, an advertising man's dream.) Suppose that this firm cannot affect the price of either product, that it takes each price as given, and that it can sell as much as it wants of each product at these prices. If it maximizes profits, how much of each product will the firm choose to produce?

---

[1]Let the total cost be $C(Q)$, where Q is the output rate. The total profit per period is

$$\Pi = PQ - C(Q)$$

where P is the price of the product. If Π is a maximum,

$$P - \frac{dC(Q)}{dQ} = 0$$

or price must equal marginal cost. The second-order condition for a maximum is

$$\frac{d^2C(Q)}{dQ^2} > 0$$

For simplicity, we shall assume that the firm has some given quantity of resources: plant, equipment, and so forth. Using this fixed total quantity of resources, the firm can produce various combinations of windshield wipers and hearing aids. For example, the possible combinations of quantities of these two products, given this amount of resources, might be given by T_1 in Figure 7.4. This curve depends, of course, on the amount of resources used by the firm. For example, T_2 is a curve that pertains to a higher level of resources.

Curves like T_1 and T_2 are called *product transformation curves.* A product transformation curve must have a negative slope, since an increase in the output of one product must result in a decrease in the output of the other product.[2] The negative of the slope of the product transformation curve is called the *marginal rate of product transformation* between the two products. It is generally assumed that the marginal rate of product transformation increases as we move to the right along a product transformation curve and decreases as we move to the left. In other words, product transformation curves are generally expected to be concave. For each additional unit of the one product that is given up, the increase in the output of the other product becomes smaller and smaller.

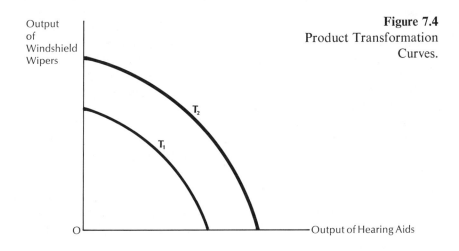

Output of Windshield Wipers

Figure 7.4
Product Transformation Curves.

T_2

T_1

O

Output of Hearing Aids

---

[2]Suppose that $g(Z_1, Z_2) = k$ is the product transformation curve, where Z_1 is the output of one good and Z_2 is the output of the other good. The total differential is

$$dk = \frac{\partial g}{\partial Z_1} dZ_1 + \frac{\partial g}{\partial Z_2} dZ_2$$

Since k is a constant, $dk = 0$, and the slope of the product transformation curve, dZ_2/dZ_1, is $-\partial g/\partial Z_1 \div \partial g/\partial Z_2$.

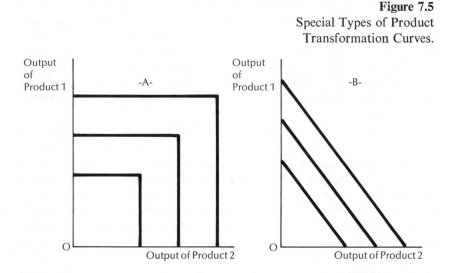

Figure 7.5

Special Types of Product
Transformation Curves.

However, two special cases exist where this is not the case. Panel A of Figure 7.5 shows the case in which there is no substitutability at all between the two outputs. This might occur if the products in question (product 1 and product 2) are joint products that occur in fixed proportions. Panel B of Figure 7.5 shows the case in which there is complete substitutability between the two products. This might occur if the two products (again called product 1 and product 2 in Figure 7.5) are two versions of the same commodity. In the rest of this section we assume that some substitutability is possible but that it is less than complete.

Since the firm's costs are fixed (because it is using a fixed set of resources), it will maximize profit by maximizing the total revenue from the two products. If π_1 is the price of windshield wipers and π_2 is the price of hearing aids, the total revenue is

$$V = X_1\pi_1 + X_2\pi_2$$

where X_1 is the amount of windshield wipers produced and X_2 is the amount of hearing aids produced. Thus, if the firm takes the prices as given, we can draw an *isorevenue line*,

$$X_2 = \frac{V}{\pi_2} - \frac{\pi_1}{\pi_2} X_1$$

which shows all combinations of outputs of the two commodities that result in a total revenue of V. There is a different isorevenue line for each value of

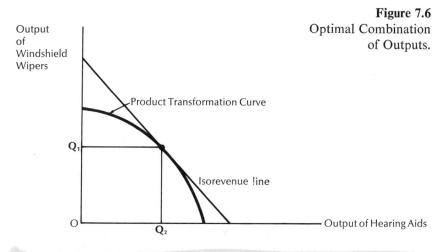

Figure 7.6
Optimal Combination
of Outputs.

V, but the slope of all such lines is the same and equal to the negative of π_1/π_2. The higher the value of V, the higher the isorevenue line.

By superimposing isorevenue lines on the graph showing the product transformation curve, we can obtain a graphical solution to the firm's problem. Figure 7.6 shows that the optimal combination of outputs is OQ_1 of windshield wipers and OQ_2 of hearing aids. This is the point on the product transformation curve that lies on the highest isorevenue line. If the firm were to produce elsewhere on the product transformation curve, it would be on a lower isorevenue line. Clearly, the isorevenue line is tangent to the product transformation curve at the optimum point. Therefore, π_1/π_2 (the negative of the slope of the isorevenue line) must equal the marginal rate of product transformation (the negative of the slope of the product transformation curve) at the optimum point.

5.   Decision-Making in Defense: An Application

The sort of analysis described in the previous section has a wide range of applications and is useful for many problems confronting public agencies as well as private firms. For example, suppose that the Defense Department is concerned with the allocation of a military budget between the procurement of two forces: a strategic bombing force and an air defense force. The total amount to be spent on both forces is fixed, and the problem is how it should be allocated. For simplicity, suppose further that the output of the strategic bombing force can be measured by the expected number of enemy targets it could destroy and that the output of the air defense force can be measured by the number of attacking bombers it could be expected to shoot down.

This problem can be viewed in much the same light as the firm's problem of finding the optimal combination of outputs. The Defense Department can be regarded as having to choose the optimal combination of two outputs: the output of the strategic bombing force and the output of the air defense force. Given the total budget, the various combinations of these two outputs that can be produced is shown in Figure 7.7. This, of course, is a product transformation curve, pure and simple. The points on this curve, like any product transformation curve, are efficient points in the sense that, holding constant the quantity produced of one output, they show the maximum amount that can be produced of the other output.

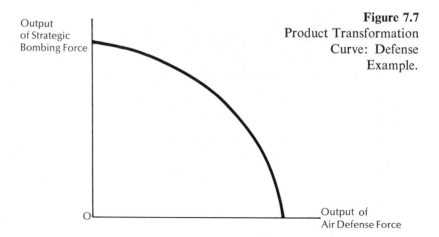

Figure 7.7
Product Transformation
Curve: Defense
Example.

Which of the infinity of points on the product transformation curve should the Department of Defense choose? At one extreme, one point on this curve provides no offensive capability; at the other extreme, another point on this curve provides no defensive capability. Clearly the answer lies somewhere in between, but where? In principle, the solution is simple: Choose that point which maximizes the "military worth" or "effectiveness" of the combined forces. Suppose that each curve, like *A*, *B*, and *C*, in Figure 7.8

represents a set of combinations of the two outputs with equal "military worth." These curves are analogous to the isorevenue lines of the previous section. (They are curved, not straight, because the relative "worth" of the two outputs is assumed constant in the previous section, but not here.) Thus the optimal combination is *P*, the point at which the product transformation curve touches the highest "isorevenue" line.

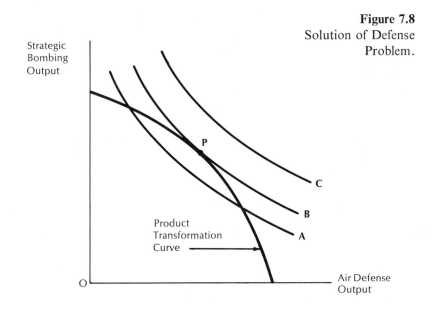

Figure 7.8
Solution of Defense Problem.

In practice, of course, the measurement of "military worth" often presents extremely difficult problems, with the result that it is not possible to draw curves like *A*, *B*, and *C* with confidence. Thus, unlike many of the illustrative cases in this and other chapters, it is often impossible in this case to generate a relatively clear-cut answer. Nevertheless, this does not mean that this type of analysis is not useful. On the contrary, it is very useful, since it provides a correct way of thinking about the problem. It focuses attention on the relevant factors, and it puts them in their proper place. The ultimate choice will often depend on the intuition of the decision-maker concerning the position of the "isorevenue lines," but this could hardly be avoided.[3]

---

[3]C. Hitch and R. McKean, *The Economics of Defense in the Nuclear Age*, Cambridge: Harvard University Press, 1960. This book is a classic in the field. The example in section 5 is discussed in pp. 110–114.

6. Linear Programming[4]

Previous sections of this chapter have shown how the profit-maximizing firm chooses its output level—or its combination of output levels, if it produces more than one commodity—in the short run, given that it takes the price of each of its inputs and outputs as given. At this point, we could go on to the theory of price and output in perfectly competitive markets. However, we choose to take a somewhat different path. In the rest of this chapter, we describe linear programming and reexamine the theory of the firm from the point of view of linear programming. Then, in Chapter 8, we discuss the theory of price and output in perfectly competitive markets.

Linear programming is the most famous of the mathematical programming methods that have come into existence since World War II. It is a technique that allows decision-makers to solve maximization and minimization problems where there are certain constraints that limit what can be done. One of the principal figures in the development of linear programming was George Dantzig, an American mathematician now at Stanford. First used shortly after World War II to help schedule the procurement activities of the United States Air Force, linear programming has become an extremely important part of microeconomic theory and a very powerful tool for the solution of managerial problems. Its remarkable growth has been helped along by the development of computers which can handle the many computations that are required to solve large linear programming problems.

Although linear programming is an important tool of microeconomists, it is purely a mathematical technique. By itself it can only tell us the implications of the data that the decision-maker or the analyst has gathered (or assumed). If these data (or assumptions) are wrong, the solution will in general be wrong, too. The great advantage of linear programming is that it provides computational advantages, not that it performs magic.

Why is it important to reexamine the theory of production from the point of view of linear programming? There are at least two reasons. First, the programming analysis is more fundamental in one respect than the conventional analysis presented in Chapters 5 and 6. The conventional theory is built on the foundation of the production function, which assumes that the technically efficient production processes have been determined and

---

[4]This chapter and Chapter 8 have been written so that the reader who is not interested in linear programming can go directly to Chapter 8 at this point. An understanding of the material in Chapter 8 does not depend on a reading of the material on linear programming.

given to the economist before he attacks the problem. But in the real world, the economist is usually confronted with a number of feasible production processes, and it is very difficult to tell which ones—or which combinations— are efficient. The choice of the optimal combination of production processes is an extremely important decision, and it can be analyzed by linear programming.

Second, the programming analysis seems to conform more closely to the way that businessmen tend to view production. The language and concepts of linear programming, though abstract and by no means the same as those of management, seem to be closer to those of management people than the ones used by the conventional theory. Although this is less important than the first reason, it is of some importance, since it makes it easier to apply linear programming than conventional theory. The development of linear programming has enabled the economist to solve many types of production problems for industry and government.

7. The Firm's Production Decisions as a Linear Programming Problem

Linear programming views the technology available to the firm as being composed of a finite number of processes. A *process* uses inputs and produces one or more outputs. For example, a man using a wheelbarrow to carry bricks is a process. An important assumption in linear programming is that each process uses inputs in fixed proportions. Consequently, each process can be described by a set of technical coefficients, $(a_1 \ldots, a_m)$, that shows the amount of the first input, . . . , mth input that is needed to produce one unit of output. For example, if the first input were man-hours, the second input were wheelbarrow-hours, and a unit of output were the transportation of 1 ton-mile of bricks, the technical coefficients for the "man-wheelbarrow" process might be $(5, 5)$, which would indicate that it takes 5 man-hours of labor and 5 hours of use of the wheelbarrow to "produce" 1 ton-mile of transportation of bricks.

Each process can be operated at various *activity levels*, the activity level of a process being the number of units of output that is produced with the process. For example, if 2 ton-miles of bricks are "produced" with the "man-wheelbarrow" process described above, its activity level is 2; on the other hand, if 0.5 ton-miles of bricks are transported with this process, its activity level is 0.5. It is assumed that, if the output of any process is varied, the inputs used by the process vary proportionately with the output of the process. Thus the quantity of any input used by a process is equal to the activity level of the process multiplied by the input's technical coefficient for this process. For example, the amount of labor used by the "man-wheelbarrow" process is $5 \times 5 = 25$ man-hours, if this process is operated at an activity level of 5. When two or more processes are used simultaneously, it is assumed that they do not interfere with one another or make each other more productive. (In other words, it is assumed that the processes are additive in the inputs.)

Viewed in the context of linear programming, the firm's production problem is as follows: The firm has certain fixed amounts of a number of inputs at its disposal. For example, if the firm is a steel mill, it has a limited amount of land, raw materials, managerial labor, and equipment of various types. (These limitations on the amounts of inputs that the firm can use are called *constraints.*) Each unit of output resulting from a particular process yields the firm a certain amount of profit. This amount of profit varies in general from process to process; indeed the product itself may vary from process to process. Knowing the profit to be made from a unit of output from each process and bearing in mind the limited amount of inputs at its disposal, the firm must determine the activity level at which each process should be operated to maximize profit.

8. The Finishing of Cotton Cloth: An Illustration

The previous section provided a general description of the firm's production decision, as it is pictured from the viewpoint of linear programming. But such a description is of limited use unless it is supplemented by illustrations. Recognizing this fact, the next few sections of this chapter are devoted to a fairly detailed description of several cases that illustrate how linear programming can be used to solve the production problems of the firm.

To begin with, consider the following situation. Suppose that one of the operations of a textile mill is the finishing of cotton cloth. The output rate of the finishing department is limited by the capacity of its finishing equipment and the amount of skilled labor available to carry out the work. The firm is considering three finishing processes: processes 1, 2, and 3. Suppose that the firm knows that the profit per batch of cotton cloth finished with process 1 is $1.00; similarly, it is $0.90 for process 2, and $1.10 for process 3. Suppose too that process 1 uses 3 machine-hours of finishing capacity per batch of cotton cloth processed, that process 2 uses 2.50 machine-hours, and that process 3 uses 5.25 machine-hours. Also, suppose that process 1 uses 0.4 man-hours of skilled labor per batch of cotton cloth processed, that process 2 uses 0.50 man-hours, and that process 3 uses 0.35 man-hours. These are the technical coefficients.[5] Finally, suppose that 6000 machine-hours per week is the maximum finishing capacity, and 600 man-hours per week is the maximum amount of skilled labor that the firm can use.

If Q_1 is the number of batches of cotton cloth processed per week on process 1, Q_2 is the number processed on process 2, and Q_3 is the number processed on process 3, the firm's production problem can be regarded as the following linear programming problem: Maximize

$$\pi = 1.00Q_1 + 0.90Q_2 + 1.10Q_3 \tag{7.1}$$

subject to the constraints

$$3Q_1 + 2.50Q_2 + 5.25Q_3 \leq 6000 \tag{7.2}$$

$$0.40Q_1 + 0.50Q_2 + 0.35Q_3 \leq 600 \tag{7.3}$$

$$Q_1 \geq 0; \; Q_2 \geq 0; \; Q_3 \geq 0 \tag{7.4}$$

The *objective function*, sometimes called the criterion function, is the function to be maximized in a linear programming problem. In this case, it is the expression for the firm's profits given in Equation 7.1. The *constraints* are given in Inequalities 7.2 to 7.4. Inequality 7.2 states that the total machine-hours per week of finishing capacity must be less than or equal to 6000. Inequality 7.3 states that the total man-hours of skilled labor per week must be less than or equal to 600. Inequality 7.4 contains nonnegativity constraints, which may seem so obvious as to be unnecessary to state. But they are not obvious to a dumb electronic computer, which might otherwise come up with a solution with a negative output. Finally, note that the objective function and the constraints are all linear in Q_1, Q_2 and Q_3, the levels at which the processes are operated.

To see how this problem can be solved, we begin by providing a graphical representation of the feasible input combinations and of a process.[6] Figure 7.9, which has the total man-hours per week of skilled labor-time used by all three processes along the horizontal axis and the total machine-hours

---

[5]If machine-time is the first input and skilled labor is the second input, the a's, in the terminology of Section 7, are $(3, 0.4)$ for process 1, $(2.50, 0.5)$ for process 2, and $(5.25, 0.35)$ for process 3, a unit of output being a batch of cotton cloth finished.
[6]The ensuing discussion of this problem is similar in many respects (although the problem itself is quite different) to W. Baumol, *Economic Theory and Operations Analysis*, Englewood Cliffs: Prentice-Hall, 1965, pp. 272–86. Baumol's discussions in Chapters 5, 6, and 12 of his book are highly recommended for those readers who are interested in a more detailed treatment of linear programming.

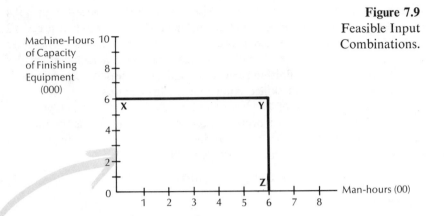

Figure 7.9
Feasible Input
Combinations.

per week of finishing capacity used by all three processes along the vertical axis, shows the combinations of total man-hours and total machine-hours that are feasible. The feasible region is the rectangle $OXYZ$, since a maximum of 600 man-hours and 6000 machine-hours are available.

Recall that a process is defined to have fixed input proportions. Since all points where input proportions are unchanged lie along a straight line through the origin, we can represent each process by such a line, or *ray*. In Figure 7.10, the ray OR_1 represents process 1. Process 1 uses 3 machine-hours of finishing capacity and 0.4 hours of skilled labor per batch processed. That is, it uses 7.5 machine-hours of finishing capacity for every hour of skilled labor. Thus the ray OR_1 includes all points at which finishing capacity is combined with skilled labor in the ratio of 7.5 : 1. Each point on this ray implies a certain output level. For example, point A, where 100 hours of labor and 750 machine-hours of finishing capacity are used, implies an output

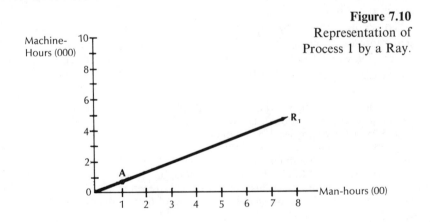

Figure 7.10
Representation of
Process 1 by a Ray.

of 250 batches per week, since process 1 uses 0.4 hours of skilled labor and 3 machine-hours of finishing capacity per batch. Moreover, since all points at which labor and finishing capacity are combined in the ratio of 7.5 : 1 are included in the ray OR_1, every possible output corresponds to some point on OR_1.

9. Isoquants

It is possible to construct rays representing each of the three processes. Figure 7.11 shows all of them, OR_2 representing process 2, and OR_3 representing process 3. Each ray is constructed in the same way as OR_1 was constructed for process 1. Using these rays, we can draw isoquants—curves that include all input combinations that can produce a particular amount of output. An isoquant means the same thing here as in Chapter 5; the only difference is that an isoquant here does not exhibit the smoothness of the isoquants in Chapter 5.

To begin with, we focus on processes 1 and 3. In Figure 7.11, point A_1 on OR_1 is the point corresponding to an output of 250 batches per week, and point A_3 on OR_3 is the point corresponding to an output of 250 batches

Figure 7.11
Rays for Processes 1, 2, and 3.

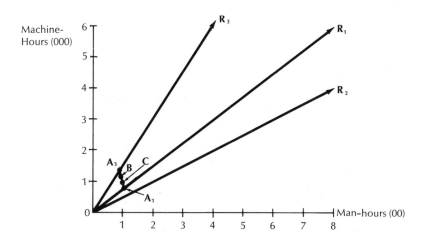

per week. Thus A_1 and A_3 are points on the isoquant corresponding to an output of 250 batches per week. Moreover, any point on the line segment that joins A_1 to A_3 is also on this isoquant, because the firm can simultaneously use both process 1 and process 3 to produce 250 batches per week. For example, point B corresponds to the case in which process 1 is used to produce 25 batches and process 3 is used to produce 225 batches, and point C corresponds to the case in which process 1 is used to produce 150 batches and process 3 is used to produce 100 batches. By varying the proportion of total output produced by each process, one can obtain all points on the line segment that joins A_1 to A_3.

In Figure 7.12, to complete the isoquant corresponding to an output of 250 batches per week, we join A_1 to A_2, the point on OR_2 that represents an output of 250 batches per week. Thus the entire isoquant is $A_3A_1A_2$. (At first glance, one might wonder why the line segment joining A_3 to A_2 is not part of the isoquant. After all, it does represent various combinations of skilled labor and finishing capacity that can produce 250 batches a week. The reason for its exclusion is that all points on the line segment joining A_3 to A_2 are inefficient. They use as much of one input and more of the other input than some point on $A_3A_1A_2$. Thus the points on A_3A_2 are clearly not on the isoquant—and they are not part of the solution to the firm's problem.) Other isoquants are also shown in Figure 7.12, $B_3B_1B_2$ being the isoquant corresponding to an output of 500 batches per week and $C_3C_1C_2$ being the isoquant corresponding to an output of 750 batches per week.

Figure 7.12
Isoquants for Selected Output Levels.

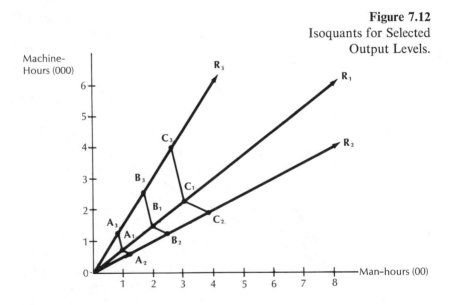

Several things should be noted about the characteristic shape of isoquants in linear programming problems. First, they consist of a series of connected line segments, not the smooth curves of conventional theory. If the number of possible processes is very large, however, the isoquants may approximate the smooth conventional curves.[7] Second, their slope is negative, or at least nonpositive. Third, they are convex, which means that the marginal rate of technical substitution of one input for another decreases as more of the first input is substituted for the other. Disregarding the fact that they do not exhibit the smoothness assumed in conventional theory, the isoquants of linear programming have the same basic shape as the isoquants of conventional theory.

Since the isoquants show a decreasing marginal rate of technical substitution of one input for another, linear programming is quite compatible with the law of diminishing returns, which plays an important role in conventional theory. However, the linearity assumptions in linear programming problems imply that there are neither diminishing nor increasing returns to scale. In other words, the production function is always assumed to be linear and homogeneous, which means that there are constant returns to scale.

10. Isoprofit Curves and a Graphical Solution

Returning to the firm's problem, our next step toward a solution of this linear programming problem is the construction of isoprofit curves. Once this is done, we can obtain a solution by graphical means. Just as each isoquant in Figure 7.12 represents the locus of input combinations that can produce a given output, each *isoprofit curve* is constructed to include all input combinations that can produce a given level of profit.

For example, suppose that we construct the isoprofit curve corresponding to a profit of $200. Since the profit per batch is $1.00 for process 1, the point on OR_1 corresponding to an output of 200 batches per week is on this isoprofit curve. Since each batch produced with process 1 requires 3 machine-hours of finishing capacity and 0.4 man-hours of labor, the point on OR_1 corresponding to an output of 200 batches per week is A in Figure 7.13. Similarly, since the profit per batch is $0.90 for process 2, the point on

---

[7]The basic reason why they are not smooth is that only a finite number of processes are assumed to be available to the firm. As the number of processes grows larger and larger, the isoquants become closer and closer to the smooth isoquants of conventional theory.

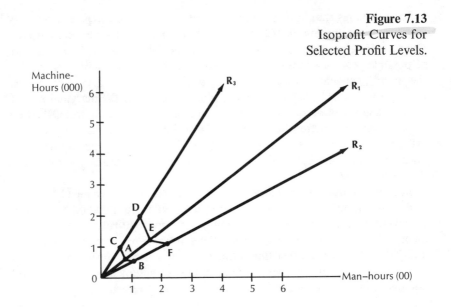

Figure 7.13
Isoprofit Curves for
Selected Profit Levels.

OR_2 corresponding to an output of 222.2 batches per week is on this isoprofit curve. This is point B. Moreover, since the profit per batch is $1.10 for process 3, the point on OR_3 corresponding to an output of 181.8 batches per week is also on this isoprofit curve. This is point C. Finally, for the same reason as in the case of the isoquants, we can also include all points on the lines that join these points. Thus the isoprofit curve corresponding to a profit of $200 per week is CAB in Figure 7.13.

Isoprofit curves corresponding to other levels of profit can be constructed in a similar manner. As in the case of the isoquants in Figure 7.12, the isoprofit curves in Figure 7.13 are parallel to one another. For example, if we compare DEF, the isoprofit curve corresponding to $400, with CAB, the isoprofit curve corresponding to $200, we find that they are parallel. That is, the slope of CA equals the slope of DE, and the slope of AB equals the slope of EF.

Given the isoprofit curves, we can easily solve the firm's problem. All that we need to do is to add the isoprofit curves to the diagram (Figure 7.9) showing the feasible input combinations. This is done in Figure 7.14. Clearly, the problem is to find the point in the rectangle $OXYZ$ of feasible input combinations that lies on the highest isoprofit curve. It is evident from Figure 7.14 that this optimal point is Y. If we construct various isoprofit curves, like $U_3U_1U_2$, $V_3V_1V_2$, and so forth, the highest isoprofit

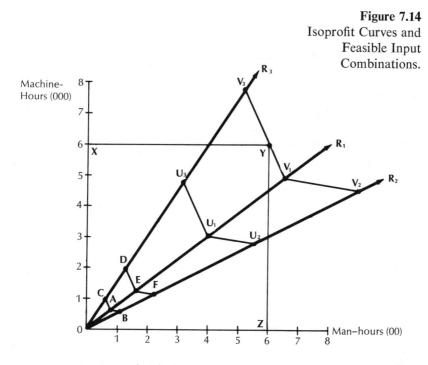

Figure 7.14
Isoprofit Curves and
Feasible Input
Combinations.

curve we can construct that includes any points in $OXYZ$ is $V_3V_1V_2$. And the only point in $OXYZ$ that lies on $V_3V_1V_2$ is Y.

Granting that Y is the optimum point, how can we tell what the optimal values of Q_1, Q_2, and Q_3 are? First, since Y lies on the line segment V_3V_1, it means that it is optimal only to use processes 3 and 1. This illustrates the fact that the optimal solution of a linear programming problem of this sort will generally entail the use of no more processes than there are constraints: two, in this case (excluding the nonnegativity constraints). Second, since Y is the point where a total of 6000 machine-hours of finishing capacity and 600 hours of skilled labor are used,

$$3Q_1 + 5.25Q_3 = 6000 \tag{7.5}$$

$$0.40Q_1 + 0.35Q_3 = 600 \tag{7.6}$$

Solving Equations 7.5 and 7.6 simultaneously, we find that the optimal values are $Q_3 = 571.4$ and $Q_1 = 1000$. In other words, the firm will maximize its profit if it produces about 571 batches per week on process 3 and 1000 batches per week on process 1.

11. Minimization of Costs

As another simple illustration of the use of linear programming in solving production problems, consider a variant of the above example. Suppose that the textile firm is no longer constrained by limits on the amount of skilled labor and finishing capacity it can use. Instead, it can hire all of the skilled labor it wants at $3.00 an hour, and it can rent all of the finishing capacity it wants at $0.40 per machine-hour. Suppose that it can use any of the three processes just described, and that its problem is to choose that combination of processes that will produce 400 batches per week of finished cotton cloth at minimum cost. The price received per batch is the same for all processes. (Note that the figures given in Section 8 concerning the profit per batch made by each process are no longer valid, since the price received per batch is now the same for all processes.)

In this case the firm's production problem can be regarded as the following linear programming problem: Minimize

$$C = 2.40Q_1 + 2.50Q_2 + 3.15Q_3 \qquad (7.7)$$

subject to the constraints

$$Q_1 + Q_2 + Q_3 = 400 \qquad (7.8)$$

$$Q_1 \geq 0; \; Q_2 \geq 0; \; Q_3 \geq 0 \qquad (7.9)$$

The objective function in this case is cost, C, which is given in Equation 7.7. To derive this equation, note that the cost of each batch produced by process 1 is $2.40, since process 1 requires 3 machine-hours of finishing capacity (at $0.40 a machine-hour) and 0.4 man-hours of skilled labor (at $3.00 an hour). Thus the total cost of the batches produced by process 1 is $2.40Q_1$. Similarly, the total cost of the batches produced by process 2 is $2.50Q_2$, and the total cost of the batches produced by process 3 is $3.15Q_3$. The only constraint, other than the nonnegativity constraints in Inequality 7.9, is Equation 7.8, which states that the total production from all processes must equal 400.

It is easy to solve this problem. Using the methods described in Section 9, we can construct the isoquant corresponding to an output of 400 batches per week. This isoquant, labeled *ABC*, is shown in Figure 7.15. Next we can construct isocost curves, each of which shows the various combinations of quantities of skilled labor and finishing capacity that can be obtained at a given level of cost. The isocost curves corresponding to costs of $1000

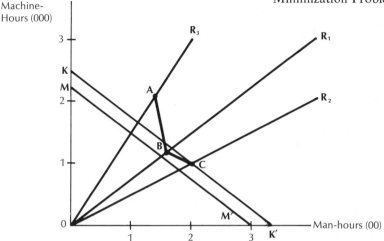

Figure 7.15
Optimal Solution: Cost
Minimization Problem.

and $900 are labeled *KK'* and *MM'* in Figure 7.15. Clearly, the problem is to find the point on the isoquant, *ABC*, that lies on the lowest isocost curve. It is evident that the optimal point is *B*, which means that all of the output should be produced with process 1.

Two things should be noted at this point. First, a comparison of this problem with the one at the end of Section 3 of Chapter 6 shows that they are one and the same. In both cases, we are determining the input combination and production technique that minimize the cost of producing a given output. Moreover, Figure 6.3 on p. 153, which shows the solution according to conventional theory, is very similar to Figure 7.15, which shows the solution in this case. What is the difference between the two cases? It boils down to the fact that in Chapter 6 we assumed that we were somehow given a smooth production function, whereas here we assume that there are three processes that can be used and that their characteristics are as described here and in Section 8.

Second, was it really necessary to use linear programming—even the simplified version relying only on graphical techniques that we use here—to solve this problem? The answer clearly is no. All that the problem entails is a choice among three methods of production in a case in which the unit costs of production are constant for each process and there is no constraint on the amount that can be produced using a particular process. In such a case the answer is obvious: Produce the required volume of output with the process with the lowest unit cost. The moral is clear. Although relatively high-powered analytical devices like linear programming are often required to help solve large and complicated problems, nothing is gained by using them to handle problems that can just as readily be solved by simpler means. Students—and economists long out of school—sometimes become so infatuated with new tools that they use them even when much simpler methods would do just as well.

12.   The Production of Automobiles and Trucks: Another Illustration

Turning now to a more complex case, suppose that a firm produces two kinds of output, automobiles and trucks.[8] It has four kinds of facilities, each of which is fixed in capacity: automobile assembly, truck assembly, engine assembly, and sheet metal stamping. The problem is: How many automobiles and how many trucks should the firm produce? The profit per automobile or the profit per truck depends on the price of an automobile or a truck, the variable costs of producing an automobile or a truck, and the firm's fixed costs. Assume that the price and average variable cost of each product are constant; that is, they do not vary with output in the relevant range. Specifically, assume that the price of an automobile is $2000, the price of a truck is $4000, the average variable costs of an automobile are $1700, and the average variable costs of a truck are $3750.

The firm wants to maximize profits. Neglecting fixed costs (which will be the same regardless of what the firm does), the firm's profits equal

$$\pi = 300Q_a + 250Q_t \tag{7.10}$$

where Q_a is the number of automobiles produced by the firm per hour and Q_t is the number of trucks produced by the firm per hour. Since the firm receives $300 ($2000 − $1700) above the variable cost for each automobile that it produces, and since the firm receives $250 ($4000 − $3750) above the variable cost for each truck it produces, the firm's profits (before deducting fixed costs) must equal $300 times the output of automobiles plus $250 times the output of trucks.

---

[8]This is an adaptation of the well-known example found in R. Dorfman, "Mathematical or Linear Programming," *American Economic Review*, Dec. 1953. Different numbers have been used to simplify the results.

The constraints on the firm's decisions are the fixed capacities for automobile assembly, truck assembly, engine assembly, and sheet metal stamping. Table 7.3 shows the proportion of each facility's total capacity required to produce one automobile or one truck. From this table, we can represent the constraints on the production of automobiles and trucks by the following inequalities:

$$.05Q_a \leq 1 \tag{7.11}$$

$$.04Q_t \leq 1 \tag{7.12}$$

$$.02Q_a + .033Q_t \leq 1 \tag{7.13}$$

$$.033Q_a + .025Q_t \leq 1 \tag{7.14}$$

$$Q_a \geq 0; \quad Q_t \geq 0 \tag{7.15}$$

To begin with, Inequalities 7.11 and 7.12 represent the constraints imposed by existing automobile and truck assembly capacity. Since each automobile that is produced per hour takes up 5 percent of the automobile assembly capacity, it follows that .05 times the output per hour of automobiles must be less than or equal to one. Figure 7.16 plots the firm's automobile production against its truck production. The vertical line at 20 automobiles per hour shows the effects of this constraint, since 20 is the maximum automobile output compatible with this constraint. Similarly, since each truck that is produced per hour takes up 4 percent of the truck assembly capacity, it follows that .04 times the output per hour of trucks must be less than or equal to one. The horizontal line in Figure 7.16 at 25 trucks per hour shows the effects of this constraint, since 25 is the maximum truck output compatible with this constraint.

Table 7.3. Percent of Capacity of Each Division of Plant Required to Make a Car or a Truck (per hour).

CAPACITY	CAR	TRUCK
Auto assembly	5	0
Engine assembly	2	$3\frac{1}{3}$
Sheet metal	$3\frac{1}{3}$	$2\frac{1}{2}$
Truck assembly	0	4

Inequality 7.13 states that no more than the existing capacity for engine assembly can be used. Since each automobile produced per hour takes up

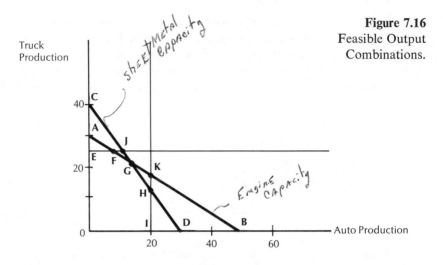

Figure 7.16
Feasible Output
Combinations.

2 percent of the existing engine assembly capacity and since each truck produced per hour takes up 3 1/3 percent of the existing engine assembly capacity, it follows that .02 times the output per hour of automobiles plus .033 times the output per hour of trucks, must be less than or equal to one. Thus the line *AB* in Figure 7.16 separates feasible combinations of automobile and truck outputs from those that are beyond the existing engine assembly capacity. To be feasible, the combination of outputs must be on, or within, the triangle *OAB*.

   Inequality 7.14 states that no more than the existing sheet metal stamping capacity can be used. Since each automobile produced per hour takes up 3 1/3 percent of the available metal stamping capacity and since each truck produced per hour takes up 2 1/2 percent of the available metal stamping capacity, it follows that .033 times the output per hour of automobiles plus .025 times the output per hour of trucks, must be less than or equal to one. Thus the line *CD* in Figure 7.16 separates feasible combinations of automobile and truck outputs from those that are beyond the existing sheet metal stamping capacity. To be feasible, the combination of outputs must be on, or within, the triangle *OCD*.

   Combining these constraints, the combination of output of automobiles and trucks must lie within the area *OEFGHI* in Figure 7.16. Any point outside this area violates at least one of the constraints. For example, point *C* uses more engine assembly capacity and truck assembly capacity than is available, and point *K* uses more sheet metal stamping capacity than is available.

This is a linear programming problem. The objective function is given by Equation 7.10, and the constraints are given in Inequalities 7.11 to 7.15. There are two processes, automobile production and truck production, each of which uses the four types of capacities in fixed (but different) proportions. The optimal solution to this problem can be found graphically by adding a family of isoprofit lines to Figure 7.16. This is done in Figure 7.17. Each broken line shows the various combinations of automobile production and truck production that will result in the same total profit (gross of fixed costs). If π is this profit, the equation for an isoprofit line is

$$Q_t = \frac{\pi}{250} - \frac{300}{250} Q_a \tag{7.16}$$

Obviously, one should find that point in the feasible area, *OEFGHI*, that lies on the highest isoprofit line, i.e., the highest broken line.

Figure 7.17 shows that the optimal solution is at point *G*, where the firm produces 13.6 automobiles and 21.8 trucks per hour. With these output rates, the firm's profit (gross of fixed costs) is $9547 per hour.[9]

Before leaving this example, it is important to note that this problem is

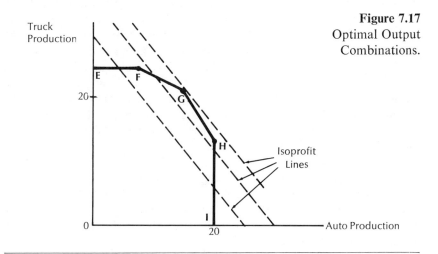

Truck
Production

Figure 7.17
Optimal Output
Combinations.

---

[9]How can a firm produce 13.6 autos per hour? By producing 68 autos every 5 hours. In cases in which the solution must be composed of integers, an extension of linear programming called integer programming must be used. See W. Baumol, *op. cit.*, Chapter 8. Note that it is easy to find the coordinates of *G* by making inequalities 7.13 and 7.14 into equations and solving them simultaneously for Q_a and Q_t.

almost exactly the same as the problem we solved with conventional theory in Section 4 of this chapter. In both cases, the firm, taking the price of each product as given, is faced with the task of deciding how much of each product to produce. A comparison of Figure 7.17 with Figure 7.6 (p. 195) shows the similarities quite clearly. In both cases, there are isoprofit lines plotted against a product transformation curve, the isorevenue line in Figure 7.6 being the same as an isoprofit line under the circumstances posited there. However, an important dissimilarity is that in Section 4 we had to assume that someone handed us a production function; here we assume only that we are given the technological data in Table 7.3.

13.   Computational Efficiency and the Comparison of Solutions at "Extreme Points"

Thus far, we have emphasized the similarities between the conventional theory of production and production theory based on linear programming. Given that there are so many similarities, one might ask why there is any advantage in the linear programming approach. As we pointed out in Section 6, one important reason why the linear programming approach is used is that powerful computational techniques have been developed to find the numerical solutions to linear programming problems. These computational techniques make use of the following fact: The optimal solution will lie at one of the "extreme points"—or "corners"—of the feasible area.[10] This rule is consistent with the cases discussed in the previous paragraphs. For example, in Figure 7.17, the optimal point, G, was an "extreme point" of the feasible area OEFGHI; and in Figure 7.14, the optimal point, Y, was an "extreme point" of the feasible area OXYZ. This fact reduces very greatly the number of points that must be examined to find the optimal solution, since it shows that all one needs to bother with are the "extreme points" of the feasible area.

To illustrate, consider Figure 7.17. There are 6 "extreme points" of the feasible area OEFGHI. To find the optimal solution, we need only compute the profit (gross of fixed costs) at each of these points. At the origin O,

---

[10]Of course, it sometimes happens that other points are as good as (but not better than) any extreme point. See A. Charnes, W. Cooper, and A. Henderson, *Introduction to Linear Programming*, New York: John Wiley and Sons, 1953.

profit obviously is zero. At $E(Q_a = 0$ and $Q_t = 25)$, profit is \$6250. At $I(Q_a = 20$ and $Q_t = 0)$, profit is \$6000. We must find the coordinates of the other three "extreme points" before we can compute the level of profit at them. To find the coordinates of F, we must make (7.12) and (7.13) into equations and solve them simultaneously; to find the coordinates of G, we must make (7.13) and (7.14) into equations and solve them simultaneously; and to find the coordinates of H, we must make (7.11) and (7.14) into equations and solve them simultaneously. We find that point F is $Q_a = 8\,1/3$ and $Q_t = 25$, the result being that profit is \$8750. Point G is $Q_a = 13.6$ and $Q_t = 21.8$, the result being that profit is \$9547. Point H is $Q_a = 20$ and $Q_t = 13\,1/3$, the result being that profit is \$9333 1/3. Thus, on the basis of these few computations, we know that point G must be the optimal solution.

In problems where the number of processes and constraints are too large for the graphical analysis used in previous sections, this kind of comparison of "extreme point" or "corner" solutions is employed to find the optimal solution. The *simplex method*, which is generally used for this purpose, is a systematic procedure for comparing "extreme point" or "corner" solutions. Combined with the speed and capacity of modern computers, it can solve extremely large problems in a very short period of time. There is a large literature on the simplex method, much of it involving a good deal of mathematics.[11] For present purposes, it is only necessary to know of the existence and general nature of this method.

14. The Dual Problem and Shadow Prices

Linear programming can do more than just find an optimal production program, the objective discussed in previous sections of this chapter. It can also find values to be placed on particular resources or inputs. For example, one could carry out the programming problem considered in Section 12 under the assumption that the firm had a small amount of additional engine assembly capacity. Then one could compare the maximum profit obtainable with the extra amount of engine assembly capacity with the maximum profit obtainable without it. The increase, if there is an increase, in maximum

---

[11]For example, see G. Dantzig, *Linear Programming and Extensions*, Princeton, N.J.: Princeton University Press, 1963.

profit is, of course, a measure of the value of the extra amount of engine assembly capacity.

Although this method of finding the value of an extra unit of a particular input is perfectly correct, it is cumbersome. A very interesting characteristic of linear programming problems is that one can obtain such values without going through this cumbersome procedure. Every linear programming problem has a corresponding problem called its *dual*, the original problem being called the *primal* problem. If the primal is a maximization problem, the dual is a minimization problem; if the primal is a minimization problem, the dual is a maximization problem. The solutions to the dual are *shadow prices*, the values we seek.

For example, the shadow price of each type of capacity (in the problem in Section 12) tells us what would happen to the firm's profits if the company were somehow able to increase this type of capacity. Obviously, these shadow prices are of great practical importance. They show which types of capacity are bottlenecks, or effective constraints on output, since capacity that is underutilized receives a zero shadow price. More important, they indicate how much it would be worth to management to expand each type of capacity. A comparison can then be made between the extra profit due to expansion and the extra costs that must be incurred. If the costs are lower than the extra profits, as indicated by the shadow price, the expansion seems desirable. For example, if the firm producing automobiles and trucks can rent an additional 1 percent of engine assembly capacity at $100 an hour and if an extra 1 percent of such capacity would increase profits by $200, it would be well worth it to rent the extra capacity.[12]

15. Application of Linear Programming in the Petroleum Industry

Linear programming has been used in countless ways by many segments of industry and government. To illustrate the sorts of problems it has helped to solve, we present in this section one of its applications in the petroleum industry. The petroleum industry became aware of linear programming through the pioneering studies in the early fifties by Charnes, Cooper, and

---

[12]See R. Dorfman, P. Samuelson, and R. Solow, *Linear Programming and Economic Analysis*, New York: McGraw-Hill, 1958.

Mellon; and Manne.[13] As is true of most new techniques, it took some time before the industry recognized linear programming's full potentialities, but once the initial educational process was over, its use spread very rapidly.

The petroleum industry is composed of various phases: exploration, production, refining, and distribution and marketing. An integrated oil firm must explore in order to locate places where oil is most likely to be found. It must drill for oil, and refine it to produce gasoline and other products. It must transport the oil, both to and from the refinery. Finally, the oil and oil products enter the distribution system and are marketed by the firm. The petroleum industry is extremely complex and extremely large, the international oil companies like Standard Oil of New Jersey being among the giants of American industry.

Each phase of the petroleum business is full of unanswered problems and questions. The oil potentialities of a region can be explored in various ways. How should these ways be combined for maximum effectiveness? There are a number of different ways of planning and organizing production in an oil field. Which is best? A modern oil refinery is an extremely complex type of plant. What is the best way of operating it? And what do we mean by "best"? Of course, linear programming has not been able to solve all of these problems, but it has helped to solve some of them. For example, it has been useful in solving the following problem, which obviously is an important one to oil producers.

Consider the production phase of the petroleum industry. Suppose that a firm has a number of oil fields, or reservoirs, which are producing at various rates. The total production of the reservoirs must be adjusted to meet a commitment, such as keeping a pipeline full or a refinery supplied. An outside source of crude oil also exists. Technological factors require that the production rates do not exceed certain levels. The profit per barrel of crude oil produced is given, as is the number of years the operation is to be run on this basis. The problem is to determine a schedule of production rates so that the profit over the entire period is a maximum.

This can be viewed as a linear programming problem. For simplicity, assume that the firm has only two reservoirs and that the firm is planning for only two years. The results can easily be extended to larger numbers of reservoirs and longer periods of time. Let Q_{11} be the number of gallons of

---

[13]See A. Charnes, W. Cooper, and B. Mellon, "Blending Aviation Gasolines," *Econometrica*, Apr. 1952; "A Model for Programming and Sensitivity Analysis in an Integrated Oil Company," *Econometrica*, Apr. 1954. Also A. Manne, *Scheduling of Petroleum Refinery Operations*, Cambridge, Mass.: Harvard University Press, 1956.

crude oil produced from the first reservoir in the first year, Q_{12} be the number of gallons of crude oil produced from the first reservoir in the second year, Q_{21} be the number of gallons of crude oil produced from the second reservoir in the first year and Q_{22} be the number of gallons of crude oil produced from the second reservoir in the second year. Let Q_1 be the number of barrels of crude oil purchased from the outside source in the first year, and Q_2 be the corresponding number in the second year.

The objective function is the total profit over the two years, which is

$$\Pi = C_{11}Q_{11} + C_{12}Q_{12} + C_{21}Q_{21} + C_{22}Q_{22}$$
$$+ C_1Q_1 + C_2Q_2 \qquad (7.17)$$

where C_{11} is the profit per barrel of crude oil produced from the first reservoir in the first year, C_{12} is the profit per barrel of crude oil produced from the first reservoir in the second year, C_{21} is the profit per barrel of crude oil produced from the second reservoir in the first year, C_{22} is the profit per barrel of crude oil produced from the second reservoir in the second year, C_1 is the profit per barrel of crude oil obtained from the outside source in the first year, and C_2 is the profit per barrel of crude oil obtained from the outside source in the second year.

The constraints are as follows. First, there are certain maximum levels of production. Thus,

$$Q_{11} \leq Q_{11}^* \qquad (7.18)$$

$$Q_{12} \leq Q_{12}^* \qquad (7.19)$$

$$Q_{21} \leq Q_{21}^* \qquad (7.20)$$

$$Q_{22} \leq Q_{22}^* \qquad (7.21)$$

where Q_{11}^* is the maximum production level of the first reservoir in the first year, Q_{12}^* is the maximum production level of the first reservoir in the second year, Q_{21}^* is the maximum production level of the second reservoir in the first year, and Q_{22}^* is the maximum production level of the second reservoir in the second year.[14]

Second, the total production from the two reservoirs in each year plus the amount purchased from the outside source must equal the commitment

---

[14]See W. Garvin, H. Crandall, J. John, and R. Spellman, "Applications of Linear Programming in the Oil Industry," *Management Science*, July 1957. This section is based largely on their paper. The model in the text is simplified in various respects to make it more easily comprehensible to students. In particular, the constraints in (7.18) to (7.21) are not the only ones that were actually used. But this should make little difference in this context.

for that year. That is,

$$Q_{11} + Q_{21} + Q_1 = K_1 \qquad\qquad (7.22)$$

$$Q_{12} + Q_{22} + Q_2 = K_2 \qquad\qquad (7.23)$$

where K_1 is the commitment for the first year and K_2 the commitment for the second year. Also, $Q_{11}, Q_{12}, Q_{21}, Q_{22}, Q_1$ and Q_2 must be nonnegative.

Using linear programming, this problem can be solved to determine the values of $Q_{11}, Q_{12}, Q_{21}, Q_{22}, Q_1$, and Q_2 that maximize the firm's profits. The Magnolia Petroleum Company and the Arabian American Oil Company have done a considerable amount of work on this problem, using a simple model like that described above and more complicated variants of this model. The results have been useful to these companies and others in the industry.[15]

16. Summary

If the firm takes the price of its product as given, it maximizes profit—or minimizes losses—in the short run by producing the quantity of output at which marginal cost equals the price of the product. However, if the price of the product is less than the firm's average variable cost for any quantity of output, the firm will minimize losses by discontinuing production. If a firm produces two products and takes the price of each product as given, it will maximize profit by choosing the output levels of the two products so that the marginal rate of product transformation is equal to the ratio of the prices of the two products. The marginal rate of product transformation is the negative of the slope of the product transformation curve.

Linear programming is the most famous of the mathematical programming methods that have come into existence since World War II. It is a technique that allows decision-makers to solve maximization and minimization problems where there are certain constraints that limit what can be done. It is useful to look at production decisions from the programming point of view because, unlike conventional theory, it does not take the production function as being given to the economist before he attacks the problem. Also the programming analysis is easier to apply in many respects, and powerful computational techniques are available to obtain solutions.

---

[15]*Ibid.* As presented above, the problem is, of course, much simpler than the one dealt with by these companies. (As it stands, it can be solved in an elementary way.) For present purposes, it seemed wise to strip it down to its simplest form.

Linear programming views the technology available to the firm as being a finite number of processes, each of which uses inputs in fixed proportions. The firm has a certain amount of each of the inputs at its disposal. Each unit of output resulting from a particular process yields the firm a certain amount of profit, this amount of profit varying from process to process. Knowing the profit to be made from a unit of output from each process and bearing in mind the limited amount of the various inputs at its command, the firm is visualized as attempting to determine the output from each process that will maximize profit.

To illustrate the use of linear programming, we discussed a case in which a hypothetical textile firm had to choose which combination of a number of alternative processes to use, given that it has only a limited amount of certain inputs. We solved the problem by graphical techniques. Isoprofit curves were constructed and superimposed on a diagram showing the feasible input combinations, and the point was chosen that, among those that were feasible, was on the highest isoprofit curve. In addition, we considered a variant of this problem in which the firm is no longer constrained by limitations on inputs.

Turning to a more complex case, we discussed the problem of a firm that produces more than one product and has various fixed facilities which set limits on the amount of each product that can be produced. The problem is to determine the optimal combination of outputs of the two products. This problem was also solved by graphical means, isoprofit lines being superimposed on a diagram showing feasible output combinations. In addition, in the context of this example, we discussed the fact that the optimal solution of a linear programming problem will lie at one of the "extreme points" or "corners" of the feasible area.

Every linear programming problem has a corresponding problem called its dual, the original problem being the primal problem. If the primal is a maximization problem, the dual is a minimization problem; if the primal is a minimization problem, the dual is a maximization problem. In the example concerning the optimal combination of outputs of two products, whereas the primal looked for optimal output rates for the two products, the dual seeks to impute values to the fixed facilities. These imputed values, or shadow prices, are very useful, since they show what would happen to the firm's profits if the company somehow were able to increase each type of capacity. Finally, we presented an application of linear programming to an important practical problem of the petroleum industry. The problem is to determine the optimal schedule of production rates for a number of oil fields, or reservoirs.

SELECTED REFERENCES

Baumol, William, *Economic Theory and Operations Analysis*, Englewood Cliffs, N.J.: Prentice-Hall, 1965.

Dorfman, Robert, Paul Samuelson, and Robert Solow, *Linear Programming and Economic Analysis*, New York: McGraw-Hill, 1958.

Dantzig, George, *Linear Programming and Extensions*, Princeton, N.J.: Princeton University Press, 1963.

Henderson, A. and R. Schlaifer, "Mathematical Programming" in Edwin Mansfield, *Managerial Economics and Operations Research*, New York: Norton, revised edition, 1970.

Hitch, Charles and Roland McKean, *The Economics of Defense in the Nuclear Age*, Cambridge, Mass.: Harvard University Press, 1960.

8

Price and Output under Perfect Competition

1. Market Structure: An Introduction

Previous chapters have provided models of the behavior of consumers and firms. In Chapters 8 to 11 we turn to the analysis of markets, our principal purpose being to explain the behavior of price and output. We will be concerned with questions of the following sort: What determines the price of a product? What determines how much of a product is produced? How are resources allocated among alternative uses? These are some of the most basic—and most important—questions in economics.

To begin with, we must distinguish between various types of markets. Economists have found it useful to classify markets into four general types: perfect competition, monopoly, monopolistic competition, and oligopoly. This classification is based largely on the number of firms in the industry that supplies the product. In perfect competition and monopolistic competition, there are many sellers, each of which produces only a small part of the industry's output.   In monopoly, on the other hand, the industry consists of only a single firm.   Oligopoly is an intermediate case where there are a few sellers.

In this chapter we investigate how price and output are determined in perfectly competitive markets.   Monopoly, monopolistic competition, and oligopoly are taken up in subsequent chapters.   The analysis in this chapter brings together, and builds on, the topics discussed in previous chapters. The theory of consumer demand (the topic of Chapters 2 to 4) provides insight into the revenue side of a firm's operations.   The theory of production and cost (the topics of Chapters 5 to 7) provides insight into the expenditure and supply side of a firm's operations.   Put together, the revenue and expenditure sides of a firm's operations, and their reflection in the demand and supply conditions in the market, determine price and output in the firm and the industry.

2.   Perfect Competition

What do economists mean by perfect competition?   When first exposed to this concept, students sometimes find it difficult to grasp because it is quite different from the concept of competition used by their fathers and brothers in the business world.   When a businessman speaks of a highly competitive market, he generally means a market where each firm is keenly aware of its rivalry with a few others and where advertising, packaging, styling, and other competitive weapons are used to attract business away from them. In contrast, the basic feature of the economist's definition of perfect competition is its impersonality.   Because there are so many firms in the industry, no firm views another as a competitor, any more than one small wheat farmer views another small wheat farmer as a competitor.

More specifically, perfect competition is defined by four conditions. First, perfect competition requires that the product of any one seller be the same as the product of any other seller.   This is an important condition because it makes sure that buyers do not care whether they purchase the product from one seller or another, as long as the price is the same.   Note that the "product" may be defined by a great deal more than the physical characteristics of the good.   Although various English pubs may serve the same beer, their products may not be identical because the barmaids may be prettier in one place than another, the location may be better, and so forth.

Second, perfect competition requires each participant in the market, whether buyer or seller, to be so small, in relation to the entire market, that he cannot affect the product's price. Each buyer must be so small that he cannot wangle a better price from the sellers than some other buyer. Each seller must be so small that he cannot influence the price by altering his output rate. Of course, if all producers act together, changes in output will certainly affect price, but any producer acting alone cannot do so. It will be recalled from Chapter 4 that this means that the firm's demand curve is horizontal.

Third, perfect competition requires that all resources be completely mobile. In other words, each resource must be able to enter or leave the market, and switch from one use to another, very readily.[1] More specifically, it means that labor must be able to move from region to region and from job to job; it means that raw materials must not be monopolized; and it means that new firms can enter and leave an industry. Needless to say, this condition is often not fulfilled in a world where considerable retraining is required to allow a worker to move from one job to another and where patents, large investment requirements, and economies of scale make difficult the entry of new firms.

Fourth, perfect competition requires that consumers, firms, and resource owners have perfect knowledge of the relevant economic and technological data. Consumers must be aware of all prices. Laborers and owners of capital must be aware of how much their resources will bring in all possible uses. Firms must know the prices of all inputs and the characteristics of all relevant technologies. Moreover, in its purest sense, perfect competition requires that all of these economic decision-making units have an accurate knowledge of the future together with the past and present.

Having described these four requirements, it is obvious that no industry is perfectly competitive. Some agricultural markets may be reasonably close, since the first three requirements are frequently met; but even they do not meet all of the requirements.[2] Nevertheless, this does not mean that the study of the behavior of perfectly competitive markets is useless. Recall from Chapter 1 that a model may be quite useful even though some of its

---

[1]Of course, this does not mean that such movements of resources do not take time. In the short run, many resources cannot be transferred from one use to another.
[2]Some agricultural markets in which the conditions would otherwise be reasonably close to perfect competition are heavily affected by government programs. See Sections 15 and 16 at the end of this Chapter.

assumptions are unrealistic. The conclusions derived from the model of perfect competition have proved very useful in explaining and predicting behavior in the real world. They have permitted a reasonably accurate view of resource allocation in important segments of our economy.

3. Price Determination in the Market Period

Beside the short run and the long run, discussed in previous chapters, there is also the market period during which the supply of a good is fixed. For example, retailers may have only a certain number of Beatles records in stock, and it may take a certain period of time before they can obtain more from the producers. Or the quantity of an agricultural commodity may be fixed for some time after a harvest. Also, in some cases, the quantity of a certain commodity may be fixed for a long period of time. For example, the quantity of Van Gogh paintings cannot be augmented—although forgers sometimes try.

Whereas the quantity of output is variable in the short and long runs, it is fixed in the *market period*, the consequence being that the *supply curve*, the curve that shows the quantity of output supplied at each price, is a vertical straight line. For example, in Figure 8.1, the quantity available for sale is OA, and the market supply curve is AA'. Since each seller has a fixed supply that it sells for the market-established price, the behavior of the sellers is perfectly straightforward: They simply sell what they have for as much as they can get.[3]

Equilibrium is achieved, of course, at that price which clears the market by equating the amount demanded with the amount supplied. At a lower price, buyers will want more of the commodity than exists in the market; at a higher price they will want less of the commodity than exists in the market. In Figure 8.1, if the market demand curve is DD', the equilibrium price is OP_0. If the demand curve were higher (like D_1D_1') the equilibrium price would be higher (like OP_1). If the demand curve were lower (like D_2D_2'), the equilibrium price would be lower (like OP_2). But

---

[3]Of course, the sellers themselves may be among those who can use and want the good, the result being that their demand is included in the market demand curve. If this is the case, it may turn out that they sell some of the good to themselves: that is, they keep it.

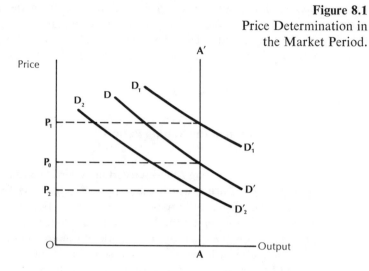

Figure 8.1
Price Determination in
the Market Period.

the equilibrium quantity would be the same, since it is fixed. Consequently, in the market period, quantity is set by supply alone and (given supply) price is set by demand alone.

The role played by prices as rationing devices is particularly obvious in the market period, where this is the major function of price. When the market equilibrium price is reached, the available supply has been rationed, without resort to fights among consumers or government intervention. Those consumers who can and will pay the price have the commodity—and there are just enough such consumers to exhaust the available supply.

4. The Supply Curve of the Firm in the Short Run

Having dealt with the determination of price and output in the market period, we proceed to the case of price and output determination in the short run. The first step is to construct each firm's short-run supply curve: the curve that shows how much the firm will produce at each price. Based on the results in Chapter 7, it is a simple matter to derive the firm's short-run supply curve. Recall from Chapter 7 that a firm that takes the price of its product as given (and can sell all it wants at that price) will choose the output level at which price equals marginal cost. Or if the price is less than the firm's average variable cost at any output, the firm will discontinue produc-

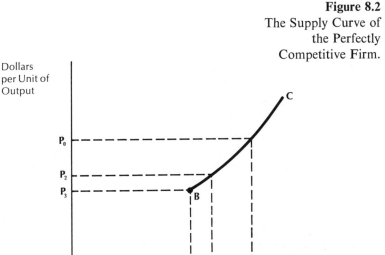

Figure 8.2
The Supply Curve of
the Perfectly
Competitive Firm.

tion. Thus, suppose that the firm's short-run cost curves are those in Figure 7.3 (p. 191). The marginal cost curve intersects the average variable cost curve at the latter's minimum point, *B*. If the price of the product is below OP_3, the firm will produce nothing, because there is no output level where price exceeds average variable cost.

If the price of the product exceeds OP_3, the firm will set its output rate at the point at which price equals marginal cost. This is the output rate that maximizes profit, as we saw in Chapter 7. Thus, if the price is OP_0, the firm will produce OX; if the price is OP_2, the firm will produce OY, and so forth. The resulting supply curve is that shown in Figure 8.2 as OP_3BC. *Given the way it was constructed, this curve is exactly the same as the firm's short-run marginal cost curve for prices above OP_3; at or below OP_3, the supply curve coincides with the price axis.*

5.   Short-Run Supply Curve of the Industry

The price of the industry's product in the short run was given to us in the previous section. What we want to do is to see how it is determined. This price is influenced by both the consumers that demand the good and the firms that supply it. The determinants of the industry demand curve have been discussed in previous chapters, particularly in Chapter 4. In this section, we discuss the determinants of the short-run industry supply curve, and in the next section, we combine the demand and supply curves and show how the industry's price and output are determined in the short run.

As a rough approximation, the industry's short-run supply curve can be regarded as the horizontal summation of the short-run supply curves of all of the firms in the industry. For example, if there were three firms in the industry and if their supply curves were OSS_1S_1', OSS_2S_2', and OSS_3S_3' in Figure 8.3, the industry's supply curve would be $OSS'S''$, since $OSS'S''$ shows the amounts of the product that all of the firms together would supply at various prices. Of course, if there were only three firms, the industry would not be perfectly competitive, but we can ignore this inconsistency. The point of Figure 8.3 is to illustrate the fact that the industry supply curve is the horizontal summation of the firm supply curves, at least under one important assumption.

The assumption underlying this construction of the short-run industry supply curve is that supplies of inputs to the industry as a whole are perfectly elastic. In other words, it is assumed that increases or decreases in output by all firms simultaneously do not affect input prices. This is a strong assumption. Although changes in the output of one firm alone often cannot affect input prices, the simultaneous expansion or contraction of output by all firms may well alter input prices, the result being that the individual firm's cost curves—and supply curve—will shift. For example, an expansion of

Figure 8.3
Horizontal Summation
of Short-Run Supply
Curves of Firms.

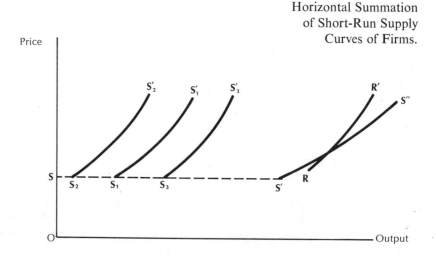

the whole industry may bid up the price of certain inputs, the result being that the cost curves of the individual firms will be pushed upward.[4]

If, contrary to the assumption underlying Figure 8.3, input prices are influenced in this way by expansion of the industry, what will be the effect on the short-run industry supply curve? It will make the short-run industry supply curve less elastic than $OSS'S''$. In the relevant price range, the curve might be more like RR'. To see this, note that expansion of the industry causes the short-run average cost curve and the short-run marginal cost curve to move upward, because of the resulting increase in input prices. But if the marginal cost curve moves upward, price will equal marginal cost at a lower output than would have been the case if the marginal cost curve had not moved.

In summary, the shape of the short-run supply curve is determined by the number of firms in the industry, the size of the plant and other factors determining the shape of the marginal cost curve of each firm, and the effect of changes in industry output on input prices.

6.   Short-Run Equilibrium Price and Output for the Industry

The short-run equilibrium price level is the price at which the quantity demanded and the quantity supplied of the product in the short run are equal. For example, if the demand curve is DD' and the supply curve is SS' in Figure 8.4, the equilibrium price is OP and the equilibrium industry output is OQ, this point being the intersection of the demand and supply curves. Once enough time has elapsed for firms to adjust their utilization of the variable inputs, the price will tend to equal this equilibrium level, aside from the effects of certain factors that will be discussed in Section 12. If the price is above this equilibrium level, the quantity supplied will tend to exceed the quantity demanded, with the result that the price will tend to fall. If the price is below this equilibrium level, the quantity demanded will tend to exceed the quantity supplied, with the result that the price will tend to rise. There is no tendency for the price to move in one direction or the other if and only if it is at the equilibrium level.

---

[4]More will be said about the effect of industry output on individual cost curves in subsequent sections of this chapter. Note, too, that in this chapter (and the rest of this book) we go back to the conventional, rather than the linear programming, view of production.

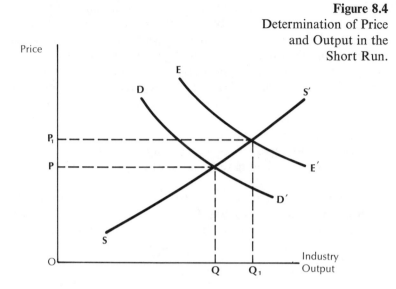

Figure 8.4
Determination of Price
and Output in the
Short Run.

At the equilibrium price, price will equal marginal cost for all firms that choose to produce, rather than shut down their plants. Price may be above or below average total cost, since there is no necessity that profits be zero or that fixed costs be covered in the short run. An increase in demand will increase equilibrium price and output in the short run. For example, suppose that demand shifts from DD' to EE' in Figure 8.4. The shift in the demand curve will cause a shortage at the old price, OP, the result being that the price will eventually be pushed up to OP_1. At the same time, each firm will adjust its output rate upward so that its marginal cost will equal the higher price, the result being that industry output will grow to OQ_1.

7. The Long-Run Adjustment Process

In the long run, the firm can change its plant size. This means that established firms may leave an industry if the industry has below-average profits, or that new firms may enter an industry if the industry has above-average profits. The next two sections are concerned with the long-run equilibrium of a perfectly competitive industry. We begin in this section by describing the adjustment process for an established firm.

Suppose that the firm has a plant with short-run average and marginal cost curves of A_0A_0' and M_0M_0', shown in Figure 8.5. Suppose that the

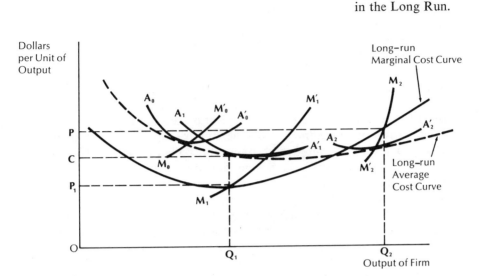

Figure 8.5
Change of Plant Size
in the Long Run.

price of the product is *OP*. With its existing plant the firm makes a small profit on each unit of output. However, in the long run, the firm is not limited to this plant. The firm could build a plant corresponding to any of the short-run cost curves in Figure 8.5. For example, it could build a medium-sized plant corresponding to short-run cost curves of $A_1 A_1'$ and $M_1 M_1'$, or it could build a large plant corresponding to short-run cost curves of $A_2 A_2'$ and $M_2 M_2'$. What will the firm do in the long run? If it attempts to maximize profit, it will choose to build the plant corresponding to short-run cost curves of $A_2 A_2'$ and $M_2 M_2'$. The maximum attainable profit under the postulated circumstances will be earned by using this plant and producing OQ_2 units of output per period of time.

In general, maximum profit will be obtained by producing at an output rate and with a plant such that the *long-run marginal cost is equal to price at the point where the short-run marginal cost of the plant is equal to price.* This, of course, is true at the output of OQ_2 units and with the plant corresponding to short-run cost curves $A_2 A_2'$ and $M_2 M_2'$ in Figure 8.5. The plant will be chosen so that long-run marginal cost equals price, since this clearly is a condition for profit maximization in the long run. To maximize profit, the firm will operate this plant at the point where short-run marginal cost equals price. Thus the equality of long-run marginal cost, short-run marginal cost, and price follows from the assumption of profit maximization. (See footnote 10, Chapter 6.)

If all firms in the industry except this one had plants of optimal size, the expansion of this one firm would have no significant influence on price. Consequently, since OP is greater than the average cost of producing OQ_2 units, all firms would be earning a profit. Recall from Chapter 6 that costs, as reckoned by economists (but not accountants), include the returns that could be gotten from the most lucrative alternative use of the firm's resources. Consequently, an *economic profit* means that the firm is making more than it could make with its resources in other industries. Of course, the existence of above-average profits in this industry attracts new entrants; when these new firms enter the industry, the adjustment process must go on.

The arrival of new entrants shifts the industry supply curve to the right. That is, more will be supplied at a given price than before. For example, suppose that the industry supply curve shifts from SS' to S_1S_1' in Figure 8.6, the result being that the price drops from OP to OP_1 and industry output increases from OQ to OQ_1. Although total industry output increases (because of the new entrants), the output of each of the firms is smaller. Given that the price is now OP_1 the optimal output of each firm is OQ_1, rather than OQ_2. (See Figure 8.5.) And the optimal plant is the one corresponding to the short-run cost curves A_1A_1' and M_1M_1'. Firms that have built plants corresponding to the short-run cost curves A_2A_2' and M_2M_2' will lose a great deal of money. But even those firms that are lucky enough to be able to switch to plants of optimal size (corresponding to the short-run cost curves A_1A_1' and M_1M_1') will lose P_1C dollars per unit.

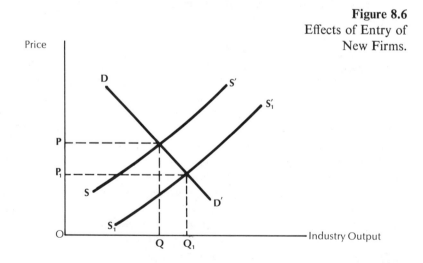

Figure 8.6
Effects of Entry of
New Firms.

This does not mean that the firms with the new plants of optimal size are not maximizing profits. On the contrary, it is evident from Figure 8.5 that, with the price at OP_1, long-run marginal cost equals short-run marginal cost equals price when the firm produces OQ_1 units of output with the plant corresponding to the short-run cost curves, A_1A_1' and M_1M_1'. Thus this is the profit-maximizing solution for the firm. The trouble is that, even if the firm does the best it can, it cannot make an economic profit. The result will be an out-migration of firms from the industry. Since the returns that could be obtained from the firm's resources are greater in other industries, entrepreneurs will transfer these resources to other industries. In this way, the adjustment process will go on, since the exit of the firms will shift the industry's supply curve to the left.

8. Long-Run Equilibrium of the Firm

When and where will this adjustment process end? Eventually, enough firms will leave the industry so that economic profits are eliminated, but losses are avoided, too. At this point the remaining firms will be in equilibrium. In other words, the long-run equilibrium position of the firm is at the point at which its long-run average total costs equal price. If price is in excess of average total costs for any firm, economic profits are being earned and new firms will enter the industry. If price is less than average total costs for any firm, that firm will eventually leave the industry.

Going a step further, we can show that price must be equal to the *lowest value* of long-run average total costs. In other words, firms must be producing at the minimum point on their long-run average cost curves. The reason for this is as follows: To maximize their profits, firms must operate where price equals long-run marginal cost. Also, we have just seen that they must operate where price equals long-run average cost. But if both of these conditions are satisfied, it follows that long-run marginal cost must equal long-run average cost. And we know from Chapter 6 that long-run marginal cost is equal to long-run average cost only at the point at which long-run average cost is a minimum. Thus this must be the equilibrium position of the firm.

This equilibrium position is illustrated in Figure 8.7. When all adjustments are made, price equals OB. Since the demand curve is horizontal, the marginal revenue curve is the same as the demand curve, both being *BB'*. The equilibrium output of the firm is *OV*, and its plant corresponds to short-run average and marginal cost curves, *AA'* and *MM'*. At this output and with this plant, long-run marginal cost equals short-run marginal cost equals price: This insures that the firm is maximizing profit. Also, long-run average cost equals short-run average cost equals price: This insures that economic profits are zero. Since the long-run marginal cost and long-run average cost must be equal, the equilibrium point is at the bottom of the long-run average cost curve.

Figure 8.7
Long-Run Equilibrium
of a Perfectly
Competitive Firm.

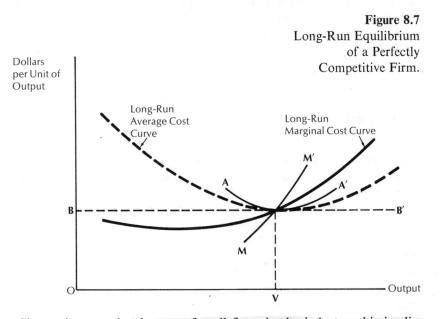

Since price must be the same for all firms in the industry, this implies that the minimum of the long-run average cost curve must be the same for all firms. However, this is not as unrealistic as it appears at first glance. Firms that appear to have lower costs than others in the industry often have unusually good resources or particularly able managements. The owners of superior resources (including management ability) can obtain a higher price for them if they are put to alternative uses than more ordinary resources. Consequently, the alternative costs, or implicit costs, of one's using superior resources are higher than those of using ordinary resources. If this is taken into account, and if these superior resources are costed properly, the firms with apparently lower costs have no lower costs at all.

9.   Constant Cost Industries

In the previous two sections, it was assumed implicitly that the industry exhibited "constant costs," which means that expansion of the industry does not result in an increase in input prices. Figure 8.8 shows long-run equilibrium under conditions of constant cost. The left-hand panel shows the short- and long-run cost curves of a typical firm in the industry. The right-hand panel shows the demand and supply curves in the market as a whole, DD' being the original demand curve and SS' being the original short-run supply curve. It is assumed that the industry is in long-run equilibrium, with the result that the price line is tangent to the long-run (and short-run) average cost curve at its minimum point (OP being the price).

Assume now that the demand curve shifts to D_1D_1'. In the short run, with the number of firms fixed, the price of the product will rise from OP to OP_1; each firm will expand output from OQ to OQ_1; and each firm will be making economic profits since OP_1 exceeds the short-run average costs of the firm at OQ_1. The consequence is that firms will enter the industry

Figure 8.8
Long-Run Equilibrium:
Constant Cost Industry.

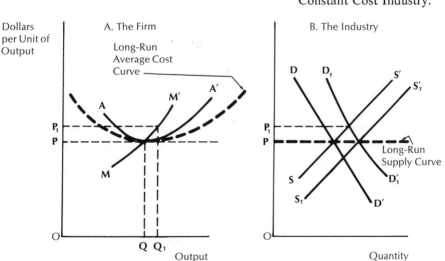

and shift the supply curve to the right. In the case of a constant cost industry, the entrance of the new firms does not affect the costs of the existing firms. The inputs used by this industry are used by many other industries as well, and the appearance of the new firms in this industry does not bid up the price of inputs and consequently raise the costs of existing firms. Neither does the appearance of the new firms lower the costs of existing firms.

Consequently, *a constant cost industry has a horizontal long-run supply curve.* Since output can be increased by increasing the number of firms producing OQ units at an average cost of OP, the long-run supply curve is horizontal at OP. So long as the industry remains in a state of constant costs, its output can be increased indefinitely. If price exceeds OP, firms would enter the industry; if price were less than OP, firms would leave the industry. Thus long-run equilibrium can only occur in this industry when price is OP. And industry output can be expanded or contracted, in accord with demand conditions, without altering this long-run equilibrium price.

10.   Increasing and Decreasing Cost Industries

An increasing cost industry is shown in Figure 8.9. The original conditions are the same as in Figure 8.8, DD' being the original demand curve, SS' being the original supply curve, OP being the equilibrium price and the long-run and short-run average cost curves of each firm being LL' and AA' in the left panel. As in Figure 8.8, the original position is one of long-run equilibrium, since the price line is tangent to the average cost curves at their minima.

Now suppose that the demand curve shifts to D_1D_1', the result being that the price of the product increases and firms earn economic profits, thus attracting new entrants. More and more inputs are required by the industry, and in an increasing cost industry, the price of inputs increases with the amount used by the industry. Consequently, the cost of inputs increases for the established firms as well as the new entrants, the average cost curves being pushed up to L_1L_1' and A_1A_1'.

If the marginal cost curve of each firm is shifted to the left by the increase in input prices, the industry supply curve will also tend to shift to the left. However, this tendency is more than counterbalanced by the effects of the increase in the number of firms, which shifts the industry supply curve to the right. The latter effect must more than offset the former effect because otherwise there would be no expansion in total industry output. (No new

Figure 8.9
Long-Run Equilibrium:
Increasing Cost Industry.

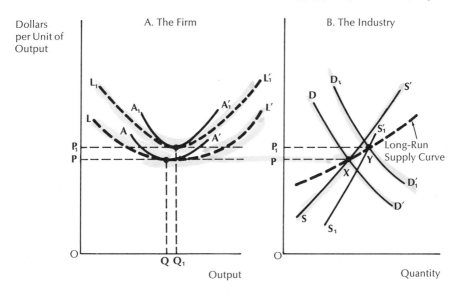

resources would have been attracted to the industry.) The process of adjustment must go on until a new point of long-run equilibrium is reached. In
Figure 8.9, this point is where the price of the product is OP_1 and each firm
produces OQ_1 units, the new short-run supply curve being S_1S_1'.

An increasing cost industry has a positively sloped long-run supply curve.
That is, after long-run equilibrium is achieved, increases in output require
increases in the price of the product. For example, points X and Y in Figure 8.9 are both on the long-run supply curve for this industry. The difference between constant cost and increasing cost industries is as follows: In
constant cost industries, new firms enter in response to an increase in demand
until price returns to its original level; whereas in increasing cost industries,
new firms enter until the minimum point on the long-run cost curve has
increased to the point where it equals the new price.

A decreasing cost industry is shown in Figure 8.10. Once again, we begin
with an industry in long-run equilibrium, the demand curve being DD', the
short-run supply curve being SS', price being OP, and the long-run and
short-run average cost curves of each firm being LL' and AA'. As before,
we postulate an increase in demand to D_1D_1', the result being economic
profit for established firms and the entry of new firms. However, in the case
of a decreasing cost industry, the expansion of the industry results in a de-

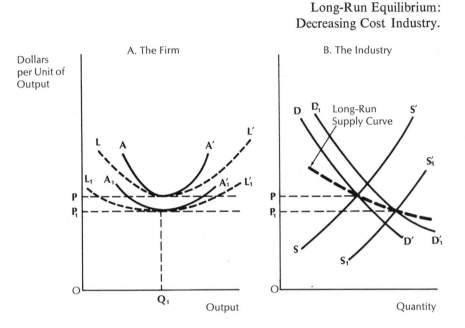

Figure 8.10
Long-Run Equilibrium:
Decreasing Cost Industry.

crease in the costs of the established firms. Thus, the new long-run equilibrium is at a price of OP_1, the equilibrium output of each firm being OQ_1, and the new long-run and short-run average cost curves being L_1L_1' and A_1A_1'.

A decreasing cost industry has a negatively sloped long-run supply curve. That is, after long-run equilibrium is reached, increases in output are accompanied by decreases in price. *External economies,* which are cost reductions that occur when the industry expands, may be responsible for the existence of decreasing cost industries. An example of an external economy is an improvement in transportation that is due to the expansion of an industry and that reduces the costs of each firm in the industry. If there are important external economies, an industry may be subject to decreasing costs. Note that external economies are quite different from economies of scale: The individual firm has no control over external economies.

Most economists seem to regard increasing cost industries as being the most frequently encountered of the three types. Decreasing cost industries are the most unusual situation, although quite young industries may fall into this category. In Section 13, we present estimates of the shape of the long-run supply curve in various industries.

11. The Allocation Process: Short and Long Run

At this point, it is instructive to describe the process by which a perfectly competitive economy—an economy composed of perfectly competitive industries—would allocate resources. In Chapter 1, we noted that the allocation of resources among alternative uses is one of the major functions of an economic system. Equipped with the concepts of this and previous chapters, we can now go much farther than we could in Chapter 1 in describing how a perfectly competitive economy goes about shifting resources in accord with changes in consumer demand.

To be specific, suppose that a change occurs in tastes, consumers being more favorably disposed toward corn and less favorably disposed toward potatoes than in the past. What will happen in the short run? The increase in the demand for corn increases the price of corn, and results in some increase in the output of corn. However, the output of corn cannot be increased very substantially because the capacity of the industry cannot be expanded in the short run. Similarly, the fall in the demand for potatoes reduces the price of potatoes, and results in some reduction in the output of potatoes. But the output of potatoes will not be curtailed greatly because firms will continue to produce as long as they can cover variable costs.

The change in the relative prices of corn and potatoes tells producers that a reallocation of resources is called for. Because of the increase in the price of corn and the decrease in the price of potatoes, corn producers are earning economic profits and potato producers are showing economic losses. This will trigger a redeployment of resources. If some variable inputs in the production of potatoes can be used as effectively in the production of corn, these variable inputs may be withdrawn from potato production and switched to corn production. Even if there are no variable inputs that are used in both corn and potato production, adjustment can occur in various interrelated markets, with the result that corn production gains resources and potato production loses resources.

When short-run equilibrium is attained in both the corn and potato industries, the reallocation of resources is not yet complete since there has not been enough time for producers to build new capacity or liquidate old capacity. In particular neither. industry is operating at minimum average cost. The corn producers are operating at greater than the output level where average cost is a minimum; and the potato producers are operating at less than the output level where average cost is a minimum.

What will happen in the long run? The shift in consumer demand from potatoes to corn will result in greater adjustments in production and smaller adjustments in price than in the short run. In the long run, existing firms can leave potato production and new firms can enter corn production. Because of short-run economic losses in potato production, some potato land and related equipment will be allowed to run down, and some firms engaged in potato production will be liquidated. As firms leave potato production, the supply curve shifts to the left, causing the price to rise above its short-run level. The transfer of resources out of potato production will stop when the price has increased, and costs have decreased, to the point where losses are avoided.

While potato production is losing resources, corn production is gaining them. The short-run economic profits in corn production will result in the entry of new firms. The increased demand for inputs will raise input prices and cost curves in corn production, and the price of corn will be depressed by the movement to the right of the supply curve because of the entry of new firms. Entry ceases when economic profits are no longer being earned. At that point, when long-run equilibrium is achieved, there will be more firms and more resources used in the industry than in the short run.

Finally, long-run equilibrium is established in both industries, and the reallocation of resources is complete. It is important to note that this reallocation can affect industries other than corn and potatoes. If potato land and equipment can be easily adapted to the production of corn, which seems unlikely, potato producers can simply change to the production of corn. If not, the resources used in potato production are converted to some use other than corn, and the resources that enter corn production come from some use other than potato production. The full repercussions can be analyzed by general equilibrium analysis, which is discussed in Chapter 14.

12.   The Path to Equilibrium and the Cobweb Theorem

A great deal of attention has been devoted in this chapter to the equilibrium levels of price and output. However, disequilibrium, rather than equilibrium, has to be the usual state of most real-life markets. Demand curves are constantly shifting in response to changes in tastes and incomes, among other things. Supply curves are constantly shifting in response to changes in technology and resource limitations, among other things. Thus the equilibrium levels of prices are constantly changing, and actual prices differ from them. It is important to recognize the importance of disequilibrium but it would be a mistake to conclude from this that theories based on equilibrium prices are of no use. On the contrary, equilibrium theories help us to predict the direction of change of price and output. With careful study one can sometimes say a good deal about the way in which price and output are likely to move.

To illustrate how actual price may converge on the equilibrium price, consider one of the simplest dynamic models[5] in economics, the cobweb model or theorem.[6] Suppose that the amount supplied of a commodity, say hogs, is a function of price in the *previous* period. This might be the case because it takes one period to raise a hog. On the other hand, suppose that the amount demanded of the commodity is a function of price in the *present* period. Finally, suppose that the demand and supply functions are DD' and SS' in Figure 8.11 and OP_0 was the price in the previous period.

Under these assumptions, the amount supplied in the first period will be OQ_1. But given that OQ_1 is supplied, the demand curve shows that the price will be OP_1 in the first period. With this price in the first period, the supply curve shows that the amount supplied in the second period will be OQ_2. And with OQ_2 as the amount supplied in the second period, the demand curve

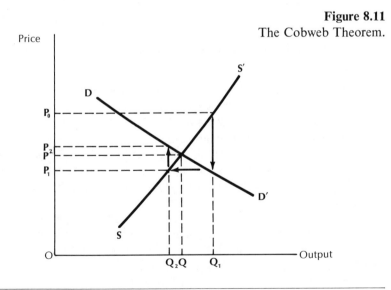

Figure 8.11

The Cobweb Theorem.

[5]Dynamic models indicate the movement over a period of time of economic variables and the way in which such variables move from one equilibrium to another (or one disequilibrium to another).
[6]The name, "cobweb," is derived from the appearance of diagrams like Figure 8.11.

shows that the price in the second period will be OP_2. This process will go on and on, price and output each moving in a cycle. In one period, price is above the equilibrium level, the result being that the quantity supplied in the next period is above the equilibrium level. Because quantity is then above the equilibrium level, price will be below the equilibrium level. And so on.

In the case described in Figure 8.11, the process converges, the actual price and output becoming closer and closer to the equilibrium levels, OP and OQ. This is because the supply curve is steeper than the demand curve. If the slopes of the demand and supply curves are equal (in absolute value), the cycles of price and output continue undiminished. If the demand curve is steeper than the supply curve, the amplitude of the cycles increases over time.

Although the cobweb model is extremely simple and mechanical, it may be of use in explaining why the prices and outputs of some commodities have shown pronounced cyclical movements. Jan Tinbergen of the Netherlands, a recent Nobel laureate, has suggested that this model may be relevant in explaining the patterns of hog prices. Clearly, however, the cobweb theorem is a very simple model that captures only a limited amount of the richness of the real world.

13.   Estimates of Elasticity of Supply

Previous sections of this chapter have dealt at length with the role of demand curves and supply curves, both short-run and long-run, in the determination of price. Chapter 4 presented the results of various empirical studies of the demand curve for selected commodities. In this section we present the results of various empirical studies of the supply curve for selected commodities. The econometric techniques used to estimate the supply curve are much like those used to estimate the demand curve, which were discussed in Chapter 4.

To illustrate the kind of studies that have been carried out, consider the investigation by George Dean and Earl Heady of the elasticity of supply of hog production in the United States.[7] They analyzed data concerning hog production, hog prices, and other variables in the United States during 1924–1937 and 1938–1956. Holding constant the effects of other variables (like the price of corn, which is important), they found a significant relation-

---

[7]See G. Dean and E. Heady, "Changes in Supply Response and Elasticity of Hogs," *Journal of Farm Economics*, Nov. 1958.

ship between hog price and hog production, the elasticity of supply (in the spring farrowing period) being 0.60 in 1938–1956 and 0.50 in 1924–1937. According to Dean and Heady, technological change may have resulted in the increase in the elasticity of supply, producers now being able to increase (decrease) spring production more easily in response to price increases (decreases) than formerly.

Of course, there is a considerable difference between short-run and long-run elasticities of supply. Marc Nerlove and William Addison have estimated short-run and long-run elasticities of supply for a number of vegetables produced for fresh market in the United States during 1919–1955. The short-run elasticity is defined to be the elasticity over one production period. The results are shown in Table 8.1.[8] Note that the short-run elasticities are

Table 8.1.   Estimated Elasticities of Supply.

	PRICE ELASTICITY	
COMMODITY	SHORT RUN	LONG RUN
Green lima beans	0.10	1.70
Green snap beans	0.15	∞*
Cabbage	0.36	1.20
Carrots	0.14	1.00
Cucumbers	0.29	2.20
Lettuce	0.03	0.16
Onions	0.34	1.00
Green peas	0.31	4.40
Green peppers	0.07	0.26
Tomatoes	0.16	0.90
Watermelons	0.23	0.48
Beets	0.13	1.00
Cantalopes	0.02	0.04
Cauliflower	0.14	1.10
Celery	0.14	0.95
Eggplant	0.16	0.34
Kale (Va. only)	0.20	0.23
Spinach	0.20	4.70
Shallots (La. only)	0.12	0.31

*According to Nerlove and Addison, this estimate holds only for a limited range of output.

[8] M. Nerlove and W. Addison, "Statistical Estimation of Long-Run Elasticities of Supply and Demand," *Journal of Farm Economics*, Nov. 1958.

considerably lower than the long-run elasticities, as would be expected. For example, the short-run elasticity of supply for cabbage is estimated to be 0.36, whereas the long-run elasticity is estimated to be 1.2. According to these estimates the long-run elasticity of supply is greater for cucumbers, green peas, and spinach than for the other commodities. Although these estimates are based on quite sophisticated techniques, Nerlove and Addison caution that they are tentative and presented mainly for purposes of illustration.

14. The Cotton Textile Industry: A Case Study[9]

The cotton textile industry has been described as being closer to perfect competition than any other manufacturing industry in the United States. The industry's major product, gray cotton print cloth, can be viewed as homogeneous. Many buyers and sellers exist, no one of which is big enough to influence the price. Entry into the industry is not difficult. Looking at the cotton textile industry during the interwar period, how closely did its behavior accord with the theory presented in this chapter?

Considerable excess capacity existed in the cotton textile industry from about 1924 to 1936. Evidence of this over-capacity is presented in Table 8.2, which shows that the profit rate in cotton textiles was considerably below

Table 8.2. Profits as a Percent of Capitalization, Cotton Textile Industry and All Manufacturing, 1919–1936.

PERIOD	COTTON TEXTILES	ALL MANUFACTURING
1919–1923	15.3	11.0
1924–1928	4.7	11.0
1933–1936	2.4	4.3

Source: Lloyd Reynolds, "Competition in the Cotton Textile Industry," in W. Adams and D. Traywick, *Readings in Economics*, New York: Macmillan, 1948.

[9]This section is based largely on L. Reynolds, "Competition in the Textile Industry," in W. Adams and L. Traywick (ed.), *Readings in Economics*, New York: Macmillan, 1948. K. Cohen and R. Cyert, *Theory of the Firm*, Englewood Cliffs, N.J.: Prentice-Hall, 1965, pp. 157–59, have also drawn on Reynolds' paper and used it in a similar way.

that in other manufacturing. For example, during 1924–1928 and 1933–1936, textile profits averaged less than 4 percent of the firms' capitalization, whereas profits as a percent of capitalization in all manufacturing averaged 8 percent. It is also important to note that profit rates in cotton textiles were higher in the South than in the North. Profits in the South averaged 6 percent, whereas profits in the North averaged 1 percent. This was due to the fact that the prices of many inputs—like labor and raw cotton—were lower in the South.

If we are given a situation of this sort, what would the perfectly competitive model predict? Clearly, the industry was not in long-run equilibrium, since the industry was not earning as great a return as other manufacturing industries and the returns obtained by mills in the South were greater than those obtained by mills in the North. What sort of changes would be required to make the industry approach long-run equilibrium? First, many firms would have to leave the industry, until eventually the profit rate in cotton textiles would increase to the point at which it approximated the profit rate in other industries. Second, the industry would tend to become concentrated more heavily in the South, the exit rate being higher in the North than in the South. It should be obvious from previous sections that the model would predict these two occurrences.

In fact, did the industry perform as expected on the basis of the model? According to careful studies of the industry's history during this period, the answer is yes. Under the pressure of economic losses, elimination of weaker firms proceeded steadily, the total number of spindles falling from a peak of 38 million in 1925 to 27 million in 1938. Moreover, the chief loser of capacity was the North, not the South. As one observer put it, "Competition has thus performed, though tardily and haphazardly, its traditional function of adjusting productive capacity to effective demand."[10]

15. Agricultural Prices and Output: An Application

Perhaps the most important sector of the American economy that contains industries that are reasonably close to perfect competition is agriculture. Farming is still our most important single industry, although it includes a much smaller percentage of our people than it once did. One of the most important points to note about American agriculture is that agricultural

---

[10]L. Reynolds, *ibid.*, p. 151.

prices have generally been falling, relative to other prices, in the past 60 years. That is, if we correct for changes in the general price level resulting from over-all inflation, there has been a declining trend in farm prices. Another important fact is that farm incomes vary between good times and bad to a much greater extent than nonfarm incomes, whereas farm output is much more stable than industrial output.

The theory presented in this and previous chapters is useful in explaining the reasons for these characteristics of American agriculture. Figure 8.12 shows the demand and supply curves for farm products at various points in time. Since we know from Chapter 4 that the demand for food does not grow very rapidly in this country, we would expect the demand curve to shift relatively slowly to the right, from DD' in the first period to D_1D_1' in the second period to D_2D_2' in the third period. On the other hand, because of very great technological improvements in agriculture, the supply curve has been shifting relatively rapidly to the right, from SS' in the first period to S_1S_1' in the second period to S_2S_2' in the third period. The consequence is that agriculture prices have fallen (relative to other prices) from OP to OP_1 to OP_2.

Figure 8.12
Shifts in Demand and
Supply: Agriculture.

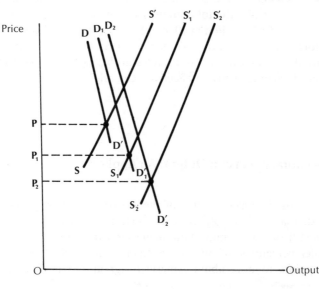

It is also easy to see why farm incomes are so unstable. We know from Chapter 4 that the demand curve for basic farm products is relatively inelastic. Also, the supply curve for basic farm products is relatively inelastic in the short run. Since both the demand curve and the supply curve are inelastic, a small shift (to the right or left) in either curve, or both, results in a large change in price. To illustrate, consider Figure 8.13. In panel A, the demand and supply curves are much less elastic than in panel B, the result being that a small shift in the demand curve results in a much bigger change in price in panel A than in panel B.[11]

Figure 8.13
Relationship between
Elasticity of Supply
and Demand and
Instability of Price.

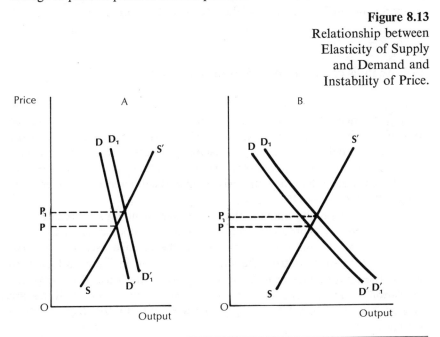

---

[11]For simplicity, suppose that the demand and supply curves exhibit the same elasticity at each point, in which case

$$Q_D = \alpha_0 P^{-\beta_0} \tag{8.1}$$
$$Q_S = \alpha_1 P^{\beta_1} \tag{8.2}$$

where P is price, Q_D the quantity demanded, and Q_S the quantity supplied. Equation 8.1 is the demand function, β_0 being the price elasticity of demand. Equation 8.2 is the supply function, β_1 being the price elasticity of supply. Suppose that the demand curve shifted slightly, α_0 increasing or decreasing by a small amount. What would be the effect on the equilibrium price? Suppose that the supply curve shifted slightly, α_1 increasing or decreasing by a small amount. What would be the effect on the equilibrium price?

Another important fact about American agriculture that must be added to this picture is government intervention and aid. Both Figures 8.12 and 8.13 are based on the supposition that agricultural markets are free. For about half of all farm products, the government has price "support" programs of one sort or another. These programs vary in many respects, but the general idea behind them is that the federal government tries to increase farm prices in various ways. For products where such programs exist, the perfectly competitive model is clearly an inappropriate device to predict price and output. But, as we shall see in the next section, the basic elements of the theory remain useful in analyzing the effects of these programs.

16. Analysis of Government Subsidy Programs

More specifically, these programs can be described in terms of Figure 8.14. A support price, OP', is set which is above the equilibrium price, OP, the consequence being that output equals OQ_1, consumers buy OQ_2, and the rest (which equals $OQ_1 - OQ_2$) must be purchased by the government. The imposition of the support price means, of course, that farmers receive more for their crop than they otherwise would, the difference in their receipts being $OP' \times OQ_1 - OP \times OQ$.

To cut down on the amount that the government must purchase (and store or dispose of), production controls may be imposed as well. These controls often take the form of quotas on the acreage used to grow the product. With such controls the situation is shown in Figure 8.15, where OQ_3 is the total quota—in terms of output—for all farms. Because of the imposition of the production control, the government's expenditures are reduced from $OP' \times (OQ_1 - OQ_2)$ in Figure 8.14 to $OP'(OQ_3 - OQ_2)$ in Figure 8.15.

Since $Q_D = Q_S (= Q)$ in equilibrium, it follows from Equations 8.1 and 8.2 that

$$\log P = \frac{\log \alpha_0 - \log \alpha_1}{\beta_0 + \beta_1}$$

Thus,

$$\frac{dP}{P} \div \frac{d\alpha_0}{\alpha_0} = \frac{1}{\beta_0 + \beta_1}$$

$$\frac{dP}{P} \div \frac{d\alpha_1}{\alpha_1} = \frac{-1}{\beta_0 + \beta_1}$$

Consequently, as stated in the text, the relative change in price resulting from a small relative change in α_0 or α_1 is bigger if β_0 and β_1 are small than if β_0 or β_1 is large.

Figure 8.14
Effect of Price Support.

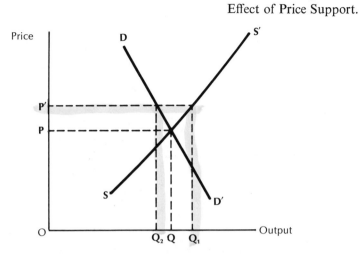

An alternative plan, proposed by President Truman's Secretary of Agriculture, Charles Brannan, and President Eisenhower's Secretary, Ezra Taft Benson, can be illustrated by Figure 8.16. According to this plan, farmers are still guaranteed the price of OP', but rather than allow the amount the government buys (which equals $OQ_3 - OQ_2$) to waste in storage, they

Figure 8.15
Effect of Price Support
and Production Control.

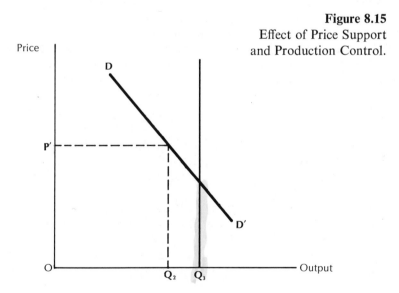

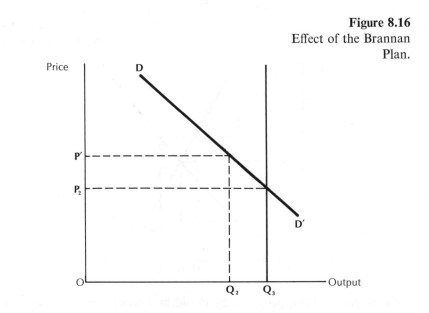

Figure 8.16
Effect of the Brannan
Plan.

would sell this amount at whatever consumers would pay for it. Or, what amounts to the same thing, they would let the competitive market alone, the result being that an output of OQ_3 would be produced and sold at a price of OP_2; then they would have the government issue subsidy checks to farmers to cover the difference between the price they received and the support price, OP'.

Clearly, the cost to the government under the Brannan plan would be $(OP' - OP_2) \times OQ_3$. An important question is: Will the cost to the Treasury be greater than under the support plan shown in Figure 8.15? The answer depends on the elasticity of demand. If demand is inelastic, it will be greater; if demand is elastic, it will be smaller. To prove this, recall that the cost under the Brannan plan would be $(OP' - OP_2)OQ_3$, and the cost in Figure 8.15 would be $OP'(OQ_3 - OQ_2)$. Thus the former cost would be less than the latter if $OP_2 \times OQ_3 > OP' \times OQ_2$. But since $OP_2 \times OQ_3$ is the revenue at price OP_2 and $OP' \times OQ_2$ is the revenue at price OP', the former will be more than the latter only if the elasticity of demand exceeds one.

Since the demand for agricultural products is generally inelastic, this means that the Brannan plan would cost the Treasury more than the support plan in Figure 8.15. But this is not a necessarily overwhelming argument against the Brannan plan. It should be recalled that the total cost to the consumers and taxpayers together is the same in each case, although the burden on low- and high-income groups is likely to be different. More will be.said about the economic advantages and disadvantages of various types of agricultural price support plans in Chapter 15, where we continue this discussion of agricultural subsidies.

17. Summary

Perfect competition is defined by four conditions: No participant in the market can influence price; output must be homogeneous; resources must be mobile; and there must be perfect knowledge. In the market period, where the quantity supplied is fixed, the price of a product is demand-determined. In the short run the firm maximizes profit or minimizes losses by producing the output at which marginal cost equals price. However, if market price is less than the firm's average variable costs at all levels of output, the firm will minimize losses by discontinuing production. The firm's short-run supply curve is the same as its marginal cost curve, as long as price exceeds average variable cost.

The short-run price of a product is determined by the interaction between the demand and supply sides of the market. As a rough approximation, the industry's short-run supply curve can be regarded as the horizontal summation of the short-run supply curves of the individual firms. However, this is not the case if the supply of inputs to the industry is not perfectly elastic. The short-run equilibrium price level is the price at which the quantity demanded and the quantity supplied in the short run are equal. At the equilibrium price, price will equal marginal cost for all firms that choose to produce, rather than shut down their plants.

In the long run, firms can change their plant size and leave or enter the industry. The long-run equilibrium position of the firm is at the point at which its long-run average costs equal price. Moreover, firms must be operating at the minimum point on their long-run average cost curves. Industries can be divided into three types: constant cost, increasing cost, and decreasing cost. Constant cost industries have horizontal long-run supply curves; increasing cost industries have positively sloped long-run supply curves; and decreasing cost industries have negatively sloped long-run supply curves. Increasing cost industries are generally regarded as being the most numerous of the three types.

Having presented this basic theory, we described the way in which resources are allocated in a perfectly competitive economy. Then we discussed the process by which actual price may converge on the equilibrium price, using as an illustration the cobweb model. Next we presented estimates of the elasticity of supply for a number of commodities. Finally, after a brief case study of the cotton textile industry, we used the theory to explain some of the characteristics of American agriculture and to analyze government subsidy programs.

SELECTED REFERENCES

Knight, Frank, *Risk, Uncertainty, and Profit*, London School Reprints of Scarce Works, No. 16, 1933.

Marshall, Alfred, *Principles of Economics*, London: Macmillan, 1920.

American Economic Association, *Readings in Price Theory*, edited by George Stigler and Kenneth Boulding, Homewood: Richard D. Irwin, 1952.

Smith, Vernon, "An Experimental Study of Competitive Market Behavior," *Journal of Political Economy*, April 1962.

Samuelson, Paul, *Foundations of Economic Analysis*, Cambridge: Harvard University Press, 1947. (Advanced)

9

Price and Output under Pure Monopoly

1. Pure Monopoly

Most Americans are familiar with the word *monopoly*. On rainy afternoons, children in the United States often play a game called Monopoly in which they try hard to become the sole owners of related pieces of property. (According to the rules of the game, the amount that a player can get from the other players is greater if he is the sole owner of related pieces of property.) Whether or not you have ever played this game, the concept of a monopoly is probably familiar: A monopoly is a situation where there is a single source of supply.

In microeconomics, pure monopoly, like perfect competition, is a useful model. The conditions defining pure monopoly are easy to state: There must exist one, and only one, seller in a market. Pure monopoly, like perfect competition, does not correspond more than approximately to conditions in real industries. But, as we have noted several times before, a model must be judged by its predictive ability, not the "realism" of its assumptions. The theory of pure monopoly has proved to be a very useful analytical device.

253

Pure monopoly and perfect competition are opposites in the following sense: The firm in a perfectly competitive market has so many rivals that competition becomes impersonal in the extreme; the firm under pure monopoly has no rivals at all. Under pure monopoly, one firm is the sole supplier. There is no competition.

Having said this, it is important to add that the policies adopted by a pure monopolist are affected by certain indirect and potential forms of competition. Clearly, the monopolist is not completely insulated from the effects of actions taken in the rest of the economy. All commodities are rivals for the consumer's favor, as we saw in Chapter 2: Clearly this rivalry occurs among different products, as well as among the producers of a given commodity. For example, meat competes in this sense with butter, eggs, and even men's suits. Of course, the extent of the competition from other products depends on the extent to which other products are substitutes for the monopolist's product. For example, even if a firm somehow could obtain a monopoly on the supply of steel in a particular market, it would still face considerable competition from producers of aluminum, plastics, and other materials that are reasonably good substitutes for steel.

In addition, the threat of potential competition also acts as a brake on the policies of the monopolist. The monopolist often can maintain his monopoly position only if he does not extract as much short-run profit as possible. If he sets prices above a certain point, other firms may enter his market and try to break his monopoly. If entry can occur, the monopolist must take this possibility into account. Failure to do so may make him an ex-monopolist.

2. Reasons for Monopoly

Why do monopolies arise? There are many reasons, but four seem particularly important. First, a single firm may control the entire supply of a basic input that is required to manufacture a given product. The example that is cited repeatedly to illustrate this situation is the pre-war aluminum industry. Bauxite is an input used to produce aluminum; and for some time, practically every source of bauxite in the United States was controlled by the Aluminum Company of America (Alcoa). For this reason (and others), Alcoa was, for a long time, the sole producer of aluminum in the United States. More will be said about the case of Alcoa in Section 16.

Second, a firm may become a monopolist because the average cost of producing the product reaches a minimum at an output rate that is big enough to satisfy the entire market at a price that is profitable. In a situation of this sort, if there is more than one firm producing the product, each must be producing at a higher-than-minimum level of average cost. Each may be inclined to cut the price to increase its output rate and reduce its average costs. The result is likely to be economic warfare—and the survival of a single victor, the monopolist. Cases in which costs behave in this fashion are called "natural monopolies." When an industry is a "natural monopoly," the public often insists that its behavior be regulated by the government.

Third, a firm may acquire a monopoly over the production of a good by having patents on the product or on certain basic processes that are used in its production. The patent laws of the United States permit an inventor to get the exclusive right to make a certain product or to use a particular process, the patent being in force for 17 years. Patents can be very important in keeping competitors out. For example, Aloca held important patents on basic production processes used to make aluminum. However, it is often possible to "invent around" another company's patents. That is, although a firm cannot use a product or process on which another firm has a patent (without the latter's permission), it may be able to develop a closely related product or process and obtain a patent on it. Further discussion of the patent system is contained in Chapter 16.

Fourth, a firm may become a monopolist because it is awarded a market franchise by a government agency. The firm is granted the exclusive privilege to produce a given good or service in a particular area. In exchange for this right, the firm agrees to allow the government to regulate certain aspects of its behavior and operations. For example, as we shall see in Section 15, the government may set the firm's price. Regardless of the form of regulation, the important point is that the monopoly has been created by the government.

3. The Monopolist's Demand Curve

Since the monopolist is the only firm producing a product, it is obvious that the monopolist's demand curve is precisely the same as the demand curve for the product. Consequently, the factors determining the shape of the monopolist's demand curve are the same factors that determine the shape of the demand curve for the product. As we saw in Chapter 4 these factors are the prices of other related products (substitutes and complements),

incomes, and tastes. However, it should be noted that the monopolist sometimes can affect the prices of related products, as well as consumer tastes.
To influence consumer tastes, monopolists often make considerable expenditures on advertising, the purpose being, of course, to shift the demand
curve to the right or to make it more inelastic.

Since the monopolist's demand curve is negatively sloped (because the
demand curve for a product is negatively sloped, save for a few cases of
little significance), average and marginal revenue are not the same. This
is quite different from the case of perfect competition where average and
marginal revenue were equal. To illustrate the situation faced by a monopolist, consider the hypothetical case in Table 9.1. The price at which each

Table 9.1.   Demand and Revenue of a Monopolist.

QUANTITY	PRICE	TOTAL REVENUE	MARGINAL REVENUE*
3	$100.00	$ 300.00	—
8	80.00	640.00	$68.0 $(= \frac{340}{5})$
15	74.00	1110.00	67.1 $(= \frac{470}{7})$
21	70.00	1470.00	60.0 $(= \frac{360}{6})$
26	67.50	1755.00	57.0 $(= \frac{285}{5})$
30	65.50	1965.00	52.5 $(= \frac{210}{4})$
33	62.00	2046.00	27.0 $(= \frac{81}{3})$
35	60.00	2100.00	27.0 $(= \frac{54}{2})$

*These figures pertain to the interval between the indicated quantity
of output and one unit less than the indicated quantity of output.

quantity (shown in column 1) can be sold is shown in column 2. The total
revenue, the product of the first two columns, is shown in column 3. Obviously, the average revenue corresponding to each output is the price
corresponding to that output.

Marginal revenue is of great importance to the profit-maximizing firm.
How can we estimate marginal revenue from the figures in Table 9.1?
Marginal revenue between q and $(q - 1)$ units of output is defined as
$R(q) - R(q - 1)$, where $R(q)$ is the total revenue when the output equals q.
The problem in Table 9.1 is that the data are not provided for each level of
output; we only have data for $q = 3, 8, 15$, and so on. To cope with this
problem, we assume that $R(q)$ is approximately a linear function of q between 3 and 8, 8 and 15, 15 and 21, and so on. If this is the case, the marginal
revenue is ($640 - $300) ÷ 5 at an output of between 7 and 8, ($1110 -
$640) ÷ 7 at an output of between 14 and 15, and so forth. The results are
shown in the last column of Table 9.1.

4. The Monopolist's Costs

Although a firm is a monopolist in the product market, it may be a perfect competitor in the market for inputs, in which case it buys so small a proportion of the total supply of each input that it cannot affect input prices. If this is the case, there is no need to dwell further on the monopolist's costs, since the theory in Chapter 6 will apply without modification.

In many cases, however, the monopolist is not a perfect competitor in the input markets, because it buys a large proportion of certain specialized resources that have little use other than to produce the commodity in question. In a case of this sort, the price that the firm has to pay for this input depends on how much it buys. The more the firm wants of this resource, the more it will generally have to pay. Cases of this sort are discussed at some length in Chapter 13. In the present chapter we assume that the firm is a perfect competitor in the market for inputs.

Table 9.2 shows the costs of our hypothetical monopolist. Column 1

Table 9.2 Costs of a Monopolist.

OUTPUT	TOTAL VARIABLE COST	FIXED COST	TOTAL COST	MARGINAL COST*
0	$ 0	$500	$ 500	—
3	110	500	610	$ 36.67 $(= \frac{110}{3})$
8	240	500	740	26.00 $(= \frac{130}{5})$
15	390	500	890	21.43 $(= \frac{150}{7})$
21	560	500	1060	28.33 $(= \frac{170}{6})$
26	750	500	1250	38.00 $(= \frac{190}{5})$
30	960	500	1460	52.50 $(= \frac{210}{4})$
33	1190	500	1690	76.67 $(= \frac{230}{3})$
35	1440	500	1940	125.00 $(= \frac{250}{2})$

*These figures pertain to the interval between the indicated quantity of output and one unit less than the indicated quantity of output.

shows various output rates, column 2 shows the total variable cost at each output rate, and column 3 shows the firm's fixed costs. Finally, column 4 shows the firm's total cost at each output rate, and column 5 shows the firm's marginal costs.

5.   Short-Run Equilibrium Price and Output

If the monopolist is unregulated and free to maximize profits, he will, of course, choose the price and output at which the difference between total revenue and total cost is largest. For example, combining the data from Tables 9.1 and 9.2 into Table 9.3, we find that our hypothetical monopolist

Table 9.3.   Cost, Revenue, and Profit of Monopolist.

OUTPUT	TOTAL REVENUE	TOTAL COST	TOTAL PROFIT
3	$ 300	$ 610	$−310
8	640	740	−100
15	1110	890	220
21	1470	1060	310
26	1755	1250	505
30	1965	1460	505
33	2046	1690	356
35	2100	1940	160

will choose an output rate of either 26 or 30 units per time period and a price of $65.50 or $67.50. Figure 9.1 shows the situation graphically.

Note that either of these optimal output rates is less than the output rate where price equals marginal cost. Under perfect competition, the profit-maximizing output was the one at which price equals marginal cost; indeed,

Table 9.4.   Marginal Cost and Marginal Revenue of Monopolist.

OUTPUT	MARGINAL COST*	MARGINAL REVENUE*	TOTAL PROFIT
3	$ 36.7	—	$−310
8	26.0	$68.0	−100
15	21.4	67.1	220
21	28.3	60.0	310
26	38.0	57.0	505
30	52.5	52.5	505
33	76.7	27.0	356
35	125.0	27.0	160

*These figures pertain to the interval between the indicated quantity of output and one unit less than the indicated quantity of output.

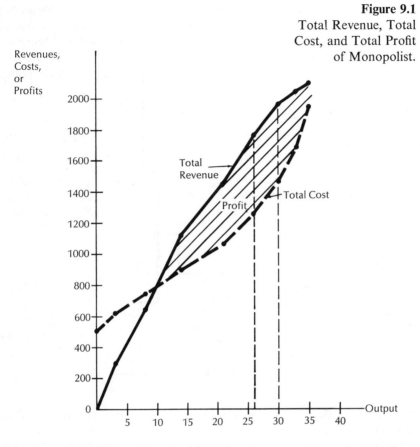

Figure 9.1
Total Revenue, Total
Cost, and Total Profit
of Monopolist.

this fact was used to derive the firm's supply curve. It is obvious from Tables 9.1 and 9.2 that this result is not true for pure monopoly.

Under monopoly, the firm will maximize profit if it sets its output rate at the point at which marginal cost equals marginal revenue. Table 9.4 and Figure 9.2 show that this is true in this example. It is easy to prove that this is generally a necessary condition for profit maximization. At any output rate at which marginal revenue exceeds marginal cost, profit can be increased by increasing output, since the extra revenue will exceed the extra cost. Thus profit will not be a maximum when marginal revenue exceeds marginal cost. At any output rate at which marginal cost exceeds marginal revenue, profit can be increased by reducing output, since the decrease in cost will exceed the decrease in revenue. Thus profit will not be a maximum when marginal cost exceeds marginal revenue. Since profit is not a maximum when marginal revenue exceeds marginal cost or when marginal cost exceeds

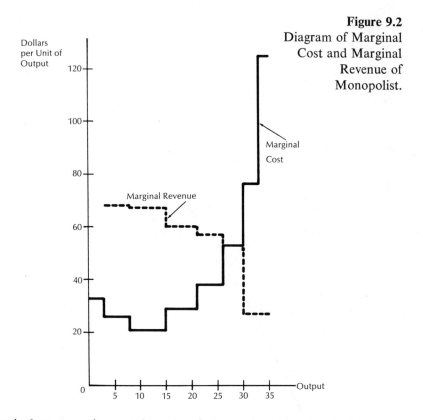

Figure 9.2
Diagram of Marginal
Cost and Marginal
Revenue of
Monopolist.

marginal revenue, it must be a maximum only when marginal revenue equals marginal cost.[1]

Using this result, it is also simple to represent graphically the short-run equilibrium of the monopolist. Figure 9.3 shows the demand curve (*DD'*),

---

[1]Suppose that the monopolist's demand function is $P = D(q)$, where P is price and q is output. Let $C(q)$ be the monopolist's total cost function. Then the monopolist's profit is

$$\Pi = qD(q) - C(q)$$

and

$$\frac{d\Pi}{dq} = D(q) + qD'(q) - C'(q)$$

Setting $d\Pi/dq = 0$ to obtain the conditions under which profit is a maximum, we find that

$$D(q) + qD'(q) = C'(q)$$

Thus marginal revenue must equal marginal cost when profits are maximized, since the expression on the left-hand side is marginal revenue and the expression on the right-hand side is marginal cost. Of course, this is only the first-order condition for a local maximum. The second-order conditions must also be met, and the maximum may be only a local maximum.

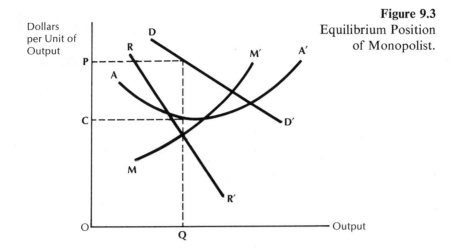

Figure 9.3
Equilibrium Position
of Monopolist.

the marginal revenue curve (*RR'*), the marginal cost curve (*MM'*), and the average total cost curve (*AA'*) faced by the firm. Short-run equilibrium will occur at the output, *OQ*, where the *MM'* curve intersects the *RR'* curve. If the monopolist produces *OQ* units, the demand curve shows that it must set a price of *OP*. Moreover, since the average cost curve shows that average costs are *OC* at an output of *OQ* units, the profit per unit of output is (*OP* − *OC*), and the firm's total profit is *OQ*[*OP* − *OC*].

In this case, the monopolist earns a profit, but this need not always be the case. It does not follow that a firm that holds a monopoly over the production of a particular product must make a profit. The demand curve for the product may be such that, even when the firm produces at the point at which marginal revenue equals marginal cost, average cost exceeds price. For example, even if one could somehow obtain a monopoly on the sale of cigar-store Indians, it might not be a profitable business to enter. Moreover, it is even possible that a monopolist cannot cover its variable costs, although it produces at the point at which marginal revenue equals marginal cost. In this case, the firm will discontinue production.

6.   Relationship between Price and Output

In perfect competition, one can define a unique relationship between the price of the product and the amount supplied. This is the industry's supply curve, which we discussed in Section 5 of Chapter 8. In monopoly, there is no such unique relationship between the product's price and the amount supplied. At first, this is likely to strike the reader as being extremely strange;

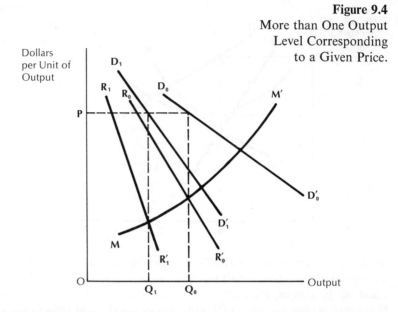

Figure 9.4
More than One Output
Level Corresponding
to a Given Price.

indeed, he can be pardoned if he has reservations about its being so. The rest
of this section is aimed at convincing the reader that it is true.

Figure 9.4 shows the marginal cost curve (*MM'*) of the monopolist. It is
assumed that the demand curve shifts from $D_0 D_0'$ to $D_1 D_1'$. When the
demand curve is $D_0 D_0'$, the firm produces OQ_0 units (since the *MM'* curve
intersects the marginal revenue curve, $R_0 R_0'$, at OQ_0) and the price must
be *OP*. When the demand curve is $D_1 D_1'$, the firm produces OQ_1 units
(since the *MM'* curve intersects the new marginal revenue curve, $R_1 R_1'$, at
OQ_1) and the price must be *OP*. This result shows that there is no unique
relationship between price and quantity. A price of *OP* can result in an
output of OQ_0 or OQ_1. Thus a particular price can result in a wide variety
of output levels, depending on the shape and level of the demand curve.

7. Long-Run Equilibrium Price and Output

In contrast to perfect competition, the long-run equilibrium of a monopolistic industry is not marked by the absence of economic profits or losses.
If a monopolist earns a short-run economic profit, it will not be confronted
in the long run with competitors, unless the industry is no longer a monopoly.

(The entrance of additional firms into the industry is, of course, not compatible with the existence of monopoly.) Thus the long-run equilibrium of an industry under monopoly may be characterized by economic profits.

On the other hand, if the monopolist incurs a short-run economic loss, he will be forced to look for other, more profitable uses for his resources. One possibility is that his existing plant is not optimal and that he can earn economic profits if he alters the scale and characteristics of his plant appropriately. If this is the case, he will make these alterations in the long run and remain in the industry. However, if there is no scale of plant that will enable the monopolist to avoid economic losses, he will leave the industry in the long run.

Returning to the case in which the monopolist earns short-run profits, he must decide in the long run whether he can make even larger profits by altering his plant. For example, Figure 9.5 illustrates the situation. The market demand and marginal revenue curves are DD' and RR'. The monopolist's long-run average cost curve is LL', and his long-run marginal cost curve is MM'. Suppose that the firm currently has a plant corresponding to short-run average cost curve, A_0A_0', and short-run marginal cost curve, M_0M_0'. In the short run, it will produce OQ_0 units and set a price of OP_0. Since short-run average cost is OB, the firm's short-run profits will be $OQ_0[OP_0 - OB]$.

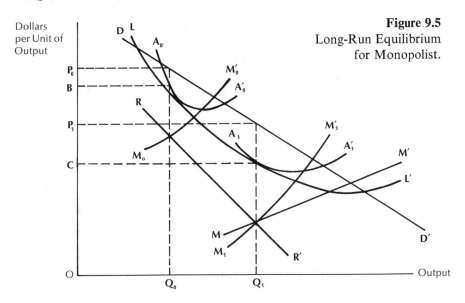

Figure 9.5
Long-Run Equilibrium
for Monopolist.

However, the firm can adjust its plant in the long run so as to make bigger profits than $OQ_0[OP_0 - OB]$. It is easy to show that the monopolist will maximize profit in the long run when he produces the output at which long-run marginal cost equals long-run marginal revenue. The reasoning behind this rule is precisely the same as that given in Section 5. Thus the firm will produce OQ_1 units in the long run, since this is the point at which the long-run marginal cost curve intersects the marginal revenue curve. The long-run average cost will be OC, the price will be OP_1, and total profit will be $OQ_1[OP_1 - OC]$. The resulting plant will have short-run average and marginal cost curves of A_1A_1' and M_1M_1', respectively.

8. Multiplant Monopoly

In previous sections we have assumed that the monopolist operated only one plant. This, of course, is an unrealistic assumption in many industries. Even readers with the most superficial knowledge of the structure of various industries will recognize that many firms operate more than one plant and that cost conditions may vary among these plants. This section extends the analysis in previous sections to cover the case where the monopolist operates more than one plant.

An illustrative case is shown in Table 9.5, which assumes that the monopolist operates two plants with marginal cost curves shown in columns 2 and 3, output being shown in column 1. Judging from the figures in these columns, if the firm decides to produce only one unit of output, it should use plant A, since the marginal cost between zero and one unit is lower in plant A than plant B. Thus, for the firm as a whole, the marginal cost between zero and one unit of output is $5 (the marginal cost between zero

Table 9.5. Costs of Multiplant Monopoly.

OUTPUT	MARGINAL COST* PLANT A	PLANT B	MARGINAL COST FOR FIRM*	PRICE	MARGINAL REVENUE*
1	$ 5	$ 7	$5	$20.00	—
2	6	9	6	15.00	$10
3	7	11	7	13.00	9
4	10	13	7	11.50	7
5	12	15	9	8.00	−6

*These figures pertain to the interval between the indicated output and one unit less than the indicated output.

and one unit for plant A). Similarly, if the firm decides to produce two units of output, both should be produced in plant A, and the marginal cost between the first and second unit of output for the firm as a whole is $6 (the marginal cost between the first and second unit in plant A). If the firm decides to produce three units of output, two should be produced in plant A and one in plant B, and the marginal cost between the second and third unit of output for the firm as a whole is $7 (the marginal cost between zero and one unit of output for plant B). Alternatively, all three could be produced at plant A.

Continuing in this fashion, we can derive the marginal cost curve for the firm as a whole, shown in column 4 of Table 9.5. To maximize profits, the firm should find that output at which marginal revenue equals the marginal cost of the firm as a whole. This is the optimum output. In this case, it is 3 or 4 units: Suppose that the firm picks 4 units.[2] To find out what price to charge, the firm must see what price corresponds to this output on the demand curve. In this case, the answer is $11.50.

This solves most of the monopolist's problems, but not quite all. Given that he will produce 4 units of output per year, how should he divide this production between the two plants? The answer is that he should set the marginal cost in plant A equal to the marginal cost in plant B. Table 9.5 shows that this means that plant A will produce 3 units per year and plant B will produce 1 unit per year. It should also be noted that the common value of the marginal costs of the two plants is also the marginal cost of the firm as a whole. Consequently, this common value must also be set equal to marginal revenue if the firm is maximizing profits.

In the long run the firm can vary the number and size of its plants. The monopolist can construct each plant of optimal size. In other words, in Figure 9.6, the short-run average cost, AA', will equal the long-run average cost, and it will be at the minimum point on the long-run average cost curve, LL'. The firm will build plants, each of which produces Oq units of output at an average cost of Ou dollars per unit. Thus, once it has reached Oq units of output, further expansion of output will be accommodated by building more plants of optimal size. Consequently the long-run marginal cost curve is a horizontal line at Ou. Since long-run marginal cost must equal marginal revenue, RR', the firm's total output in the long run will be Oz; it will operate $Oz \div Oq$ plants; and it will charge a price of OP.[3]

---

[2] If the firm maximizes profit, it is a matter of indifference to the firm whether it produces 3 or 4 units since the profit is the same. Suppose that the firm flips a coin to determine which output it will choose and that 4 units is the winner.

[3] Of course, we ignore here the problem that Oz/Oq may not be an integer. For simplicity we assume that it is an integer. Also, Oz will generally be bigger than Oq, the scale in Panel A of Figure 9.6 being different from that in Panel B.

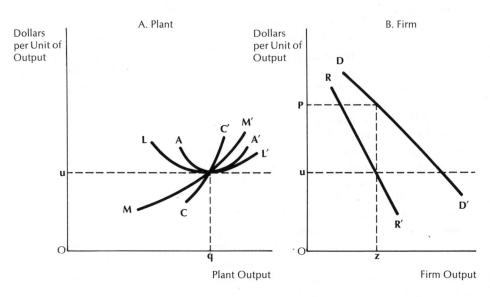

Figure 9.6
Equilibrium in the
Long Run of a
Multiplant Monopoly.

9. Effects of Changes in Demand and Cost

When the demand curve for a product shifts to the right, one ordinarily thinks that the product's price will rise. This expectation is correct under perfect competition, as long as the supply curve does not change (and is upward sloping). But under monopoly it may not be the case. For example, suppose that the monopolist's marginal cost curve is horizontal in the relevant range. Moreover, suppose that, at the price that prevailed before the shift in the demand curve, the elasticity of demand was 3; but that, at the price that prevailed after the shift in the demand curve, the elasticity of demand was 4. That is, the demand curve, when it shifted to the right, also became more elastic. Will such a shift in the demand curve increase price?

The answer is no. To prove this, note that, if the firm maximized profits before the shift in demand, it set marginal cost equal to marginal revenue. Thus,

$$M_1 = P_1 \left(1 - \frac{1}{n_1}\right)$$

(9.1)

where M_1 is marginal cost before the shift in demand, P_1 is price before the shift in demand, and n_1 is the elasticity of demand before the shift in demand. As shown in Chapter 4, the right-hand side of Equation 9.1 equals marginal revenue. Similarly, if the firm maximized profits after the shift in demand, it set

$$M_2 = P_2 \left(1 - \frac{1}{n_2}\right) \tag{9.2}$$

where M_2 is marginal cost after the shift in demand, P_2 is price after the shift in demand, and n_2 is the elasticity of demand after the shift in demand. Since the marginal cost curve is assumed horizontal, $M_1 = M_2$. And since $n_1 = 3$ and $n_2 = 4$, it follows that $P_2 = \frac{8}{9}P_1$. Thus price will be reduced by about 11 percent, despite the shift of the demand curve to the right.

If a monopolist's costs increase, one might think that the monopolist would pass all of the additional costs along to the consumer. For example, suppose that an excise tax were imposed on the monopolist's product, the result being that his marginal cost curve shifts from MM' to NN' in Figure 9.7. For simplicity we assume again that the marginal cost curve is horizontal in the relevant range. Under these conditions, will the monopolist increase his price by an amount equal to the vertical distance between MM' and NN'? Or will he pass along only part of the additional costs to the consumer, in which case his price will increase by an amount less than the vertical distance between MM' and NN'?

The answer is: He will pass along only part of the additional costs to the

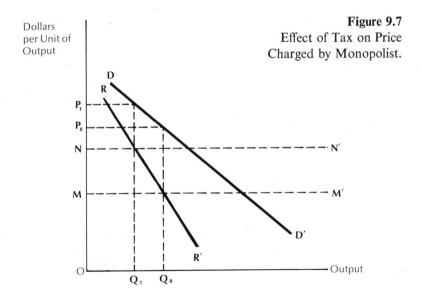

Figure 9.7
Effect of Tax on Price
Charged by Monopolist.

consumer. If the monopolist maximized profits, he set marginal revenue equal to OM before the tax, the result being that he produced OQ_0 units of output and the price was OP_0 (Figure 9.7). After the imposition of the tax, he sets marginal revenue equal to ON, the result being he produces OQ_1 units of output and the price is OP_1. It is obvious from Figure 9.7 that the difference between OP_1 and OP_0 is less than the difference between ON and OM, which means that he passes along only part of the additional costs.

10.   Comparison of Monopoly with Perfect Competition

It is important to note the differences between the long-run equilibrium of a monopoly and a perfectly competitive industry. Suppose that we could perform an experiment in which an industry was first operated under conditions of perfect competition and then under conditions of monopoly. Assuming that the demand curve for the industry's product and the industry's cost curves would be the same in either case,[4] what would be the difference in the long-run equilibrium?

First, under perfect competition, each firm operates at the point at which both long-run and short-run average costs are a minimum. However, under monopoly, although the plant that is used will produce the monopolist's long-run equilibrium output at minimum average cost, it is not the plant that will produce the product at the lowest possible average cost. In general, if the monopolist expanded his long-run equilibrium output, he could utilize a plant with lower average costs. This is clearly shown by Figure 9.8 (which compares the long-run equilibrium under perfect competition and monopoly). Consequently, society's resources tend to be used more effectively in perfectly competitive industries than in monopolized industries.[5] More will be said about this in Chapter 15.

Second, the output of a perfectly competitive industry tends to be greater and price tends to be lower than under monopoly. This, too, is clearly indicated by Figure 9.8, the competitive price and output being OP_1 and OQ_1 and the monopoly price and output being OP_2 and OQ_2. The perfectly

---

[4]However, the cost and demand curves need not be the same, as we noted above. For further discussion of this point, see George Stigler, *Theory of Price*, New York: Macmillan, 1966, Chapter 11.

[5]In multiplant monopoly the monopolist operates fewer plants than would a competitive industry.

Figure 9.8
Comparison of
Long-Run Equilibria.

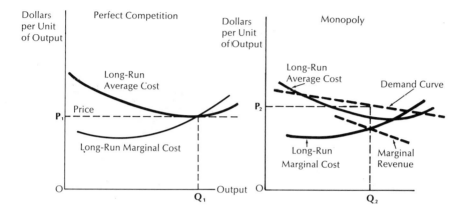

competitive firm operates at the point at which price equals marginal cost, whereas the monopolist operates at a point at which price exceeds marginal cost. Under various circumstances, as we shall see in Chapter 15, price is a good indicator of the marginal social value of the good, and marginal cost is a good indicator of the marginal social cost of the good. Consequently, under these conditions, a monopoly produces at a point at which the marginal social value of the good exceeds the good's marginal social cost. In a static sense, society would be better off if more resources were devoted to the production of the good, and if the marginal social value of the product were set equal to the marginal social cost of the product—as it is in perfect competition. Again, more will be said on this score in Chapter 15.

Assuming that the demand curve for the product is linear (DD') and that the marginal cost is constant (MM'), we compare the equilibrium price and output in monopoly and perfect competition in Figure 9.9. The monopoly price is OP_1 and the competitive price is OM; the monopoly output is OQ_1 and the competitive output is OQ_0. It is assumed, of course, that the MM' curve is the long-run supply curve in perfect competition. Under these very special assumptions, the monopoly output will be exactly one-half the competitive output, the reason being that the marginal revenue curve, RR', cuts in half any horizontal line from the vertical axis to the demand curve.[6]

---

[6]For a proof of this point, see Chapter 4, Section 9.

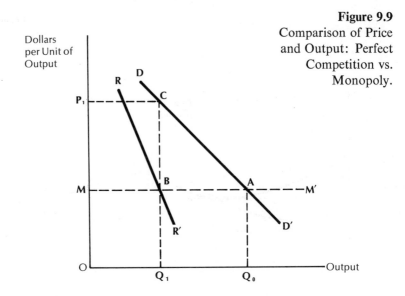

Figure 9.9
Comparison of Price
and Output: Perfect
Competition vs.
Monopoly.

In general, of course, the ratio of the monopoly to the competitive output could be more or less than one-half, depending on the shape of the demand and cost curves.

Using the concept of consumer's surplus described in Chapter 3, some economists believe that the welfare loss to society due to monopoly, rather than perfect competition, can be measured by the so-called "welfare triangle," *ABC*, in Figure 9.9. Basically, the idea is that the value to society of the extra output resulting from perfect competition is equal to Q_1CAQ_0, whereas the cost to society of the extra output is equal to Q_1BAQ_0. Thus the net loss due to the smaller output under monopoly is equal to *ABC*. One important limitation of this kind of measure is that it assumes that one can simply add up the "utilities" gained and lost by various members of society. No attention is paid to the effects of monopoly on the distribution of income.

11.   Bilateral Monopoly

Bilateral monopoly occurs when a monopolistic seller is confronted with only a single buyer. In other words, it is a case where the market is composed of a single buyer and a single seller. For example, if all tin plate were produced by a single firm and if only a single firm used tin plate, this would be a case of bilateral monopoly. Clearly, there are few cases of this sort, except perhaps in the labor markets. The market for labor may be dominated, particularly in small areas, by a single firm and a single union.[7]

Suppose that the seller's marginal cost curve is SS' in Figure 9.10. Also suppose that the buyer's demand curve is DD' in Figure 9.10. More specifically, DD' shows the number of units of output demanded by the buyer at each price, given that the price is determined outside the control of the buyer. Under these conditions, the seller would like to set a price that will maximize his profits. Taking the buyer's demand curve, DD', as given, the seller's marginal revenue curve is RR'; and he would like to operate at the point at which his marginal revenue curve intersects his marginal cost curve. Thus he would like to charge a price of OP_0 and supply OQ_0 units of the good.

Turning to the buyer, what price would he like to pay and how many units of output would he like to buy? The buyer views the seller's marginal cost curve as a supply curve. Given a certain price, determined outside the control of the seller, we know that this curve, SS', shows how much the seller will

Figure 9.10
Bilateral Monopoly.

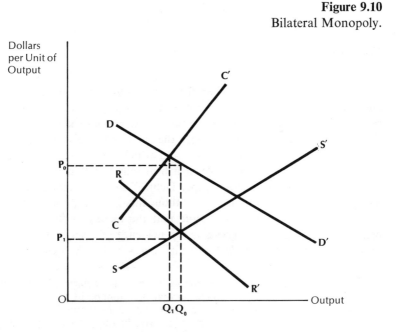

<hr />

[7]However, even here there are problems in applying the theory. As pointed out in Chapter 13, the assumption that labor unions can be represented in this way implies a very special kind of motivation on the part of unions.

supply.[8] Like the seller, the buyer would like to maximize his profits. The buyer's profits will be maximized when the curve showing the buyer's marginal expenditure on the good intersects the buyer's demand curve. The marginal expenditure on the good when between x and $(x - 1)$ units are bought is $R(x) - R(x - 1)$, where $R(x)$ is the amount spent by the buyer on x units. The marginal expenditure on the good is shown by the CC' curve in Figure 9.10. Thus the buyer would like to operate at the point at which the CC' curve intersects the DD' curve, which means that he would like to pay a price of OP_1 and buy OQ_1 units of output.

The price and output that will result in a situation of this sort is indeterminate. It seems likely that the price will lie somewhere between OP_0 and OP_1 and that output will lie somewhere between OQ_0 and OQ_1, but we cannot make any more specific predictions. A theory based on profit maximization is unable to yield a more specific prediction. Other factors, like bargaining power and negotiating skill and public opinion, are likely to play an important role in determining the nature of the final outcome.

12. Price Discrimination

Price discrimination occurs when the same commodity is sold at more than one price. For example, an operation to cure a particular form of cancer may be "sold" to a rich man for $500 and to a poor man for $100. Even if the commodities are not precisely the same, price discrimination is said to occur if very similar products are sold at prices that are in different ratios to marginal costs. For example, if a firm sells fountain pens with a label (cost of label: 1 cent) saying "Super Deluxe" in rich neighborhoods for $2 and sells the same fountain pens without this label in poor neighborhoods for $1, this is discrimination. Note that the mere fact that differences in price exist among similar goods is not evidence of discrimination. Only if these differences do not reflect cost differences is there evidence of this sort.

---

[8]In Section 6, we showed that a monopoly has no supply curve. The curve, SS', is a supply curve only under the condition that the monopolist is constrained to sell at fixed prices outside its control. In other words, the monopolist is assumed to be stripped of its monopoly power. Similarly, in the preceding paragraph, the monopsonist is assumed to be stripped of its monopsony power. These assumptions are made to obtain a range within which the outcome is likely to be.

Under what conditions will a monopolist be able and willing to engage in price discrimination? The necessary conditions are that buyers fall into classes with considerable differences in the elasticity of demand for the product, and that these classes can be identified and segregated at moderate cost. Clearly, it is important that buyers be unable to transfer the commodity easily from one class to another, since otherwise it would be possible for persons to make money by buying the commodity from the low-price classes and selling it to the high-price classes, thus making it difficult to maintain the price differentials between classes. The differences between classes of buyers in the elasticity of demand may be due to differences between classes in income level, differences between classes in tastes, or differences between classes in the availability of substitutes. For example, the elasticity of demand for a particular good may be lower for the rich than the poor.

If a monopolist practices discrimination of this sort, he must decide two questions: How much output should he allocate to each class of buyer, and what price should he charge each class of buyer? To avoid unnecessary complications, let us assume that there are only two classes of buyers. Also, for the moment, assume that the monopolist has already decided on his total output, and consequently that the only real question is how it should be allocated between the two classes. In each class, there is a demand curve showing how many units of output would be bought by buyers in this class at various prices. In each class, there is also a marginal revenue curve that can be derived from the demand curve.

Given these marginal revenue curves, the monopolist will maximize his profits by allocating the total output between the two classes in such a way that marginal revenue in one class is equal to marginal revenue in the other class. The reason for this is clear. For example, if marginal revenue in the first class is \$5 and marginal revenue in the second class is \$3, the allocation is not optimal, since profits can be increased by allocating one less unit of output to the second class and one more unit of output to the first class. Only if the two marginal revenues are equal is the allocation optimal. And if the marginal revenues in the two classes are equal, the ratio of the price in the first class to the price in the second class will equal

$$\left(1 - \frac{1}{n_2}\right) \div \left(1 - \frac{1}{n_1}\right)$$

where n_1 is the elasticity of demand in the first class and n_2 is the elasticity of demand in the second class. Thus it will not pay to discriminate if the two elasticities are equal. Moreover, if discrimination does pay, the price will be lower in the class in which demand is more elastic.

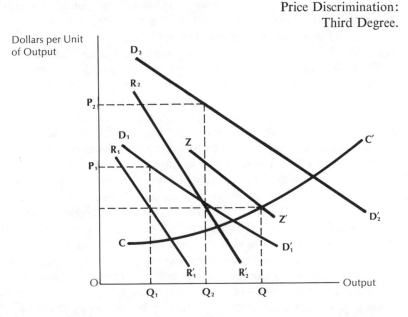

Figure 9.11
Price Discrimination:
Third Degree.

Next consider the more realistic case where the monopolist must also decide on his total output. In this case, the monopolist must look at his costs, as well as demand in the two classes. It can be shown that he will choose the output where the marginal cost of the monopolist's entire output is equal to the common value of the marginal revenue in the two classes. To see this, consider Figure 9.11, which shows $D_1 D_1'$, the demand curve in class 1; $D_2 D_2'$, the demand curve in class 2; $R_1 R_1'$, the marginal revenue curve in class 1; $R_2 R_2'$, the marginal revenue curve in class 2; and CC', the firm's marginal cost curve. The monopolist begins to determine his total output by summing horizontally over the two marginal revenue curves, $R_1 R_1'$ and $R_2 R_2'$. The curve representing the horizontal summation of the two marginal revenue curves is ZZ'. This curve shows, for each level of marginal revenue, the total output that is needed if marginal revenue in each class is to be maintained at this level. The optimal output is shown by the point where the ZZ' curve intersects the CC' curve, since marginal cost must be equal to the common value of marginal revenue in each class. If this were not the case, profits could be increased by expanding output (if marginal cost were less than marginal revenue) or by contracting output (if marginal cost were greater than marginal revenue). Thus the firm will produce an output of

OQ units and sell OQ_1 units in the class 1 market and OQ_2 units in the class 2 market. Price will be OP_1 in the class 1 market and OP_2 in the class 2 market.[9]

13. Other Types of Price Discrimination

Price discrimination can take a number of forms. The type discussed in the previous section is often called *third-degree price discrimination*, this expression having been invented by A. C. Pigou, the English economist.[10]

---

[9]Let p_1 be the price in the first class, p_2 the price in the second class, q_1 the quantity sold in the first class, and q_2 the quantity sold in the second class. If $C(q)$ is the monopolist's total cost, q being equal to the sum of q_1 and q_2,
$$\Pi = p_1q_1 + p_2q_2 - C(q)$$
where Π is the monopolist's profits. Then
$$\frac{\partial\Pi}{\partial q_1} = \frac{\partial(p_1q_1)}{\partial q_1} - \frac{\partial C(q)}{\partial q_1} = \frac{d(p_1q_1)}{dq_1} - \frac{dC(q)}{dq}\frac{\partial q}{\partial q_1}$$
$$= \frac{d(p_1q_1)}{dq_1} - \frac{dC(q)}{dq} = 0$$
$$\frac{\partial\Pi}{\partial q_2} = \frac{\partial(p_2q_2)}{\partial q_2} - \frac{\partial C(q)}{\partial q_2} = \frac{d(p_2q_2)}{dq_2} - \frac{dC(q)}{dq}\frac{\partial q}{\partial q_2}$$
$$= \frac{d(p_2q_2)}{dq_2} - \frac{dC(q)}{dq} = 0$$
Thus, if Π is to be a maximum,
$$\frac{d(p_1q_1)}{dq_1} = \frac{d(p_2q_2)}{dq_2} = \frac{dC(q)}{dq}$$
In other words, $MR_1 = MR_2 = MC$, where MR_1 is marginal revenue in the first class, MR_2 is marginal revenue in the second class, and MC is marginal cost. Since
$$MR_1 = P_1\left(1 - \frac{1}{n_1}\right) \quad \text{and} \quad MR_2 = P_2\left(1 - \frac{1}{n_2}\right),$$
as proved in Chapter 4, it follows that, if $MR_1 = MR_2$,
$$P_1\left(1 - \frac{1}{n_1}\right) = P_2\left(1 - \frac{1}{n_2}\right)$$
$$\frac{P_1}{P_2} = \frac{[1 - (1/n_2)]}{[1 - (1/n_1)]}$$
[10]A. C. Pigou, *The Economics of Welfare*, London: Macmillan, 1950, 4th ed.

Besides third-degree price discrimination, there are also first-degree and second-degree price discrimination. In *discrimination of the first degree*, the monopolist is aware of the maximum amount that each and every consumer will pay for each amount of the commodity. Since it is assumed that the product cannot be resold, the monopolist can charge each consumer a different price. And since he is assumed to be a profit-maximizer, he will establish prices so as to extract from each consumer the full value of his consumer's surplus.

To illustrate this case, suppose that each consumer buys only one unit of the commodity. In this very simple case, the monopolist will establish a price for each consumer that is so high that the consumer is on the verge of refusing to buy the commodity. In the more realistic case, where each consumer can buy more than one unit of the commodity, it is assumed that the monopolist knows each consumer's demand curve for the commodity and that he adjusts his offer accordingly. For example, suppose that the maximum amount that a particular consumer would pay for 20 units of the commodity is $50 and that 20 units is the profit-maximizing amount for the monopolist to sell to this consumer. Then the monopolist will make an all-or-nothing offer of 20 units of the commodity for $50.

First-degree price discrimination is a limiting case that could occur only in the few cases when a monopolist has a small number of buyers and when he is able to guess the maximum prices they are willing to accept. *Second-degree price discrimination* is an intermediate case. In second-degree price discrimination, the monopolist takes part, but not all, of the buyers' consumers' surpluses. For example, consider the case of a gas company. Suppose that each of its consumers has the demand curve, DD', shown in Figure 9.12. The company charges a high price, OP_0, if the consumer purchases less than OX units of gas per month. For any amount beyond OX units per month, the company charges a medium price, OP_1. For purchases beyond OY, the company charges an even lower price, OP_2. Consequently, the company's total revenues from each consumer are equal to the shaded area in Figure 9.12, since the consumer will purchase OX units at a price of OP_0, $(OY - OX)$ units at a price of OP_1, and $(OZ - OY)$ units at a price of OP_2.[11]

It is obvious that the gas company, by charging different prices for various amounts of the commodity, is able to increase its revenue and profits considerably. After all, if it were permitted to charge only one price and if it wanted to sell OZ units, it would have to charge a price of OP_2. Thus the firm's total revenue would equal only the rectangle, OP_2EZ, which is considerably less than the shaded area in Figure 9.12. By charging different

---

[11]Of course, this assumes for simplicity that each consumer purchases OZ units.

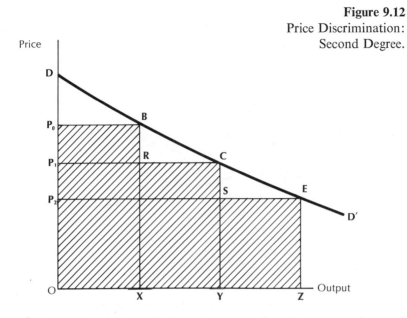

Figure 9.12
Price Discrimination:
Second Degree.

prices, the monopolist is able to take part of the consumers' surplus. According to some authorities, the schedules of rates charged by many public
utilities—gas, water, electricity, and others—can be viewed as a type of
second-degree price discrimination.[12]

14.   Discrimination and the Existence of the Industry

Economists generally regard price discrimination as a socially inefficient way
of pricing a commodity, for reasons discussed in Chapter 15. It should be
recognized, however, that a good or service sometimes cannot be produced
without discrimination. For example, consider the case in Figure 9.13, where
there are two types of consumers, their demand curves between $D_0 D_0'$, and
$D_1 D_1'$. Adding the two demand curves, we find that the total demand for
the commodity is $D_0 UV$. Since the monopolist's average total cost curve
is AA', no output exists at which price is greater than or equal to average

---

[12]Ralph Davidson, *Price Determination in Selling Gas and Electricity*, Baltimore:
Johns Hopkins University Press, 1955.

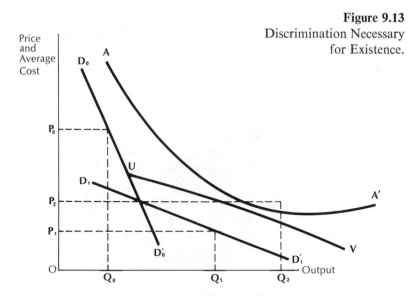

Figure 9.13
Discrimination Necessary
for Existence.

total cost if price discrimination is not practiced. However, with price discrimination, an output of OQ_0 can be sold at a price of OP_0 to one type of consumer; an output of OQ_1 can be sold at a price of OP_1 to the second type of consumer; and the total output (which equals OQ_2) brings an average price of OP_2, which is greater than average total costs.

15.   Public Regulation of Monopoly

State regulatory commissions often have substantial power over the prices charged by public utilities like gas and electric companies. For example, consider the firm in Figure 9.14. The demand curve it faces is DD', the marginal revenue curve RR', the average cost curve AA', and the marginal cost curve MM'. Without regulation, the firm would charge a price of OP_0 and it would produce OQ_0 units of the commodity. By setting a maximum price of OP_1, the commission can make the monopolist increase output, thus making price and output correspond more closely to what they would be if the industry were organized competitively. For instance, if the commission imposes a maximum price of OP_1, the firm's demand curve becomes P_1BD', its marginal revenue curve becomes P_1BCR', its optimum output

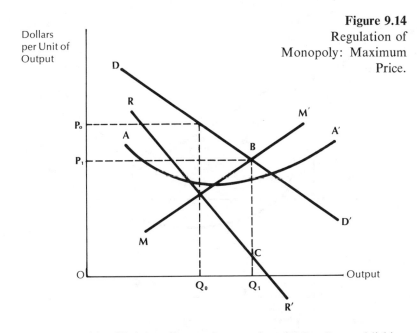

Figure 9.14
Regulation of
Monopoly: Maximum
Price.

becomes OQ_1, and it will charge the maximum price of OP_1. By establishing the maximum price, the commission helps consumers who pay a lower price for more of the good. By the same token, the commission deprives the monopolist of some of his monopoly power.

Commissions often set the price—or the maximum price—at the level at which it equals average total cost, including a "fair" rate of return on the company's investment. For example, in Figure 9.15, the price would be established by the commission at OP_2, where the demand curve, DD', intersects the average total cost curve, AA', the latter including what the commission regards as a "fair" profit per unit of output. Needless to say, there has been considerable controversy over what constitutes a "fair" rate of return. There has also been a good deal of controversy over what should be included in the company's "investment" on which the fair rate of return is to be earned. For example, these questions have been discussed, argued, and examined in great detail—and sometimes with heat—in connection with the telephone industry in the famous A. T. and T. investigation conducted by the Federal Communications Commission in the late sixties. One suggestion is that public utilities should set price equal to marginal cost, not average cost. This suggestion will be discussed in Chapter 15.

The regulatory commissions also govern the extent to which price discrimination is used by the public utilities. Intricate systems of price dis-

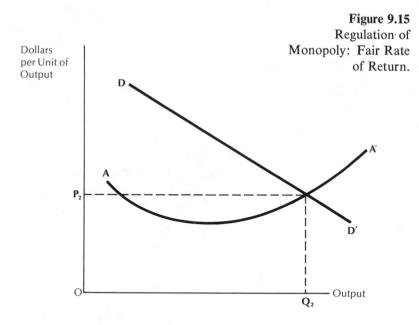

Figure 9.15
Regulation of
Monopoly: Fair Rate
of Return.

crimination exist in the rate structures of the railroads, the electric and gas companies, the telephone companies, and so forth. Although some types of discrimination are prohibited, other types can be practiced if they are "reasonable." For example, a company may be permitted to charge a lower rate for a service where it must meet stiff competition. It should be noted that rate discrimination raises important questions of equity and of redistribution of income, as well as questions regarding economic efficiency. Particularly in transportation, some of the most nettlesome problems of rate regulation are concerned with questions of discrimination.

16. Alcoa: A Case Study of Unregulated Monopoly

The Aluminum Company of America was the sole manufacturer of virgin aluminum ingot in the United States from its inception in the late nineteenth century until World War II. Its monopoly position was based originally on patents regarding the production process. These patents terminated in

1909, and Alcoa attempted to maintain its monopoly position by (1) agreements with foreign aluminum producers not to export into their markets in exchange for their not intruding into its market, and (2) long-term contracts with companies controlling sources of raw materials to bar these companies from selling their raw materials to companies other than Alcoa. However, these agreements and contracts were nullified by the courts in 1912.

Alcoa maintained its monopoly position after 1912 largely by the constant expansion of its productive capacity to meet the increased demand for aluminum at the established price. According to Judge Learned Hand, Alcoa "insists that it never excluded competitors; but we can think of no more effective exclusion than progressively to embrace each new opportunity as it opened, and to face every newcomer with new capacity already geared into a great organization, having the advantage of experience, trade connections, and the elite of personnel."[13]

With regard to pricing, Alcoa did not attempt to maximize short-run profits. Instead, it recognized that foreign imports would be stimulated if it set its prices above a certain point. Moreover, according to some observers, it recognized "the advantages accruing to the company from an orderly reduction of aluminum prices over the years as necessary to penetrate new markets, coupled with a policy of stabilized prices between price reductions ... This policy also served to discourage potential competitors."[14] Thus Alcoa seemed to gear its pricing policy to the pursuit of long-run profits, recognizing the importance from its point of view of discouraging entry.

An antitrust suit was instituted against Alcoa in the forties. The company denied that it was a monopoly, arguing that it had many competitors: sellers of secondary aluminum ingot, foreign producers, and producers of other materials that to some extent are substitutes for aluminum. However, Judge Hand ruled that Alcoa had a monopoly position since it controlled over 90 percent of the domestic market for virgin aluminum ingots (foreign producers supplying the rest). In a subsequent antitrust case, it was ruled that Alcoa should not be broken up, since Reynolds and Kaiser had entered the industry and had become domestic producers of virgin aluminum ingot.[15]

---

[13]See A. Papandreau and J. Wheeler, *Competition and its Regulation*, Englewood Cliffs, N.J.: Prentice-Hall, 1954, p. 318.

[14]R. Lanzillotti, "The Aluminum Industry," *The Structure of American Industry*, W. Adams, ed., New York: Macmillan, 1961, pp. 209–11.

[15]This case is frequently used to illustrate pure monopoly. For a somewhat similar account, see K. Cohen and R. Cyert, *Theory of the Firm,* Englewood Cliffs, N.J.: Prentice-Hall, 1965, pp. 200–03.

17.   The Michigan Telephone Industry: A Case Study of Regulation

The previous section described a case of unregulated monopoly. To illustrate the case of regulated monopoly, we turn to the telephone industry in Michigan. According to C. Emery Troxel,[16] the two groups that play a key role in the regulation of the telephone industry in Michigan are one firm, Michigan Bell Telephone System (a subsidiary of A. T. & T.), and one commission, the Public Service Commission in Michigan. Although Michigan Bell is not the only telephone company in the state, it is the dominant firm, and there is no direct competition in the industry between firms. The Commission, which is composed of three members appointed by the Governor, has had authority over the telephone industry for about 50 years.

A general-rate case, according to Troxel, is the common sort of regulatory "contest" in the Michigan telephone industry. In the past 20 years, all such cases have been initiated by the firms and have been based on company claims that earnings are deficient and a higher price level is required. It is generally assumed, though not proved, that demand is inelastic and that higher prices will mean greater revenues. During this period, only one of the requests was approved in its entirety, and some were turned down completely. Thus the industry received less than it asked for. Moreover, Commission decisions have lagged behind the industry's revenue requests. However, it should be recognized that the fact that the Commission does not approve all Bell requests does not mean that the company is being constrained much by the Commission. The company may ask for more than it thinks it will get. There is some debate over the extent to which regulatory commissions of this kind really regulate the industries they oversee. Little is really known about many important aspects of the effects of regulation.

According to Troxel, nothing in public utility controls is more conventional, more securely established in regulatory methods, than the idea of a "reasonable return on the value of a firm's existing plant."[17] This is what the Commission is interested in establishing. Yet there are a host of questions, some obvious to the most naïve housewife, others difficult for a trained engineer or accountant to understand, concerning what is a "reasonable return" and what is "the value of a firm's existing plant." The original

---

[16]See C. E. Troxel, "Telephone Regulation in Michigan," in W. G. Shepherd and T. Gies, *Utility Regulation*, New York: Random House, 1966.
[17]*Ibid.*, p. 162.

cost or historical cost of the plant is the measure on which the Commission bases its estimates of the value of the plant; Michigan Bell would like to use replacement-cost valuations instead. In the early sixties, Michigan Bell sought a rate of return of about 7.5 percent; the Commission approved a rate of return of about 6.7 percent. There are lots of detailed and difficult questions in each case of this sort that provide employment for a great many lawyers, accountants, engineers, and economists.

18. Summary

Pure monopoly exists when there is one, and only one, seller in a market. From some points of view, pure monopoly and perfect competition are polar opposites. Monopolies arise because a single firm controls the entire supply of a basic input, because a firm has a patent on the product or on certain basic processes, because the average cost of producing the product reaches a minimum at an output rate that is big enough to satisfy the entire market at a price that is profitable, because the firm is awarded a franchise, or for other reasons. The demand curve facing the monopolist is the demand for the product. The cost conditions facing a monopolist may be no different from those facing a perfectly competitive firm, if the monopolist is a perfect competitor in the input markets.

Under monopoly, the firm will maximize profit if it sets its output rate at the point where marginal cost equals marginal revenue. It does not follow that a firm that holds a monopoly over the production of a particular product must make a profit. If the monopolist cannot cover his variable costs, he will shut down, even in the short run. Under monopoly, there is no unique relationship between the product's price and the amount supplied. The long-run equilibrium of the industry is not necessarily marked by the absence of economic profits. If the monopolist has more than one plant, he should allocate production among his plants so that marginal costs are the same in each plant, and he should set his over-all output rate so that this common marginal cost equals marginal revenue.

There are a number of important differences between the long-run equilibrium of a monopoly and of a perfectly competitive industry. Under perfect competition, each firm operates at the point where both long-run and short-run average costs are at a minimum; under monopoly, if the monopolist expanded his long-run equilibrium output, he could utilize a plant with lower average costs. The output of a perfectly competitive industry tends to be greater and price tends to be lower than under monopoly. The perfectly competitive firm operates at the point where price equals marginal cost, whereas the monopolist operates at a point where price exceeds marginal cost. Some economists measure the loss in economic welfare due to monopoly by the "welfare triangle."

Bilateral monopoly occurs when a monopolistic seller confronts a monopsonistic buyer. The price and output that will result in this situation is indeterminate. Price discrimination occurs when the same commodity is sold at more than one price, or when similar products are sold at prices that are in different ratios to marginal costs. A monopolist will be able and willing to practice price discrimination if various classes of buyers with different elasticities of demand can be identified and segregated. There are three types of price discrimination, and we have discussed the monopolist's behavior in each case. Economists generally regard price discrimination as a socially inefficient way of pricing a commodity, but it is sometimes true that, without discrimination, a commodity cannot be produced at all.

Regulatory commissions frequently have the power to set the prices charged by public utilities like gas or electric companies. They often set the price— or the maximum price—at the level at which it equals average total cost, including a "fair" rate of return on the company's investment. There has been considerable controversy over what constitutes a "fair" rate of return, and over what should be included in the company's "investment." Finally, we presented two very brief case studies, the history of the Aluminum Company of America illustrating the case of an unregulated monopoly, the telephone industry in Michigan illustrating the case of a regulated monopoly.

SELECTED REFERENCES

Harrod, Roy, "Doctrines of Imperfect Competition," *Quarterly Journal of Economics*, 1934.

Hicks, John, "Annual Survey of Economic Theory: The Theory of Monopoly," *Econometrica*, 1935.

Mansfield, Edwin, *Monopoly Power and Economic Performance*, New York: Norton, revised edition, 1968.

Machlup, Fritz, *The Political Economy of Monopoly*, Baltimore: Johns Hopkins Press, 1952.

Ferguson, C., *Microeconomic Theory*, Homewood, Ill.: Richard D. Irwin, 1969.

Robinson, Joan, *The Economics of Imperfect Competition*, London: Macmillan, 1933.

10

Price and Output under Monopolistic Competition

1. Historical Background

Perfect competition and pure monopoly are two polar extremes. There is an extremely large number of firms in a perfectly competitive industry, but only one firm in a pure monopoly. For many years economists felt that these two models enabled them to analyze any market. They knew that some markets were quite different from either perfect competition or pure monopoly, but it was felt that the two models could be combined somehow to treat such cases. With the exception of a few over-simplified duopoly models, discussed in the following chapter, the whole of price theory consisted of the theory of perfect competition and the theory of pure monopoly. This situation lasted until the late twenties and early thirties.

During the twenties and thirties there was a marked change in attitude. Economists began to stress the importance of more and better research to develop models to handle the important "middle ground" between perfect competition and pure monopoly. An English economist, Piero Sraffa,[1]

---

[1]P. Sraffa, "The Laws of Returns under Competitive Conditions," *Economic Journal*, 1926.

was one of the first to emphasize this point, and he was soon joined by many others who shared his feeling that the theories of perfect competition and pure monopoly dealt with polar extremes, between which fell practically all of the empirically relevant cases.

In response to this challenge, there was a flurry of activity in this area among the members of the economics profession in the period around 1930. One of the most noteworthy achievements that were produced was the theory of "monopolistic competition," put forth by Harvard's Edward Chamberlin.[2] In this chapter, we present a detailed description of Chamberlin's theory, which unquestionably has had an important impact on the development of microeconomic theory in the past 40 years. In addition, we discuss some of the criticisms that have been made of this theory.

2. Product Differentiation, the Group, and Other Assumptions

The basic idea behind Chamberlin's theory is that most firms face relatively close substitutes and that most commodities are not completely homogeneous from one producer to another. For example, General Motors has a monopoly on the production and sale of Chevrolets. However, other firms can produce roughly similar automobiles like Fords, Plymouths, Ramblers, and so forth. Each firm has a monopoly over the sale of its own product, but the various brands are close substitutes.

This is a case of *product differentiation*. In other words, there is no single, homogeneous commodity called an automobile; instead, each producer differentiates its product from that of the next producer. This, of course, is a prevalent case in American markets. Each producer tries to make his product a little different, by altering the physical makeup of his product, the services he offers, and other such variables. Other differences—which may be spurious—are based on brand name, "image" making, advertising claims, and so forth. In this way, each producer has some amount of monopoly power, but it usually is small, because the products of other firms are very similar.

---

[2]E. Chamberlin, *The Theory of Monopolistic Competition*, Cambridge, Mass.: Harvard University Press, 1933. Another very important work of the same period was J. Robinson, *The Economics of Imperfect Competition*, New York: Macmillan, 1933.

In perfect competition, the firms included in an industry are easy to determine, because they all produce the same product. But if there is product differentiation, it is no longer easy to define an industry, since each firm produces a somewhat different product. Nevertheless, Chamberlin believes that it is useful to group together firms producing similar products and call them a *product group*. For example, we can formulate a product group called "automobiles" or "trucks." Of course, the process by which we combine firms into product groups is bound to be somewhat arbitrary, since there is no way to decide how close a pair of substitutes must be in order to be included in the same product group. However, Chamberlin asserts that meaningful product groups can be formulated.

The assumptions underlying Chamberlin's theory are as follows: First, he assumes that the product, which is differentiated, is produced by a large number of firms, each firm's product being a fairly close substitute for the products of the other firms in the product group. Second, he assumes that the number of firms in the product group is sufficiently large so that each firm expects its actions to go unheeded by its rivals and to be unimpeded by any retaliatory measures on their part. Third, he assumes that both demand and cost curves are the same for all of the firms in the group. This, of course, is a very restrictive assumption since, if the products are dissimilar, one would ordinarily expect their demand and cost curves to be dissimilar, too.

A firm under monopolistic competition can do three things to affect its rate of sales. It can change its price, change the characteristics of its product, or change its advertising and promotional expenditures. We take up each of these three types of decisions in the following sections, Sections 3 to 5 being concerned with price variation, Section 6 with product variation, and Section 7 with selling costs.

3. Demand Curves under Monopolistic Competition

Two kinds of demand curves play an important role in the theory of monopolistic competition. On the one hand, there is a demand curve that shows how much the firm will sell if it varies its price from the going level and if other firms maintain their existing prices. As an example of this demand curve, consider the situation in Figure 10.1. The firm is currently in equilibrium at the point A, with price OP and output OQ. If the firm reduces its price and if other firms maintain their prices, the firm can expect a considerable increase in sales, since it will be able to attract buyers away from other firms in the group (and increase sales to existing customers). If the firm increases its price and if other firms maintain their prices, the firm can expect a considerable decrease in sales, since it will lose business to other firms in the group (because buyers will switch allegiance). Thus, assuming that each firm expects its actions to go unheeded by its rivals, each firm believes its demand curve to be quite elastic. This demand curve is shown as *dd'* in Figure 10.1.

In addition, there is another important type of demand curve, based on the supposition that *all* firms raise or lower their prices by the same amount as this firm. This demand curve is shown as DD' in Figure 10.1. Thus, if this firm reduces its price to OP_1 and all other firms reduce their prices to OP_1 as well, this firm will sell OQ_1 units of output. Similarly, if this firm increases its price to OP_2 and all other firms increase their price to OP_2 as well, this firm will sell OQ_2 units of output. Of course, this second type of demand curve, DD', is less elastic than the first type, *dd'*, since price reductions by this firm will expand its sales by a greater amount if other firms do not meet the price reduction, and price increases by this firm will decrease its sales by a greater amount if other firms do not meet the price increase. For example, if other firms do not meet the price reduction, this firm's sales will increase to OQ_3, rather than OQ_1, if it reduces its price to OP_1.

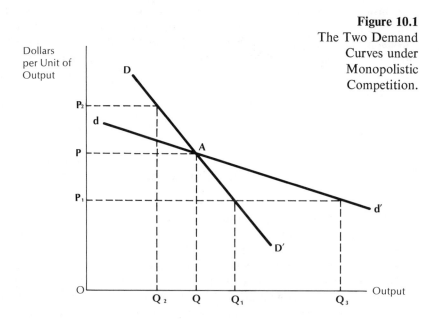

Figure 10.1
The Two Demand Curves under Monopolistic Competition.

4. Equilibrium Price and Output in the Short Run

In discussing the pricing behavior of firms under monopolistic competition, it simplifies matters to assume that the firms have already decided on the characteristics of product and extent of selling expense that are most profitable. (In Sections 6 and 7, we shall deal with the way in which firms determine these variables.) It is also convenient to analyze the behavior of a product group in terms of a "representative firm." Since the demand and cost functions of each firm are assumed to be identical, it is legitimate to think in terms of a "representative firm."

To see how the equilibrium price and output of each firm in the group is determined in the short run, consider the situation in Figure 10.2. The market price is OP_0 and the firm is producing and selling OQ_0 units. Suppose that the firm believes that any alteration in its price will not be matched by its rivals in the group, and that it tries to act as a monopolist. Then *dd'* is the relevant demand curve, *RR'* is the relevant marginal revenue curve,

Figure 10.2
Initial Change of
Price and Output.

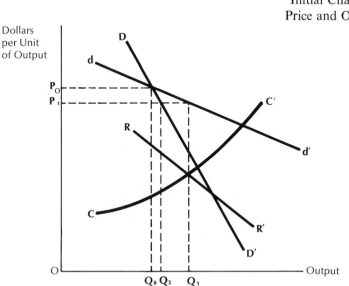

and the firm will decide to produce and sell an output of OQ_1, since this is the output at which the marginal cost curve, CC', intersects the marginal revenue curve, RR'. The price charged by the firm will change to OP_1.

This new price would boost the firm's profits, if the firm were correct in believing that the price charged by other firms in the group would remain constant. However, since all of the firms in the group are confronted with the same situation and since they all make the assumption that the other firms will not change price, they all do the same thing. Thus every firm changes its price to OP_1 and DD', not dd', becomes the relevant demand curve. This means that OQ_2, not OQ_1, units of output are sold by each firm at the new price, OP_1.

The results are shown in Figure 10.3. Because all firms are now charging a price of OP_1, the dd' demand curve has now moved down until it intersects the DD' demand curve at OP_1. Clearly, the new dd' demand curve must intersect the DD' demand curve at OP_1, since the new dd' demand curve shows how much the firm will sell at various prices if other firms' prices remain constant at OP_1, not OP_0. Thus, at the point on the dd' demand curve corresponding to a price of OP_1, all firms are charging a price of OP_1, and the firm's sales must correspond to the point on the DD' demand curve corresponding to OP_1.

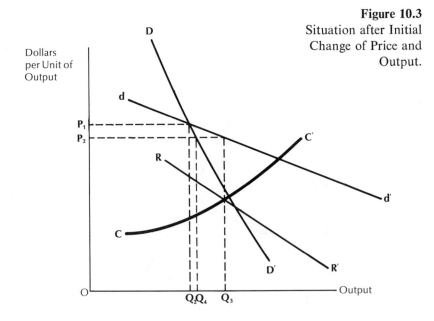

Figure 10.3
Situation after Initial Change of Price and Output.

Again, the firm acts as a monopolist and attempts to maximize profits on the basis of the new *dd'* demand curve. It sets a price of OP_2 and expects to produce and sell OQ_3 units of output. But since this change in price seems profitable for all firms, they all take the same action, with the result that the *DD'* demand curve, not the new *dd'* demand curve, is the relevant one. Consequently, each firm produces OQ_4, not OQ_3, units of output. Again the *dd'* demand curve shifts to intersect the *DD'* demand curve at the new price, OP_2. And the process goes on.

Figure 10.4
Short-Run Equilibrium.

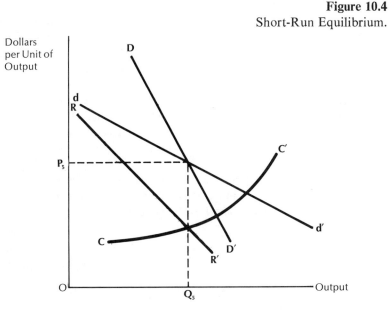

This process goes on until a point is reached where the firm has no reason to change its price. In the short run, an equilibrium will be reached when the situation is like that in Figure 10.4. That is, the short-run equilibrium price and output of each firm are OP_5 and OQ_5, respectively. It can easily be verified that the firm has no incentive to change its price from OP_5. Since marginal revenue based on the *dd'* demand curve and a going price of OP_5 equals marginal cost at an output of OQ_5, the firm believes that it is maximizing profits by maintaining its price at OP_5. Of course, the representative firm may not earn profits in short-run equilibrium. But as long as OP_5 exceeds the firm's average variable costs, the firm will continue to produce in the short run.

5.   Equilibrium Price and Output in the Long Run

As in perfect competition, firms in the long run are able to change the scale
of their plant and to leave or enter the industry. The long-run equilibrium
price and output of the representative firm are shown in Figure 10.5, the
equilibrium price being *OP* and the equilibrium output being *OQ*. Since
there is free entry and exit in a monopolistic competitive industry, the
long-run equilibrium is a situation in which all firms in the industry, although
they are maximizing profits, have zero economic profits. This, of course,
is similar to the long-run equilibrium in a perfectly competitive industry.
Note that the cost curves in Figure 10.5 are long-run cost curves, not the
short-run cost curves shown in Figure 10.4.   The long-run equilibrium
position is the point where (1) the long-run average cost curve, *LL′*, is
tangent to the *dd′* demand curve, and where (2) the *DD′* demand curve
intersects the *dd′* demand curve and the *LL′* curve at the tangency point.
(The marginal revenue curve is *RR′*, and the long-run marginal cost curve
is *MM′*.)

How is this long-run equilibrium position reached? The adjustments that
take place can be described in terms of changes in the *dd′* demand curve and
in the *DD′* demand curve. The *DD′* demand curve shifts in response to the

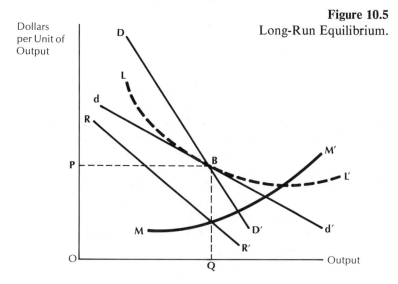

Figure 10.5
Long-Run Equilibrium.

entry of new firms and the exit of old firms. Increases in the number of firms in the industry shift the *DD'* demand curve facing the representative firm to the left, because the market (which is relatively fixed) must be divided among more firms. Reductions in the number of firms shift the *DD'* demand curve facing the representative firm to the right, because the market must be divided among fewer firms. As a result of entry and exit, the *DD'* demand curve is pushed toward the equilibrium position, where it intersects the *dd'* demand curve at the point at which the *dd'* demand curve is tangent to the long-run average cost curve, *LL'*.

Consider Figure 10.6, where $D_1 D_1'$ is the initial *DD'* demand curve and *LL'* is the long-run average cost curve. This firm (and the others in the group) is making an economic profit since the current price is OP_0. Thus, it follows that entry is encouraged and the *DD'* demand curve shifts to the left. Simultaneously, the *dd'* demand curve also moves to the left from $d_1 d_1'$. As entry continues, the *DD'* demand curve may shift to $D_2 D_2'$. If so, one might think that point *A* would be a long-run equilibrium position, since the *DD'* demand curve, $D_2 D_2'$, intersects the *LL'* curve at point *A*. However, this is not the case, since the *dd'* demand curve, $d_2 d_2'$, lies above the *LL'* curve for outputs above OQ_1. Thus each firm believes that it is profitable to expand.

Only when at last the situation in Figure 10.5 is reached will a long-run equilibrium be established. At point *B* in Figure 10.5, the *DD'* demand

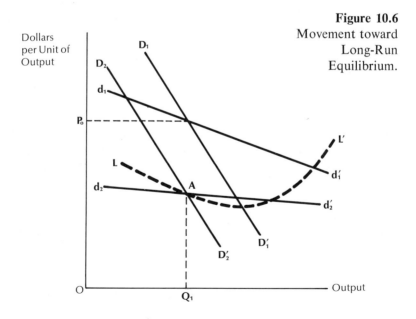

Figure 10.6
Movement toward
Long-Run
Equilibrium.

curve intersects the long-run average cost curve, *LL'*, the result being that there is no incentive for entry or exit, since economic profits are nonexistent. Moreover, at point *B*, the *dd'* demand curve is always below the long-run average cost curve, *LL'*, except at point *B* where the two curves intersect. Thus the firm has no incentive to change its price or output, since any such change appears to be unprofitable.

6. Product Variation

In his theory Chamberlin recognizes that firms can change the characteristics of their product as well as change their price. With regard to product variation, we can begin to find the optimal strategy for the representative firm by assuming that the price and product characteristics of its competitors are fixed. Then we can take each possible variant of the firm's product; and after calculating the effect on profits of alternative prices, we can find the most profitable price for each variant of the product, given the prices and product characteristics of competitors. Next, we can compare the (maximum) profits that can be made with each variant of the product, and we can find the most profitable of all the variants of the product. The representative firm will choose this variant of the product and charge the price that renders it most profitable.

Of course, this change in the characteristics and price of the firm's product may have repercussions on the product characteristics and prices of other firms in the product group; and the change in the product characteristics and prices of other firms is likely to make further change on the part of this firm profitable. Eventually, however, an equilibrium position is reached. In terms of Figure 10.5, changes in the firm's product characteristics result in changes in all three curves (*LL'*, the *DD'* demand curve, and the *dd'* demand curve), since changes in a product generally mean changes in its costs and demand. In long-run equilibrium, however, the relationships among the curves must be like those in Figure 10.5, regardless of which product characteristics are chosen by the firm and its rivals. In other words, the position of the *LL'* curve, the *DD'* demand curve, and the *dd'* demand curve will vary with the product characteristics that are chosen, but it will always be true that the equilibrium point occurs where the *LL'* curve is tangent to the *dd'* demand curve and where at the same time the *DD'* demand curve intersects the *dd'* demand curve and the *LL'* curve at the tangency point. This follows from the fact that the analysis in Section 5 is applicable regardless of which variant of the product is picked.

Monopolistic competition, as visualized by Chamberlin and others, is characterized by considerable product variety. Some firms may decide to cater to the portion of the market that is very price-conscious, with the result that their product is inexpensive and of relatively low quality. Other firms may decide to cater to the portion of the market that is quality-conscious, with the result that their product is of high quality but costly. Still other firms may attempt to add stylish "gimmicks" to their product, in the hope that they will attract sales. Whether this proliferation of product varieties is worth its cost is a very important question which, as we shall see below, is unsettled.

7. Selling Expenses

Besides varying price and the characteristics of their products, firms can also vary the extent of their selling expenses. To determine the optimal selling expense for the representative firm, it is convenient to begin by assuming that price and the characteristics of the firm's product are already determined. Suppose that Figure 10.7 represents the situation faced initially by the representative firm. The ZZ' curve is the long-run average cost curve when production, but not selling, costs are considered. The TT' curve is the ZZ' curve plus the amount of selling expenses (per unit of output) necessary to sell the relevant output, given that the other firms in the product group hold constant their selling expenses. For example, to sell an output of OQ_1, the total selling expenses by this firm must be $OQ_1 \times BA$; thus the average total cost—of both production and selling—of OQ_1 units is OA, OB being the average cost of production and BA being the average cost of selling.

For the representative firm in Figure 10.7, we assume that the initial price is OP_0 and that output is OQ_0, with the result that the firm is incurring a loss of P_0W per unit. This does not appear to be the most profitable output level for the firm. The UU' curve is the marginal curve corresponding to the TT' average cost curve; that is, it shows the total additional cost—both of production and selling—required to make and market the last unit sold. More specifically, if $V(q)$ is the total cost of producing and selling q units of output, the UU' curve shows $[V(q) - V(q-1)]$ between each value of q and $(q-1)$. Since we assume that price is given (and fixed), marginal revenue is constant and equal to the price, OP_0. Consequently, the most profitable output for this firm seems to be OQ_2 units, since this is the output at which the total marginal cost curve, UU', intersects the marginal revenue curve, P_0C. To sell this output, the firm's selling expenses per unit of output must be increased to ED.

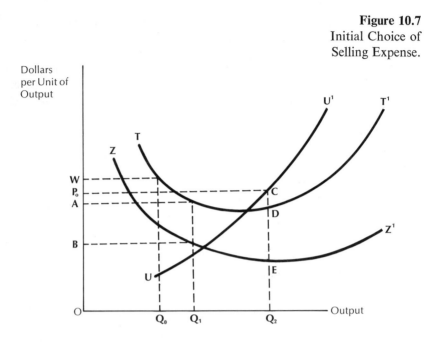

Figure 10.7
Initial Choice of
Selling Expense.

However, the firm may not be able to earn the expected profits by this course of action. For example, if greater selling expenses do not raise the market demand curve, and if all firms attempt to increase their selling expenses in this way, the sales of the representative firm will remain OQ_0, but the firm's average total costs will rise because of the higher selling costs. Eventually, the TT' curve will rise to the point where it is tangent to the price line, and the firm will then have no reason to alter its selling costs. In the long run, when firms can enter or leave the product group, changes in the number of firms will go on until economic profits or losses are eliminated. Long-run equilibrium will be attained when economic profits are zero and when, if other firms' selling expenses remain constant, there is no apparent gain from any firm's altering its own selling expenses.

Thus Figure 10.8 shows the full long-run equilibrium when the firm is allowed to manipulate all variables: price, product characteristics, and selling expenses. The SS' curve shows the average total costs of the firm, assuming that the actual selling expense currently being incurred will be maintained at each output level. At the equilibrium solution, the dd' demand curve is tangent to the SS' curve at a price of OP and an output of OQ, and the DD' demand curve intersects the dd' demand curve and the TT' curve at the tangency point. This is the full long-run equilibrium because no

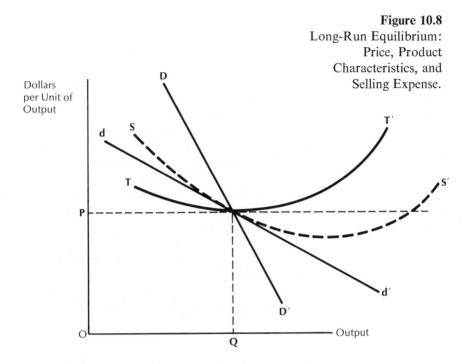

Figure 10.8
Long-Run Equilibrium:
Price, Product
Characteristics, and
Selling Expense.

incentive exists for entry or exit since economic profits are zero, and because
there is no apparent advantage to be achieved by any firm from changing its
price, product characteristics, or selling expense, as long as other firms in
the product group make no such changes.

8. Excess Capacity in Monopolistic Competition

Economists[3] have generally regarded the *ideal output* of a firm to be the
output where long-run average cost is a minimum. For example, in Figure 10.9, the ideal output is OQ_0. Similarly, the *ideal plant* is the one with
the short-run average cost curve, AA', which is tangent to the long-run aver-

[3]For example, see J. Cassels, "Excess Capacity and Monopolistic Competition,"
Quarterly Journal of Economics, 1936–1937, and R. Harrod, "Doctrines of Imperfect Competition," *Quarterly Journal of Economics*, 1934–1935.

age cost curve, *LL'*, at the ideal output. *Excess capacity* is the difference between the ideal output and the actual output in long-run equilibrium. For example, if the firm's output in long-run equilibrium is OQ_1, excess capacity in Figure 10.9 is $(OQ_0 - OQ_1)$.

A famous and somewhat controversial conclusion of the theory of monopolistic competition is that firms under this form of market organization will tend to operate with excess capacity. In other words, the firm will not construct the minimum-cost size of plant or operate the one it does construct at the minimum-cost rate of output. This conclusion can be deduced from Figure 10.5 (p. 292). The firm will not produce the ideal output or build the ideal plant because average cost at the ideal output would be greater than price, the result being that the firm would incur losses at this output. In long-run equilibrium, the firm will produce that quantity of output at which the *dd'* demand curve is tangent to the long-run average cost curve. But since the *dd'* demand curve slopes downward, the long-run average cost curve must also be downward sloping at the output the firm produces in long-run equilibrium. Thus, since the long-run average cost curve slopes downward only at outputs that are less than the ideal output, it follows that the output produced by the firm in long-run equilibrium must be less than the ideal output. In other words, there is excess capacity.

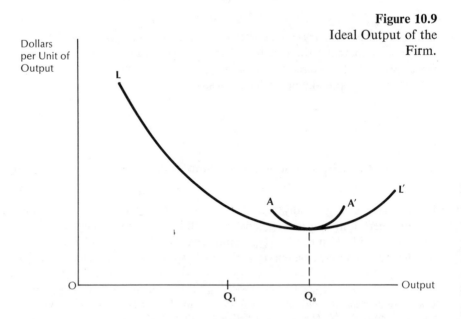

Figure 10.9
Ideal Output of the
Firm.

Since each firm builds a smaller than ideal plant and produces a smaller than ideal output, more firms can exist under these circumstances than if there were no excess capacity. Thus there is likely to be some "overcrowding" of the industry. It is difficult to know whether particular industries in the real world that are close to the monopolistic competitive model are in fact overcrowded in this sense. To be sure that such overcrowding occurred, one would have to know the ideal output of firms in each industry. However, on the basis of relatively casual empiricism, it is often asserted that a number of cases of this sort exist. For example, in the case of gas stations and grocery stores, both of which bear some resemblance to monopolistic competition, it is sometimes asserted that there are too many firms.

9. Comparisons with Perfect Competition and Monopoly

Frequently, attempts are made to compare the long-run equilibria that result from various market organizations. If we suppose that an industry were monopolistically competitive, rather than purely competitive or purely monopolistic, what difference would it make in the long-run behavior of the industry? It is difficult to interpret this question in a meaningful way, let alone answer it, since the output of the industry would be heterogeneous in one case and homogeneous in the other, and since the cost curves of the industry would probably vary with its organization. Nevertheless, many economists seem to believe that differences of the following kinds can be expected.

First, the firm under monopolistic competition is likely to produce less, and charge a higher price, than under pure competition. The demand curve confronting the monopolistic competitor is not perfectly elastic, as it is in perfect competition. Since marginal revenue is less than price in monopolistic competition, the firm will produce less than the amount at which price equals marginal cost, the consequence being that it will produce less than under perfect competition. However, the difference may not be very great, since the demand curve facing the firm under monopolistic competition may be very close to perfectly elastic.

Second, relative to pure monopoly, monopolistically competitive firms are likely to have lower profits, greater output, and lower prices. The firms in a product group might obtain economic profits if they were to collude and behave as a monopolist. For example, in Figure 10.5, the DD' demand curve is above the long-run average cost curve for outputs less than OQ. Of course, the increase in profits resulting from the monopoly would make the producers better off, but consumers would be worse off because of higher prices and a smaller output of goods.

Third, as noted in the previous section, firms in monopolistic competition may be somewhat inefficient because they tend to operate with excess capacity. Of course, inefficiences of this sort would not be expected under perfect competition. However, these inefficiencies may not be very great, since the demand curve confronting the monopolistically competitive firm is likely to be highly elastic; and the more elastic it is, the less excess capacity the firm will have.

A good deal of effort has been devoted by economists to determine the effects on social welfare of monopolistic competition. Thus far, these efforts have not been very successful, and little or nothing can be said concerning the social desirability or undesirability of monopolistic competition. On the one hand, some economists are impressed by the apparent waste in monopolistic competition. They think it results in too many firms, too many brands, too much selling effort, and too much spurious product differentiation. On the other hand if the differences among products are real and are understood by consumers, the greater variety of alternatives available under monopolistic competition may be worth a great deal to consumers. The unfortunate truth is that economics is not yet in a position to tell whether the market imperfections associated with product differentiation decrease or enhance the welfare of consumers.

10. Criticisms of the Theory of Monopolistic Competition

According to some social philosophers (mostly very young or very old), life begins at forty. Chamberlin's theory of monopolistic competition celebrates its fortieth birthday in the near future, but there is still a good deal of argument concerning its significance. A number of important criticisms have been made of the theory. For example, Chicago's George Stigler and others have argued that the definition of the group of firms included in the product group is extremely ambiguous. It may contain only one firm or all of the firms in the economy. Moreover, in Stigler's view, the concept of the group is not salvaged by the assumption that each firm neglects the effects of its decisions on other firms in the group, and that each firm has essentially the same demand and cost curves.

Indeed, according to Stigler, the firms in the group must be selling homogeneous commodities if the assumption of similar demand and cost curves for all firms in the group is to be at all realistic. But if the commodities are homogeneous, there is no reason why firms should have downward-sloping demand curves. If one loosens the assumption that the demand and cost curves are the same for all firms, other criticisms can be made of the analysis. Stigler states that "In the general case we cannot make a single statement about economic events in the world we sought to analyze . . . [although] many such statements are made by Chamberlin . . ."[4]

In addition, a number of economists have questioned the conclusion that excess capacity will be present under monopolistic competition. For example, Oxford's Roy Harrod believes that the argument leading to this conclusion contains inconsistencies since the firm uses a short-run marginal revenue curve and a long-run marginal cost curve to determine its output and size of plant. Thus the firm sets the price at a level that attracts the entry of other firms, which in turn shifts its marginal revenue curve downward. The supposedly rational entrepreneur is unaccountably short-sighted. Harrod's own analysis, which attempts to eliminate this inconsistency, results in the conclusion that excess capacity will be less, if existent at all, than Chamberlin suggests.

Still other economists claim that there are few, if any, markets in the real world where the model of monopolistic competition is relevant. There certainly is a great deal to be said for this view, the assumptions underlying the theory being quite stringent.

In conclusion, it must be granted that these criticisms have a considerable amount of merit. Although there was a good deal of enthusiasm for the theory soon after its development, the passage of time seems to have pushed the theory farther and farther from the center of the stage. However, it remains a standard part of most courses in microeconomic theory, perhaps partly in the hope that it will lead to more adequate models of the "middle ground" between perfect competition and pure monopoly. Incipient economic theorists take note.[5]

---

[4]G. Stigler, *Five Lectures on Economic Problems*, London: Longmans Green, 1949, pp. 18–19.

[5]For an excellent brief discussion of the criticisms of Chamberlin's theory, see K. Cohen and R. Cyert, *Theory of the Firm*, Englewood Cliffs, N.J.: Prentice-Hall, 1965, pp. 221–26.

11. Summary

The theory of monopolistic competition is based on the following assumptions. First, there is assumed to be a large number of firms producing a differentiated product, each firm's product being a fairly close substitute for the product of every other firm in the product group. Second, the number of firms in the product group is assumed to be sufficiently large so that each firm expects its actions to go unheeded by its rivals and to be unimpeded by any retaliatory measures on their part. Third, it is assumed that both demand and cost curves are the same for all of the firms in the group.

In the theory of monopolistic competition, there are two kinds of demand curves. On the one hand, there is the *dd'* demand curve, which shows how much the firm will sell if it varies its price from the going level and if other firms maintain their existing prices. On the other hand, there is the *DD'* demand curve, which shows how much the firm will sell if all firms raise or lower their prices by the same amount as this firm. In discussing the pricing behavior of firms under monopolistic competition, it simplifies matters to assume that the firms have already decided on the characteristics of product and the extent of selling expenses that are most profitable.

In the short run, equilibrium price and output occur when marginal revenue based on the *dd'* demand curve equals marginal cost at the existing output, while the *dd'* demand curve intersects the *DD'* demand curve at the existing price (and output). In the long run, firms, as in perfect competition, are able to change the scale of their plant and to leave or enter the industry. The long-run equilibrium position is the point at which (1) the long-run average cost curve is tangent to the *dd'* demand curve, and (2) the *DD'* demand curve intersects the *dd'* demand curve and the long-run average cost curve at the tangency point.

Under monopolistic competition, firms can vary the characteristics of the product as well as price. It is assumed that they choose the product characteristics that appear most profitable. Firms also can vary their selling expenses. Long-run equilibrium will be attained when economic profits are zero and when, if other firms' selling expenses remain constant, there is no apparent gain from any firm's altering its own selling expenses.

A famous, and somewhat controversial, conclusion of the theory of monopolistic competition is that firms under this form of market organization will tend to operate with excess capacity. That is, the firm will not construct the minimum-cost size of plant or operate the one it does construct at the minimum-cost rate of output. There have been a number of attacks on this conclusion, as well as on other aspects of the theory. Attempts have been made to determine the effects on social welfare of monopolistic competition, but little or no success has been achieved.

SELECTED REFERENCES

Chamberlin, Edward, *The Theory of Monopolistic Competition*, Cambridge, Mass.: Harvard University Press, 1933.

Robinson, Joan, *The Economics of Imperfect Competition*, London: Macmillan, 1933.

Triffin, Robert, *Monopolistic Competition and General Equilibrium Theory*, Cambridge, Mass.: Harvard University Press, 1949.

Cohen, Kalman, and Richard Cyert, *Theory of the Firm*, Englewood Cliffs, N.J.: Prentice-Hall, 1965.

Stigler, George, *Five Lectures on Economic Problems*, London: Longmans Green, 1949.

11

Price and Output
under Oligopoly

1. Oligopoly: Definition, Causes, and Classification

Previous chapters have dealt with perfect competition, monopoly, and monopolistic competition. In this chapter, we turn to oligopoly, a market structure characterized by a small number of firms and a great deal of interdependence, actual and perceived, among firms. Each oligopolist formulates his policies with an eye to their effect on his rivals. Since an oligopoly contains a small number of firms, any change in the firm's price or output influences the sales and profits of competitors. Moreover, since there are only a few firms, each firm must recognize that changes in his own policies are likely to elicit changes in the policies of his competitors as well.

A good example of an oligopoly is the American steel industry where four firms have accounted in recent years for about 60 percent of the industry's ingot capacity. Each of the major steel firms must take account of the reaction of the others when it formulates its price and output policy, since its policy is likely to affect theirs. Thus, when U. S. Steel reportedly lowered its price in response to the threat of foreign imports in 1968, it had to take into account the likelihood that other American steel producers might follow suit. And in fact this is what occurred: Bethlehem slashed its price in response. Afterwards, however, prices were raised again.

Oligopoly is a common market structure in the United States, many industries being dominated by a few firms. The automobile industry is dominated by three firms—General Motors, Ford, and Chrysler. Many parts of the electrical equipment industry are dominated by General Electric and Westinghouse. The can industry has been dominated by two firms: American Can and Continental Can. And these are only a few highly visible examples. Not all oligopolists are large firms. If two grocery stores exist in an isolated community, they are oligopolists, too; the fact that they are small firms does not change the situation.

There are many reasons for oligopoly, one being economies of scale. In some industries, low costs cannot be achieved unless a firm is producing an output equal to a substantial percentage of the total available market, the consequence being that the number of firms will tend to be rather small. In addition, there may be economies of scale in sales promotion as well as in production, and this too may promote oligopoly. Further, there may be barriers that make it very difficult to enter the industry. A variety of such barriers are discussed in Section 14. Finally, of course, the number of firms in an industry may decrease in response to the desire to weaken competitive pressures.

Oligopolistic industries can be classified in various ways. If the firms produce a homogeneous product, like steel or cement, the industry is called a *pure oligopoly*. If the firms produce a differentiated product, like automobiles, the industry is called a *differentiated oligopoly*. Throughout most of this chapter, we shall deal with the case of pure oligopoly. Also, oligopolistic industries may be marked by *collusion* or *independent action*. In Sections 2 to 8, we take up cases where oligopolists act independently. In Sections 9 to 11, we take up cases of collusion, perfect and imperfect.

2. The Cournot Model

To begin with, we consider a theory put forth by Augustin Cournot[1] well over a hundred years ago. Although this theory is too simple to capture much of the richness of the oligopolistic situation, it has attracted considerable attention and is still cited. Cournot considers the case in which there are two sellers, i.e., the case of *duopoly;* but his model can easily be generalized to include the case of three or more sellers. To describe his model, it is convenient to assume that the two firms, firm I and firm II, produce the same product, have the same cost functions, and are perfectly aware of the demand

---

[1] A. Cournot, *Recherches sur les Principes Mathématiques de la Théorie des Riches* (translated by Nathaniel Bacon), New York: Macmillan, 1897. He first published his model in 1838.

curve for their product, which is supposed to be linear. More specifically, Cournot discusses the case of two firms selling spring water, the cost of production being zero for each firm.

Turning to behavioral assumptions, both firms are supposed to maximize profits. Each assumes that, regardless of what output it produces, the other will hold its output constant at the existing level. Taking the other firm's output level as given, each firm chooses its own output level to maximize profit. Suppose that firm I is the first to act. It sells the monopoly output, 1000 units, according to the situation in Figure 11.1. It chooses this output level because it assumes that firm II will continue to produce nothing. If this is the case, firm I's marginal revenue (RR') equals its marginal cost (which is zero) at 1000 units if the demand function for the product is DD'.

Now it is firm II's turn to act. Contrary to firm I's expectation, firm II is seriously considering changing its current output level, which is zero. Taking firm I's output level (of 1000) as given, firm II believes that the demand curve for its product is the total market demand curve less 1000, or EE' in Figure 11.1. Thus firm II chooses an output level of 500, where the marginal revenue, R_1R_1', based on the demand curve EE' equals its marginal cost, which is zero.

The spotlight now moves back to firm I, which is assumed to have the next move. Again, firm I assumes that firm II has chosen an output level that will be maintained regardless of what it, firm I, does. Consequently, firm I believes that the demand curve for its product is the total demand curve less

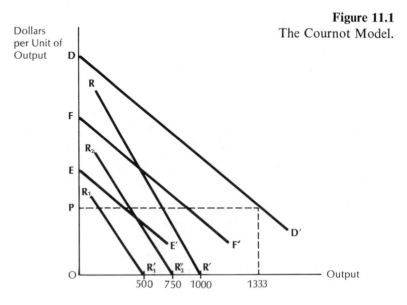

Figure 11.1
The Cournot Model.

500, or *FF'* in Figure 11.1. Thus firm I chooses an output level of 750, where marginal revenue (R_2R_2') based on the demand curve *FF'* equals the firm's marginal cost, which is zero.

This process goes on indefinitely, each firm taking the other firm's output as given and choosing the output that maximizes its own profits. Firm I's output is 1000, then 750, then 22,000 ÷ 32, $\cdots$[2] Firm II's output is 0, then 500, then 20,000 ÷ 32, $\cdots$[3] Ultimately, it can be shown that the output of each firm tends to 666 2/3.[4] Thus the price that eventually is maintained is *OP*. If price were set equal to marginal cost, it would equal zero and the industry's output would be 2000. This is the perfectly competitive solution. Thus the equilibrium output under duopoly in the Cournot model is 2/3 of the competitive output. Since the monopoly output would be 1000, it is 4/3 of the monopoly output.[5]

---

[2]How do we get 22,000/32? It can be shown that firm I will produce $1/2C$, $3/8C$, $11/32C$, $\cdots$, where C is the competitive output (2000 in this case). Try to prove this as an exercise.

[3]It can be shown that firm II will produce 0, $1/4C$, $5/16C$, $\cdots$, where C is the competitive output (2000 in this case). Prove this as an exercise. See Footnote 2.

[4]Firm I's output in the limit can be represented as
$$C[1 - (\tfrac{1}{2} + \tfrac{1}{8} + \tfrac{1}{32} + \cdots)] = C[1 - \tfrac{1}{2}(1 + \tfrac{1}{4} + (\tfrac{1}{4})^2 + \cdots)]$$
which equals
$$C\left[1 - \frac{1}{2}\left(\frac{1}{1 - \tfrac{1}{4}}\right)\right] = C(1 - \tfrac{2}{3}) = \frac{C}{3}$$
Firm II's output in the limit can be represented as
$$C(\tfrac{1}{4} + \tfrac{1}{16} + \tfrac{1}{64} + \cdots)$$
which equals
$$\tfrac{1}{4}C[1 + \tfrac{1}{4} + (\tfrac{1}{4})^2 + \cdots] = \tfrac{1}{4}C\left(\frac{1}{1 - \tfrac{1}{4}}\right) = \frac{C}{3}.$$
C is the competitive output.

[5]Another way to describe the Cournot model is as follows: There is a demand curve for the industry's product, $p = f(q_1 + q_2)$, where q_1 is the output of firm I, q_2 is the output of firm II, and p is the price of the product. The total cost function of firm I is $C_1(q_1)$ and the total cost function of firm II is $C_2(q_2)$. Thus the profit of firm I is
$$\Pi_1 = q_1 f(q_1 + q_2) - C_1(q_1)$$
and the profit of firm II is
$$\Pi_2 = q_2 f(q_1 + q_2) - C_2(q_2)$$
If each firm takes the other firm's output as given and maximizes profit
$$\frac{\partial \Pi_1}{\partial q_1} = f(q_1 + q_2) + q_1 \frac{\partial f(q_1 + q_2)}{\partial q_1} - \frac{\partial C_1}{\partial q_1} = 0$$
$$\frac{\partial \Pi_2}{\partial q_2} = f(q_1 + q_2) + q_2 \frac{\partial f(q_1 + q_2)}{\partial q_2} - \frac{\partial C_2}{\partial q_2} = 0$$
Solving these two equations simultaneously, we obtain the equilibrium q_1 and q_2, which in turn tells us what the equilibrium value of p will be.

3. The Edgeworth Model

Cournot's model was criticized by Joseph Bertrand and F. Y. Edgeworth,[6] who believed that it was better to assume that firms think that their rivals will hold price, rather than quantity, constant. In his model, Edgeworth followed Cournot in assuming that the industry is composed of two firms that sell a homogeneous product at zero marginal cost. He assumed that each firm faces the same demand curve for its product, this demand curve being represented by D_0D_0' in Figure 11.2. In addition, he assumed that each firm has a maximum output rate, this output rate being OB in Figure 11.2.

Suppose once again that firm I is the first to act and that it chooses to produce the output where marginal revenue (R_0R_0') equals marginal cost: that is, it produces OC units. It is then firm II's turn to act. Expecting that firm I will maintain its price, OP_1, firm II decides to set a price slightly below OP_1, since at that price it will take enough business away from firm I to

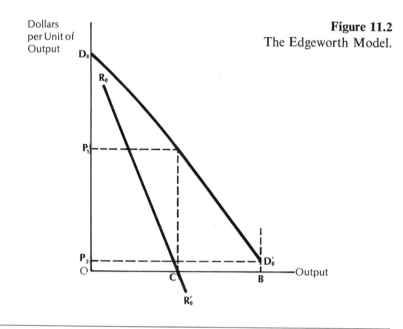

Figure 11.2
The Edgeworth Model.

[6]J. Bertrand, "Theory Mathématique de la Richesse Sociale," *Journal des Savants,* Paris, 1883; and F. Edgeworth, "La Teoria Pura del Monopolio," *Giornale degli Economisti,* 1897.

operate at its maximum output rate. Assuming that firm II will maintain its price, firm I sets a price somewhat below that set by firm II, firm I's expectation being that it will obtain enough of the market to operate at its maximum output rate.

According to Edgeworth, this process of successive price cutting goes on until price reaches OP_2. At OP_2, both firms sell their maximum output levels. But once price reaches OP_2, one of the firms, according to Edgeworth, notes that, if the other firm maintains a price of OP_2, the other firm will sell its maximum output. Thus, this firm, say firm I, raises the price to OP_1, the monopoly price, assuming that the other firm, firm II, will maintain its price of OP_2 and sell its maximum output. But once firm I raises its price to OP_1, firm II sets a price somewhat lower than OP_1, firm I sets a somewhat lower price, and the process is repeated. Thus price moves continually between OP_1 and OP_2.

Both the Cournot and Edgeworth models are extremely naïve. They make the unrealistic assumption that a firm continually makes the mistake of assuming that its rivals will not alter their output or price in response to the firm's own changes in output and price. In addition, the Edgeworth model makes the assumption that firms have maximum output levels, whereas output in the long run is generally augmentable. The Cournot and Edgeworth models are worth studying, because they are important forerunners of more realistic models, but taken by themselves they have very limited use.

4. The Chamberlin Model

A more realistic model was put forth by Edward Chamberlin of Harvard University.[7] He makes the same basic assumptions as Cournot: There are two firms, each selling water at zero marginal cost, and the demand curve for their combined output is DD' in Figure 11.3. Firm I is the first to act, and it chooses the monopoly output, 1000 units. Firm II, taking firm I's output as given, faces a demand curve of EE', and thus decides to produce 500 units. All of this is precisely the same as the Cournot model.

But Chamberlin takes a different path at the next step in the process. Firm I does not assume that firm II will maintain its output rate at 500 units, regardless of what firm I does. Instead of making this naïve assumption, which is characteristic of the Cournot model, firm I recognizes that firm II

---

[7]E. Chamberlin, *The Theory of Monopolistic Competition*, Cambridge, Mass.: Harvard University Press, 1933.

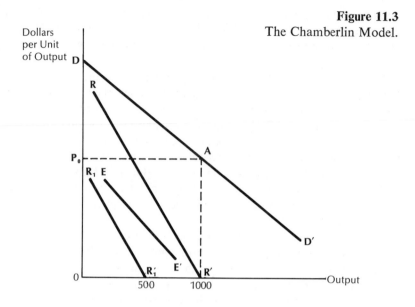

Figure 11.3

The Chamberlin Model.

will react to firm I's actions. After some deliberation, firm I concludes that the best thing that it and firm II can do is to share the monopoly profit—the profit of $OR'AP_0$. Firm II reaches the same conclusion. Thus firm I reduces its output to 500 units, and firm II keeps its output at 500 units, the result being that total output in the industry is 1000 units, price is OP_0, and the two firms share the monopoly level of profits.

An important thing to note regarding Chamberlin's model is the fact that the solution is quite stable. In contrast to Edgeworth's model, and to some extent Cournot's, price will not tend to fluctuate a great deal in Chamberlin's model. This is an advantage of Chamberlin's model, because the facts seem to indicate that prices in oligopolistic markets tend to be quite stable. For example, as we shall see in the following section, the price of one oligopolistic product, steel rails, remained essentially fixed for over a decade. Although this may be an extreme case, it illustrates the stability of prices in oligopolistic industries.

Chamberlin's model showed how firms may decide to set identical prices and maximize their joint profits, even though there is no collusion among them. They may do so, according to the Chamberlin model, without any form of agreement. Whether or not their profits are large or small depends, of course, on the individual case. Just as a monopolist may earn little or no profit, so may a Chamberlin type of oligopoly. It is difficult to know how often non-collusive behavior of this sort occurs, but it is a reasonable possibility in at least some oligopolistic markets.

5. The Kinked Demand Curve

In the previous section, we noted that empirical studies of pricing in oligopolistic markets have often concluded that prices in such markets tend to be rigid. A classic example occurred in the steel industry. From 1901 to 1916, the price of steel rails remained at $28 a ton, and from 1922 to 1933, it remained at $43 a ton. These were periods when considerable shifts occurred in demand and cost; yet the industry's price remained constant. This example is somewhat extreme, but it illustrates the basic point, which is that prices in oligopolistic industries commonly remain unchanged for fairly long periods.[8]

Of course, one would not expect prices always to respond quickly to small changes in demand and cost. It costs money for a firm to change prices, and it costs the consumer time and trouble—and perhaps money, too—to learn about them. Moreover, although quoted prices may not vary very much, this does not necessarily imply that actual prices do not vary considerably. For example, in periods when demand is low, concessions (secret or fairly open) from the quoted prices may be made to buyers. Nevertheless, taking these things into account, it is frequently concluded that prices in oligopolistic markets tend to be rigid.

A well-known theory designed to explain the rigidity of prices in oligopolistic markets was advanced by Paul Sweezy[9] in 1939. He asserted that, if an oligopolist cuts its price, it can be pretty sure that its rivals will meet the reduction. On the other hand, if an oligopolist increases its price, it is likely to find that its rivals will not change their prices. In such a case, the demand curve for the oligopolist's product would be much more elastic for price increases than for price decreases.

Figure 11.4 shows the situation, the oligopolist's demand curve being represented by $D_1 V D_1'$ and the current price being OP_0. Because of the "kink" in the demand curve, the marginal revenue curve is not continuous: It consists of two segments MA and BM'. Given that the firm's marginal cost curve is CC', marginal revenue does not equal marginal cost at any level of output. But it can be shown that OQ_0 is the most profitable output of the firm. Moreover, OQ_0 remains the most profitable output—and OP_0

---

[8]H. Purdy, M. Lindahl, and W. Carter, *Corporate Concentration and Public Policy*, Englewood Cliffs, N.J.: Prentice-Hall, 1950, p. 646.

[9]P. Sweezy, "Demand under Conditions of Oligopoly," *Journal of Political Economy*, 1939.

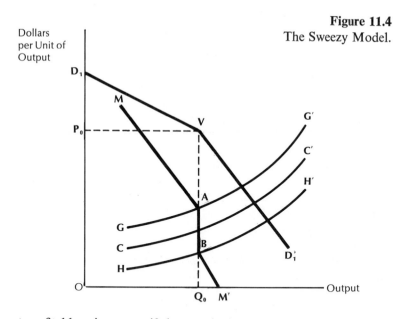

Figure 11.4
The Sweezy Model.

the most profitable price—even if the marginal cost curve changes considerably. For example, it remains the most profitable output if the marginal cost curve shifts to *GG'* or *HH'*. Also, OQ_0 remains the most profitable output —and OP_0 the most profitable price—for some changes in demand, as long as the kink remains at the same price level. Thus, under these circumstances, one might expect price to be quite rigid.

Soon after Sweezy's theory first appeared, it was regarded by some economists as a general theory of oligopoly. However, subsequent research has cast doubt on its general usefulness. For example, George Stigler found that, in seven oligopolistic industries, there was little indication that an increase in price by one firm would not be matched, in general, by other firms.[10] Thus, in these industries at least, there seemed to be little evidence for the existence of a kink in the demand curve. Moreover, although this theory may be useful under some circumstances in explaining why price tends to remain at a certain level (OP_0 in Figure 11.4), it is of no use in explaining why this level, rather than another, currently prevails. For example, it simply takes as given that the current price is OP_0 in Figure 11.4; it does not explain why the current price is OP_0. Thus this theory is an incomplete model of oligopolistic pricing.

[10]G. Stigler, "The Kinky Oligopoly Demand Curve and Rigid Prices," *Journal of Political Economy*, 1947.

6. The Theory of Games

As we have seen in previous sections, a basic feature of oligopoly is that each firm must take account of its rivals' reactions to its own actions. For this reason an oligopolistic firm cannot tell what effect a change in its output will have on the price of its product and on its profits, unless it can guess how its rivals will respond to this change in its output. Thus oligopolistic behavior has some of the characteristics of a game. One of the most interesting developments in the theory of oligopoly in the postwar period was the appearance of the *Theory of Games and Economic Behavior*, by John von Neumann and Oskar Morgenstern.[11] Although the theory of games has not shed as much light on oligopolistic behavior as was originally hoped, it has enriched oligopoly theory considerably. In this section, we provide a basic description of the objectives and concepts of game theory, as well as a very simple example of a two-person constant-sum game.

Game theory attempts to study decision-making in conflict situations. A game is a competitive situation where two or more persons pursue their own interests and no person can dictate the outcome. For example, poker is a game, and so is a situation in which two firms are engaged in competitive advertising campaigns. A game is described in terms of the players, the rules of the game, the payoffs of the game, and the information conditions that exist during the game. These elements, common to all conflict situations, are the fundamental characteristics of a game.

More specifically, a *player*, which may be a single person or an organization, is a decision-making unit. Each player has a certain amount of resources; the *rules of the game* describe how these resources can be used. For example, the rules of poker indicate how bets can be made and which hands are better than other hands. A *strategy* is a complete specification of what a player will do under each contingency in the playing of the game. For example, a corporation president might tell his subordinates how he wants an advertising campaign to start, and what should be done at subsequent points in time in response to various actions of competing firms.

The game's outcome clearly depends on the strategies used by each player. A player's *payoff* varies from game to game: It is win, lose, or draw in checkers, and various sums of money in poker. For simplicity we restrict

---

[11]J. von Neumann and O. Morgenstern, *Theory of Games and Economic Behavior*, Princeton, N.J.: Princeton University Press, 1944.

our attention to *two-person games*, games with only two players. Moreover, we restrict our attention to *zero-sum games*, games in which the amount that one player wins is exactly equal to the amount that the other player loses. Duopoly situations are frequently not of this type, but there are cases that can be described by a zero-sum game. Zero-sum games are the simplest sort, and thus we will describe them here.

The relevant features of a two-person, zero-sum game can be shown by constructing a *payoff matrix*. To illustrate, suppose that two firms are about to stage rival advertising campaigns and that each firm has a choice of strategies. Firm I can choose strategy A or B, and firm II can choose strategy 1, 2, or 3. The payoff, expressed in terms of profits, for firm I is shown in Table 11.1 for each combination of strategies. For example, if firm I adopts strategy A and firm II adopts strategy 2, firm I makes a gain of $2 million. And since it is a zero-sum game, firm II loses $2 million. If firm I adopts strategy B and firm II adopts strategy 1, firm I gains $1 million and firm II loses $1 million.

This game is *strictly determined* because, upon examination of the payoff matrix, there is a definite optimal choice for each firm. To see that this is the case, suppose that firm I is allowed to select his strategy first and he chooses strategy B. Firm II would respond by choosing strategy 1 to minimize his losses. Assuming that each firm knows the payoff matrix, this would therefore be a foolish move on firm I's part. Firm I knows that, whatever strategy it chooses, firm II will choose its strategy so as to minimize firm II's losses—and minimize firm I's gains. Consequently, firm I focuses its attention on the row minima, shown in the last column of Table 11.1. Thus firm I will choose strategy A, since it provides firm I with the greatest gain. Similarly, firm II focuses its attention on the column maxima, since it knows that firm I's response to its strategy will be to pick a strategy that maximizes the payoff to firm I. Thus firm II will choose strategy 2, since it provides firm II with the smallest loss.

Consequently, it turns out that the solution to this game is quite simple. Firm I chooses strategy A, and firm II chooses strategy 2. Firm I adopts a *maximin* policy: It maximizes the row minima. Firm II adopts a *minimax* policy: It minimizes the column maxima. Firm I gains $2 million, and firm II loses $2 million. This game is strictly determined, since there is a unique strategy that each player chooses. The maximum of the row minima equals the minimum of the column maxima. Consequently, firm I can guarantee itself a gain of $2 million, and firm II can guarantee that firm I's gain, which is at firm II's expense, will not exceed $2 million. This is the best that either player—that is, either firm—can do.

Table 11.1.   Payoff Matrix.

POSSIBLE STRATEGIES FOR FIRM I	POSSIBLE STRATEGIES FOR FIRM II			
	1	2	3	ROW MINIMUM
	[Profits for Firm I, or Losses for Firm II]			
A	$3 million	$2 million	$4 million	$2 million
B	$1 million	$1.5 million	$3 million	$1 million
Column maximum	$3 million	$2 million	$4 million	

7.   Mixed Strategies

Not all games are strictly determined. For example, suppose that the payoff matrix is the one shown in Table 11.2 rather than that in Table 11.1. If so, firm I is in bad shape if it chooses strategy A, since firm II can impose a $5 million loss on firm I by adopting strategy 1. It is also in bad shape if it chooses strategy B, since firm II can impose a $5 million loss on firm I by adopting strategy 3. What can firm I do? According to von Neumann and Morgenstern, the answer lies in the concept of a *mixed strategy*. Firm I can assign probabilities to the two pure strategies (A and B) and choose a strategy in accord with these probabilities.

Suppose that firm I chooses strategy A with probability x_1 and strategy B with probability $(1 - x_1)$. Suppose that firm II chooses strategy 1 with probability y_1, strategy 2 with probability y_2, and strategy 3 with probability $(1 - y_1 - y_2)$. Because of the uncertainty of the outcome, the firms can no longer try to maximize or minimize the particular payoff, since this payoff has no unique value. Instead they are assumed to maximize the *expected value* of the game, which can be derived from the payoff matrix by multiplying each payoff in the matrix by the probability that it occurs and summing these products for all entries in the payoff matrix.

Thus, in the case at hand, the expected gain for firm I is

$$-5x_1 + 6(1 - x_1) = 6 - 11x_1,$$

if firm II uses strategy 1. It is $3x_1 + 3(1 - x_1) = 3$, if firm II uses strategy 2. And it equals $6x_1 - 5(1 - x_1)$ if firm II uses strategy 3. Given whatever

Table 11.2. Payoff Matrix: Game Not Strictly Determined.

POSSIBLE STRATEGIES FOR FIRM I	POSSIBLE STRATEGIES FOR FIRM II			
	1	2	3	ROW MINIMUM
	[Profits for Firm I, or Losses for Firm II]			
A	−$5 million	$3 million	$6 million	−$5 million
B	$6 million	$3 million	−$5 million	−$5 million
Column maximum	$6 million	$3 million	$6 million	

value of x_1 it chooses, firm I can be sure that it will receive no less than the lowest of these three values.

Figure 11.5 shows firm I's expected gain if it adopts various values of x_1 and if firm II adopts strategies 1, 2, or 3. Suppose that firm I is interested in choosing x_1 so as to put the highest possible floor under its expected gain. It is clear from Figure 11.5 that, if firm I chooses a value of x_1 that is less than 1/2, the worst thing that can happen to it is if firm II adopts strategy 3. Similarly, it is clear that, if firm I chooses a value of x_1 that is more than

Figure 11.5
Firm I's Expected Gain,
Given Its Choice of X_1.

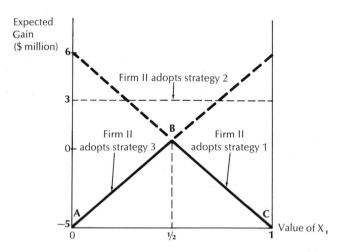

M. Shubik, "The Uses of Game Theory in Management Science," *Management Science*, Oct. 1955.

1/2, the worst thing that can happen to it is if firm II adopts strategy 1. Thus, if firm II adopts the strategy that from firm I's point of view is worst, the expected gain to firm I corresponding to each value of x_1 is given by ABC.

Consequently, if firm I puts the highest possible floor under its expected gain, it will choose $x_1 = 1/2$. That is, it will attach a probability of 1/2 to strategy A and a probability of 1/2 to strategy B. It can then be sure that its expected gain is at least \$500,000. This is termed an *optimal mixed strategy* for firm I. It can be shown that the optimal mixed strategy for firm II is $y_1 = 1/2$ and $y_2 = 0$. That is, firm II will attach a probability of 1/2 to strategy 1, a probability of 0 to strategy 2, and a probability of 1/2 to strategy 3.[12]

Von Neumann and Morgenstern proved that a pair of mixed strategies will always exist which are an equilibrium pair insofar as neither player can improve his position when each uses his optimal mixed strategy. It is easy to see that there is an equilibrium of this sort in the case just described. By choosing $x_1 = 1/2$, firm I can guarantee itself an expected gain of \$500,000. No other value of x_1 can guarantee firm I more. By choosing $y_1 = 1/2$ and $y_2 = 0$, firm II can guarantee that its expected loss is \$500,000. No other values of y_1 and y_2 can guarantee firm II more. The fact that such an equilibrium always exists in two-person zero-sum games is remarkable indeed.[13]

8. More Complicated Games and Limitations of Game Theory

Thus far the discussion has dealt only with two-person constant-sum[14] games. Most economic problems are not of the constant-sum variety. For

---

[12]The payoff matrix and solution of this example are taken from M. Shubik, "The Uses of Game Theory in Management Science," *Management Science*, Oct. 1955. The payoff matrix in Table 11.2 is also similar to one in Shubik's article.

[13]Note that there is a relationship between games and linear programming. See, for example, R. Dorfman, P. Samuelson, and R. Solow, *Linear Programming and Economic Analysis*, New York: McGraw-Hill, 1958; and W. Baumol, *Economic Theory and Operations Analysis*, Englewood Cliffs, N.J.: Prentice-Hall, 1965, pp. 538–541.

[14]Strictly speaking we have dealt only with *zero-sum games*, but there is no problem in extending the analysis to include *constant-sum games*. A constant-sum game is a case where the sum of the winnings and losses of the players is a constant, but not necessarily zero. For example, if the gambling house takes a certain amount out of each pot, the sum of winnings and losses will be a negative constant equal to the gambling house's take.

example, two firms can often increase their total profits by collusion; it is not necessary for one to gain only at the expense of the other. Although the theory is not so well developed when we leave the realm of constant-sum games, a considerable literature exists concerning both *noncooperative* games (where collusion does not occur) and *cooperative* games (where collusion does occur) that are not constant-sum. In the case of cooperative games, it is often claimed that the players will wind up on the contract curve discussed in Chapter 2. When we consider games with more than two players, added difficulties are encountered and fewer results are available.

Game theory has been criticized on several grounds, one being that the minimax principle is too conservative. According to the minimax principle, which is fundamental to the theory, a player maximizes his payoff under the assumption that his opponent will adopt the strategy that is most damaging to him. Many economists feel that this is an unnecessarily pessimistic outlook for the player, and they wonder whether such an attitude is a realistic representation of how firms actually do view competitive situations. If a player adopts a minimax strategy and his competitor does not, the former is likely to forego considerable extra profit. Despite this limitation and others, the theory of games is a useful addition to the tool kit of the microeconomist. It is useful as a suggestive framework for analysis. One can structure formerly intractable problems and think about them in terms of this theory. However, in its present state, game theory cannot be used to derive specific predictions of the behavior of oligopolists, and despite the high hopes of 25 years ago, it has permitted only a modest advance in oligopoly theory.

9. Collusion and Cartels

In previous sections we have presented theories of oligopolistic behavior based on the assumption that oligopolists do not collude.[15] However, conditions in oligopolistic industries tend to promote collusion, since the number of firms is small and the firms recognize their interdependence. The advantages to the firms of collusion seem obvious: increased profits, decreased uncertainty, and a better opportunity to prevent entry. However, collusive arrangements are often hard to maintain, since once a collusive agreement is made, any of the firms can increase its profits by "cheating"

[15]Of course, the theory of cooperative games is concerned with collusion. This is an exception to the statement in the text.

on the agreement. Moreover, collusive arrangements generally are illegal, at least in the United States.

When a collusive arrangement is made openly and formally, it is called a *cartel*. In many countries in Europe, cartels are common and legally acceptable. In the United States, most collusive agreements, whether secret or open cartels, were declared illegal by the Sherman Antitrust Act, which dates back to 1890. However, this does not mean that such agreements do not exist. For example, as we shall see in section 11, there was widespread collusion among American electrical equipment manufacturers during the 1950's. Moreover, trade associations and professional organizations may sometimes perform functions somewhat similar to a cartel. In addition, some types of cartels have the official sanction of the U. S. government.[16]

Suppose that a cartel is established to set a uniform price for a particular (homogeneous) product. What price will it charge? To begin with, the cartel must estimate the marginal cost curve for the cartel as a whole. If input prices do not increase as the cartel expands, this marginal cost curve is the horizontal sum of the marginal cost curves of the individual firms. Suppose that the resulting marginal cost curve for the cartel is CC' in Figure 11.6.

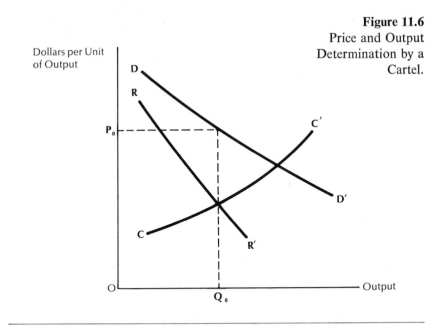

Figure 11.6
Price and Output Determination by a Cartel.

---

[16]For example, airlines flying transatlantic routes are members of the International Air Transport Association, which can agree on uniform prices for transatlantic flights.

If the demand curve for the industry's product is DD', the relevant marginal revenue curve is RR', and the output that maximizes the total profit of the cartel members is OQ_0. Thus, if it maximizes cartel profits, the cartel will choose a price of OP_0. This, of course, is the monopoly price.

Another important task of a cartel is to distribute the industry's total sales among the firms belonging to the cartel. If the aim of the cartel is to maximize cartel profits, it will allocate sales to firms in such a way that the marginal cost of all firms is equal. Otherwise the cartel could make more money by reallocating output among firms so as to reduce the cost of producing the cartel's total output. For example, if the marginal cost at firm I was higher than at firm II, the cartel can increase its total profits by transferring some production from firm I to firm II.

However, this allocation of output—sometimes called the "ideal" allocation by economists—is unlikely to occur, since allocation decisions are the result of negotiation between firms with varying interests and varying capabilities. This is a political process in which various firms have different amounts of influence. Those with the most influence and the shrewdest negotiators are likely to receive the largest sales quotas, even though this increases total cartel costs. Moreover, high-cost firms are likely to receive larger sales quotas than cost minimization would dictate, since they would be unwilling to accept the small quotas dictated by cost minimization. In practice, there is some evidence that sales are often distributed in accord with a firm's level of sales in the past, or the extent of its productive capacity. Also, a cartel sometimes divides a market geographically, some firms being given certain regions or countries and other firms being given other regions or countries.

10.   The Instability of Cartels

We have already noted that collusive agreements tend to break down. Of course, the difficulty in keeping a cartel from breaking down increases with the number of firms in the cartel. To see why firms are tempted to leave the cartel consider the case of the firm in Figure 11.7. If this firm were to leave the cartel, it would be faced with a demand curve of DD' as long as the other firms in the cartel maintain a price of OP_0. This demand curve is very elastic, the firm being able to expand its sales considerably by small reductions

Figure 11.7
The Instability of
Cartels.

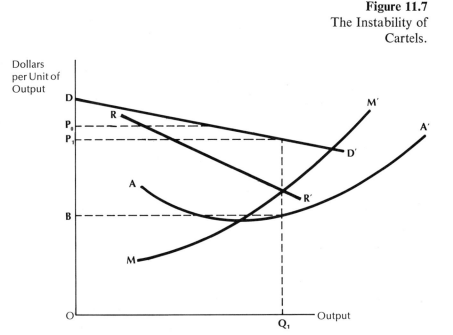

in price. Even if the firm were not to leave the cartel, but if it were to grant secret price concessions, the same sort of demand curve would be present.

Under these circumstances the firm's maximum profit if it leaves the cartel or secretly lowers price will be attained if it sells an output of OQ_1, at a price of OP_1, since MM' is its marginal cost curve and RR' is its marginal revenue curve. Since AA' is its average cost curve, this price would result in a profit of $OQ_1 \times BP_1$, which is likely to be higher than if the firm conforms to the price and sales quota dictated by the cartel. A firm that breaks away from a cartel—or secretly cheats—can increase its profits as long as other firms do not do the same thing and as long as the cartel does not punish it in some way. But if all firms do this, the cartel breaks down.

Consequently, as long as a cartel is not maintained by legal provisions, there is a constant threat to its existence. Its members have an incentive to cheat, and once a few do so, others may follow. Price concessions made secretly by a few "chiselers" or openly by a few malcontents cut into the sales of cooperative members of the cartel who are induced to match them. Thus the ranks of the unfaithful are expanded; and ultimately the cartel may break down completely.

11. Collusion in the Electrical Equipment Industry

In early 1960 the Department of Justice charged that a large number of companies and individuals in the electrical equipment industry were guilty of fixing prices and dividing up the market for circuit breakers, switchgear, and other important products. Most of the defendants were found guilty, and the companies, including General Electric and Westinghouse, received fines, and some of the guilty executives were sent to prison. This was a very interesting and instructive modern example of collusive oligopoly behavior.

The price-fixing agreements were reached in various ways. Many of the meetings occurred at conventions of the National Electrical Manufacturers Association and other trade groups. Some agreements were made through telephone calls and written memoranda transmitted from one sales executive to another. Efforts were made to keep the meetings and agreements secret. For example, codes were used, and the participants at meetings sometimes disguised their records and did not use their companies' names when registering at hotels. The executives recognized that these agreements were illegal.

To see how these agreements worked, consider the case of circuit breakers. In 1958, there were only five manufacturers of circuit breakers, and it was decided that General Electric would receive about 40 percent of the sealed-bid business; Westinghouse, about 31 percent; Allis-Chalmers, about 9 percent; Federal Pacific, about 16 percent; and I-T-E, 4 percent. According to a statement to the court, this is how it worked:

> At a working level meeting where a particular job was up for discussion, the percentages initially would be reviewed in light of what was known on the ledger list, which had on it recent sealed-bid jobs given to the other defendants. In light of that ledger list it was decided which of the companies, to keep the percentages constant, would get the job. Now if that company was prepared to say the price at which it was going to bid, then the other companies could discuss among themselves what they would bid, add on for accessories, to make sure to give . . . the company . . . whose turn it was to get the job, the best shot at it . . . . If the company whose job the particular rigged job was supposed to be did not know the price, there would be later communication, either by phone to homes with just the first names used, or by letter to homes with just first names of senders, with no return address, and . . . [using] code.[17]

In view of the discussion in the previous section, it is interesting to note that many of these agreements tended to be unstable. In the early and mid-

---

[17]*Wall Street Journal*, 1961. This appears in E. Mansfield, *Monopoly Power and Economic Performance*, New York: W. W. Norton, 1968, p. 95.

fifties, as well as in the period after 1958, there were agreements of this sort, but eventually overcapacity in the industry led to "chiseling" by various firms. This problem persisted in the late fifties as well. For example, price-cutting in sales of power switching machinery to Government agencies was regarded as a major problem in late 1958. One collusive agreement after another was drawn up, but after a while some firms began in each case to pursue an independent price policy.

12. Price Leadership

Another model of oligopolistic behavior is based on the supposition that one of the firms in the industry is the price leader. This form of behavior seems to be quite common in oligopolistic industries, one or a few firms apparently setting the price and the rest following their lead. Examples of industries that have been characterized by price leadership, according to various studies, are steel, nonferrous alloys, agricultural implements, and retail groceries.[18] Two forms of price leadership are discussed in this section, the dominant-firm model and the barometric-firm model.

The *dominant-firm* model applies to industries in which there is a single large dominant firm in the industry and a number of small firms. It is assumed that the dominant firm sets the price for the industry, but that it lets the small firms sell all they want at that price. Whatever amount the small firms do not supply at that price is supplied by the dominant firm. If this model holds, it is easy to derive the price that the dominant firm will set if it maximizes profits. Since each small firm takes the price as given, it produces the output at which price equals marginal cost. Thus a supply curve for all small firms combined can be drawn by summing horizontally the marginal cost curves of the small firms. This supply curve is labeled SS' in Figure 11.8. The demand curve for the dominant firm can be derived by subtracting the amount supplied by the small firms at each price from the total amount demanded at that price. Consequently, if DD' is the demand curve for the industry's product, the demand curve for the output of the dominant firm, dd', can be determined by finding the horizontal difference at each price between the DD' curve and the SS' curve.

---

[18]See A. Kaplan, J. Dirlam, and R. Lanzillotti, *Pricing in Big Business*, Washington, D.C.: Brookings Institution, 1958; M. Colberg, D. Forbush, and G. Whitaker, *Business Economics*, Homewood, Illinois: Irwin, 1964; and C. Wilcox, *Competition and Monopoly in American Industry*, TNEC Monograph 21, Washington, D.C., 1940.

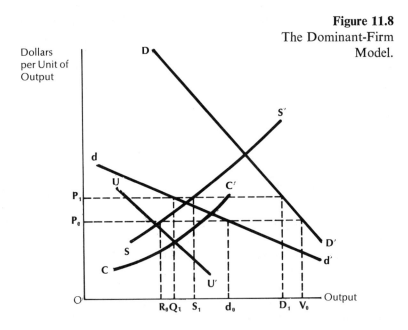

Figure 11.8
The Dominant-Firm
Model.

To illustrate the derivation of *dd'*, suppose that the dominant firm sets a price of OP_0. The *SS'* curve shows that the small firms will supply OR_0, and the *DD'* curve shows that the total amount demanded will be OV_0. Thus the amount to be supplied by the dominant firm is $OV_0 - OR_0$, which is the quantity on the *dd'* curve at price OP_0. In other words, Od_0 is set equal to $OV_0 - OR_0$. The process by which the other points on the *dd'* curve are determined is exactly the same, this procedure being repeated at various price levels.

Given the demand curve for the output of the dominant firm, *dd'*, and the dominant firm's marginal cost curve, *CC'*, it is a simple matter to determine the price and output that will maximize the profits of the dominant firm. The dominant firm's marginal revenue curve, *UU'*, can be derived from the dominant firm's demand curve, *dd'*, in the usual way. The optimal output for the dominant firm is the output, OQ_1, where its marginal cost equals its marginal revenue. This output will be achieved if the dominant firm sets a price of OP_1. The total industry output will be OD_1, and the small firms will supply $OS_1 (= OD_1 - OQ_1)$.

The *barometric-firm* model applies to another form of price leadership in which one firm usually is the first to make changes in price that are generally accepted by other firms in the industry. The barometric firm may not be the largest, or most powerful, firm. Instead it is a reasonably accurate interpreter of changes in basic cost and demand conditions in the industry as a whole.

According to Kaplan, Dirlam, and Lanzillotti, barometric price leadership frequently occurs as a response to a period of violent price fluctuation and cut-throat competition in an industry, during which many firms suffer and greater stability is widely sought.[19]

13. Cost-Plus Pricing

Empirical studies have often suggested that cost-plus pricing is used by many oligopolists. There are two basic steps in this approach to pricing. First, the firm estimates the cost per unit of output of the product. Since this cost will generally vary with output, the firm must base this computation on some assumed output level. Usually, firms seem to use for this purpose some percentage, generally between two-thirds and three-quarters, of capacity. Second, the firm adds a *markup* (generally put in the form of a percentage) to the estimated average cost. This markup is meant to include certain costs that cannot be allocated to any specific product and to provide a return on the firm's investment. The size of the markup depends on the rate of profit that the firm believes it can earn. Some firms have set up a *target return* figure that they hope to earn, which determines the markup. Table 11.3 shows the target rate of return for a few major companies.

There is considerable controversy over the extent to which cost-plus pricing is compatible with profit maximization. At first glance, it seems extremely unlikely that this form of pricing can result in the maximization of profits. Indeed, this pricing technique seems naive, since it takes no account, explicitly at least, of the extent or elasticity of demand or of the size of marginal, rather than average, costs. Nevertheless, some economists believe that cost-plus pricing may result in firms, under oligopolistic circumstances, coming close to maximum profits. They argue that cost-plus pricing is used to "stabilize" competition and lessen uncertainty. Moreover, if average variable costs are relatively constant over the relevant range, and if the elasticity of demand remains relatively constant, cost-plus pricing could result in something approaching profit maximization.

Unquestionably, many firms do compute prices on the basis of this sort of procedure. However, a model of this sort is incomplete unless it specifies more precisely the determinants of the size of the markup. Although firms

---

[19]A. Kaplan, J. Dirlam, and R: Lanzillotti, *Pricing in Big Business*, Washington, D.C.: Brookings Institution, 1958, p. 271.

Table 11.3.   Target Rates of Return (after Taxes),
Selected Firms.

	TARGET RETURN ON INVESTMENT (%)	ACTUAL RETURN ON INVESTMENT, 1947–1955 (%)
General Electric	20	21.4
General Motors	20	26.0
Sears Roebuck	10–15	5.4
U. S. Steel	8	10.3

Source: R. Lanzillotti, "Pricing Objectives in Large Companies,"
American Economic Review, Dec. 1958.

may construct these markups to yield a certain target rate of return, it is clear from Table 11.3 that these markups frequently do not prevail, since the firm's actual rates of return frequently vary considerably from the target rates of return. The simple cost-plus pricing model is silent on this score.

14.   The Long Run and Barriers to Entry

So far, we have been concerned primarily with oligopolistic behavior in the short run. In the long run it may be possible for entry or exit of firms to occur. We are already familiar, of course, with the in-migration and out-migration of firms, these phenomena having been described in our discussions of other market structures in Chapters 8 to 10. However, the importance of the entry of new firms—and the exit of old firms—in modifying the structure of an industry should be noted once more. In particular, an oligopolistic industry may not be oligopolistic for long if every Tom, Dick, and Harry can enter.

Whether or not the industry remains oligopolistic in the face of relatively easy entry depends on the size of the market for the product relative to the optimum size of firm. Above-average profits will attract new firms. If the market is small relative to the optimum size of firm in this industry, the number of firms will remain sufficiently small so that the industry will still be an oligopoly. If the market is large relative to the optimum size of the firm, the number of firms will grow sufficiently large so that the industry is no longer an oligopoly.

Ease of entry also tends to erode collusive agreements. We saw in Section 10 that existing firms are tempted continually to "cheat" on a collusive agreement, since they can attract business from their rivals by lowering prices. The situation is similar for entrants. They, too, are faced by a relatively elastic demand curve as long as existing firms adhere to collusive agreements to maintain price at its existing level. As long as profits exist in the industry, firms will be tempted to enter and take business away from the collusive group by lowering the price a bit. Once entry of this sort occurs, it becomes more and more difficult to keep a cartel together.

Since it may not be possible to maintain an oligopoly for long if firms can enter the industry, it is important that we discuss the various kinds of barriers to entry. The first barrier to entry, already noted, is smallness of the market relative to the optimum size of firm. For example, suppose that the industry demand curve is DD' in Figure 11.9. Thus, if the industry is composed of two identical duopolists producing a homogeneous product, each firm faces a demand curve of EE', which is half of DD' at each price. On the other hand, if the industry is composed of three identical oligopolists producing a homogeneous product, each firm faces a demand curve of FF', which is one-third of DD' at each price. If the average cost curve of a firm in this industry is AA', only two firms can exist in this industry; once there are two firms, there is an effective barrier to entry.

Another barrier to entry is the requirement in some industries that a firm build and maintain a large, complicated, and expensive plant. It is difficult to obtain the funds required to build a modern automobile or steel plant, which may cost hundreds of millions of dollars. Also, skilled personnel

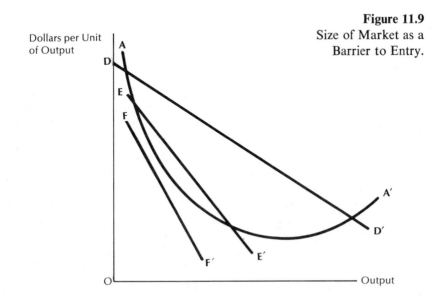

Figure 11.9
Size of Market as a
Barrier to Entry.

must be acquired, distribution channels must be established, and various types of productive and repair facilities must be set up. Because of the scale of the undertaking, as well as for other reasons, there has been little entry in recent years in industries like steel and autos.

Still another barrier to entry is the unavailability of natural resources. This factor is often cited in the case of nickel, sulfur, diamonds, and bauxite. A further barrier to entry is the existence of important patents. The holder of these patents, which may relate to the product itself or key processes by which the product is made, may license only a few firms to produce the product. Moreover, the firms in an industry may allow one another to use their patents but refuse to permit any outsider to use them. Finally, the government is sometimes responsible for other important barriers to entry. For example, taxicabs and buses must obtain franchises, and local licensing laws may be used to limit the number of plumbers, barbers, and so on.

In some oligopolistic industries it is sometimes asserted that firms set price so as to bar entry. This is called *limit pricing*. A limit price is a price that discourages or prevents entry. Firms that practice limit pricing give up short-run profits in order to earn larger, longer-term profits. The limit price must lie somewhere below the price that would maximize profits if entry were impossible regardless of price. The exact level of the limit price will depend on how difficult it is to enter the industry. Of course, the firms already in the industry must agree, at least within certain bounds, concerning the advisability and proper level of a limit price.

15. Nonprice Competition

In many oligopolistic industries, firms tend to use advertising and variation in product characteristics, more than price, as competitive weapons. They seem to view price cutting as a dangerous tactic, since it can start a price war that may have grave consequences. On the other hand, advertising and product variation are viewed as less risky ways of wooing customers away from competitors.

When a firm advertises, it attempts to shift the demand curve for its product to the right or to make it more inelastic. An effective advertising campaign will make it possible for a firm to sell more at the same price. Firms use advertising to differentiate their product from those of their competitors. In this way customers may be induced to stick with a particular brand name, even though the products of all firms in the industry are much the same. For example, various brands of cigarettes are quite similar, although not identical. The cigarette industry spends over \$200 million a year on advertising to impress their brand names, and whatever differences exist among brands, on the consumer.[20]

Sometimes advertising expenditures only have the effect of raising the costs of the entire industry, since one firm's advertising campaign causes other firms to increase their advertising. The total market for the industry's product may not increase in response to the increased advertising, and the effects on the sales of individual firms may be small, since the effects of the advertising may cancel out. However, once every firm has increased its advertising expenditures, no single firm can reduce them to their former size without losing sales. Thus the cost curves—including both production and selling costs—of the firms in the industry are pushed upward.

Frequently a firm varies the characteristics of its product as well as advertises in order to differentiate its product from those of its competitors. Like advertising, the purpose of varying the firm's product is to manipulate the firm's demand curve and to reduce the elasticity of demand for its product. Of course, changes in product, like other competitive tactics, often result in retaliatory moves by competitors. Successful changes in product design or product quality tend to be imitated by competitors, although with a lag of varying length. The costs of competition through style and quality of product can be very great. For example, the automobile industry has been engaged for many years in intense competition of this sort, the cost of model changes during the 1950's being approximately \$5 billion per year.[21]

16. Effects of Oligopoly

This chapter has taken up some of the oligopoly models that economists have constructed. Since there is no agreement that any of these models is an adequate general representation of oligopolistic behavior, it is difficult to estimate the effects of an oligopolistic market structure on price, output, and profits. Nevertheless, a few things can be said.

First, the models we have discussed usually indicate that price will be higher than under perfect competition. The difference between the oligopoly price and the perfectly competitive price will depend, of course, on the

---

[20]Other industries spending \$200 million or more on advertising in 1957 were department stores, retail food stores, drugs and medicines, and beer. See L. Telser, "Advertising and Cigarettes," *Journal of Business*, 1963.

[21]F. Fisher, Z. Griliches, and C. Kaysen, "The Cost of Automobile Model Changes since 1949," *Journal of Political Economy*, Oct. 1962.

number of firms in the industry and the ease of entry. The larger the number of firms and the easier it is to enter the industry, the closer the oligopoly price will be to the perfectly competitive level. Also, prices will tend to be more inflexible under oligopolistic conditions than under perfect competition.

Second, if the demand curve is the same under oligopoly as under perfect competition, it also follows that output will be less under oligopoly than under perfect competition. However, it is not always reasonable to assume that the demand curve is the same under oligopoly as under perfect competition, since the large expenditures for advertising and product variation that are incurred by some oligopolies may tend to shift the demand curve to the right. Consequently in some cases both price and output may tend to be higher under oligopoly than under perfect competition.

Third, we have already noted that oligopolistic industries tend to spend large amounts on advertising and product variation. The use of some resources for these purposes is certainly worthwhile, since advertising provides buyers with information, and product variation allows greater freedom of choice. Whether or not oligopolies spend too much for these purposes is by no means obvious. However, there is a widespread feeling among economists, based largely on empirical studies (and hunch), that in some oligopolistic industries such expenditures have been expanded beyond the levels that are socially optimal.[22]

Fourth, one would expect on the basis of the models presented in this chapter that the profits earned by oligopolists should be higher, on the average, than the profits earned by perfectly competitive firms. This conclusion is supported by substantial statistical evidence. For example, Joe Bain, of the University of California, has found that firms in industries in which the largest few firms had a high proportion of total sales tended to have higher rates of return than firms in industries in which the largest few firms had a small proportion of total sales.[23]

17. Summary

Oligopoly is characterized by a small number of firms and a great deal of interdependence, actual and perceived, among them. A good example of an

---

[22]Note that we are not talking here about expenditures on relatively fundamental research and development, when we talk about product variation. A great deal of existing product variation is based on relatively superficial differences among products. For some discussion of research and development, see Chapter 16.

[23]J. Bain, "Relation of Profit Rate to Industry Concentration: American Manufacturing, 1936–1940," *Quarterly Journal of Economics*, Aug. 1951.

oligopoly is the American steel industry, where a small number of firms account for the bulk of the industry's capacity. Oligopolistic industries may be marked by independent action or collusion. Two early models based on the supposition that firms act independently are the Cournot and Edgeworth models, both of which make naïve assumptions concerning the ability (or inability) of firms to learn. Somewhat more realistic models are those put forth by Chamberlin and Sweezy. An interesting development of the postwar period was the theory of games, which enriched oligopoly theory considerably, although it has not yet lived up to early expectations. One can structure formerly intractable problems and think about them in terms of game theory, but in its present state game theory cannot be used to derive specific predictions of the behavior of oligopolists.

Conditions in oligopolistic industries tend to promote collusion, since the number of firms is small and firms recognize their interdependence. The advantages to the firms of collusion seem obvious: increased profits, decreased uncertainty, and a better opportunity to control the entry of new firms. However, collusive arrangements are often hard to maintain, since once a collusive agreement is made, any of the firms can increase its profits by "cheating" on the agreement. Also, such arrangements are illegal in the United States. An interesting example of collusion took place in the electrical equipment industry during the fifties.

Another model of oligopolistic behavior is based on the supposition that one of the firms in the industry is a price leader, either because it is a dominant firm or a barometric firm. Still other models assume that oligopolists use cost-plus pricing or limit pricing. The effects of oligopoly are difficult to predict, but it appears that price and profits will be higher than under perfect competition. Also, oligopolists engage in nonprice competition, perhaps excessively in some cases from the point of view of social welfare.

SELECTED REFERENCES

Fellner, William, *Competition Among the Few*, New York: Knopf, 1949.
Shubik, Martin, *Strategy and Market Structure*, New York: John Wiley, 1959.
Cohen, Kalman, and Richard Cyert, *Theory of the Firm*, Englewood Cliffs, N.J.: Prentice-Hall, 1965.
Mansfield, Edwin, *Monopoly Power and Economic Performance*, New York: Norton, revised edition, 1968.
Modigliani, Franco, "New Developments on the Oligopoly Front," *Journal of Political Economy*, 1958.

12

Price and Employment of Inputs under Perfect Competition

1. Incomes: Distribution and Inequality

No one needs to be convinced that income is an interesting topic. Whether a person is a struggling member of the working class or a dowager whose labor is confined to endorsing dividend checks, he or she recognizes the significance of income. Moreover, no one has to be intimately acquainted with government statistics to know that there are enormous differences in the amounts of money that people make. For example, a stroll through midtown Manhattan will provide plenty of evidence of abject poverty and great affluence existing almost side by side.

Why do these differences in income exist? Why is it that one man receives so much more income than another? As we pointed out in Chapter 1, a man's income depends partly on the quantity of resources he owns. Some people own lots of land; others own none. Some people have unusual skills and talents; others do not. Some people own equipment and factories; others own little beyond their clothes (and even their clothes may not be completely paid for).

But the quantity of resources a man owns is by no means the only determinant of his income. The other important determinant is the price he obtains for the services of each type of resource that he owns. For example, if a man is a landowner with 100 acres of land, he will receive $10,000 per year if the price he obtains from the farmers who work his land is $100 per acre (annually); however, if the price goes down to $50 per acre, he will receive only $5000 per year. Similarly, a laborer's income will obviously depend on the price he receives for the services he performs.

Thus, to understand why differences in income exist, we must understand why the prices of the services of each type of resource are what they are. We must ask questions like: Why is the wage rate for physicians frequently in the neighborhood of $15 an hour while the wage rate for secretaries is often about $3 an hour? Why is the wage rate for college professors considerably higher than it was in 1960? Why is it that land of one kind yields a higher financial return than land of another kind?

In other words, we must try to understand the determinants of input prices. In a free enterprise economy, input prices are important determinants of the incomes of consumers. In the typical household the breadwinner sells his services to a firm, the wage that he receives being an input price from the viewpoint of the firm. His wage is a cost to the firm but to the worker it is an important determinant of his income, which (as we saw in Chapter 2) helps to determine his choice of consumers' goods. The distribution of income among individuals in the economy is determined to a considerable extent by the configuration of input prices.

2. Price and Employment of Inputs

The previous four chapters were concerned with the analysis of the pricing and output of consumers' goods. We turn now to the determinants of the price and employment of inputs, this being the topic of the present chapter as well as Chapter 13. This chapter assumes that there is perfect competition in both commodity and input markets; the next chapter relaxes these assumptions.

At the outset, two points should be noted. First, a good deal of the theory presented in the previous four chapters is applicable to inputs as well as commodities; for example, the price of inputs as well as commodities is determined by the interaction of supply and demand. However, the demand for inputs differs in important respects from the demand for commodities, and the supply of inputs differs in important respects from the supply of commodities. These differences stem largely from the fact that inputs are demanded by firms, not consumers; and that some important inputs, like labor, are supplied by consumers, not firms.

Second, in the nineteenth century, it was customary for economists to classify inputs into three categories: land, labor, and capital. The theory of input pricing was therefore a theory of the distribution of income among landowners, wage earners, and capitalists, three important economic and social classes. (The incomes of these three classes were rent, wages, and profits, respectively). In recent years, this simple classification of inputs has tended to go out of style, in part because each category contains such an enormous variety of inputs. For example, labor includes the services of a Nobel-Prize-winning biochemist and the services of a secretary whose typing is strictly hunt-and-peck. In this chapter we shall seldom use this tripartite classification[1]; instead we shall present our results in general terms so that the user of the model can classify inputs to fit his own particular problem.

3.   Profit Maximization and Input Employment

Fortunately, we do not have to start from scratch in constructing a model of input pricing and utilization under perfect competition. We learned a

---

[1]Toward the end of the nineteenth century, a fourth "factor of production"—or type of input—was recognized: entrepreneurship. Then profits were viewed as the return to the entrepreneur, and interest was viewed as the return on capital to the owner.

great deal that is relevant and useful in Chapters 6 and 7 when we analyzed the firm's decisions concerning input combinations and output level. A moment's reflection should convince you that, when we determined how much the firm would produce and the input combination it would use to produce this output, we in effect determined how much of each input the firm would demand under various sets of circumstances. This, of course, is an important beginning.

To make sure that the implications of our findings in Chapter 6 are clear, we shall review a few of these findings. In particular, recall the way in which a firm combines inputs in order to minimize costs. We showed that the firm will pick a combination of inputs where the ratio of each input's marginal product to its price is equal. That is, it will set

$$\frac{MP_x}{P_x} = \frac{MP_y}{P_y} = \cdots = \frac{MP_z}{P_z} \tag{12.1}$$

where MP_x is the marginal product of input x, P_x is the price of input x, MP_y is the marginal product of input y, P_y is the price of input y, and so on. If Equation 12.1 does not hold, the firm can always reduce costs by changing the utilization of certain inputs. For example, if the marginal product of input x is 2 units, the price of input x is \$1, the marginal product of input y is 6 units, and the price of input y is \$2, the firm can reduce its costs by using 1 unit less of input x—which reduces output by 2 units and cost by \$1— and by using 1/3 unit more of input y—which increases output by 2 units and cost by \$0.67. This substitution of input y for input x has no effect on output but reduces the cost by \$0.33.

Going a step further, it can be shown that, if a firm minimizes cost, each of the ratios in Equation 12.1 equals the reciprocal of the firm's marginal cost. In other words,

$$\frac{P_x}{MP_x} = \frac{P_y}{MP_y} = \cdots = \frac{P_z}{MP_z} = MC \tag{12.2}$$

where MC is its marginal cost. To prove this, consider input x. What is the cost of producing an extra unit of output if this extra unit of output is achieved by increasing the utilization of input x, while holding constant the utilization of other inputs? Since an extra unit of input x results in MP_x extra units of output, $(1/MP_x)$ units of input x will result in one unit of extra output. Since $(1/MP_x)$ units of input x will cost $(1/MP_x)P_x, P_x \div MP_x$

equals marginal cost. This same type of reasoning can be used for any input, not just input x, with the consequence that Equation 12.2 holds.[2]

As an illustration, suppose that there are only two inputs, input x and input y. Suppose that the marginal product of input x is 2 units, the price of input x is \$1, the marginal product of input y is 4 units, and the price of input y is \$2. The extra cost of producing an extra unit of product, if the extra production occurs by increasing the use of input x, is \$0.50, since an extra 1/2 unit of input x—at \$1 a unit—will result in an extra unit of output. Similarly, the extra cost of producing an extra unit of product, if the extra production comes about by increasing the use of input y, is \$0.50, since an extra 1/4 unit of input y—at \$2 a unit—will result in an extra unit of output. Thus the ratio of the price of each input to its marginal product equals marginal cost, which is \$0.50.

Going another step further, the firm, if it maximizes profit, must be operating at a point at which marginal cost equals marginal revenue. Thus

---

[2] Let $Q = f(X_1, \cdots, X_n)$, where Q is the firm's output, X_1 is the amount of the first input used by the firm, X_2 is the amount of the second input used by the firm, and so on. To minimize cost subject to the constraint that output equals Q^*, we form the Lagrangian function

$$L = \sum_{i=1}^{n} P_i X_i - \lambda(f(X_1, \cdots, X_n) - Q^*)$$

where P_i is the price of the ith input and λ is a Lagrange multiplier. Setting $\partial L/\partial X_i = 0$, we have

$$P_i - \frac{\lambda \partial f}{\partial X_i} = 0 \qquad\qquad (i = 1, \ldots, n)$$

Or

$$P_i \div \frac{\partial f}{\partial X_i} = \lambda \qquad\qquad (i = 1, \ldots, n)$$

The point in the text is that λ equals marginal cost. To prove this, note that

$$dC = \sum_{i=1}^{n} P_i \, dX_i$$

$$dQ = \sum_{i=1}^{n} \frac{\partial f}{\partial X_i} \, dX_i$$

where dC is a small change in cost, dQ is a small change in output, and dX_i is a small change in X_i. Since marginal cost equals $dC \div dQ$, it follows that marginal cost equals

$$\frac{\sum_{i=1}^{n} P_i \, dX_i}{\sum_{i=1}^{n} (\partial f / \partial X_i) \, dX_i} = \frac{\sum_{i=1}^{n} \lambda (\partial f / \partial X_i) \, dX_i}{\sum_{i=1}^{n} (\partial f / \partial X_i) \, dX_i} = \lambda$$

This proves the point in the text.

it follows that

$$\frac{P_x}{MP_x} = \frac{P_y}{MP_y} = \cdots = \frac{P_z}{MP_z} = MR \tag{12.3}$$

where MR is the firm's marginal revenue. Rearranging terms,

$$MP_x \cdot MR = P_x \tag{12.4a}$$
$$MP_y \cdot MR = P_y \tag{12.4b}$$
$$\vdots$$
$$MP_z \cdot MR = P_z \tag{12.4c}$$

Thus we conclude that the profit-maximizing firm employs each input in an amount such that the input's marginal product multiplied by the firm's marginal revenue equals the input's price. This result, as we shall see in the following section, provides the basis for the firm's demand curve for an input.

4. The Firm's Demand Curve: The Case of One Variable Input

Our first step in analyzing the demand for an input is to consider the demand curve of an individual firm for an input, assuming that this input is the only variable input in the firm's production process. In other words, the quantities of all other inputs are fixed. This assumption is relaxed in the next section. The demand curve of a firm for this input—call it input x—shows the quantity of input x that the firm will demand at each possible price of input x. Assuming that the firm maximizes its profits, it will demand that amount of input x at which the value of the extra output produced by an extra unit of input x is equal to the price of input x. This is the meaning of Equation 12.4a.

To make this more concrete, suppose that we know the firm's production function, from which we deduce that the marginal product of input x (at each level of utilization of input x) is as shown in Table 12.1. Suppose that the price of the product is \$3. Since the product market is perfectly competitive, the marginal revenue is also \$3. The value to the firm of the extra output resulting from its increasing its utilization of input x by one unit is shown in the last column of Table 12.1. This is called the *value of the marginal product* of input x, and equals $MP_x \cdot P$, where P is the price of the product. Since $P = MR$ in perfect competition, the value of the marginal product is the left-hand side of Equation 12.4a.

How many units of input x should the firm use if input x costs $10 a unit? A one-unit increase in the utilization of input x adds to the firm's revenues the amount shown in the last column of Table 12.1, and it adds $10 to the firm's costs. (Since the input markets are perfectly competitive, the firm cannot influence the price of any input.) Thus the firm should increase its utilization of input x as long as the increase in revenues exceeds the increase in costs; in other words, as long as the figure in the last column of Table 12.1 exceeds $10. For example, if the firm is using 5 units of input x, the use of an extra unit will increase revenues by $15 and increase costs by $10; consequently, the extra unit should be used. What about adding still another unit? If the firm is using 6 units of input x, the use of an extra unit will increase revenue by $12 and increase costs by $10; thus, it too should be added. Increases in the utilization of input x are profitable up to 7 units;

Table 12.1.   Value of Marginal Product of Input x.

QUANTITY OF x	MARGINAL PRODUCT*	VALUE OF MARGINAL PRODUCT*
3	8	$24
4	7	21
5	6	18
6	5	15
7	4	12
8	3	9
9	2	6

*The figures pertain to the interval between the indicated quantity of input x and one unit less than the indicated quantity of input x.

beyond this point, an extra unit of input x increases costs more than revenues. Thus the firm should use 7 units of input x.

The optimal number of units of input x is the number at which the value of the marginal product of input x equals the price of input x.[3] This, of course, is just another way of stating the result in Equation 12.4a, since under these circumstances the value of the marginal product of input x is equal to the

[3] This assumes that the quantity of the input can be varied continuously, which is often the case. However, it is not the case in Table 12.1. Since only integer values can be used, according to Table 12.1, this rule must be changed somewhat here. In this case, the optimal number of units of input x is the largest integer at which the value of the marginal product of input x is greater than or equal to the price of input x.

left-hand side of the equation and the price of input x is the right-hand side of the equation.

If the firm demands the optimal amount of input x at each price of input x, its demand schedule for input x must be the value-of-marginal-product schedule in the last column of Table 12.1. For example, if the price of input x is between $6 and $9, the firm will demand 8 units of input x; if the price of input x is between $9 and $12, the firm will demand 7 units of input x. Thus the firm's demand curve for input x is the value-of-marginal-product curve, which shows the value of input x's marginal product at each quantity of input x used. This curve will slope downward and to the right, because it is proportional to the curve showing the input's marginal productivity. From Chapter 5 we know that an input's marginal product must be decreasing in stage II, the stage where a profit-maximizing firm in perfect competition tries to operate.

5. The Firm's Demand Curve: The Case of Several Variable Inputs

Suppose now that the firm uses a number of inputs that can be varied in quantity, input x being only one of them. Under these circumstances, the firm's demand curve for input x is no longer the value-of-marginal-product curve. This is because a change in the price of input x will result in a change in the quantities of the other variable inputs used, and these changes in the quantities of the other variable inputs used will affect the quantity of input x used.

As an example, suppose that the price of input x is initially $10 and the quantity of input x used is 100 units. Holding constant the use of other inputs, suppose that the value-of-marginal-product curve is $V_1 V_1'$ in Figure 12.1. If none of the other inputs were variable, this would be the demand curve for input x. In fact, however, a number of other inputs are variable. Suppose that the price of input x falls to $6. What will happen to the quantity of input x demanded by the firm? Since the value of its marginal product exceeds its new price, the firm will tend to expand its use. But the increase in its use will shift the value-of-marginal-product curves of other inputs. For example, if another variable input is complementary to input x, its value-of-marginal-product curve will shift to the right. These shifts in the value-of-marginal-product curves of other variable inputs will result in changes in the amounts used of them. And the changes in the amounts used of other inputs will in turn shift the value-of-marginal-product curve of input x.

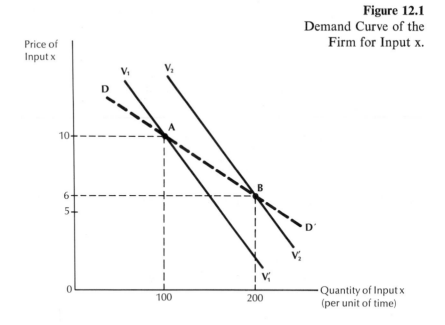

Figure 12.1
Demand Curve of the
Firm for Input x.

When all of these effects have occurred, the firm will be on another value-of-marginal-product curve for input x, say $V_2 V_2'$ in Figure 12.1. And the amount demanded of input x will be such that the value of its marginal product will be equal to its new price. Thus the firm will demand 200 units of input x. Points A and B are both on the firm's demand curve for input x. Other points can be determined in a similar fashion, the complete demand curve being DD'. It can be shown that all demand curves of this type slope down and to the right, as would be expected.[4]

---

[4]In passing, we should note that economists of the past were bothered by the question of whether or not, if each input was paid the value of its marginal product, the total amount paid by firms for inputs would be equal to the firm's revenues. Much of the discussion of this question was beside the point, and need not concern us here. (See P. Samuelson, *Foundations of Economic Analysis*, Cambridge, Mass.: Harvard University Press, 1947, pp. 81–87.) However, it may be worth noting that, if the production function exhibits constant returns to scale, Euler's Theorem states that the total physical output of a firm will be identically equal to the sum of the amount of each input used multiplied by the input's marginal product:

$$Q = X_1 MP_1 + X_2 MP_2 + \cdots + X_n MP_n \qquad (12.5)$$

where Q is the firm's output level, X_1 is the amount of the first input used by the firm, X_2 is the amount of the second input used by the firm, X_n is the amount of

6. The Market Demand Curve

When we derived a market demand curve for a commodity in Chapter 4, we summed horizontally over the demand curves of individual consumers of the commodity. At first glance it may seem that we can derive the market demand curve for an input by simply summing horizontally over the demand curves of individual firms for the input. Although this would provide a first approximation, it would not yield the correct result because it neglects the effect of changes in the input price on the product price.

Each firm's demand curve for the input is based on the supposition that the firm's decisions cannot affect the price of its output. For example, in Table 12.1, the firm assumes that the price of its product will be $3, regardless of how it alters its utilization of input x in response to changes in the price of input x. This is a perfectly reasonable assumption for the firm to make, because it is only a very small portion of the industry. But this is not the situation underlying the market demand curve. The market demand curve shows the total amount of the input demanded at various possible prices of the input. Thus it shows the effect of changes in input price on the utilization of the input *when all firms in the industry respond at the same time.*

Suppose that the price of input x decreases substantially. This will result in increased utilization of input x by all firms in the industry and in increased output by all members of the industry. Although the increased output by any single firm cannot affect the price of the industry's product, the combined

---

the nth input used by the firm, MP_1 is the marginal product of the first input, MP_2 is the marginal product of the second input, MP_n is the marginal product of the nth input, and n is the number of inputs used by the firm. Thus, multiplying both sides of Equation 12.5 by P, the price of the product, we have

$$PQ = X_1P(MP_1) + X_2P(MP_2) + \cdots + X_nP(MP_n) \tag{12.6}$$

If each input is paid the value of its marginal product, it follows that

$$PQ = X_1P_1 + X_2P_2 + \cdots + X_nP_n \tag{12.7}$$

where P_1 is the price of the first input, P_2 is the price of the second input, and P_n is the price of the nth input. The left-hand side of Equation 12.7 is the firm's receipts. The right-hand side of Equation 12.7 is the total amount paid by the firm to inputs. Thus, if there are constant returns to scale, the firm's total receipts will be identically equal to the amount necessary to pay all inputs the value of their marginal products. Finally, note that Equation 12.7 is an identity under these circumstances. In general, Equation 12.7 holds as a condition of long-run competitive equilibrium. (See Samuelson, *ibid.*)

expansion of output by all firms results in a decrease in the price of the product. This decrease in the price of the product shifts each firm's value-of-marginal-product curve, and consequently it shifts each firm's demand curve for input x.

To derive the market demand curve for input x, suppose that its initial price is $8 and that each firm in the market is in equilibrium, its demand curve for input x being dd' in Figure 12.2. Each firm uses Oq units of input x. Multiplying Oq by the number of firms in the market we get OQ, the total amount taken off the market at a price of $8. Thus, A is a point on the market demand curve.

Suppose that the price of input x falls to $6. Each firm will increase its use of input x and increase output, the consequence being that the price of the product will fall and the individual firm demand curves for input x will shift toward ee'. When all adjustments have been made, each firm will be using Or units of input x. This is less than the Os units that each would have used if it had remained on the demand curve, dd'. Multiplying Or by the number of firms in the market, we get OR, the total amount taken off the market at a price of $6. Thus, B is another point on the market demand curve. Other points on the market demand curve can be obtained in similar fashion, the complete market demand curve for input x being CC'.

Figure 12.2
Derivation of Market
Demand Curve for
Input x.

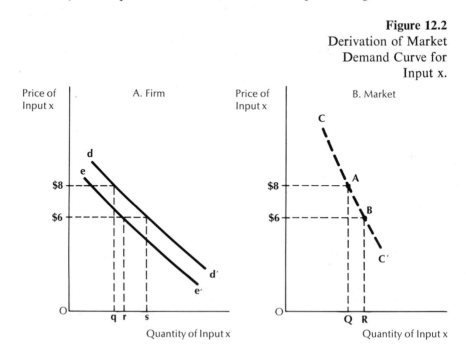

7.   Determinants of the Elasticity of Demand for an Input

In Chapter 4 we pointed out that, in the case of commodities, the price elasticity of market demand varies enormously, the quantity demanded of some commodities being very sensitive to price changes, and the quantity demanded of other commodities being quite insensitive to price changes. This is true of inputs as well. The quantity demanded of some inputs is very sensitive to price changes, whereas the quantity demanded of other inputs is not at all sensitive to price changes. Why is this the case? What determines whether the price elasticity of demand for a particular input will be high or low? Several rules are important.

First, the more easily other inputs can be substituted for a certain input, say input x, the more price elastic is the demand for input x. This certainly makes sense. If the technologies of the firms using input x allow these firms to substitute other inputs readily for input x, a small increase in the price of input x may result in a substantial decrease in its use. But if these firms cannot substitute other inputs readily for input x, a large increase in the price of input x may result in only a small decrease in its use.

Second, the larger the price elasticity of demand for the product that input x helps to produce, the larger the price elasticity of demand for input x. This, too, seems clear enough. The demand for an input is prompted by the demand for the product it produces; in other words, the demand for an input is a *derived demand*. The greater the price elasticity of demand of the product, the more sensitive is the output of the commodity to changes in its price that occur in response to changes in the price of input x.

Third, the greater the price elasticity of supply of other inputs, the greater is the price elasticity of demand for input x. The supply curve for an input is the relationship between the amount of the input that is supplied and the input's price. The price elasticity of supply of an input is the percentage increase in the quantity supplied of the input resulting from a 1 percent increase in the price of the input.[5] Thus, if small increases in price bring forth large increases in the quantity of other inputs supplied, this will mean that the demand for input x will be more price elastic than if large increases in price are required to bring forth small increases in the quantity supplied of other inputs.

---

[5]More accurately, the price elasticity of supply is $dQ/dP \div Q/P$, where Q is the quantity supplied of the input and P is its price.

Finally, the price elasticity of demand for an input is likely to be greater in the long run than in the short run. The reasoning here is like that underlying the similar proposition in Chapter 4 concerning the demand for commodities. Basically, the point is that it takes time to adjust fully to a price change. For example, if the price of skilled labor increases, it may not be possible for many plants to reduce very greatly the quantity of skilled labor demanded in the short run, since their plants are built to use fairly rigidly defined amounts of this input. But in the long run, firms can build new plants to reduce their utilization of skilled labor.[6]

8. The Market Supply Curve

Under perfect competition, the supply of an input to an individual firm is infinitely elastic. In other words, the firm can buy all it wants without influencing the price of the input. When we consider the market supply curve, which is the relationship between the price of the input and the total amount of the input supplied in the entire market, it is often untrue that the supply is infinitely elastic. In many cases, the total amount of the input supplied in the entire market will increase only if the price of the input is increased. Indeed, in some cases it is alleged that the market supply curve is perfectly inelastic, i.e., the total amount of the input supplied in the entire market is fixed and unresponsive to the price of the input.

There is, of course, no contradiction between the assertion that the supply of an input to an individual firm is perfectly elastic under perfect competition and the assertion that the market supply curve may not be perfectly elastic under perfect competition. For example, arable land might be available to any one farmer in as great an amount as he could possibly use at a given price; yet the aggregate amount of arable land available to all farmers may increase little with increases in the price per acre. The situation is similar to the sale of commodities: We saw in Chapter 8 that any firm under perfect competition believes that it can sell all it wants at the existing price; yet the total amount of a commodity sold in a given market can usually be increased only by reducing price.

---

[6]Another proposition that is frequently advanced is that the demand for an input will be less elastic if the payments to this input are a small, rather than a large, proportion of the total cost of the product. There is a good deal of truth in this proposition, but it does not always hold. See M. Bronfenbrenner, "Note on the Elasticity of Derived Demand," *Oxford Economic Papers*, Oct. 1961, as well as the accompanying note by J. Hicks.

There is sometimes a tendency to underestimate the extent to which the market supply of an input will be increased in response to an increase in the price of the input. For example, it is sometimes argued that the nation is provided with a certain amount of land and mineral resources, and that there is no way to change these amounts. For this reason, it is assumed that their market supply is perfectly inelastic, the available supply being completely unresponsive to price. But this can be quite wrong. For present purposes, what is important is the amount of land and mineral resources that are used, not the amount in existence. A large increase in price generally will increase the amount of these resources in use. This will occur because a higher price will result in more exploration for resources, in the reopening of high-cost mines and farms, and in the irrigation and upgrading of poorer land.

9. The Market Supply Curve: The Backward-Bending Case

Most inputs are *intermediate goods*, goods that are bought from other business firms. For example, an important input in the electric power industry is coal, which is bought from the coal industry. The supply curve for inputs of this kind is already familiar, and there is no need to discuss once again the determinants of the nature and shape of the market supply curve in these cases.

However, not all inputs are supplied by business firms. One of the most significant inputs—labor—is provided by individuals. In addition, individuals provide other inputs like savings. When an individual supplies an input like labor, he is supplying something that he himself can use, since the time that he does not work can be used for leisure activities. Thus each seller of these inputs wants to keep some of them for himself. And the amount of these inputs that is supplied to firms depends on the quantities of these inputs that are produced and the quantities that the suppliers want to keep for themselves.

In Chapter 8, we saw that the market supply curve for inputs supplied by business firms will generally slope upward and to the right. In other words, higher prices generally are required to bring forth an increased supply. An interesting feature of the market supply function for inputs supplied by individuals is that it, unlike the supply function for inputs supplied by business firms, may be backward-bending. That is, increases in price may result in smaller amounts of the input being supplied. An example of a backward-bending supply curve is SS' in Figure 12.3.

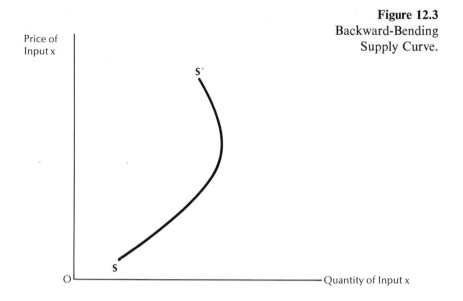

Figure 12.3
Backward-Bending
Supply Curve.

To see how such a case can occur, consider the labor time supplied by a single worker, Bill Jones. Jones has 24 hours a day to allocate between work and leisure. To him leisure time is a commodity he desires, its price being the hourly wage rate: the amount of money he gives up to enjoy an hour of leisure time. What will be the effect of an increase in the wage rate on the amount of leisure time that Jones will demand? Clearly, this is a problem of consumer choice, since the question can be restated: What is the effect of an increase in the price of leisure time on the quantity of leisure time that Jones demands? The theoretical tools discussed in Chapter 3 can help us to answer this question.

As we learned in Chapter 3, we can divide the effect of the price increase into two parts: the substitution effect and the income effect. The substitution effect is the effect of the increase in the cost of leisure relative to other commodities. Since other consumer goods will become relatively less expensive, the substitution effect will result in his reducing his leisure time and increasing his purchase of other consumer goods. Thus the substitution effect will result in his increasing the amount of labor time he puts forth.

In addition, there is an income effect, which is quite different from the income effect in the case of the purchase of most consumer products. In the first place, the income effect here works in the opposite direction from the income effect in the case of the purchase of the typical consumer product. As we saw in Chapter 3, the income effect of a price increase of a good is generally to reduce the consumption of the good, since the price increase reduces the consumer's real purchasing power. But this is not the case here. An increase in the price of his leisure time due to an increase in his wage makes Jones more affluent and better able to afford the things he wants, including leisure. Thus the income effect of an increase in the price of leisure is likely to be an increase in the demand for leisure.

The income effect in this case differs from the income effect for most consumer products in another important respect: It is likely to be much stronger than for most consumer products. In general, the consumer spends only a small percentage of his budget on the product in question, the result being that an increase in its price has only a small impact on his real income. However, in the case of leisure, an increase in its price will almost certainly have a great effect on his real income, since most of his income is likely to stem from the sale of his labor. (Remember that the price of leisure time is equal to the wage rate.) Thus an increase in the price of leisure time is likely to have a great effect on Jones's income and on his consumption pattern.

The income effect may offset the substitution effect, the result being that an increase in the wage rate may reduce the supply of labor. In other words, an increase in the price of leisure time may increase the quantity demanded of leisure time. Of course, institutional constraints often prevent workers from choosing their own working hours; for example, the 40-hour week is commonly worked in industry. But the typical, or average, work week responds to the shape of the supply curve for labor. As workers have become more affluent the average work week has tended to decrease.

10.   Determination of Price and Employment of an Input

The market demand and supply curves for an input determine the input's equilibrium price. The price of the input will tend in equilibrium to the level at which the quantity of the input demanded equals the quantity of the input supplied. Thus, in Figure 12.4, the equilibrium price of the input is OP_0. If the price were higher than OP_0, the quantity supplied would exceed the quantity demanded, and there would be downward pressure on the price. If the price were lower than OP_0, the quantity supplied would fall short of the quantity demanded, and there would be upward pressure on the price.

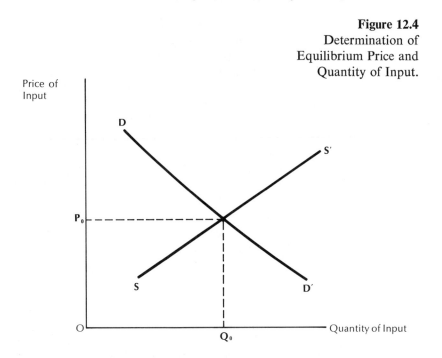

Figure 12.4
Determination of
Equilibrium Price and
Quantity of Input.

The equilibrium amount of the input that is employed is also given by the intersection of the market demand and supply curves. For example, in Figure 12.4, OQ_0 units of the input will be employed in equilibrium. In equilibrium the value of the marginal product of an input will be equal in each and every place where the input is used. In all uses the value of the marginal product of an input will equal the price of the input—and the price of the input will, of course, be the same to all firms under perfect competition.

11.   The Cost of a Volunteer Army: An Application

At this point it is advisable to pause for a moment and illustrate how the theory we have been discussing has been put to use. In 1964, President Johnson directed that a study be made to determine whether it would be possible to shift from the current reliance on the draft to a system in which defense manpower needs would be met entirely by volunteers. Part of this study entailed the estimation of the costs to the Defense Department[7] of shifting to an all-volunteer system. Estimates of this sort were made by Stuart Altman of Brown University and Alan Fechter of the Institute for Defense Analysis.[8] Essentially these estimates were applications of the kind of analysis described in this chapter, the basic approach being to estimate the supply curve for a particular input—manpower—to the defense establishment.

The effect of pay on the labor supply was estimated by analyzing the extent to which regional variations in military pay (as a percent of civilian pay) seemed to influence voluntary enlistments. The resulting supply equation for all military services is

$$\log (1 - C) = 5.0334 - .10914 \log Y - .03540 \log U$$

where C is the proportion of the male population of relevant age that enlists, Y is the ratio of first-term military to civilian pay, and U is the unemployment rate in the region. Note that the negative signs before Y and U indicate that higher military pay and higher unemployment result in higher enlistment rates, which is what we would expect: The supply curve would be expected to slope upward and to the right. To get a better idea of exactly what this equation means, consult Figure 12.5, which shows the relationship between the proportion that enlists and the level of military pay (as a percent of civilian pay) when the unemployment rate is held constant at two alternative levels.

Using this supply equation, one can determine (for given values of the unemployment rate) the level of military pay that would be required to bring forth the number of extra enlistments needed to eliminate the draft. That is, assuming U is given, if we know how big C must be to eliminate the draft, we can tell from the equation how large Y must be to result in the required value of C. How many enlistments are required to eliminate the draft? According to Altman and Fechter, an increase in enlistments of about 60 to 90 percent would be required. To bring forth these extra enlistments, they estimate on the basis of this supply equation that first-term military pay for enlisted men would have to be increased by about 110 percent if the unemployment rate were about 5.5 percent and by about 160 percent if the unemployment rate were about 4.0 percent. Using 1964 military earnings as a base, increases in first-term pay for enlisted men

---

[7]Note that the costs to the Defense Department and the social costs may be quite different. The draft has affected both the structure and level of military pay. See, for example, W. Oi, "The Economic Cost of the Draft," *American Economic Review*, May 1967.

[8]S. Altman and A. Fechter, "The Supply of Military Personnel in the Absence of a Draft," *American Economic Review*, May 1967.

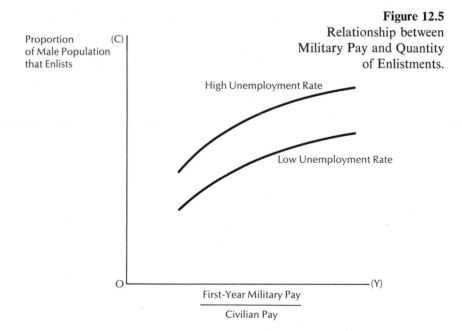

Figure 12.5
Relationship between
Military Pay and Quantity
of Enlistments.

would have to be about $3000 at a 5.5-percent unemployment level and about $5000 at a 4.0-percent unemployment level.

These estimates are based on the assumption that the nation must attract enough volunteers to maintain a 2.65 million men defense force in the early seventies. A smaller pay raise would be required if a smaller defense force were regarded as sufficient. Conversely, if circumstances were to make it necessary to have a larger force, the pay raises would have to be higher.

How big an increase in the total payroll costs of the Defense Department would be required to eliminate the draft? Multiplying 2.65 million by the average increase in pay,[9] Altman and Fechter find that the estimated increase is about $5 billion per year if there is a 5.5-percent unemployment rate or about $8 billion per year if there is a 4.0-percent unemployment rate. These figures are only crude estimates, as Altman and Fechter stress, since the supply function is subject to errors of many kinds and the assumptions on which the analysis rests are only first approximations. However, the results are an interesting illustration of how economists use the basic economic concepts in this chapter to help solve important problems.

[9]Note that the average increase in pay is less than the average increase in first-term pay. The way in which the authors proceed from the latter to the former is described in their work.

12.   The Concept of Rent

In Section 8, we stated that there is sometimes a tendency to underestimate the extent to which the market supply of an input will be increased in response to an increase in the price of the input.   Nevertheless, some inputs, like certain types of land, may be in relatively fixed supply.   Suppose that the supply of an input is completely fixed: Increases in its price will not increase its supply and decreases in its price will not decrease its supply.   Following the terminology of the classical economists of the nineteenth century, the price of such an input is rent.   This use of the word, rent, is quite different from everyday usage, according to which "rent" is the price of using an apartment or a car or some other object owned by someone else.

If the supply of an input is fixed, its supply curve is a vertical line, SS', as shown in Figure 12.6.   Thus the price of this input, i.e., its rent, is determined entirely by the demand curve for the input.   For example, if the demand curve is DD', the rent is OP; if the demand curve is $D_0 D_0'$, the rent is OP_0.   Since the supply of the input is fixed, the price of the input can be lowered without influencing the amount of the input that is supplied.

Figure 12.6
An Input in Completely
Fixed Supply.

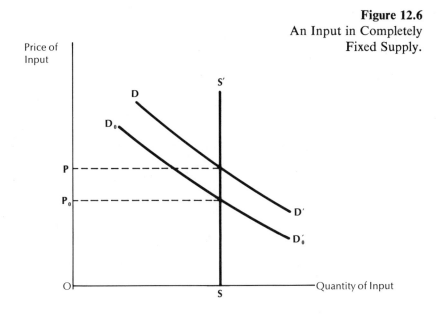

Thus a rent is a payment above the minimum necessary to attract this amount of the input.[10]

In recent years, there has been a tendency among economists to extend the use of the word rent to encompass all payments to inputs that are above the minimum required to make these inputs available to the industry or to the economy. To a great extent these payments are costs to individual firms, since these firms must make such payments in order to attract and keep these inputs, which are useful to other firms in the industry. But, if the inputs have no use in other industries, these payments are not costs to the industry as a whole (or to the economy as a whole) because the inputs would be available to the industry whether or not these payments are made.

Why is it important to know whether or not a certain payment for inputs is a rent? Because a reduction of the payment will not influence the availability and use of the inputs if the payment is a rent; whereas, if it is not a rent, a reduction of the payment is likely to change the allocation of resources. For example, if the government imposes a tax on rents, there will be no effect on the supply of resources to the economy.

13.   Quasi-Rents

The payment to any input in temporarily fixed supply is called a quasi-rent. In previous chapters, we have seen that many inputs are in fixed supply to a firm in the short run. For example, a firm's plant cannot be changed appreciably. In the short run, fixed inputs cannot be withdrawn from their current use and transferred to a use where the returns are higher. Also, fixed inputs cannot be supplemented with other similar inputs in the short run. Thus the payments to the fixed inputs are determined differently from the payments to the variable inputs. Whereas inputs that are variable in quantity are free to move where the returns are highest, fixed inputs are stuck where they are, at least in the short run. Consequently, firms must pay the variable

---

[10]Note that whether rent is or is not price-determined depends on whether we are looking at the matter from the point of view of a firm, a small industry, a large industry, or the whole economy. Although a payment to an input that is in fixed supply to the whole society or a large industry may be a rent from the point of view of the society or the industry, it may appear to be a cost-determining cost to an individual small firm or a small industry.

inputs as much as they can earn in alternative uses, and the fixed inputs receive whatever is left over.

The return to the fixed inputs is a quasi-rent. It is a residual. To understand its nature, it is useful to consider the diagram in Figure 12.7, which shows a firm's short-run cost curves. Suppose that the price is OP_0, the result being that the firm will produce OQ_0 units and its total variable costs will be $OGBQ_0$ (since MM' is the firm's marginal cost curve and VV' is the firm's average variable cost curve). This area, $OGBQ_0$, represents the amount that the firm must pay in order to attract and keep the amount of variable inputs corresponding to an output of OQ_0. It cannot pay less and expect to keep them. The fixed inputs get the residual, which is GP_0CB. This is the quasi-rent.

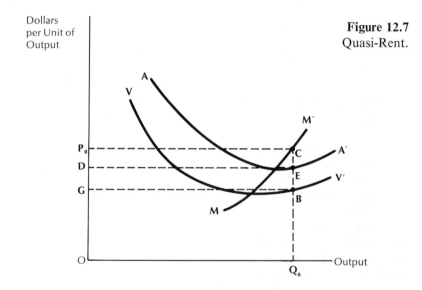

Figure 12.7
Quasi-Rent.

The short-run average total cost curve includes both the average variable costs and the average fixed costs. To determine the average fixed costs, we see what the returns on the firm's fixed assets would be if the rate of return were equal to that available elsewhere in the economy. Thus, since AA' is the firm's average total cost curve, the total fixed costs of the firm are equal to $GDEB$. Consequently, this amount of the quasi-rent is not pure economic profit; only DP_0CE is economic profit. Needless to say, quasi-rent need not be greater than total fixed costs. Firms with pure economic losses do not have quasi-rents that are large enough to cover total fixed costs.

14. Qualitative Differences in Inputs

In previous sections we have dealt with inputs that have been assumed to be homogeneous. In this section, we take account of the fact that inputs may differ in productive capacity. For example, some carpenters may be more skillful than others. Suppose that there are two types of carpenters: skilled and unskilled. Then the firm, if it maximizes profit, should hire each type of carpenter up to the point at which

$$MP_s \cdot MR = P_s \tag{12.8a}$$

$$MP_u \cdot MR = P_u \tag{12.8b}$$

where MP_s is the marginal product of skilled carpenters, MP_u is the marginal product of unskilled carpenters, P_s is the wage rate for skilled carpenters, P_u is the wage rate for unskilled carpenters, and MR is marginal revenue. This follows directly from Equations 12.4a to 12.4c. Equations 12.8a and 12.8b show that the differential in wages between skilled and unskilled carpenters will equal the differential in their marginal products, that is, $P_s \div P_u = MP_s \div MP_u$.

Suppose that we can no longer divide workers into two groups, since each worker differs from the next in the value of his output. Then the difference in wages paid to workers will equal the difference in the total value of their output. For example, suppose that Joe (together with the appropriate tools and materials) produces output worth $1000 per month and Bill (with the same tools and materials) produces output worth $900 per month. In equilibrium, Joe will earn $100 more per month than Bill. If the difference in wages were less than $100, Bill's employer would find it profitable to replace Bill with Joe, since this would increase the value of output by $100 and cost less than $100. If the difference were more than $100, Joe's employer would find it profitable to replace Joe with Bill; although this would reduce the value of output by $100, it would reduce costs by more than $100.

This kind of analysis has been applied repeatedly to explain differences in land rents. According to the classical discussions of this subject, only the better tracts of land will be used at a given point in time, the less productive lands not being in use because they are not sufficiently productive to earn a profit. The least productive lands in use earn neither a profit nor a loss; consequently their price is zero, since no one would be willing to pay more for them. The rent of any other tract of land in use will equal the difference between its value yield and the value yield of this zero-priced *marginal land*, the area of the plot being held constant. Thus the tracts of land (that are worked) will rent at a variety of levels, but after subtracting rental costs they will earn an equal net profit for those who work them.

15.   Wage Differentials among Labor of Similar Quality

In previous sections we pointed out that variable inputs will be transferred from one use to another in response to differences in the return they can yield. Thus labor will move from uses in which its wages are low to uses in which its wages are high. This migration from low-wage uses to high-wage uses tends to equalize the wage level for labor of comparable quality, but it does not eliminate all wage differentials among such labor. Even if all workers were identical, even to their fingerprints (a criminal's paradise), some wage differentials would still be required to offset differences in the characteristics of various occupations and areas.[11]

For example, some occupations require large investments in training, while other occupations require a much smaller investment in training. A physicist must spend about 8 years in undergraduate and graduate training. During each year of his training, he incurs direct expenses for books, tuition, etc., and he loses the income that he could make if he were to work rather than go to school. Clearly, if his net remuneration is to be as high in physics as in other jobs he might take, he must make a greater wage when he gets through than a comparable person whose job requires no training beyond high school; the difference in wages must be at least sufficient to compensate for his investment in extra training.

Similarly, members of some occupations incur larger occupational expenses than others. For example, a psychologist may have to buy testing materials and subscribe to expensive journals. In order for net compensation to be equalized, such workers must be paid more than others. Also, some jobs are more unstable than others. For example, some types of workers may be subject to frequent layoffs and have little job security, whereas others may be assured stable and secure employment. If the former jobs are to be as attractive as the latter, they must pay more than the latter.

In addition, there are other differences among jobs that must be offset by wage differentials if the net remuneration is to be equalized. For instance,

---

[11]In addition, of course, such wage differentials may arise because of less than perfect mobility of inputs and frictions of various kinds.

there are differences among regions and communities in the cost of living, living costs generally being lower in small towns than in big cities. Also, some jobs are more prestigious than others, the result being that people would be willing to accept them even though they paid less than others. (However, it seems to be the case that high-paying jobs tend to be the more prestigious ones.)

16. The Elasticity of Substitution and the Distribution of Income

The elasticity of substitution measures the extent to which the capital-labor ratio changes in response to changes in the ratio of the price of capital to the price of labor. More precisely, the elasticity of substitution equals

$$S = - \left(\frac{\Delta(X_c/X_L)}{X_c/X_L} \div \frac{\Delta(P_c/P_L)}{P_c/P_L} \right) \tag{12.9}$$

where X_c is the quantity of capital employed, X_L the quantity of labor employed, P_c the price of capital, and P_L the price of labor. The level of output is held constant.

The elasticity of substitution is an important determinant of how a change in the price of labor or in the price of capital will alter the share of total income going to labor or capital. Since capital's total income is $X_c P_c$ and labor's total income is $X_L P_L$, the ratio of capital's share of total income to labor's share is

$$X_c P_c \div X_L P_L \quad \text{or} \quad \frac{X_c}{X_L} \div \frac{P_c}{P_L}$$

Suppose that P_c/P_L decreases by 1 percent. Then, if $S > 1$, this decrease in the price of capital relative to the price of labor results in a more than 1-percent increase in the capital-labor ratio. If $S = 1$, it results in a 1-percent increase in the capital-labor ratio. If $S < 1$, it results in less than a 1-percent increase in the capital-labor ratio.

Given the value of S, one can determine the effect of a change in the price of labor or in the price of capital on the ratio of capital's total income to labor's total income. For example, suppose that the price of labor increases relative to the price of capital. If $S < 1$, the relative increase in X_c/X_L is less than the relative decrease in P_c/P_L, the result being that $X_c/X_L \div P_c/P_L$ must decrease. If $S = 1$, the relative increase in X_c/X_L is just equal to the relative decrease in P_c/P_L, the result being that $X_c/X_L \div P_c/P_L$ does not change. If $S > 1$, the relative increase in X_c/X_L is greater than the relative decrease in P_c/P_L, the result being that $X_c/X_L \div P_c/P_L$ must increase. Thus, when the price of labor increases relative to that of capital, if $S < 1$, the ratio of capital's share to labor's share will decrease; if $S = 1$, it will stay the same; and if $S > 1$, it will increase.

According to many observers, the share of income going to labor and capital has been relatively constant in the United States. Over the past 75 years, labor has received about 70 to 85 percent of the total real income, the exact number varying with the definition of labor income that is used. Some economists have tried to explain this phenomenon by asserting that the aggregate production function exhibits an elasticity of substitution of one. For example, former Senator Paul Douglas conjectured that the appropriate production function might be the Cobb-Douglas function (discussed in Chapter 5), which exhibits an elasticity of substitution of one. Three points should be noted in this regard. First, not all observers are impressed by the constancy of shares. Second, technological change as well as the elasticity of substitution influences the ratio of capital's share to labor's share. Third, we have relatively little evidence concerning the value of the elasticity of substitution.

17. Shortages of Scientists and Engineers: Another Application

During the fifties and early sixties, there was a widespread fear among government officials and among senior scientists that a serious shortage of scientists and engineers existed in the United States. For example, in response to a government survey in 1953, more than half of the firms included in the survey reported that they were unable to hire enough research scientists and engineers to meet their needs. Many questions were raised concerning the workings of the market for scientists and engineers, some people feeling that government action was required.

Using the analytical tools described in this chapter, Kenneth Arrow and William Capron developed a model to explain the observed symptoms of a "shortage." They pointed out that the demand curve for scientists and engineers had moved to the right in response to the increased demand for research and development, the situation being like that in Figure 12.8, where the demand curve shifts from $D_1 D_1'$ to $D_2 D_2'$. Under these circumstances the wage that would bring supply and demand into balance is OP_2. But it

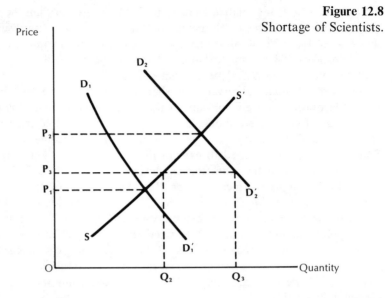

Figure 12.8
Shortage of Scientists.

will take time for the wage to move from OP_1 to OP_2. During the transition period—the period when the wage is moving from OP_1 to OP_2—the firms in the market will experience a "shortage" in the sense that they will not be able to hire as many scientists and engineers as they would like at the existing wage. For example, when the wage is OP_3, firms would like to hire OQ_3 scientists and engineers but they will only be able to obtain OQ_2 scientists and engineers.

A "shortage" of this sort can exist for a number of years if the demand curve continues to shift to the right (as it unquestionably did during this period) and if the wages of scientists and engineers tend to be "sticky" and to increase slowly in response to the excess demand. Arrow and Capron argue that these conditions were met during this period in the market for scientists and engineers. In their view, the wage was "sticky" because of "the prevalence of long-term contracts, the influence of the heterogeneity of the market in slowing the diffusion of information, and the dominance of a relatively small number of firms in research and development."[12] They conclude that

---

[12]K. Arrow and W. Capron, "Dynamic Shortages and Price Rises: The Engineer-Scientist Case," *Quarterly Journal of Economics*, May 1959, p. 303. (An excerpt from this paper is reprinted in D. Watson, *Price Theory in Action*, Boston: Houghton Mifflin, 1965.) The assumption of perfect competition is not entirely appropriate in this case, but the analysis does not depend on this assumption. Note also that the reported "shortage" might be explained partly by the fact that the relevant markets are imperfect.

the "shortage" will be over when the necessary wage increases occur. "While the . . . [wage] rise required to restore the market to equilibrium may seem to be very great, it is only by permitting the market to react to the rising demand that, in our view, it can allocate engineer-scientists in the short run and call forth the desired increase in supply in the long run."[13] This study had a considerable influence in clarifying the issues and helping to guide policy in this area.[14]

18. Summary

The importance of understanding the determinants of input prices is obvious. In a free enterprise economy input prices are an important determinant of any consumer's income. Our first step in analyzing the demand for an input is to consider the demand curve of an individual firm. If there is only one variable input, the firm's demand curve is the same as the value-of-marginal-product schedule. If there is more than one variable input, the situation is somewhat more complicated. The market demand curve for the input can be derived from the demand curves of the individual firms in the market; however, it cannot be derived by simply taking their horizontal sum.

Under perfect competition, the supply of an input to an individual firm is infinitely elastic. However, when we consider the market supply curve, which is the relationship between the price of the input and the amount of the input supplied in the entire market, it is often not true that supply is infinitely elastic. Many inputs are supplied by business firms, and the factors influencing their supply have been discussed in previous chapters. But other inputs—notably labor—are supplied by individuals, not business firms. For inputs supplied by individuals, the supply curve may be backward bending; that is, increases in input price may result in a smaller supply of the input, at least over some range of variation of input price.

Given the market demand and supply curves for an input, the price of the input will tend in equilibrium to the level at which the quantity of the input demanded equals the quantity of the input supplied. The equilibrum amount of the input that is utilized is also given by the intersection of the

---

[13]*Ibid.*, p. 308.

[14]In the past year or so, scientists and policymakers have been concerned that an "over-supply" of certain kinds of scientists and engineers may have developed. The tools of microeconomics are, of course, equally suited to analyze this situation.

market demand and supply curves. To illustrate how these concepts can be used to help solve important problems of public policy, we described how economists have estimated the costs to the Defense Department of shifting to an all-volunteer army.

The payment to an input that is completely fixed in supply is called a rent; and the payment to an input in temporarily fixed supply is a quasi-rent. One can extend the analysis to take account of qualitative differences among inputs. Wage differentials are due to such differences, as well as differences among jobs in training required, occupational expenses, security, and other factors. Finally, the elasticity of substitution, which measures the extent to which the capital-labor ratio changes in response to changes in the ratio of the price of capital to the price of labor, is an important determinant of how a change in the price of labor or capital affects the share of total income going to labor or capital.

SELECTED REFERENCES

American Economic Association, *Readings in the Theory of Income Distribution*, New York: Blakiston, 1946.

Hicks, John, *The Theory of Wages*, New York: Macmillan, 1932.

Kaldor, Nicholas, "Alternative Theories of Distribution," *Review of Economic Studies*, 1955–6.

Samuelson, Paul, *Foundations of Economic Analysis*, Cambridge, Mass.: Harvard University Press, 1947. (Advanced)

Stigler, George, *Production and Distribution Theories*, New York: Macmillan, 1941.

13

Price and Employment of Inputs under Imperfect Competition

1. Introduction

The previous chapter took up the determinants of the price and employment of inputs under perfect competition. In this chapter we continue to be concerned with the determinants of the price and employment of inputs, but we relax the assumption that there is perfect competition. More specifically, this chapter is divided into three parts. In the first part, we consider the case in which there is perfect competition in the market for the input, but imperfect competition (i.e., monopoly, oligopoly, or monopolistic competition) in the relevant product markets. In other words, we allow some of the firms that are potential buyers of the input to have some monopoly power in the sale of their products. In the second part, we take up the case in which there is only a single buyer of an input. In the third part, we discuss an important and highly visible form of market imperfection in the market for labor—the labor union.[1]

---

[1] Of course, this is only a brief introduction to the economics of collective bargaining; readers with a special interest in this field should take a specialized course in labor economics. The material presented here is chosen and viewed from the vantage point of microeconomic theory. Some of the leading texts in labor economics are listed at the end of this chapter.

2. Profit Maximization and Input Employment: Imperfect Competition in the Product Market

In Section 3 of the previous chapter we showed that a firm, if it maximizes profit, will employ inputs in such a way that each input's marginal product multiplied by the firm's marginal revenue will equal the price of the input. Put in symbols, this condition for profit maximization is

$$MP_x \cdot MR = P_x \tag{13.1a}$$

$$MP_y \cdot MR = P_y \tag{13.1b}$$

$$\vdots$$

$$MP_z \cdot MR = P_z \tag{13.1c}$$

where MP_x is the marginal product of input x, MP_y is the marginal product of input y, MP_z is the marginal product of input z, P_x is the price of input x, P_y is the price of input y, P_z is the price of input z, and MR is the marginal revenue of the firm's output.

Suppose that the firm is a monopolist or an oligopolist or a monopolistic competitor, rather than a perfect competitor as assumed in the previous chapter. Will the firm still employ inputs in the way described by Equations 13.1a, 13.1b, . . . , 13.1c if it maximizes profit? The answer is yes. As long as the market for the input is perfectly competitive and the firm cannot influence the price of the input by its purchases, it must conform to Equations 13.1a, 13.1b, . . . , 13.1c if it maximizes profit. It is a simple matter to prove to yourself that this is the case: Merely turn back to Section 3 of Chapter 12 and work through the derivation of the conditions in Equations 12.4a, 12.4b, . . . , 12.4c. Nowhere in that derivation is it assumed that the firm's product is sold in a perfectly competitive market. Thus the results hold whether the firm is a perfect competitor or an imperfect competitor in the product market.

3. The Firm's Demand Curve: The Case of One Variable Input

Equations 13.1a, 13.1b, . . . , 13.1c are the basis for the theory of input demand under imperfect competition in the product market (just as they are under perfect competition in the product market). As in the previous chapter our first step in analyzing the demand for an input is to consider the demand of an individual firm for an input, assuming that this input is the only variable input in the firm's production process. In other words, the quantities of all other inputs are fixed. This assumption is relaxed in the next section. In Section 5 we discuss the market demand for the input and the determination of input price and employment.

Suppose that the only variable input is input x. The demand curve of a firm for this input shows the quantity of input x that the firm will take at various possible prices of input x. Assuming that the firm maximizes its profits, it will take that amount of input x at which the value of the extra output produced by an extra unit of input x is equal to the price of a unit of input x. This is the meaning of Equation 13.1a.

To be more specific, suppose that the marginal product of input x at various levels of utilization of input x is that shown in Table 13.1, the total amount of output that can be derived from each number of units of input x being shown in the third column of Table 13.1. Because the firm is an imperfect competitor, the price of its product will vary with the amount it sells, the fourth column of Table 13.1 providing the price that corresponds to each output in the third column. Multiplying the output in the third column by the price in the fourth column, we get the total revenue corresponding to each number of units of input x used; this is shown in column 5.

Table 13.1. Marginal Revenue Product of Input x.

QUANTITY OF x	MARGINAL PRODUCT OF x*	TOTAL OUTPUT	PRICE OF GOOD	TOTAL REVENUE	MARGINAL REVENUE PRODUCT OF x*
3	10	33	$20.00	$ 660.00	—
4	9	42	19.50	819.00	$159.00
5	8	50	19.00	950.00	131.00
6	7	57	18.50	1054.50	104.50
7	6	63	18.00	1134.00	79.50
8	5	68	17.50	1190.00	56.00
9	4	72	17.00	1224.00	34.00

*These figures pertain to the interval between the indicated amount of input x and one unit less than the indicated amount of input x.

Finally, in column 6 of Table 13.1 we show the increase in total revenue that stems from the use of each additional unit of input x. For example, the fifth unit of input x (i.e., going from 4 units to 5 units of input x) increases the firm's total revenue by $131. Similarly, the seventh unit of input x

(i.e., going from 6 units to 7 units of input x) increases the firm's total revenue by $79.50. The increase in total revenue due to the use of an additional unit of input x is called the *marginal revenue product* of input x, which explains the heading of column 6. The marginal revenue product of input x is equal to the marginal physical product of input x times the firm's marginal revenue.[2] Thus it is equal to the left-hand side of Equation 13.1a.

If the firm maximizes profit it sets the marginal revenue product of input x equal to the price of input x. This is the meaning of Equation 13.1a. Thus the firm's demand schedule for input x must be the marginal-revenue-product schedule in column 6 of Table 13.1. For example, suppose that the price of input x is $56. Then according to Equation 13.1a the firm will set the marginal revenue product of input x equal to $56, which means that it will demand 8 units of input x. Or suppose that the price of input x is $34. Then the firm will set the marginal revenue product of input x equal to $34, which means that it will demand 9 units of input x. Thus the number of units of input x that the firm will demand at any price is given by the marginal-revenue-product curve, which shows the marginal revenue product of input x at various quantities of input x used. This curve is shown in Figure 13.1.

Two points should be noted concerning the marginal-revenue-product curve. First, it will slope downward and to the right (as a demand curve should for an input) for two reasons: the input's marginal product will decrease as more of it is used, and the firm's marginal revenue will decrease as its output increases. Since the marginal revenue product is the product of the input's marginal product and the firm's marginal revenue, it will decrease for both reasons as more of the input is used. Second, the value-of-marginal-product schedule in the previous chapter can be regarded as a special case of the marginal-revenue-product schedule. If marginal revenue is equal to price (as it is in perfect competition), the marginal-revenue-product schedule becomes precisely the same as the value-of-marginal-product schedule.

---

[2]It is easy to prove that the marginal revenue product (*MRP*) is the product of the marginal product (*MP*) and marginal revenue (*MR*). By definition,

$$MRP = \frac{\Delta R}{\Delta I}$$

where ΔR is the change in total revenue and ΔI is the change in the quantity of the input. Since $MR = \Delta R \div \Delta Q$, where ΔQ is the change in output, it follows that

$$MRP = \frac{MR \, \Delta Q}{\Delta I}$$

But since $MP = \Delta Q \div \Delta I$, it also follows that

$$MRP = MR \times MP$$

which is what we set out to prove.

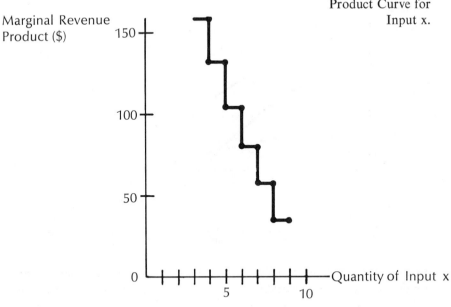

Figure 13.1
Marginal-Revenue-
Product Curve for
Input x.

4. The Firm's Demand Curve: The Case of Several Variable Inputs

Suppose that the firm uses a number of inputs that can be varied in quantity, input x being only one of them. As in the case of perfect competition, the firm's demand curve for input x is no longer its marginal-revenue-product curve. This is because a change in the price of input x will result in changes in the quantities used of other variable inputs, and these changes in the quantities used of other inputs will affect the quantity used of input x.

For example, suppose that the price of input x is initially $5 and that 80 units of input x are used at this price. Holding constant the use of other inputs, the marginal-revenue-product curve is assumed to be M_1M_1' in Figure 13.2. This would be the demand curve for input x if the other inputs were not variable. Suppose that the price of input x falls to $4. Since the marginal revenue product of input x exceeds its new price, the firm will

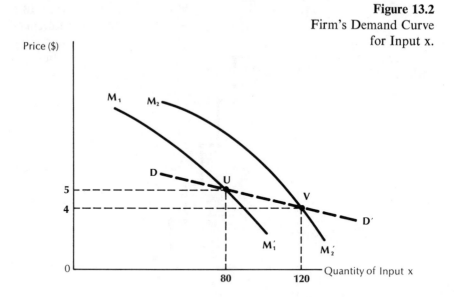

Figure 13.2
Firm's Demand Curve
for Input x.

tend to increase its use of input x. But this will shift the marginal-revenue-product curves of other variable inputs, which in turn will change the amount used of them, which in turn will shift the marginal-revenue-product curve of input x.

When all of these effects have taken place, the firm will be on another marginal-revenue-product curve for input x, say $M_2 M_2'$ in Figure 13.2. Since the amount demanded of input x will be such that the marginal revenue product of input x will equal its new price, the firm will demand 120 units. Points U and V are both on the firm's demand curve for input x. Other points can be determined in similar fashion, the complete demand curve being DD'.

5. The Market Demand Curve and Input Price

The previous sections derived the demand curve of an individual firm for an input. The next step is to combine the demand curves of the individual firms in the market (for the input) into a single market demand curve for the input. This step can be accomplished in different ways, depending on whether the firms are all monopolists or whether some are oligopolists or monopolistic competitors. If all firms are monopolists in their product markets, the market demand curve for the input would simply be the horizontal summation of the demand curves of the individual firms.

On the other hand, if some of the firms are oligopolists or monopolistic competitors, one cannot simply sum (horizontally) the demand curves of the individual firms to derive the market demand curve. This will not work for the same reason that it would not work in the case of perfect competition (discussed in the previous chapter): A change in the price of the input will affect both the output of the individual firm and the outputs of its competitors. Because of the change in its competitors' outputs, the demand curve for its own product will change, and this in turn will change its demand curve for the input. In a case of this sort, the market demand curve for the input can be determined only by finding at each price the amount of the input that will maximize the profits of each firm in the market, and by summing these amounts over all firms in the market.

Given the market demand curve for the input, the equilibrium price of the input will be the price at which this demand curve intersects the input's market supply curve. Moreover, the total amount of the input that will be used in equilibrium in this market is also determined in the usual way by the intersection of this demand curve and this supply curve. The nature and determinants of an input's market supply curve, discussed in the previous chapter, need not be altered by the existence of imperfect competition in the product market.

6. Monopsony

Up to this point we have assumed that there is perfect competition in the input market. Now we change this assumption. We begin by considering the case of monopsony. Monopsony is a situation in which there is a single buyer. For example, a group of small firms may be set up to provide tooling, supplies, or materials for a single large manufacturing firm, and because this large firm is the only one of its type in the area and its requirements are highly specialized, this large firm may be the only buyer for the product of the small firms. This is a case of monopsony.

Note the difference between monopsony and monopoly: Monopsony is a case of a single buyer; monopoly is a case of a single seller. Other market situations that could also be studied are oligopsony (where there are a few buyers) and monopsonistic competition (where there are many buyers but the inputs are not homogeneous and some buyers prefer some sellers' inputs to other sellers' inputs). However, it is sufficient for present purposes to limit our attention to monopsony.

Monopsony can occur for various reasons. In some cases, a particular type of input is much more productive in one kind of use than in others. For example, some land that is rich in iron ore may be much more profitably devoted to iron mining than to any other use. Or a person with certain specialized skills may be much more profitably employed using these skills than working at other jobs. If there is only one firm that rents such land or hires such labor, the result is a monopsonistic situation.

The classic case of monopsony is the company town in which a single firm is the sole buyer of labor services. Many "mill towns" and "mining towns" have been dominated by a single firm. As long as workers are unable or unwilling to move elsewhere to work, this firm is a monopsonist. If the mobility of labor can be increased, the monopsony can be broken, at least partially. However, the difficulties in increasing the mobility of labor should not be underestimated: Workers become emotionally attached to a particular area and to their friends and family located there; they often are ignorant of opportunities elsewhere; and they sometimes lack the money and skills that are required to move.

7. Input Supply Curves and Marginal Expenditure Curves

The supply curve of the input facing the monopsonist is the market supply curve: This is the key feature of monopsony. The reason why the monopsonist faces the market supply curve of the input is that the monopsonist is the entire market for the input: It is the sole buyer. Since the market supply curve of an input is generally upward sloping, as we saw in the previous chapter, this means that the supply curve for the input that the monopsonist faces is upward sloping. In other words, the monopsonist is forced to increase the price of the input if he wishes to use more of it, and he can reduce its price if he chooses to use less of it.

The contrast between this situation and the situation under perfect competition in the input market should be noted. In the case of perfect competition in the input market, each firm buys only a very small proportion of the total supply of any input, the consequence being that each firm faces a perfectly elastic supply curve for the input. In other words, each firm can buy all it wants of an input without affecting the input's price.

The situation under monopsony is illustrated by the case in Table 13.2. Suppose that a firm is a monopsonist with respect to input x. Suppose that the market supply schedule for input x is that shown in columns 1 and 2.

Table 13.2. Marginal Expenditure for Input x.

QUANTITY OF x	PRICE OF x	TOTAL COST OF x	MARGINAL EXPENDITURE FOR x*
8	$10.00	$ 80.00	—
9	10.50	94.50	$14.50
10	11.00	110.00	15.50
11	11.50	126.50	16.50
12	12.00	144.00	17.50
13	12.50	162.50	18.50
14	13.00	182.00	19.50

*Each figure pertains to the interval between the indicated amount of input x and one unit less than the indicated amount of input x.

For example, 8 units of input x will be supplied if the price of input x is $10.00; 9 units of input x will be supplied if the price of input x is $10.50; and so forth. Column 3 shows the total cost to the firm of buying the quantities of input x in column 1. For example, the total cost of 8 units of input x is $80.00; and the total cost of 9 units of input x is $94.50. Of course, column 3 is simply the product of the figures in column 1 and column 2.

Column 4 shows the additional cost to the firm of increasing its utilization of input x by one unit. This is called the *marginal expenditure* for input x. For example, the marginal expenditure for the 9th unit of input x is $14.50; and the marginal expenditure for the 10th unit of input x is $15.50. When the market supply curve for the input is upward sloping, the marginal expenditure for the input will be greater than the input price. The reason for this is simple. Suppose, for example, that the firm in Table 13.2 increases its use of input x from 8 units to 9 units. If it did not have to increase the price of input x in order to expand the supply of the input, it would have to pay only the price, $10, of another unit. But because the supply curve *is* upward sloping, the firm *will* have to increase the price of input x in order to increase the supply. *Moreover, this will mean paying all 9 units the higher price, not just paying more for the 9th unit.* Consequently, the marginal expenditure will exceed the input's price.

Figure 13.3 shows input x's supply curve, SS'. If the input is bought by a single buyer, the monopsonist's marginal expenditure curve, which shows the marginal expenditure for the input at various quantities used of the input, is EE'. Since the supply curve is upward sloping, the marginal expenditure curve lies above it.

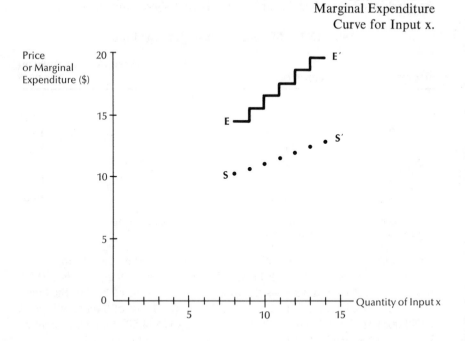

Figure 13.3
Supply Curve and
Marginal Expenditure
Curve for Input x.

8. Price and Employment: A Single Variable Input

Suppose that there is only one variable input. If the monopsonist maximizes profit, it will purchase larger amounts of the input as long as the extra revenues derived from the additional quantity of input are at least as large as the extra cost of the additional quantity of input. When this is no longer the case, the monopsonist will no longer increase its employment of the input. Indeed, if the extra revenues derived from an additional quantity of input are less than the extra cost of the additional quantity of input, the monopsonist will cut back its employment of the input.

More specifically, consider the case in Table 13.3. Column 3 shows the marginal revenue product of the input, i.e., the additional revenue derived from an additional unit of the input. For example, the addition of the 6th unit of the input results in $38 of additional revenue. Column 4 shows the marginal expenditure for the input, i.e., the additional cost of an additional

Table 13.3.   Optimal Employment of Input x: Monopsony.

QUANTITY OF INPUT x USED BY MONOPSONIST	PRICE OF x	MARGINAL REVENUE PRODUCT OF x*	MARGINAL EXPENDITURE FOR INPUT x*
5	$ 9	$40	—
6	10	38	$15
7	11	35	17
8	12	30	19
9	13	24	21
10	14	18	23
11	15	10	25
12	16	2	27

*These figures pertain to the interval between the indicated amount of input x and one unit less than the indicated amount of input x.

unit of the input. For example, the addition of the 6th unit of the input results in \$15 of additional costs.

Clearly, the monopsonist, if it maximizes profit, will employ additional units of the input as long as the marginal revenue product of the input exceeds the marginal expenditure. When the marginal revenue product no longer exceeds the marginal expenditure, it will stop adding further units of the input. Thus, in Table 13.3, the monopsonist will employ 9 units of the input. Also, in Figure 13.4, if the marginal-revenue-product curve is RR' and the marginal expenditure curve is EE', the firm will hire OQ units of the input.

Note the difference between the condition for profit maximization under monopsony and the condition for profit maximization when there is perfect competition in the input market. Under perfect competition in the input markets, we saw in the previous chapter and in Equation 13.1a of this chapter that the firm must set

$$MP_x \cdot MR = P_x \tag{13.2}$$

However, if the firm is a monopsonist, it must set

$$MP_x \cdot MR = ME_x \tag{13.3}$$

where ME_x is the marginal expenditure for input x.

The difference between Equations 13.2 and 13.3 lies in the quantities on the right-hand side: P_x in one case and ME_x in the other. Since ME_x is greater than P_x if the input's supply curve is upward sloping (see Section 7) and since the marginal revenue product of input x (which equals $MP_x \cdot MR$)

Figure 13.4
Optimal Employment of
Input x: Monopsony.

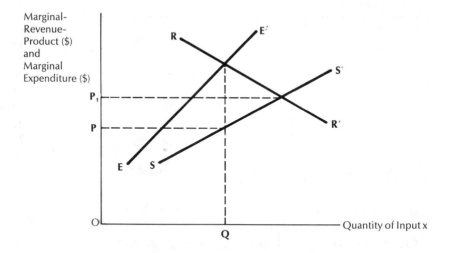

decreases as more of input x is used, it follows that less of input x is used if
Equation 13.3 is met than if Equation 13.2 is met. Thus the monopsonist
will employ less of the input than would be used if the input market were
perfectly competitive.

   The monopsonist sets the input's price at the level at which the quantity
it demands—the quantity at which marginal revenue product equals marginal
expenditure—will be supplied. Thus, in Table 13.3, it sets a price of $13.
And in Figure 13.4 it sets a price of OP, if SS' is the supply curve for input
x. Note that the price set by the monopsonist is lower than would be set
in a competitive market for the input. For example, in Figure 13.4, if RR'
were the demand curve for the input in a competitive market, the equilibrium
price of the input would be OP_1 rather than OP.

9.   Price and Employment: Several Variable Inputs

The previous section dealt with the case where the monopsonist uses only
one variable input. It is easy to generalize our results to the case in which
it uses more than one variable input. For example, suppose that there are a

number of variable inputs: input x, input y, ..., input z. For each of these inputs, it will pay the monopsonist to increase its use of the input only as long as the extra revenue derived from the additional quantity of input is at least as large as the extra cost of the additional quantity of input. Thus the monopsonist will increase its use of each input as long as the marginal revenue product of the input exceeds its marginal expenditure for the input. The firm will stop increasing its use of each input when the input's marginal revenue product equals the marginal expenditure for the input.

Thus, since an input's marginal revenue product equals its marginal product times the firm's marginal revenue, it follows that the monopsonist will hire inputs so that:

$$MP_x \cdot MR = ME_x \tag{13.4a}$$

$$MP_y \cdot MR = ME_y \tag{13.4b}$$

$$\vdots$$

$$MP_z \cdot MR = ME_z \tag{13.4c}$$

where ME_x is the marginal expenditure for input x, ME_y is the marginal expenditure for input y, and ME_z is the marginal expenditure for input z.

These equations are the basic conditions for profit maximization under monopsony. Note that Equations 13.1a ... 13.1c can be regarded as a special case of Equations 13.4a ... 13.4c. If the markets for the inputs are perfectly competitive, the marginal expenditure for each input is simply equal to the price of each input, since a firm can buy all it wants of each input without affecting its price. Thus, Equations 13.1a ... 13.1c are special cases of Equations 13.4a ... 13.4c that hold under perfect competition in the input markets.

It is often stated that a monopsonist will hire inputs so that

$$\frac{MP_x}{ME_x} = \frac{MP_y}{ME_y} = \cdots = \frac{MP_z}{ME_z} \tag{13.5}$$

To see that Equation 13.5 follows from Equations 13.4a, 13.4b, ..., 13.4c, note that Equations 13.4a, 13.4b, ..., 13.4c imply

$$MP_x \div ME_x = \frac{1}{MR}$$

$$MP_y \div ME_y = \frac{1}{MR}$$

$$\vdots$$

$$MP_z \div ME_z = \frac{1}{MR}$$

Thus Equations 13.4a, 13.4b, ..., 13.4c imply that Equation 13.5 is true. Note also that Equation 13.5 is equivalent to the standard condition for cost minimization under perfect competition,

$$\frac{MP_x}{P_x} = \frac{MP_y}{P_y} = \cdots = \frac{MP_z}{P_z}$$

if there is perfect competition in the input markets. This follows from the fact, noted previously, that the marginal expenditure for an input equals its price under perfect competition.

10.   Baseball: A Case Study[3]

Before leaving the subject of monopsony, it may be of interest to note that the labor market in professional baseball has many monopsonistic characteristics. There is a tight set of rules governing contractual arrangements between players and teams. A player is a free agent until he signs his first contract, one stipulation of this contract being that the team can renew the player's contract for the following year at a price that the club may set (as long as it is not less than 75 percent of his current salary). Another stipulation is that the team with which the player is contracted has exclusive right to the use of his services. He cannot play baseball for anyone else without the team's consent.

Consequently, once a player has signed his first contract in organized baseball, he is no longer able to sell his services in any way he chooses. He cannot move freely from one team to another. He can, of course, drop out of organized baseball and take up some other occupation. But if he stays in organized baseball, he must do what the team with his contract says. If the team assigns his contract to another team, the player must work for the assignee team. No other team in organized baseball can hire him.

A number of reasons have been given for these rules. For example, it is frequently asserted that they are necessary to maintain a relatively equal distribution of playing talent among the various teams. Without these rules, it is claimed that the wealthier clubs would buy up most of the best players, the result being that games would be uneven and attendance would drop. This argument has been challenged. According to Simon Rottenberg of Duke University and others, a free market for players would produce

[3]This section is based on S. Rottenberg, "The Baseball Players' Labor Market," *Journal of Political Economy*, June 1956. An excerpt from this article is reprinted in D. Watson, *Price Theory in Action*, Boston: Houghton Mifflin, 1965. In January 1970, the so-called "reserve clause" in the baseball players' contract received its most serious challenge in a case initiated by Curt Flood of the St. Louis Cardinals.

better results: "It appears that free markets would give as good aggregate results as any other kind of market for industries, like the baseball industry, in which all firms must be nearly equal if each is to prosper. On welfare criteria, ... the free market is superior to the others, for in such a market each worker receives the full value of his services and exploitation does not occur."[4]

11. Labor Unions

One of the most important inputs is, of course, labor, and an important feature of the labor market is the existence of unions. Over 18 million people in the United States belong to unions, the four largest unions being the Teamsters, the Steel Workers, the Auto Workers, and the Machinists. Up to the 1930's, there was strong opposition to unions, but since the passage of the Wagner Act in 1935, most manufacturing industries have become unionized. In the remainder of this chapter, we discuss briefly the ways in which unions can try to increase wages, the nature of union objectives, tactical considerations in collective bargaining, and the economic effects of unions.

For the moment, let us suppose that a union wants to increase the wage rate paid its members. How might it go about accomplishing this objective? First, the union might try to shift the supply curve of labor to the left. For example, it might shift the supply curve from SS' to S_0S_0' in Figure 13.5,

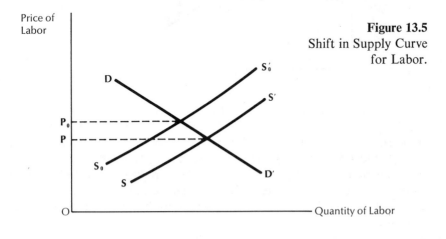

Figure 13.5
Shift in Supply Curve
for Labor.

[4]*Ibid.*

the result being that the price of labor will rise from OP to OP_0. (Of course, DD' is the demand curve for labor.) To cause this shift in the supply curve, the union might restrict entry into the union, or it might not let nonunion workers obtain jobs, or it might restrict the labor supply in other ways.

Second, the union might try to get the employers to pay a higher wage, while allowing some of the supply of labor forthcoming at this higher wage to find no opportunity for work. For example, in Figure 13.6, the union might exert pressure on the employers to get them to raise the price of labor from OP to OP_0. At OP_0, not all of the available supply of labor can find jobs, the quantity of labor supplied being OQ_1, while the amount of labor demanded is OQ_0. The effect is the same as in Figure 13.5, but in this case the union does not limit the supply directly: It lets the higher wage reduce the opportunity for work.

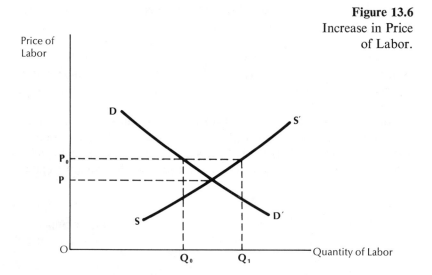

Figure 13.6
Increase in Price
of Labor.

Third, the union might try to shift the demand for labor upward and to the right. For example, in Figure 13.7 it might try to shift the demand curve from DD' to D_1D_1', the result being that the price of labor will increase from OP to OP_1. To cause this shift in the demand curve for labor, the union might help the employers advertise their products; it might help them to be more efficient and better able to compete against other industries; or it might try to get Congress to pass legislation to protect the employers from foreign competition.

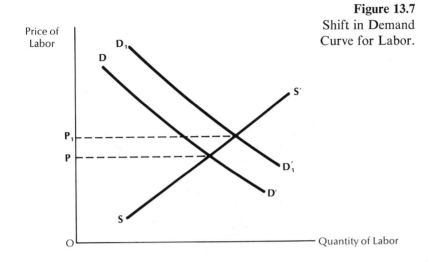

Figure 13.7
Shift in Demand
Curve for Labor.

12. Collective Bargaining and Bilateral Monopoly

In the previous section, we described various ways in which unions might influence the price of labor. But this does not tell us what the price of labor will be. Can we predict the equilibrium wage level in a unionized labor market? For simplicity, suppose that the union is confronted by a single group representing the employers. For example, the Steel Workers might be confronted by a single group representing the steel firms. To some extent, the union can be viewed as a labor monopoly in a case of this sort, and the process of wage negotiation can be viewed as a case of bilateral monopoly, the union on the one side, the management on the other.

We have already discussed price determination under bilateral monopoly in Chapter 9. If DD' in Figure 13.8 is the demand curve for labor, SS' is the union's supply curve for labor,[5] RR' is the marginal revenue curve corresponding to DD', and CC' is the curve showing the firms' marginal expenditure for labor, it will be recalled from Chapter 9 that, according to the theory of bilateral monopoly, the employers will want to set a wage rate of OX and the union will want to set a wage rate of OY. Since the wage that

---

[5]See Footnote 8, Chapter 9 (p. 272).

Figure 13.8
Bilateral Monopoly in
the Labor Market.

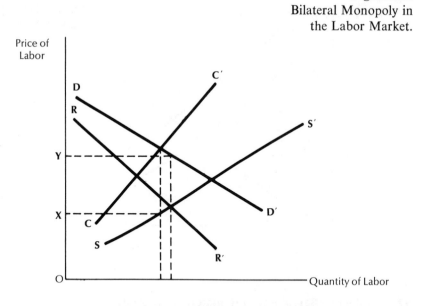

will result in such a situation is indeterminate, we cannot go any further toward predicting the wage level: The result depends on the relative bargaining power and negotiating skill of the two parties, as well as on public opinion and other factors.

Note an important problem in applying the theory of bilateral monopoly to this situation: The theory assumes that the union wants to maximize the difference between the total wages that are paid to (employed) workers and the amount of money required to bring this amount of labor onto the market if each unit of labor were paid only the price necessary to induce it to work. It is by no means obvious that this is what unions are trying to do. Indeed, a number of other assumptions concerning the objectives of unions are equally plausible, as we shall see in the next section.

13. The Nature of Union Objectives

What are the objectives of unions? This is a difficult matter to settle, since unions, like firms, have diverse goals that are not easy to encapsulate and measure. Indeed, the problem is even more difficult for unions than for firms, there being less agreement that any relatively simple objective like profits is a reasonable first approximation. Nevertheless, it is worthwhile discussing the implications of some simple hypotheses concerning union motivation that have been put forth. Three possible union objectives that are often considered are: (1) The union wants to keep its members fully employed; (2) the union wants to maximize the aggregate income of its members; and (3) the union wants to maximize the wage rate subject to the condition that a certain minimum number of its members be employed. All three hypotheses concerning union motivation have a certain amount of plausibility. It is easy to show, however, that they lead to quite different conclusions regarding union behavior.

Suppose that DD' in Figure 13.9 is the demand curve for labor that faces the union. If the union has objective 1 and if it contains OM_1 members, it will have to accept a wage of OP_1, since this is the highest wage that will enable all of its members to find work.

But suppose that it has objective 2. Then it will choose OP_2, since this is the wage that maximizes the total wage bill of the union. To prove this, note that the wage bill is the union's total revenue from its product, labor; and that consequently the wage bill is maximized when the union's marginal revenue is zero. Using the techniques described in Chapter 4, one can

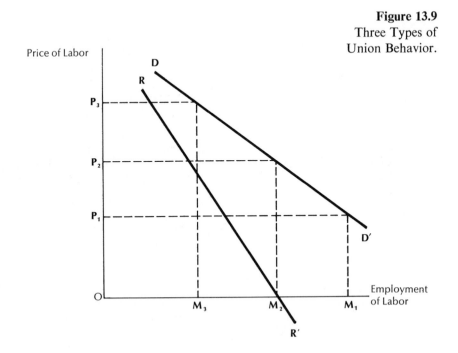

Figure 13.9
Three Types of
Union Behavior.

derive the union's marginal revenue curve from the demand curve, DD', the result being RR'. Since this marginal revenue curve intersects the horizontal axis at OM_2, the union's wage bill is maximized when OM_2 workers are employed, which means that the wage must be OP_2. Note that, if the union has objective 2, it must be prepared to see a great many of its members out of work.[6]

On the other hand, suppose that the union has objective 3. Specifically, suppose that it wants to maximize the wage rate subject to the condition that OM_3 of its members are employed, these members being perhaps those with considerable seniority. If this is its objective, it will choose a wage of OP_3, since this is the highest wage at which the employment level is at least OM_3.

It is clear that the wage desired by the union—and the supply of labor—will vary considerably, depending on which of these objectives is pursued. After all, OP_1, OP_2, and OP_3 are quite different wage levels, and OM_1, OM_2, and OM_3 are quite different labor supplies. Moreover, it is also perfectly clear that the three objectives stated above are only three possibilities out of a very large number. For example, the union leadership obviously has as one objective the maintenance of its own position in the union.[7]

14.   Tactical Considerations in Collective Bargaining

The wage demands made by unions depend on tactical considerations, as well as on the union's basic objectives. The initial asking figure put forth by the union is likely to be higher than the union's real expectations. The difference between the initial asking figure and the union's real expectation is governed by what the union regards as the best tactics. In most cases the union refrains from making the difference so large that the initial asking figure seems ridiculously large. On the other hand, the union often considers it unwise to make the difference so small that there is little room for "compromise."

The union's basic demand, the one for which it fundamentally is striving, is likely to be influenced considerably by what other unions are obtaining for

---

[6]And there is the difficult question of which members should be unemployed and which members should work.

[7]For an excellent discussion of this topic, see J. Dunlop, *Wage Determination Under Trade Unions*, Reprints of Economic Classics, New York: Augustus M. Kelley, 1966. This section is based largely on Dunlop's book.

their memberships. If other unions are getting increases of 30 cents an hour, the union may feel that it must do at least this well in order to show the membership that it can produce for them. Thus wage negotiations in a few major industries like autos and steel may set a pattern for other industries. Also, the union's basic wage demands will depend on the size of the industry's profits (its "ability to pay"), the mood and militancy of the membership, and the extent of the union's nonwage demands (work rules, pensions, union shop, etc.).

The employer tries, of course, to pay only what he must for what he regards to be the optimal number of employees. Like the union, he is influenced by tactical considerations in bargaining with the union concerning wages. For example, he may adopt a hard bargaining position when he thinks the union is in a relatively weak position, or an easy bargaining position when he wants to maintain a friendly group of union officials in office. He may adopt a hard bargaining position when he thinks that the union needs to be "put in its place," or an easy bargaining position when he wants to persuade the union to reduce their nonwage demands.

Given the basic objectives of the union and the employer in a particular case, the wage level that actually is negotiated is determined by the relative bargaining strength of the two parties and by their relative skill at negotiation. The strength of the employer depends on his ability to withstand a strike and to keep his head above water. The strength of the union depends on the extent of its membership, its ability to keep out nonunion workers and to enlist the support of other unions, and the size of its financial reserves.

15. Economic Effect of Unions

Given the apparent importance of labor unions in the American economy, it may seem that we should be able to describe the economic effects of unions with relative ease. Unfortunately, we are not able to do so. Although a considerable amount of research has been carried out, there is a great deal of uncertainty concerning the effects of unions. Of course, if unions provide labor with a relative bargaining advantage—or counterbalance monopsonistic pressures by employers—it would seem that the wage rate should be higher with unions than without them. But it is very difficult to isolate and measure this effect if, indeed, it exists.

Empirical studies of the effect of unions on wages have generally been based on comparisons of wage increases in unionized industries with those in nonunion industries. But the evidence based on these studies is not at all clear-cut. The results in recent years show that there is little tendency for union wages to increase more rapidly than nonunion wages. However, between 1933 and the late forties, industries that were more recently unionized tended to have greater wage increases than industries that were not unionized or that were unionized before 1933. Even if the evidence were clear-cut, comparisons of this sort are difficult to interpret because increases in union wages may prompt increases in nonunion wages, the result being that the difference in wage increases between union and nonunion fields underestimates the effect of unions on wages.

Beside influencing the general wage level, unions may influence the size of wage differentials among firms, jobs, and regions. With respect to wage differentials among firms or regions, it seems quite likely that unionization will reduce such differentials, particularly if industry-wide bargaining develops. However, if some firms or regions become unionized and others do not, differentials may increase. With respect to wage differentials among occupations, the effects of unions are even less obvious. It seems likely that unions can influence the pay of some occupations more than others, and it is clear that some occupations are more highly unionized than others. But it is not clear whether unions increase or reduce the size of the differentials between high-paid and low-paid occupations. In other words, if there were no unions, it is not clear that these differentials would widen or narrow.

16. Summary

If there is imperfect competition in product markets but perfect competition in the market for an input, a firm will use an input in such a way that the marginal revenue product of the input equals the price of the input. Thus, if there is only one variable input, the firm's demand curve for the input is the same as the marginal-revenue-product curve. If there are several variable inputs, the firm's demand curve for an input is no longer the same as the marginal-revenue-product curve, since a change in the price of one input will result in changes in the quantity used of other inputs. The market demand curve for an input can be derived by finding at each price the amount of the input that will maximize the profits of each firm in the market, and by summing these amounts over all firms in the market. The equilibrium price of the input is given by the intersection of the market demand and supply curves for the input.

Monopsony is a situation in which there is a single buyer. The supply curve of the input facing the monopsonist is the market supply curve. If the monopsonist maximizes profit, it sets the marginal expenditure for the input equal to the marginal revenue product of the input. The monopsonist will employ less of the input than would be used if the input market were perfectly competitive. Also, the monopsonist will set a lower price for the input than if the input market were perfectly competitive. The market for baseball players has some monopsonistic aspects.

An important feature of the market for labor is the existence of labor unions. To some extent, unions can be viewed as labor monopolies. However, it is difficult to know what the objectives of the union are. Under certain circumstances the union might want to keep its members fully employed. Under other circumstances, a union might want to maximize the aggregate income of its members. And these two objectives are only two possibilities out of a very large number. The wage demands made by unions depend on tactical considerations, as well as the union's basic objectives. The initial asking figure put forth by the union is likely to be higher than the union's real expectations. The wage that actually results from collective bargaining is indeterminate: It is likely to depend on the relative bargaining strength and negotiating skill of the two parties, as well as on public opinion and other factors. If unions provide labor with a relative bargaining advantage—or counterbalance monopsonistic pressures by employers—it would seem that the wage rate should be higher with unions than without them. But it is very difficult to isolate and measure this effect, if indeed it exists.

SELECTED REFERENCES

Dunlop, John, *Wage Determination Under Trade Unions*, New York: Macmillan, 1944.

Cartter, Allan, *Theory of Wages and Employment*, Homewood, Ill.: Richard D. Irwin, 1959.

Becker, Gary, *The Economics of Discrimination*, Chicago: University of Chicago Press, 1957.

Northrup, Herbert and Gordon Bloom, *Economics of Labor Relations*, Homewood, Ill.: Richard D. Irwin, 1967.

Reynolds, Lloyd, *Labor Economics and Labor Relations*, Englewood Cliffs, N.J.: Prentice-Hall, 1959.

14

General Equilibrium
Analysis and
Resource Allocation

1. Introduction

At the beginning of this book we said that microeconomics is concerned with the economic behavior of individual decision-making units like consumers, resource owners, and firms. At first glance one might interpret this statement to mean that microeconomics views the behavior of such individual units and the workings of individual markets in isolation, each unit or market being considered separately. Such an interpretation would be quite wrong. Microeconomics is also concerned in an important way with how these units and these markets fit together. Indeed, some of the intellectually most exciting, and practically most significant, parts of microeconomics deal with the interrelations among individual units and among various markets.

In previous chapters we looked in detail at the behavior of individual decision-making units and the workings of individual markets. Our approach has been like that of a movie maker who, sitting with a camera in a helicopter, depicts a battle by zooming in to get a close-up picture of what the infantry is doing, then by zooming in to get a picture of what the artillery is doing, then by zooming in to get a picture of what the commanding generals are doing, and so on. After taking these pictures, the movie maker has the problem, of course, of showing how the pieces fit together.

At this point, we face the same kind of problem. We, like the movie maker, have "zoomed in" to study the behavior of people acting as consumers; then we have "zoomed in" to study the behavior of people acting as managers and as workers. And we have "zoomed in" to look at the workings of various kinds of markets, each considered separately. Now we must show how economists have attempted to form an integrated model of the economy as a whole. This clearly is an important task: Every schoolboy knows that it is important not to get so engrossed in the trees that he loses sight of the forest.

In this chapter, we provide a brief introduction to general equilibrium analysis, the branch of microeconomics that deals with the interrelations among various decision-making units and various markets. After defining general equilibrium analysis, we see whether we can be reasonably sure that a general equilibrium exists in a perfectly competitive economy. Then we build a simple general equilibrium model and describe input-output analysis, an important application and extension of this type of model. Finally, we take up some questions concerning the optimal allocation of resources.

2. Partial Equilibrium Analysis vs. General Equilibrium Analysis

As stressed in the last section our analysis in previous chapters has focused on a single market, viewed in isolation. According to the models we have used, the price and quantity in each such market are determined by supply and demand curves, these supply and demand curves being drawn on the assumption that other prices are given. Each market is regarded as independent and self-contained for all practical purposes. In particular, it is assumed that changes in price in this market do not have significant repercussions on the prices existing in other markets.

But this assumption may be seriously wrong. No market can adjust to a change in conditions without a change in other markets, and in some cases the change in other markets may be substantial. For example, suppose that a shift to the left occurs in the demand for pork. In previous chapters, it was assumed that when the price and output of pork changed in response to this change in conditions, the prices of other products would remain fixed. However, the market for pork is not sealed off from the market for lamb, beef, and other meats.[1] (For that matter, it is not completely sealed off from the markets for other food products or from the markets for other less similar products, like washing machines and autos.) Thus the market for pork cannot adjust without disturbing the equilibrium of other markets *and without having these disturbances feed back on itself.*

An analysis that assumes that changes in price can occur without causing significant changes in price in other markets is called a *partial equilibrium analysis*. This is the kind of analysis we carried out in previous chapters. An analysis that takes account of the interrelationships among prices is called a *general equilibrium analysis*. Both kinds of analysis are very useful, each being valuable in its own way. Partial equilibrium analysis is perfectly adequate in cases in which the effect of a change in market conditions in one market has *little* repercussion on prices in other markets. For example, in studying the effects of a proposed excise tax on the production of a certain commodity, the assumption that prices of other commodities are fixed may be a good approximation to the truth. However, if the effects of a change in market conditions in one market result in *important* repercussions on other prices, a general equilibrium analysis may be required.

3.   The Nature and Existence of General Equilibrium

General equilibrium analysis, like partial equilibrium analysis, can be used to solve problems of many kinds. One of the most fundamental problems that general equilibrium analysis has been used to help solve is as follows: If we could somehow establish a perfectly competitive economy, would it be possible for equilibrium to occur simultaneously in all markets? That is, does a set of prices exist such that all of the markets would be in equilibrium simultaneously?

Approaching this problem somewhat differently, let us define a state of *general equilibrium* as a state of the economy in which the following conditions hold: (1) Every consumer chooses his preferred market basket subject to his budget line, which is determined by the prices of inputs and the prices of

---

[1]Quantitative evidence on this point was presented in Table 4.6, where the cross-elasticity of demand for beef with respect to the price of pork was given.

products; (2) every consumer supplies whatever amount of inputs he chooses, given the input and product prices that prevail; (3) every firm maximizes its profits subject to the constraints imposed by the available technology, the demand for its product, and the supply of inputs, but in the long run profits are zero; and (4) the quantity demanded equals the quantity supplied at the prevailing prices in all product and input markets.

Given this definition of a state of general equilibrium, the problem is: Can we be sure that a state of general equilibrium can be achieved? It is evident from the definition of general equilibrium that a great many conditions must be satisfied simultaneously if a state of general equilibrium is to be achieved. Can we be sure that all of these conditions can always be satisfied at the same time? Or can they all be satisfied only under certain conditions? And if so, what are these conditions? This is an important question that has received considerable attention from economic theorists in recent years.

4. The Conditions for the Existence of General Equilibrium

Modern work by Kenneth Arrow, Gerard Debreu, Lionel McKenzie, and others has established that in a perfectly competitive economy a general equilibrium can be achieved under a fairly wide set of conditions. As Robert Kuenne has put it,

> "Judged . . . against the characteristics of our abstract economic models [of consumption and production], the pragmatic assertion of a faith that our data would need to be constrained in wholly acceptable ways to guarantee a solution under all allowable conditions of their initial values seems to be well justified on the whole."[2]

---

[2]R. Kuenne, *The Theory of General Economic Equilibrium*, Princeton, N.J.: Princeton University Press, 1963, p. 566. Also see K. Arrow and G. Debreu, "Existence of an Equilibrium for a Competitive Economy," *Econometrica*, July 1954; G. Debreu, *Theory of Value*, New York: John Wiley & Sons, 1959; L. McKenzie. "On the Existence of General Equilibrium for a Competitive Market," *Econometrica*, Jan. 1959; and J. Quirk and R. Saposnik, *Introduction to General Equilibrium Theory and Welfare Economics*, New York: McGraw-Hill, 1968.

To be more specific, Arrow and Debreu show that a general equilibrium exists if increasing returns to scale exist for no firm, at least one primary input must be used to produce each commodity, the quantity of a primary input supplied by a consumer must not be greater than his initial stock of the input, each consumer can supply all primary inputs, each consumer's ordinal utility function is continuous, his wants cannot be satiated, and his indifference curves are convex. Of course, these conditions are sufficient but not necessary.

But are the prices and outputs that make up a general equilibrium unique? That is, is there only one set of prices and outputs at which supply equals demand in all markets? Clearly the answer is no. Only relative prices affect the decisions of consumers, firms, and resource owners. Thus, if all markets are in equilibrium at one set of prices, they will also be in equilibrium if all prices are increased or decreased in the same proportion. Whether there is more than one set of *relative* prices that can result in equilibrium is a more difficult question that is taken up in advanced texts but is beyond the scope of this book.

It is important to know that general equilibrium can be achieved under a wide set of conditions in a perfectly competitive economy. As we shall see in the next chapter, economists have concluded that, under certain circumstances, a perfectly competitive economy has a variety of desirable characteristics; for this reason, a perfectly competitive economy is sometimes held up as an ideal. For those who put forth this view, it would be embarrassing to find that this kind of economy is based on behavioral assumptions and market mechanisms that are incompatible in the sense that general equilibrium cannot be achieved. Fortunately, no such embarrassment is necessary.

5. A Simple Model of General Equilibrium

In the next three sections, we present in somewhat more detail a simple general-equilibrium model of the economy.[3] This model shows more completely the nature of general equilibrium in a perfectly competitive economy. Our discussion requires that the reader be familiar with the idea of, and notation for, a set of equations, the nature of the analysis being such that this is necessary. Readers who do not have this familiarity can skip to Section 8 without losing the thread of the argument.

For simplicity, we assume in this model that the economy is composed of two sectors, a business sector and a consumer sector. A diagram describing the flows of income, payments, products, and services in such an economy

---

[3]This model is similar to ones presented in J. Due and R. Clower, *Intermediate Economic Analysis*, Homewood, Illinois: Richard D. Irwin, 1966, pp. 391–397; and R. G. D. Allen, *Mathematical Economics*, London: Macmillan, 1960, pp. 317–319.

Figure 14.1
Flows in a Two-Sector
Economy.

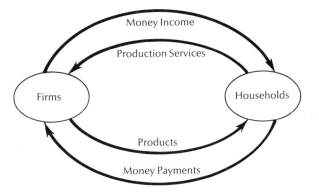

is shown in Figure 14.1. Note that there is no government sector or foreign sector. Although they could be added, the essential features of general equilibrium can be described without them. We assume that all production is done by firms (not consumers) and that all inputs come from consumers (not firms). This means that there are no intermediate goods—goods made by one firm to be used by another firm.

In addition, we assume that consumers obtain their incomes only from the sale of inputs to firms, and that this income is spent entirely on the products of these firms. Moreover, we assume that the amount of inputs supplied by each consumer is fixed and independent of the level of input prices. This assumption is made because it simplifies the analysis, not because of necessity or realism; it can easily be relaxed in more advanced treatments of this topic. Finally, we also assume that there are fixed coefficients of production. This assumption too can easily be relaxed.

When this simple two-sector model is in equilibrium, the total flow of money income from firms to households is equal to the total flow of payments from households to firms. We shall be concerned here with the characteristics of this simple economy in equilibrium, not with the path by which it moves from one equilibrium to another. Let the economy consist of A consumers, C consumer products, and D types of inputs. Thus, if there are two million consumers, 500 consumer products, and 1,000 types of inputs, A equals two million, C equals 500, and D equals 1,000. We assume that all markets are perfectly competitive.

6. Equations of the Model

There are three kinds of equations in this simple model of general equilibrium. First, there are equations representing the demand by consumers for commodities. Let r_{ca} be the amount of the cth commodity demanded by the ath consumer. We know from Chapter 4 that r_{ca} will depend on the prices of all commodities and on the tastes of the ath consumer. Also, r_{ca} will depend on the prices of all of the inputs, since they (together with the amount of each input supplied by the consumer) determine the consumer's income. Thus, there are AC equations of the form:

$$r_{ca} = r_{ca}(p_1, \cdots, p_C, W_1, \cdots, W_D) \qquad \begin{matrix} (c = 1 \cdots C) \\ (a = 1 \cdots A) \end{matrix} \qquad (14.1)$$

where p_c is the price of the cth commodity, and W_d is the price of the dth input. The consumer's tastes (and his supply of inputs) determine the functional form of each of these equations.

Letting R_c be the total quantity demanded by consumers of the cth commodity, it is obvious that

$$R_c = r_{c1} + r_{c2} + \cdots + r_{cA} \qquad (c = 1 \cdots C) \qquad (14.2)$$

Consequently, it follows from the equations in (14.1) that

$$R_c = R_c(p_1, \cdots, p_C, W_1, \cdots, W_D) \qquad (c = 1 \cdots C) \qquad (14.3)$$

In other words, the total quantity demanded of each commodity depends on all commodity and input prices, the form of the relationship differing from commodity to commodity.

Second, there are equations that ensure that the total amount of each input employed by firms is equal to the total amount of the input supplied by consumers. That is, firms cannot use more inputs than are supplied, and there is no unemployment of inputs. If u_{cd} is the amount of the dth type of input used to produce one unit of the cth consumer good, this means that

$$X_d = u_{1d}R_1 + u_{2d}R_2 + \cdots u_{cd}R_C \qquad (d = 1 \cdots D) \qquad (14.4)$$

where X_d is the total amount of the dth type of input supplied by consumers.

Third, there are equations that ensure that the long-run conditions of perfect competition are met, there being neither profit nor loss in the production of each commodity. In other words, price must equal average cost for each commodity. And since there are fixed coefficients of production, the average cost of producing the cth commodity is

$$A_c = u_{c1}W_1 + u_{c2}W_2 + \cdots u_{cD}W_D \quad (c = 1 \cdots C) \quad (14.5)$$

where W_1 is the price of the 1st input, W_2 is the price of the 2nd input, and so on. Consequently, if the price of the cth commodity equals its average cost,

$$p_c = u_{c1}W_1 + u_{c2}W_2 + \cdots + u_{cD}W_D \quad (c = 1 \cdots C) \quad (14.6)$$

7. Existence of a Solution

We have constructed a simple general equilibrium model composed of equations in (14.3), (14.4), and (14.6).[4] However, the fact that we have written down these equations does not ensure that a solution exists. In other words, it does not ensure that at least one consistent and feasible set of numbers can be assigned to all the variables so that all these equations are satisfied. One step in telling whether a solution exists is to compare the number of equations in the model with the number of variables to be determined. Table 14.1 shows the number of equations in the model and the

Table 14.1. Number of Equations vs. Number of Variables.

EQUATIONS		VARIABLES	
EQUATION	NUMBER	VARIABLE	NUMBER
(14.3)	C	R_c	C
(14.4)	$D - 1$	W_d	D
(14.6)	C	p_c	C

[4]This is an extremely simple model. For more complete accounts of general equilibrium analysis, see R. G. D. Allen, *Mathematical Economics* (London: Macmillan, 1960); and J. Quirk and R. Saposnik, *Introduction to General Equilibrium Theory and Welfare Economics* (New York: McGraw-Hill, 1968); as well as R. Kuenne, *op. cit.*

number of variables to be determined. Note that the number of equations in (14.4) is given as $(D - 1)$, rather than D. This is because one of the equations in (14.4) is not independent. If all the other equations in the model hold, it can be shown that this equation must hold too. Thus there are only $(D - 1)$ independent equations in (14.4).[5]

Table 14.1 shows that the number of equations is one less than the number of variables. This means that the model cannot determine values for each of the variables to be determined. The situation is similar to having one equation and two variables to be determined: although only certain pairs of numbers can be solutions, there is no single solution. However, we can obtain a solution if we take the price of one commodity or input as being given: If we arbitrarily select one commodity or input as the *numeraire* and assign this commodity or input a price of 1, we have an exactly determined system. This is just like setting one variable equal to 1 and solving for the other variable in a case where there are two variables and one equation. In effect, the prices of all commodities and inputs are expressed in terms of

---

[5]Suppose that each of the equations in (14.6) holds and that all but one of the equations in (14.4) hold. That is, assume that

$$p_c = \sum_d u_{cd} W_d \qquad\qquad (c = 1 \cdots C)$$

$$X_d = \sum_c u_{cd} R_c \qquad\qquad (d = 1 \cdots (D - 1))$$

It is easy to show that the remaining equation in (14.4) must hold too. Since the total amount spent by consumers must equal their total income,

$$\sum_c R_c p_c = \sum_d X_d W_d$$

And since $p_c = \sum_d u_{cd} W_d$, it follows that

$$\sum_d X_d W_d = \sum_c R_c \sum_d u_{cd} W_d$$

Moreover, since $\sum_{d=1}^{D-1} X_d W_d = \sum_{d=1}^{D-1} \sum_c u_{cd} R_c W_d$,

$$X_D W_D = \sum_c R_c \sum_d u_{cd} W_d - \sum_{d=1}^{D-1} \sum_c u_{cd} R_c W_d$$

$$= \sum_c R_c \sum_d u_{cd} W_d - \sum_c R_c \sum_{d=1}^{D-1} u_{cd} W_d$$

$$= \sum_c R_c u_{cD} W_D$$

Therefore, since $W_D > 0$, $X_D = \sum_c u_{cD} R_c$, which is what we set out to prove.

the price of the numeraire. For example, if $p_3 = 3$, this means that the price of the third commodity is 3 times the price of the numeraire.

We stated above that one step in telling whether a solution exists is to compare the number of equations in the model with the number of variables to be determined. However, for reasons that are too technical to concern us here, the equality of the number of variables and the number of equations does not always guarantee that a solution exists. Whether or not it does so depends on the functional form of the equations; and whether the solution is economically meaningful depends on the solution's satisfying various nonnegativity constraints.[6] But as we saw in Section 4, it can be shown that a general equilibrium exists under a fairly wide set of conditions.

8. Input-Output Analysis: An Extension and Application

Leon Walras,[7] a nineteenth-century French economist, was the first to construct a model of the general equilibrium of a perfectly competitive economy. His model has been modified in subsequent years but the general formulation remains much the same. Vilfredo Pareto[8] was another great nineteenth-century figure in the development of this field. In the period since these men did their pioneering work, many improvements and extensions have been made in general equilibrium analysis, some of them having been cited in previous sections. In recent years, a dominant figure in general equilibrium analysis has been Wassily Leontief,[9] the father of input-output analysis.

Input-output analysis puts general equilibrium analysis in a form that is operationally useful to governments and firms faced with a variety of important practical problems. An important feature of input-output analysis is its emphasis on the interdependence of the economy. Each industry uses the outputs of other industries as its inputs, and its own output may be used as an input by the same industries whose output it uses.[10] Recognizing

---

[6]These nonnegativity constraints are like those discussed in Chapter 7; it makes no sense for some variables, like the production of corn, to be negative.

[7]L. Walras, *Elements of Pure Economics* (translated by Jaffe), New York: Allen and Unwin, 1954. It originally appeared in French in 1874.

[8]V. Pareto, *Cours d'Economie Politique*, F. Rouge, 1897.

[9]W. Leontief, *The Structure of the American Economy*, New York: Oxford University Press, 1951.

[10]Note that this is in contrast to the model in Sections 5 to 7 that assumed that there were no intermediate goods.

this interdependence, input-output analysis attempts to determine the amount that each industry must produce in order that a specified amount of various final goods will be turned out by the economy. This type of analysis has been applied to help predict production requirements to meet estimated demands. For example, it has been applied by economic planners to problems of military mobilization and to problems of economic development in less-developed countries.

To put general equilibrium analysis in a form that is operationally useful, input-output analysis makes a number of simplifying assumptions. To begin with, it uses as variables the *total* quantity of a particular good demanded or supplied, rather than the quantity demanded by a particular consumer or the quantity supplied by a particular firm. This reduces enormously the number of variables and the number of equations that are included. Also, it is assumed that consumer demand for all commodities is given. This assumption, together with the assumption (discussed in the following paragraph) that inputs are used in fixed proportions, means that demand theory does not play an important part in input-output analysis.[11] Input-output analysis attempts to find out what can be produced, and the amount of each input and intermediate good that must be employed to produce a given output: The question is viewed as being largely a matter of technology.

Finally, it is assumed that inputs are used in fixed proportions in producing any product and that there are constant returns to scale. This is a key assumption of Leontief's input-output system. For example, in the production of steel, Leontief would assume that, for every ton of steel produced, a certain amount of iron ore, a certain amount of coke, a certain amount of fuel, and so on would be required. The amount of each input required per unit of output is assumed to be the same, regardless of the level of output. For example, if a certain amount of iron ore is required to produce 1 million tons of steel, it is assumed that 10 times that amount is required to produce 10 million tons of steel.[12]

---

[11]Strictly speaking, this is true only in Leontief's open model, which is all that is described here. In his closed model, at least some attention must be given to the determinants of demand. See H. Chenery and P. Clark, *Interindustry Economics*, New York: John Wiley & Sons, 1959.

[12]In Chapter 5, we said that the proportion in which inputs are combined can generally be altered. This, of course, is a direct contradiction of the assumption of fixed proportions in input-output analysis. But it often takes a fair amount of time for changes to be made and they are often gradual, the result being that Leontief's assumption of fixed proportions may work reasonably well in the short run despite this fact.

9. A Simple Input-Output Model

Anyone with a rudimentary understanding of the solution of simultaneous linear equations can quickly grasp the essentials of input-output analysis. For example, suppose that the economy consists of only three industries: coal, chemicals, and electric power. Suppose that each industry uses the products of the other industries in the proportions shown in Table 14.2. For

Table 14.2. Amount of Each Input Used per Dollar of Output.

TYPE OF INPUT	TYPE OF OUTPUT		
	ELECTRIC POWER	COAL	CHEMICALS
Electric power	$0.2	$0.2	$0.2
Coal	0.4	0.1	0.2
Chemicals	0.2	0.0	0.1
Labor	0.2	0.7	0.5
Total	1.0	1.0	1.0

instance, the second column of Table 14.2 states that every dollar's worth of coal requires 20 cents worth of electric power, 10 cents worth of coal, and 70 cents worth of labor.[13]

Suppose that this economy has set consumption targets of $100 million of electric power, $30 million of coal, and $40 million of chemicals. Input-output analysis is concerned with the question: How much will have to be produced by each industry in order to meet these targets? To begin to solve this problem, consider the case of coal. If electric power output is E, chemical output is C, and coal output is X (E, C, and X being measured in millions of dollars), it follows from Table 14.2 that

$$X = .4E + .1X + .2C + 30 \tag{14.7}$$

if the target is met. Why? Because an amount of coal equal in value to $.4E$ must be produced to meet the needs of the electric power industry, an amount

---

[13]In some cases, the outputs and inputs are measured in physical units rather than dollars. For example, coal output and coal input might be measured in tons per year, and labor input might be measured in man hours per year. Clearly, one can carry out the analysis in either way.

of coal equal in value to $.1X$ must be produced to meet the needs of the coal industry, an amount of coal equal in value to $.2C$ must be produced to meet the needs of the chemical industry, and an amount of coal equal in value to 30 must be produced for consumption. Thus the total output of coal must be equal to the sum of these four terms, as shown in Equation 14.7.

If we construct similar equations for electric power output and chemical output, we find that

$$E = .2E + .2X + .2C + 100 \tag{14.8}$$

$$C = .2E + .1C + 40 \tag{14.9}$$

if the targets are to be met. For example, Equation 14.9 must hold because chemical output must equal the amount needed by the electric power industry $(.2E)$ plus the amount needed by the chemical industry itself $(.1C)$ plus 40 for consumption.

Equations 14.7 to 14.9 are three simultaneous linear equations in three variables, X, E, and C. It is a simple matter to solve for these unknowns, the solution being $X = 131$, $E = 178$, and $C = 84$. This provides the answer to our question: \$131 million of coal, \$178 million of electric power, and \$84 million of chemicals must be produced if the consumption targets are to be met. Also, we can find out how much labor will be required to meet these targets, since (according to Table 14.2) the total value of labor required equals

$$.2E + .7X + .5C$$

Substituting the 131, 178, and 84 for X, E, and C, respectively, we find that \$169 million of labor are required. If this is within the available labor supply, the solution is feasible; otherwise the targets must be scaled downwards.

This simple example illustrates the fundamentals of input-output analysis. It also suggests why the assumption that inputs are used in fixed proportions is so convenient. Without this assumption, the *input-output table* in Table 14.2 would not hold for each output level of the industries; instead the numbers in the table would vary depending on how much of each commodity was produced. The added complexity that would arise if this assumption were relaxed is obvious. Even with this assumption, the computational problems and problems of estimation involved in obtaining solutions to large input-output models can be substantial. A model involving 450 industries has been constructed for the United States; usually, however, much fewer industries are included in such models.

10. Applicability of Input-Output Analysis

Whether or not input-output analysis can be applied fruitfully in a particular situation depends in part on whether the *production coefficients*—the numbers in Table 14.2, for example—remain constant. (See Footnote 12.) There are at least two important factors that might cause changes over time in such coefficients: First, changes in technology may result in smaller amounts of certain inputs, and more of other inputs, being used. For example, the amount of coal required to produce many goods has decreased considerably between 1947 and 1958. Second, changes in the relative prices of inputs may result in changes in production coefficients as cheaper inputs are substituted for more expensive ones.

In the previous section we showed how input-output analysis can be used to determine the output level of each industry, and the total amount of labor, required to meet specified target consumption levels. It is also possible to determine long-run equilibrium prices in an input-output model. In the long run, there will be no economic profits, the total revenue received by each industry being equal to its total costs. Using this proposition, it is possible to determine the level of long-run equilibrium price in each industry.[14]

The postwar period has seen a great deal of work carried out to implement and extend input-output analysis. Some of it has been basic research carried out by academic economists interested in the quantitative significance of various types of economic interdependence. Some of it has been research aimed at the formulation of techniques that would be useful in decision-making in government and business. For example, a large government-sponsored program in the United States in the early fifties was carried out to analyze problems of defense and mobilization. In other countries, programs have been carried out to determine the relationship of imports and exports to domestic production, as well as to analyze various problems of economic development.[15]

---

[14]Suppose that we have an input-output table like Table 14.2, but suppose that the production coefficients are expressed in physical units. (See Footnote 13.) If we have the price of each input, we can determine the long-run equilibrium price in each industry by solving a set of simultaneous equations. See R. Dorfman, *The Price System*, Englewood Cliffs, N.J.: Prentice-Hall, 1964.

[15]H. Chenery and P. Clark, *Interindustry Economics*, New York: John Wiley & Sons, 1959.

11. Resource Allocation and the Edgeworth Box Diagram

We now turn our attention to a somewhat different, but related, topic. In previous chapters, we have stated repeatedly that microeconomics is concerned with the way in which resources should be allocated. Once we consider more than a single market, it becomes possible to consider many interesting questions concerning the optimal allocation of resources. The rest of this chapter is devoted to a discussion of some of these questions.

In the simple models that we shall take up, the Edgeworth box diagram finds extensive use. The Edgeworth box diagram is, of course, an old friend, a comrade-in-arms that appeared in Chapter 2 to help shed light on the problem of allocating fissionable materials. (Note that good economic diagrams, unlike old soldiers, neither die nor fade away . . . unless made with substandard ink.) But since we all sometimes forget important facts about old friends, we devote this section to a review of the Edgeworth box diagram.

The Edgeworth box diagram shows the interaction between two economic activities when the total amount of commodities consumed or inputs used by these activities is fixed in quantity. To see how the Edgeworth box diagram is constructed, and how it should be interpreted, see Figure 14.2. We assume that there are two goods, food and medicine, and two consumers, Tom and Harry. The total amount of food that they have is OF and the total amount of medicine that they have is OM.

The amount of food that Tom has is measured horizontally from the origin at O. The amount of medicine that Tom has is measured vertically from O. Thus any point in the box diagram indicates a certain amount of food and a certain amount of medicine consumed by Tom. For example, the point, P, indicates that Tom consumes OR of food and OS of medicine. The amount of food that Harry consumes is measured by the horizontal distance to the left of the upper right-hand corner of the box diagram. And the amount of medicine that Harry consumes is measured by the vertical distance downward from the upper right-hand corner of the box diagram. Thus every point in the diagram indicates an amount of food and medicine consumed by Harry. For example, the point P indicates that Harry consumes $(OF - OR)$ of food and $(OM - OS)$ of medicine.

The important points to remember about the Edgeworth box diagram are that its length and width represent the total amounts of the two commodities that both consumers together have, and that each point in the box represents

Figure 14.2
Edgeworth Box
Diagram.

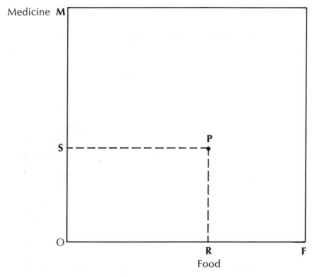

an allocation of the total supplies of these two goods between the two consumers.

The Edgeworth box diagram can be used for production problems, as well as consumption problems. For example, suppose that there are two industries, industry A and industry B, and that there are two inputs, labor and capital. Suppose that the total amount of labor available to the two industries is OL and the total amount of capital available to the two industries is OC. Figure 14.3 shows the relevant Edgeworth box diagram, the height of which equals the total amount of labor, OL, and the width of which equals the total amount of capital, OC.

Any point in the box represents an allocation of this total supply of labor and total supply of capital between the two industries. The amount of labor allocated to industry A is represented by the vertical distance upward from the origin, and the amount of capital allocated to industry A is represented by the horizontal distance to the right of the origin. For example, point Q indicates that industry A has OU of labor and OV of capital. The amount of labor allocated to industry B is represented by the distance downward from the upper right-hand corner of the box diagram, and the amount of capital allocated to industry B is represented by the distance leftward from the upper right-hand corner of the box diagram. Thus point Q indicates that industry B receives $(OL - OU)$ of labor and $(OC - OV)$ of capital.

Figure 14.3
Edgeworth Box
Diagram: Production.

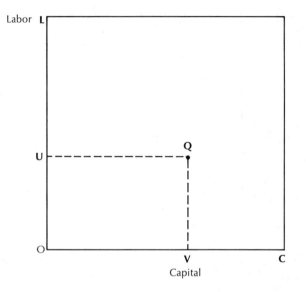

12.   Exchange

Having reviewed the Edgeworth box diagram, we must next review the process of exchange, which was also discussed in Chapter 2. To begin with, consider an economy of the simplest sort. There are only two consumers, Tom and Harry, and only two commodities, food and medicine. There is no production, the only economic problem being the allocation of a given amount of food and medicine between the two consumers. If it helps, you may regard Tom and Harry as two shipwrecked sailors marooned on a desert island with a certain amount of food and medicine that they rescued from their ship.

The amount of food and medicine brought by Tom to the island is indicated in the Edgeworth box diagram in Figure 14.4: He arrives with OH units of food and OI units of medicine. The amount of food and medicine brought by Harry to the island is also indicated in Figure 14.4: He arrives with $(OF - OH)$ units of food and $(OM - OI)$ units of medicine. The

Figure 14.4
Exchange.

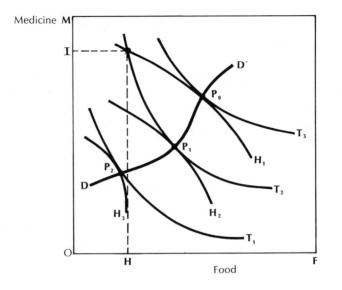

total amount of food brought to the island by both men is *OF*, and the total amount of medicine brought to the island by both men is *OM*.

If the two men are free to trade with one another, what sort of trading will take place? What can be said about the optimal allocation of the commodities between the two men? To find out, we must insert the indifference curves of Tom and Harry into the Edgeworth box diagram in Figure 14.4. Three of Tom's indifference curves are T_1, T_2, and T_3. The highest indifference curve is T_3; the lowest is T_1. Three of Harry's indifference curves are H_1, H_2, and H_3. The highest indifference curve is H_3; the lowest is H_1. In general, Tom's satisfaction is increased as we move from points close to the origin to points close to the upper right-hand corner of the box. Conversely, Harry's satisfaction is increased as we move from points close to the upper right-hand corner of the box to points close to the origin.

Given the initial allocation of food and medicine, we find that Tom is on indifference curve T_2 and Harry is on indifference curve H_1. At this point, Tom's marginal rate of substitution of food for medicine is much higher than Harry's, as shown by a comparison of the slope of T_2 with the slope of H_1 at this point. Thus, if both men are free to trade, Tom will trade some medicine to Harry in exchange for some food. The exact point to which they will move cannot be predicted, however. If Tom is the more astute bargainer, he may get Harry to accept the allocation at point P_0, where

Harry is no better off than before (since he is still on indifference curve H_1) but Tom is much better off (since he has moved to indifference curve T_3). On the other hand, if Harry is the better negotiator, he may be able to get Tom to accept the allocation at point P_1, where Tom is no better off than before (since he is still on indifference curve T_2) but Harry is much better off (since he has moved to indifference curve H_2). The ultimate point of equilibrium is very likely to be between P_0 and P_1.

One thing is certain. If the object is to make the men as well off as possible, the optimal allocation of the commodities is one in which the marginal rate of substitution of food for medicine will be the same for both men. Otherwise one man can be made better off without making the other worse off. In other words, the optimal allocation is at a point at which Tom's indifference curve is tangent to Harry's. The locus of points at which such a tangency occurs is called the *contract curve*. This curve, DD', includes all points, like P_0, P_1, and P_2, where the marginal rates of substitution are equal for both consumers. The contract curve is an optimal set of points in the sense that, if the consumers are at a point *off* the contract curve, it is always preferable for them to move to a point *on* the contract curve, since one or both can gain from the move while neither incurs a loss.

13. Production[16]

In the previous section we reviewed the case in which consumers exchange quantities of commodities, there being no production. Now we move on to new territory. In this section and the next, we take up a simple case in which there is production but no consumption. Then, in Section 15, we combine the results and consider a case in which there is both consumption and production.

Consider a simple economy where only two goods are being produced, the production sector of the economy being composed of a food industry and a medicine industry. Suppose that there are two inputs, labor and capital, and that the total amount of labor to be allocated between the two industries is OL and the total amount of capital to be allocated between the two industries is OC. Suppose that the initial allocation of labor and capital is that represented by point Z in the Edgeworth box diagram in Figure 14.5.

---

[16]The following sections are based to some extent on F. Bator, "The Simple Analytics of Welfare Maximization," *American Economic Review*, 1957.

Figure 14.5
Production.

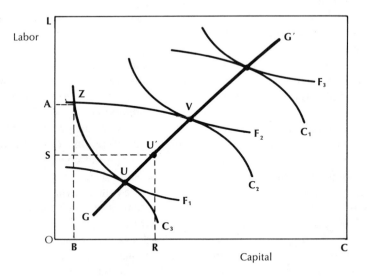

That is, the food industry has OA units of labor and OB units of capital, and the medicine industry has $(OL - OA)$ units of labor and $(OC - OB)$ units of capital.

On the basis of the production functions for food and medicine one can insert isoquants for both food production and medicine production in Figure 14.5. Three isoquants for food production are F_1, F_2, and F_3: The isoquant pertaining to the highest output level is F_3; the isoquant pertaining to the lowest output is F_1. Three isoquants for medicine production are C_1, C_2, and C_3: The isoquant pertaining to the highest output level is C_3; the isoquant pertaining to the lowest output level is C_1.

What will be the optimal allocation of inputs between the two industries? At the original allocation at point Z, the marginal rate of technical substitution of capital for labor in producing food is higher than in producing medicine. This is indicated by the fact that the slope of F_1 is steeper than the slope of C_2 at point Z. The fact that the marginal rates of technical substitution are unequal means that the inputs are not being allocated efficiently. For example, suppose that at point Z the food industry can substitute 2 units of labor for 1 unit of capital without changing its output level, while the medicine industry must substitute 1 unit of labor for 2 units of capital to maintain its output level. In this case if the medicine industry uses more labor and less capital and if the food industry uses less labor and more capital, it will be possible for one industry to expand its output without any reduction in the other industry's output. Specifically, it is possible to move to point U, where the output of food is the same as at Z but the output of medicine is at the level corresponding to C_3. It is also possible to move to point V, where the output of medicine is the same as at Z but the output of food is at the level corresponding to F_2. Or it is possible to move to a point between U and V.

Regardless of which point is chosen, production should occur at a point at which the marginal rate of technical substitution between inputs is the same for all producers, if the allocation of inputs is to be efficient in the sense that an increase in the output of one commodity can be achieved only by reducing the output of the other commodity. Thus the optimal allocation of inputs will lie somewhere along the locus of points, GG', where the marginal rates of technical substitution are equal—and consequently where a food isoquant is tangent to a medicine isoquant. This locus of points, like the analogous set in the previous section, is called the *contract curve*.[17] This curve is an optimal set of points in the sense that, if producers are at a point *off* the contract curve and if society is interested in producing as much as possible of each good, it is always socially desirable for them to move to a point *on* the contract curve, since output in one industry or the other can be increased without a reduction in the other's output.

Note that this analysis of production is entirely analogous to the analysis of exchange in the previous section. The total amounts of the two inputs determine the dimensions of the Edgeworth box in this section; the analogous quantities in the previous section are the total amounts of the two commodities. The isoquant maps play an analogous role to the indifference maps in the previous section.

14. The Product Transformation Curve

The contract curve in Figure 14.5, GG', shows the various allocations of inputs that are optimal. Corresponding to each point on this contract curve is a level of output of food and a level of output of medicine. For example, consider U. If the level of output of food corresponding to isoquant F_1 is 100 and if the level of output of medicine corresponding to isoquant C_3 is 200, then an output of 100 units of food and 200 units of medicine corresponds to the point U. Similarly, if the level of output of food correspond-

---

[17]Other terms could be used as well, but this is the term that is often applied.

ing to isoquant F_2 is 200 and if the level of output of medicine corresponding to isoquant C_2 is 100, then an output of 200 units of food and 100 units of medicine corresponds to the point V.

Proceeding in this way, we can find the pair of outputs corresponding to each point on the contract curve. Then we can plot each such pair of points in a graph like Figure 14.6, where the amount of food produced is shown on the horizontal axis and the amount of medicine produced is shown on the vertical axis. For example, the pair of outputs corresponding to point U on the contract curve are plotted as point A in Figure 14.6, and the pair of outputs corresponding to point V on the contract curve are plotted as point B in Figure 14.6. The curve, PP', which results when all of these points are plotted in Figure 14.6, is called the product transformation curve.

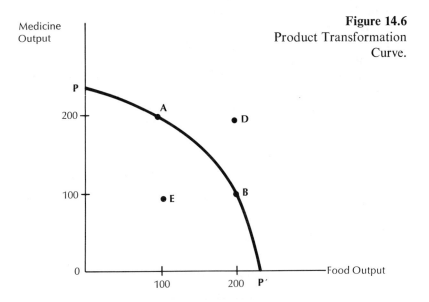

Figure 14.6
Product Transformation Curve.

The product transformation curve shows the various combinations of food output and medicine output that can be derived from the economy's input base (which is OL units of labor and OC units of capital). More specifically, it shows the maximum output of one good that can be produced, holding fixed the output of the other good. Given the economy's input base, it is impossible, given existing technology, to attain a point (like D) that is outside the product transformation curve. It is possible to attain a point like E that is inside the product transformation curve, but it would be inefficient to do so. As long as production is efficient, production occurs at some point along the product transformation curve.

15. Production and Exchange

In this section, we take up a simple model that includes both production and exchange. Our simple economy contains two consumers, Tom and Harry, and two commodities, food and medicine, and two inputs, labor and capital. As in Sections 13 and 14, this economy can use a total of OL units of labor and OC units of capital. If the input base, the utility functions of the consumers, and the production functions in the two industries are given, how should these inputs be allocated between industries, and how should the output of goods be allocated between the consumers?

If the isoquant map in each industry is that shown in Figure 14.5, we know from the previous section that the various combinations of food output and medicine output that can be derived from this input base are given by the product transformation curve, PP', in Figure 14.6. This curve, PP', is reproduced in Figure 14.7. Suppose that we know the composition of output in the economy, i.e., the amount of food and medicine that will be produced. Then we can insert an Edgeworth box diagram similar to Figure 14.4 in Figure 14.7, the upper right-hand corner of the box being the point on the

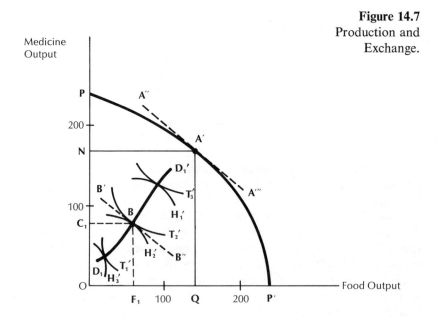

Figure 14.7
Production and
Exchange.

product transformation curve corresponding to the composition of output.

More specifically, suppose that we know that the composition of output in the economy will be represented by point A', the quantity of food produced being OQ and the quantity of medicine produced being ON. Then we can draw a box diagram with OQ as its width and ON as its height. Since OQ is the total amount of food to be distributed to Tom and Harry, and ON is the total amount of medicine to be distributed to them, this box diagram can be used to see how much of the total output of each good will go to each consumer. Figure 14.7 shows the indifference curves of each consumer (T_1', T_2', and T_3' for Tom and H_1', H_2', and H_3' for Harry) within the box, OQ $A'N$. It also shows the contract curve, $D_1D'_1$, the locus of points where Tom's indifference curves are tangent to Harry's.

We know from Section 12 that the distribution of output between the two consumers should be such that they will be on the contract curve, $D_1D'_1$. But at what point on the contract curve should they be? We show in the following section that, if the economy's output is allocated so that consumer satisfaction is maximized, the marginal rate of transformation—the slope of the product transformation curve—must equal the marginal rate of substitution. Thus, if the economy's output is allocated to maximize consumer satisfaction, the consumers should be at the point on the contract curve at which the common slope of their indifference curves equals the slope of the product transformation function at A'.

At what point on the contract curve does the common slope of their indifference curves equal the slope of the product transformation curve at A'? An examination of Figure 14.7 shows that this condition is fulfilled at point B on the contract curve, where Tom gets OF_1 units of food and OC_1 units of medicine and Harry gets $(OQ - OF_1)$ units of food and $(ON - OC_1)$ units of medicine. The slope of the indifference curves at point B equals the slope of the product transformation curve at point A', as demonstrated by the fact that the tangents, $B'B''$ and $A''A'''$ are parallel. Thus, given the amount to be produced of each commodity, we can find in this way the amount of each commodity that should be allocated to Tom and to Harry.

In addition, we can find the amount of labor and capital that should be allocated to the production of each commodity by consulting the Edgeworth box diagram in Figure 14.5 that underlies the product transformation curve. Recall from Section 14 that each point on the product transformation curve corresponds to a point on the contract curve in Figure 14.5, and that each point on the contract curve in Figure 14.5 corresponds to a particular allocation of labor and capital between the production of the two commodities. For example, point A' on the product transformation curve corresponds to point U' on the contract curve, GG', in Figure 14.5. Thus, given that the composition of output in the economy will be given by point A', we know that OS units of labor will be devoted to the production of food, $(OL - OS)$ units of labor will be devoted to the production of medicine, OR units of capital will be devoted to the production of food, and $(OC - OR)$ units of capital will be devoted to the production of medicine.

To sum up, we have answered the two questions set forth at the beginning of this section. Given the amount of each commodity to be produced, we have shown how this output should be distributed between consumers and how the available inputs should be distributed between industries if production is to be efficient and if consumer satisfaction is to be maximized. However, it is important to note that our model is incomplete even for this simple two-commodity, two-consumer, two-input economy, since we take as given the amount of each commodity to be produced. In the next chapter, we shall describe one way that economists have attempted to complete the model.

16. The Marginal Rate of Product Transformation, the Marginal Rate of Substitution, and Consumer Satisfaction

In the previous section, it was asserted that consumer satisfaction will not be maximized unless the marginal rate of product transformation between two goods is equal to the marginal rate of substitution between the two goods. The purpose of this section is to demonstrate that this is the case. For simplicity, suppose that firm A produces both food and medicine and that it supplies all of these commodities consumed by Tom. Suppose, too, that Tom initially consumes C_T units of medicine and F_T units of food, and that his marginal rate of substitution of medicine for food is X. Finally, suppose that firm A produces C units of medicine and F units of food and that the marginal rate of product transformation between food and medicine is Y.

The first thing we shall show is that consumer satisfaction is not being maximized if X is less than Y. If X is less than Y, suppose that we decrease the amount of medicine produced by firm A and the amount of medicine consumed by Tom by 1 unit. For Tom to maintain the same level of satisfaction, he can be given X additional units of food to offset the loss of the 1 unit of medicine. (This follows from the definition of the marginal rate of substitution, given in Chapter 2.)

Suppose that firm A gives him the extra X units of food. By decreasing its production of medicine by 1 unit, firm A can make an additional Y units of food. (This follows from the definition of the marginal rate of product transformation, given in Chapter 7.) After decreasing its output of medicine, firm A supplies Harry just as much medicine as before, since both its total output of medicine and Tom's consumption of medicine is reduced by 1 unit. But it can supply him with an extra $(Y - X)$ units of food (the extra Y units it can produce less the X units it has given Tom). Consequently, Harry can be made better off without hurting Tom, if X is less than Y. Thus consumer satisfaction is not being maximized if X is less than Y.[18]

The next thing we shall show is that consumer satisfaction is not being maximized if X is greater than Y. If X is greater than Y, suppose that we increase the amount of medicine produced by firm A and the amount of medicine consumed by Tom by 1 unit. For Tom to maintain the same level of satisfaction, he must give up X units of food. Suppose that he gives them to firm A. By increasing its output of medicine by 1 unit, firm A can make Y fewer units of food. Firm A can supply Harry with as much medicine as before but it can supply him with an extra $(X - Y)$ units of food (the X units Tom has given up minus the Y units by which its output of food has fallen). Consequently Harry can be made better off without hurting Tom if X is greater than Y. Thus consumer satisfaction is not being maximized if X is greater than Y.[19]

If consumer satisfaction is not being maximized if X is less than Y, and if it is not being maximized if X is greater than Y, it follows that consumer satisfaction can be maximized only if X is equal to Y. This, of course, is what we set out to prove.

---

[18]A numerical example may help make this easier. If Tom's marginal rate of substitution of medicine for food is one and if the marginal rate of product transformation between food and medicine is two, firm A can reduce its output of medicine by 1 unit and provide Tom with one less unit of medicine. Firm A can also increase its production of food by 2 units and give Tom one extra unit of food to compensate for his loss of medicine. There is 1 unit of food left over, which can make Harry better off without hurting Tom.

[19]A numerical example may help make this easier. If Tom's marginal rate of substitution of medicine for food is two and if the marginal rate of product transformation between food and medicine is one, firm A can increase its output of medicine by 1 unit and provide Tom with 1 extra unit of medicine. Firm A can also obtain 2 units of food from Tom to compensate for the extra unit of medicine, but to produce the extra unit of medicine, firm A had to produce one less unit of food. Thus firm A has 1 unit of food left over, which can make Harry better off without hurting Tom.

17. Summary

Previous chapters have been concerned with partial equilibrium analysis, which assumes that changes in price can occur in whatever market is being studied without causing significant changes in price in other markets, which in turn affect the market being studied. An analysis that takes account of the interrelationships among prices in various markets is called a general equilibrium analysis. One of the most fundamental problems that general equilibrium analysis has been used to help solve is whether or not it is possible for equilibrium to occur simultaneously in all markets in a perfectly competitive economy. Modern work has established that in a perfectly competitive economy a general equilibrium can be achieved under a fairly wide set of conditions.

General equilibrium analysis provides a framework of price and output relations for both commodities and inputs for the economy as a whole. Its purpose is to show what the equilibrium configuration of prices, outputs, and inputs will be in various markets, given a certain set of consumer preferences, production functions, and input supply functions. In the simple model studied in Sections 5 to 7, there are three kinds of equations. This model is extremely simple, since it assumes that the supply of inputs is given (and independent of prices) and that production coefficients are fixed. However, it illustrates the nature of general equilibrium models.

Input-output analysis attempts to make the general equilibrium model empirically useful. It assumes that inputs are used in fixed proportions in producing any product, that there are constant returns to scale, and that consumer demand for all commodities is given. An important feature of input-output analysis is its emphasis on the interdependence of the economy. Input-output analysis involves the solution of a number of simultaneous linear equations. A typical problem handled by input-output analysis is: If consumption targets for each of a number of industries are given, how much will have to be produced by each industry to meet these targets? Can these production levels be achieved with the available resources?

Once we consider more than a single market, it becomes possible to consider many interesting questions concerning the optimal allocation of resources. Using the Edgeworth box diagram, we showed that the optimal allocation of commodities between consumers lies on the contract curve. We also showed that the optimal allocation of inputs between industries lies on an analogous contract curve and that a production transformation curve can be constructed from the latter contract curve. Finally, we studied a simple model that included both production and exchange. It was shown that consumer satisfaction will not be maximized unless the marginal rate of product transformation between two goods is equal to the marginal rate of substitution between them.

SELECTED REFERENCES

Cassel, Gustav, *The Theory of Social Economy*, New York: Harcourt, Brace and World, 1924.

Debreu, Gerard, *Theory of Value*, New York: John Wiley, 1959.

Henderson, James, and Richard Quandt, *Microeconomic Theory*, New York: McGraw-Hill, 1958.

Leontief, Wassily, *The Structure of the American Economy*, New York: Oxford University Press, 1951.

Walras, Léon, *Elements of Pure Economics*, trans. by William Jaffé, Homewood, Ill.: Richard D. Irwin, 1954.

15

Welfare Economics

1. Introduction

At the beginning of this book, we made the claim that microeconomics is of use in clarifying public policy issues. Having made this claim, we hastened to add that microeconomics alone is seldom able to provide a clear-cut solution to such issues, but that, in combination with other relevant disciplines, it frequently can provide useful ways of structuring and analyzing these issues. The purpose of this chapter is to provide an introduction to welfare economics, the branch of microeconomics that is concerned with the nature of the policy recommendations that economists can make.

To prevent confusion, note that welfare economics is not concerned with the various government "welfare" programs you read about in the newspapers. Instead, welfare economics covers a much broader set of questions, its primary concern being with policy issues concerning the allocation of resources. In other words, it deals mainly with questions concerning the optimal allocation of inputs among industries and the optimal distribution of commodities among consumers. These are general equilibrium problems, since the optimal usage of any input cannot be determined by looking at the market for this input alone, and the optimal output of any commodity cannot be determined by looking at the market for this commodity alone. On the contrary, the optimal allocation of resources between two products depends on the relative strength of the demands for the products and their relative production costs.

We have already begun the study of welfare economics, although we have not called it by that name. The latter part of the previous chapter, devoted to resource allocation, was concerned with welfare economics in the very simple case of a two-commodity, two-consumer, two-input economy. This chapter provides a further introduction to the fundamental principles of welfare economics. We begin by considering interpersonal comparisons of utility and by taking up the conditions that must be satisfied by an optimal allocation of resources. Then we deal with the role of perfect competition, as well as rules for government planning, in promoting an optimal allocation of resources. Finally, we discuss the nature and effects of external economies and diseconomies, various criteria for welfare judgments, Arrow's impossibility theorem, and the theory of the second best.

2. Interpersonal Comparison of Utility and the Distribution of Income

At the outset it is important to recognize an important limitation of welfare economics: There is no scientifically meaningful way to compare the utility levels of various individuals. The reader will recall that in our previous discussion of utility and demand theory in Chapters 2 and 3 we were not required to make any such interpersonal comparisons.[1] This was fortunate, and intentional. There is no way that one can meaningfully state that a piece of Aunt Mary's apple pie will bring you more satisfaction than it will me, or that your headache is worse than mine. This is because there is no scale on which we can measure pleasure or pain in such a way that interpersonal comparisons can validly be made.

---

[1]However, there were two exceptions. In the treatment of the water problem in Chapter 3, we simply added the areas under the demand curves of various consumers to get an aggregate measure of the loss to consumers due to the curtailment of their use of water. We noted that this treatment, although sometimes adopted in applied work, suffers from difficulties. In this chapter, these difficulties are explained at length. Also, in Chapter 9, when we computed the "welfare loss" due to monopoly, we simply added up the areas under the demand curves of various persons. We indicated that this entailed problems discussed here in detail.

Because we cannot make interpersonal comparisons of utility, we cannot tell whether one distribution of income is better than another. For example, suppose you receive twice as much income as I do. Economics cannot tell us whether this is a better distribution of income than if I receive twice as much income as you do. This is a value judgment, pure and simple. However, most problems of public policy involve changes in the distribution of income. For example, even a decision to increase the production of numerically controlled machine tools and to reduce the production of conventional machine tools may mean that certain stockholders and workers will gain, while others will lose (since some machine tool firms specialize more heavily than others in the production of numerically controlled tools). Because it is so difficult to evaluate the effects of such a decision on the distribution of income, it is correspondingly difficult to come to any conclusion as to whether or not such a decision is good or bad.

Faced with this problem, economists have adopted a number of approaches, all of which have important difficulties. Some economists simply have paid no attention to the effects of proposed policies on the income distribution. Others have taken the existing income distribution as optimal, while still others have asserted that income distributions exhibiting less inequality of income are preferable to those exhibiting more inequality of income. Purists have argued that we really cannot be sure a change is for the better unless it hurts no member of society. Others have suggested that we must accept the judgment of Congress (or the public as a whole) as to what is an optimal distribution of income.

Much more will be said about these approaches when we discuss criteria for welfare judgments later on in this chapter. For the moment, the important point to note is that the marginal conditions for an optimal allocation of resources, described in the following section, are incomplete, since they say nothing concerning the optimal income distribution. We now turn to a discussion of these marginal conditions in Sections 3 and 4 and a discussion of one approach to the income distribution problem in Section 5.

3. Marginal Conditions for Optimal Resource Allocation

Fundamentally, there are three necessary conditions for optimal resource allocation. The first pertains to the optimal allocation of commodities among consumers. It states that *the marginal rate of substitution between any two commodities must be the same for any two consumers.* The proof that this condition is necessary to maximize consumer satisfaction is quite simple. All that need be noted is that, if the marginal rates of substitution were unequal, both consumers could benefit by trading. For example, suppose that the first consumer regards an additional unit of product A as having the same utility as two extra units of product B, whereas the second consumer regards an additional unit of product A as having the same utility as three extra units of product B. Then, if the first consumer trades one unit of product A for 2.5 units of product B from the second consumer, both consumers are better off.

This condition implies that commodities should be distributed in such a way that consumers are on their contract curve, since the contract curve is composed of points where the marginal rates of substitution are equal for the consumers. In the case of only two commodities and two consumers, we showed in the previous chapter (Section 12) that this condition must be met if consumer satisfaction is to be maximized. We are now stating the more general proposition that this condition must also be met in the more realistic case in which there are more than two commodities and two consumers.

The second condition pertains to the optimal allocation of inputs among producers. It states that *the marginal rate of technical substitution between any two inputs must be the same for any pair of producers.* If this condition does not hold, it is possible to increase total production merely by reallocating inputs among producers. For example, suppose that, for the first producer, the marginal product of input 1 is twice that of input 2, whereas for the second producer the marginal product of input 1 is three times that of input 2. Then, if the first producer gives one unit of input 1 to the second producer in exchange for 2.5 units of input 2, both firms can expand their output.

To see this, suppose that the marginal product of input 1 is M_1 for the first producer and M_2 for the second producer. Then the output of the first producer is reduced by M_1 units because of its loss of the unit of input 1, but it is increased by $2.5 \times M_1/2$ units because of its gain of the 2.5 units of input 2, the consequence being that on balance its output increases by $M_1/4$ units because of the trade. Similarly, the output of the second producer is increased by M_2 units because of its gain of the one unit of input 1, but it is decreased by $2.5 \times M_2/3$ units because of its loss of the 2.5 units of input 2, the consequence being that on balance its output increases by $M_2/6$ units because of the trade.

This condition implies that inputs should be allocated so that producers are on their contract curve, since the contract curve is made up of points at which the marginal rates of technical substitution are equal for producers. In the case of only two inputs and two producers, we showed in the previous chapter (Section 13) that this condition must be met if the output of each

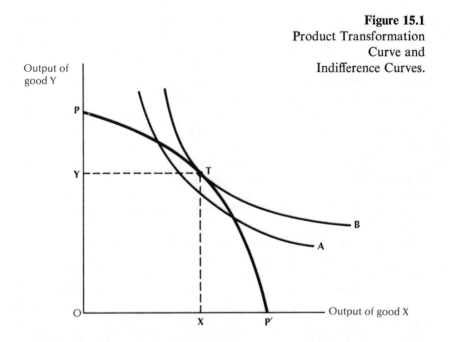

Figure 15.1
Product Transformation
Curve and
Indifference Curves.

producer is maximized, holding constant the output of the other producer. We are now stating the more general proposition that this condition must also be met in the more realistic case in which there are more than two inputs and two producers.

The third condition pertains to both the optimal allocation of inputs among industries and the optimal allocation of commodities among consumers. It states that *the marginal rate of substitution between any two commodities must be the same as the marginal rate of transformation between these two commodities for any producer.* Suppose that *PP'* in Figure 15.1 is the product transformation curve, the curve that shows the maximum amount of good X that can be produced, given various output levels for good Y. The marginal rate of transformation is the slope of the product transformation curve; it shows the number of units of good Y that society must give up in order to get an additional unit of good X.

Suppose that curves *A* and *B* in Figure 15.1 represent the indifference curves of a consumer who, for simplicity, is assumed to be the only consumer in the economy. To maximize the consumer's satisfaction, production must take place at point *T*, the output of good X being *OX* and the output of good Y being *OY*. Clearly, *T* is the point on the product transformation curve that is on the consumer's highest indifference curve. Since the product transformation curve is tangent to the indifference curve at point *T*, it follows that the marginal rate of transformation equals the marginal rate of substitution at point *T*. Thus the marginal rate of transformation equals the marginal rate of substitution if consumer satisfaction is maximized. This result will hold for any number of consumers, not just for one.

In the case of two products and two consumers, we showed in the previous chapter (Section 16) that this condition must hold if the satisfaction of one consumer is maximized, holding constant the other consumer's satisfaction. We are now stating the more general proposition that this condition must also be met in the more realistic case in which there are more than two commodities and two consumers.

4. Agricultural Price Supports: An Application

We can use these three conditions for optimal resource allocation to analyze many interesting questions, one being the choice among alternative agricultural price support schemes. From Chapter 8 it will be recalled that such schemes commonly specify that each farm can produce a certain quota, represented by *OX* in panel A of Figure 15.2. The total quota for the entire industry is *OY* in panel B of Figure 15.2. Also, there is a support price set by the government, which is *OP* in this case. Since *DD'* is the demand curve for the product, consumers will purchase OQ_1 units of the product, and the government will buy $(OY - OQ_1)$ units of the product. This is in contrast to the situation that would prevail if there were no quotas and price supports; under these circumstances, price would be OP_1 and the total output of the product would be OQ_2. The purpose of the quotas and price supports is to increase the income of farmers.

Unfortunately, this type of support scheme leads to inefficiencies of various kinds in the use of resources. First, because the marginal cost at *OX* will certainly vary from firm to firm, the industry's total output will be produced inefficiently. That is, the total cost of producing the total output could be decreased by reducing the output of firms with high marginal cost at *OX* and increasing the output of firms with low marginal cost at *OX*. Since the industry's total output is being produced inefficiently, it is clear that the second condition in the previous section is being violated. Second, part of the industry's output is unnecessary, and is taken off the market by the government. Third, since price is above marginal cost for this product (*MM'* being the marginal cost curve), the third condition in the previous section is also violated, if the prices of other goods equal marginal cost (as

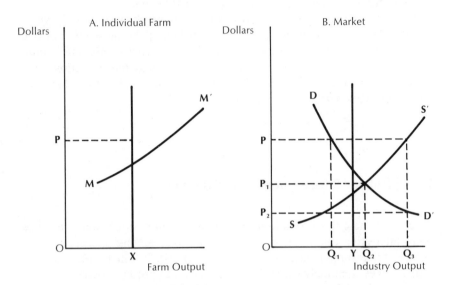

Figure 15.2
Agricultural Price
Supports.

they would in a perfectly competitive economy). The reasoning underlying this statement is explained in some detail in Section 6. For the moment, it is sufficient to accept it on faith.

It has been pointed out that a somewhat different scheme would eliminate the first and second types of inefficiency.[2] Such a plan would guarantee each farmer a price of OP, the result being that the industry would produce OQ_3 units of the product. But then it would let the free market alone, the result being that the OQ_3 units of the agricultural product would command a price of only OP_2 in the market and the government would pay each farmer $(OP - OP_2)$ per unit. The first type of inefficiency would be eliminated because each farmer would set marginal cost equal to OP, the result being that the marginal cost for each firm would be the same. The second type of inefficiency would be eliminated because the government no longer would take part of the industry's output off the market. The third type of inefficiency remains, since the price to consumers would be less than marginal cost.

However, this does not mean that this scheme is necessarily an improvement. For instance (as noted in Section 2), any choice among policies must

---

[2]See G. Stigler, *The Theory of Price*, New York: Macmillan, 1966, pp. 187–90. However, note that piece-meal attempts to induce fulfillment of the marginal conditions may not improve matters. See Section 15.

take into account their effects on the income distribution. This kind of plan would result in a different distribution of benefits and costs among consumers and farmers. For example, the abandonment of the quota system would hurt farmers who possess quotas, but not others. These aspects of the choice may outweigh all others in many people's minds; Congressmen in particular may be sensitive to the question of whose ox is gored. More will be said on this score in the next section.

5. The Utility-Possibility Curve and the Social Welfare Function[3]

In Section 2, we stated that the three conditions described in Section 3 are incomplete guides to an optimal allocation of resources, since they say nothing concerning the question of income distribution. In this section we show more explicitly how these conditions are incomplete, and we describe one way that economists have attempted to get around this problem. To do these things, it is convenient to return to the two-commodity, two-consumer, two-input case discussed at the end of the previous chapter. There are two consumers, Tom and Harry; two commodities, food and medicine; and two inputs, labor and capital. There are a total of OL units of labor and OC units of capital.

Given that the production functions are as shown in Figure 14.5 (p. 403), the previous chapter (Section 14) shows that the product transformation curve is that shown in Figure 14.6 (p. 405). This curve, PP', is reproduced in Figure 15.3. At any point on this curve, inputs are allocated so that the second condition in Section 3 is met. (See Sections 13 and 14 of Chapter 14.) If we know the amount of food and the amount of medicine that will be produced, we can construct an Edgeworth box diagram for the two consumers. For example, if the total quantity of food produced is OF and the total amount of medicine produced is OK, the Edgeworth box diagram has OF as its width and OK as its height. Figure 15.3 also shows the indifference curves of Tom and Harry (T_1'', T_2'', and T_3'' for Tom; and H_1'', H_2'', and H_3'' for Harry) and the contract curve, CC'. At any point on this contract curve, commodities are allocated so that the first condition in Section 3 is met (see Section 12 of Chapter 14).

---

[3]This section is based to a considerable extent on F. Bator, "The Simple Analytics of Welfare Maximization," *American Economic Review*, 1957.

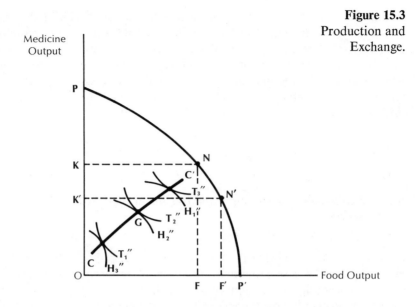

Figure 15.3
Production and
Exchange.

If the total quantity of food produced is *OF* and the total quantity of medicine produced is *OK*, the third condition in Section 3 dictates that the commodities be distributed between the consumers so that they are at point *G*. Only at point *G* does the common slope of their indifference curves (the marginal rate of substitution) equal the slope of the product transformation function at point *N* (the marginal rate of product transformation). The distribution of commodities at point *G* between Tom and Harry means that Tom achieves a certain level on his (ordinal) utility function and Harry achieves a certain level on his (ordinal) utility function. Suppose that this pair of utility levels corresponds to point *R* in Figure 15.4.

Now suppose that we take another point on the product transformation curve in Figure 15.3, say *N'*. On the basis of this amount of food output and this amount of medicine output, a new Edgeworth box diagram can be drawn, its width being *OF'* and its height being *OK'*. Drawing Tom's and Harry's indifference curves in this new Edgeworth box diagram, we can find the contract curve for this new box diagram, and we can find the point on this contract curve at which the common slope of the indifference curves (the marginal rate of substitution) equals the slope of the product transformation function at point *N'* (the marginal rate of product transformation). Then we can see what levels of Tom's utility and Harry's utility correspond to this point and we can plot these utility levels in Figure 15.4, the result being point *R'*.

Figure 15.4
Utility-Possibility
Curve and Social
Indifference Curves.

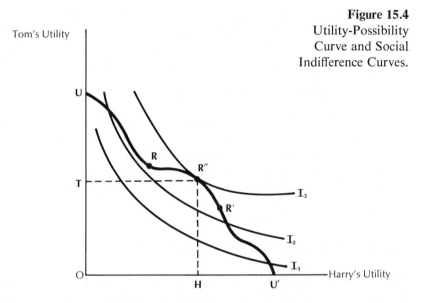

If we repeat this process for all points on the product transformation function, we shall obtain a locus of points, UU', that shows the various possible pairs of utility levels of Tom and Harry if the three conditions in Section 3 are met. This locus of points is called the *utility-possibility curve*. As would be expected, UU' is negatively sloped: if these conditions are met, the greater satisfaction obtained by Tom, the less satisfaction obtained by Harry. Some point on UU' must be chosen. Basically, the choice of a point on the utility-possibility curve is the choice of an income distribution. If this choice is made, the problem of finding an optimal allocation of resources in this case is solved.

But how can a choice be made among the points on UU'? One approach is to posit the existence of a *social welfare function*, a function that is an aggregate measure of national, or social, well-being. This function is assumed to depend solely on where Tom and Harry are on their own utility functions. It summarizes and takes into account the "deservingness" of Tom and Harry, as seen by society as a whole, or by the dictator if one exists. In a democracy it is possible under certain circumstances that such a function could be developed by voting. However, as we shall see in subsequent sections, the construction of a social welfare function is an extremely difficult business.

For present purposes, it is sufficient simply to assume that a social welfare function exists and is represented by the social indifference curves, I_1, I_2, and I_3, in Figure 15.4. Each social indifference curve includes a locus of points at which social welfare is the same. Of course, I_2 is a higher indifference curve than I_1 because both Tom's and Harry's utility levels are higher at points on I_2 than at points on I_1. Clearly, the highest attainable social indifference curve is I_3, and the optimum point in Figure 15.4 is R''. This is the chosen distribution of income, Tom's utility level being OT and Harry's utility level being OH. Thus, if there exists a social welfare function, one can obtain a complete solution to the problem of resource allocation in this case. Note that this solution answers the question left unanswered in Chapter 14: How much of each commodity should be produced? To answer this question, we need only find out what point on the product transformation curve corresponds to R''.[4]

6. Perfect Competition and Economic Efficiency

One of the most important, and most fundamental, findings of microeconomics is that a perfectly competitive economy satisfies the three sets of conditions for welfare maximization set forth in Section 3. The argument for competition can be made in various ways. For example, some people favor competition simply because it prevents the undue concentration of power and the exploitation of consumers. But to the economic theorist, the basic argument for a perfectly competitive economy is the fact that such an economy satisfies these conditions. In this section we prove that this is indeed a fact. In Sections 7 and 8, we discuss how prices can be used in planned economies and by regulated industries to achieve the same kinds of results.

The first condition in Section 3 is that the marginal rate of substitution between any pair of commodities must be the same for all consumers. To see that this condition is met under perfect competition, we must recall from Chapter 2 that, under perfect competition, consumers choose their purchases so that the marginal rate of substitution between any pair of commodities is equal to the ratio of the prices of the pair of commodities. Since prices, and thus price ratios, are the same for all buyers under perfect competition, it follows that the marginal rate of substitution between any pair of commodities must be the same for all consumers. For example, if every consumer can buy bread at 25 cents a loaf and butter at $1 a pound, each one will

---

[4]Note that this section as well as Sections 11 to 16 of Chapter 14 specify nothing about the institutional context. All that we have done is to figure out how resources should be allocated in this situation. We have not said anything about the sorts of institutional arrangements that will result in such an allocation of resources. The next few sections deal with the latter subject.

arrange his purchases so that the marginal rate of substitution of butter for bread is four. Thus the marginal rate of substitution will be the same for all consumers: four for everyone.

The second condition in Section 3 is that the marginal rate of technical substitution between any pair of inputs must be the same for all producers. To see that this condition is met under perfect competition, we must recall from Chapter 6 that, under perfect competition, producers will choose the quantity of each input so that the marginal rate of technical substitution between any pair of inputs is equal to the ratio of the prices of the pair of inputs. Since input prices, and thus price ratios, are the same for all producers under perfect competition, it follows that the marginal rate of technical substitution must be the same for all producers. For example, if every producer can buy labor services at $3 an hour and machine tool services at $6 an hour, each one will arrange the quantity of its inputs so that the marginal rate of technical substitution of machine tool services for labor is two. Thus the marginal rate of technical substitution will be the same for all producers: two for each of them.

The third condition in Section 3 is that the marginal rate of product transformation must equal the marginal rate of substitution for each pair of goods. The proof that this condition is met under perfect competition is somewhat lengthier than in the case of the other conditions. To begin with, we must note that the marginal rate of product transformation is the number of units of good A that must be given up to produce an additional unit of good B. The additional cost of producing the extra unit of good B is, of course, the marginal cost of good B. To see how many units of good A must be given up to get this extra unit of good B, we must divide the marginal cost of good B by the marginal cost of good A. This will tell us how many extra units of good A cost as much as one extra unit of good B. Thus the marginal rate of product transformation under perfect competition equals the ratio of the marginal cost of good B to the marginal cost of good A.

From Chapter 8 it will be recalled that price equals marginal cost under perfect competition. Consequently, the ratio of the marginal cost of good B to the marginal cost of good A equals the ratio of the price of good B to the price of good A under perfect competition. Coupled with the result of the previous paragraph, this means that the marginal rate of product transformation is equal to the ratio of the price of good B to the price of good A under perfect competition. But, as we noted in connection with our discussion of the first condition, the marginal rate of substitution is equal to the ratio of the price of good B to the price of good A under perfect competition. Consequently, it follows that the marginal rate of product transformation equals the marginal rate of substitution for any pair of products under perfect competition.

Referring back to Section 4 for a moment, it is obvious now why the agricultural price supports violated the third condition for optimality. Since the price of the agricultural good does not equal marginal cost (see Figure 15.2), the third condition must be violated if the prices of other goods equal marginal cost. For example, take some other good with marginal cost, MC_x, and price, P_x. The marginal rate of transformation between this good and the agricultural product is $MC_A \div MC_x$, where MC_A is the marginal cost of the agricultural good. Moreover, if consumers maximize satisfaction, the marginal rate of substitution between the two goods is $P_A \div P_x$, where P_A is the price of the agricultural product. However, since $P_x = MC_x$ and $MC_A \neq P_A$, it follows that the marginal rate of substitution does not equal the marginal rate of transformation.

Returning to the original topic of this section, we find that all three conditions for optimal resource allocation are satisfied under perfect competition. This is one of the principal reasons why economists are so enamoured of perfect competition and so wary of monopoly. If a formerly competitive economy is restructured so that some industries become monopolies, these conditions for optimal resource allocation are no longer met. As we know from Chapter 9, each monopolist produces less than the perfectly competitive industry that it replaces would have produced. Thus too few resources are devoted to the industries that are monopolized, and too many resources are devoted to the industries that remain perfectly competitive. This is one of the economist's chief charges against monopoly. It wastes resources because its actions result in an over-allocation of resources to competitive industries and an under-allocation of resources to monopolistic industries. Society is then less well off.[5]

7. Economic Planning and Marginal Cost Pricing

The previous section showed that the three conditions for optimal resource allocation are satisfied under perfect competition. Economists interested in the functioning of planned, or socialist, economies have pointed out

---

[5]In evaluating this result and judging its practical relevance, it is important to note that it stems from a very simple model that ignores such things as technological change and other dynamic considerations, risk and uncertainty, and externalities. Some of these factors are taken up in subsequent sections of this chapter and in Chapter 16. The reader should be very careful to note the qualifications and assumptions that must be made. Sometimes the argument for perfect competition is made without full recognition of these qualifications.

that a price system could be used in a similar way to increase social welfare in such economies. According to economists like California's Abba Lerner,[6] rational economic organization could be achieved in a socialist economy that is decentralized, as well as under perfect competition. For example, the government might try to solve the system of equations that is solved automatically in a perfectly competitive economy, and obtain the prices that would prevail under perfect competition. Then the government might publish this price list, together with instructions for consumers to maximize their satisfaction and for producers to maximize profit. (Of course, the wording of the instructions to consumers might be a bit less heavy-handed than "Maximize your satisfaction!")

An important advantage claimed for planning and control of this sort is that the government does not have to become involved in the intricate and detailed business of setting production targets for each plant. It need only compute the proper set of prices. As long as plant managers maximize "profits," the proper production levels will be chosen by them. Thus decentralized decision-making, rather than detailed centralized direction, could be used, the result being that administrative costs and bureaucratic disadvantages might be reduced.

The prices that the government would publish, like those prevailing in a perfectly competitive economy, would equal marginal cost. Many economists have recommended that government-owned enterprises in basically capitalist economies also adopt *marginal cost pricing*, i.e., that they set price equal to marginal cost. For example, Harold Hotelling argued that this should be the case.[7] Taking the case of a bridge where the marginal cost (the extra cost involved in allowing an additional vehicle to cross) is zero, he argued that the socially optimal price for crossing the bridge is zero, and that its costs should be defrayed by general taxation. If a toll is charged, the conditions for optimal resource allocation are violated.

Marginal cost pricing has fascinated economists during the 30 years that have elapsed since Hotelling's article.[8] But there are a number of important problems in the actual application of this idea. One of the most important is that, if (as is frequently the case in public utilities) the firm's average costs decrease with increases in its scale of output, it follows from the discussion in Chapter 6 that marginal cost must be less than average cost, the consequence being that the firm will not cover its costs if price is set equal to

[6]A. Lerner, *The Economics of Control*, New York: Macmillan, 1944.
[7]See H. Hotelling, "The General Welfare in Relation to Problems of Taxation and of Railway and Utility Rates," *Econometrica*, 1938.
[8]For example, see J. Nelson, *Marginal Cost Pricing in Practice*, Englewood Cliffs, N.J.: Prentice-Hall, 1964; and N. Ruggles, "Recent Developments in Marginal Cost Pricing," *Review of Economic Studies*, 1949–1950.

marginal cost. This means that marginal cost pricing must be accompanied by some form of subsidy if the firm is to stay in operation. However, the collection of the funds required for the payment of the subsidy may also violate the conditions for optimal resource allocation. Moreover, this subsidy means that there is a change in the income distribution favoring users of the firm's output and penalizing nonusers of its output: Whether or not marginal cost pricing results in improved economic welfare depends on how one views this change in the income distribution.

8.   Marginal Cost Pricing: A Case Study

During the mid-fifties, Électricité de France, the French nationalized electricity industry, introduced marginal cost pricing for its high tension service. The ultimate goal of the new pricing scheme was that the price paid for a kilowatt-hour of electricity at a given time of day in a given season of the year in a given region was to approximate the cost of an additional kilowatt-hour at this time in this season in this region.

Of course, a great many simplifications had to be made in computing the new price schedule. First, consider price differences at various times of day. In the winter, the day is divided into three periods: the peak daytime hour, the other daytime hours, and the night. In the summer, it is divided into two periods: day and night. A consumer in a given region must pay a different price for kilowatt-hours in each period, the differences reflecting differences in marginal costs. Next, consider price differences among regions. To estimate the marginal costs in each region, a pattern of movements of electricity from generating stations to consumption areas is derived that meets estimated demands at minimum total cost given present capacity. The marginal costs corresponding to this pattern are used to determine prices in various regions.

Finally, consider price differences among seasons. Differences among seasons in demand curves, as well as differences in hydroelectric reservoir levels and river flows, are responsible for these differences in price. The seasonal differences in demand are assumed by the industry to be like those observed in the past. Average snow and rainfall levels in each season can be used in the calculations. Since water tends to be less abundant in the winter, peak demands for electricity have to be satisfied by using less efficient thermal plants than have to be used in the summer. Also, demand for electricity tends to be higher in the winter. Both of these factors clearly influence the level of the marginal cost of electricity.

What has the new pricing scheme achieved? According to California's Thomas Marschak, who has made a careful study of the French experience, Électricité de France's marginal-cost pricing has had a number of important beneficial results. In his view, a

> "clear improvement over the [old] pricing scheme is very plausibly claimed. Preliminary observation suggests that a leveling of consumption between the daytime and the nighttime periods may be expected. One immediate result is a reduction by 5 percent in the capacity required to meet peak demands.... Another is a substantial saving of imported (American) coal in winter, since the flattening of peaks eliminates the need for some of the inefficient thermal output previously required."[9]

9. External Economies and Diseconomies

Up to this point, we have generally assumed implicitly that there is no difference between private and social benefits, or between private and social costs. For example, costs to producers have been assumed to be costs to society, and costs to society have been assumed to be costs to producers; benefits to producers have been assumed to be benefits to society, and benefits to society have been assumed to be benefits to producers. In fact, however, there are many instances in which these assumptions do not hold. Instead, producers sometimes confer benefits on other members of the economy but are unable to obtain payment for these benefits, and they sometimes act in such a way as to harm others without having to pay the full costs. In these cases, the pursuit of private gain will not promote the social welfare. The purpose of this section is to describe how differences between private and social returns are likely to arise and the ways in which these differences influence our results. The following sections apply this theory to two areas of the modern economy.

It is convenient, and customary, to classify these divergences into four types. First, there are *external economies of production.* An external economy occurs when an action taken by an economic unit results in uncompensated benefits to others; when such benefits are due to an increase in a firm's production, they are called external economies of production. The firm may benefit others directly. For example, it may train workers that eventually

---

[9]T. Marschak, "Capital Budgeting and Pricing in the French Nationalized Industries," *Journal of Business*, Jan. 1960, p. 151.

go to work for other firms that do not have to pay the training costs. Or the firm may benefit other firms indirectly because its increased output may make it more economical to provide services to other firms in the industry. For example, a great expansion in an aircraft firm may make it possible for aluminum producers to take advantage of economies of scale, with the result that other metal fabricating firms can also get cheaper aluminum. In either case, there is a difference between private and social returns, the gains to society being greater than the gains to the firm.

Second, there are *external economies of consumption*, which occur when an action taken by a consumer, rather than a producer, results in an uncompensated benefit to others. For example, if I maintain my house and lawn, this benefits my neighbors as well as myself. If I educate my children and make them more responsible citizens, this too benefits my neighbors as well as myself. The list of external economies from consumption could easily be extended, but the idea should be clear at this point.

Third, there are *external diseconomies of production*. An external diseconomy occurs when an action taken by an economic unit results in uncompensated costs to others; when such costs are due to increases in a firm's production, they are called external diseconomies of production. For example, a firm may pollute a stream by pumping out waste materials, or it may pollute the air with smoke or materials. Such actions result in costs to others; for instance, Chesapeake Bay's oyster beds and Long Island's clam beds are being threatened by water pollution. However, the private costs do not reflect the full social costs, since the firms and cities responsible for the pollution are not charged for their contribution to poorer quality water and their harm to industries dependent on good water. There are many cases of external diseconomies of production, such as traffic congestion and the defacement of scenery.

Fourth, there are *external diseconomies of consumption*, which occur when an action taken by a consumer results in an uncompensated cost to others. Some external diseconomies of consumption can be fairly subtle. For example, Mrs. White may be trying hard to keep up with the social leader in town, Mrs. Brown. If Mrs. Brown obtains a new mink coat, this may make Mrs. White worse off, since she may become dissatisfied with her old mink coat. Similarly, a family that feels that a three-year-old Chevrolet is perfectly adequate may become dissatisfied with it after moving to a community where everyone drives a new Thunderbird.

The foregoing are some of the most important cases where social and private costs and benefits differ. At first glance, these cases may not seem very important. But when all of these types of external economies and diseconomies are considered, their aggregate significance can be substantial. For example, the fact that environmental pollution of various kinds resulting from industrial output is important has been stressed repeatedly in the United States in recent years. The importance of various types of external economies of production is undeniable, and the fact that consumer tastes and well-being are determined by the tastes and well-being of other members of society is obvious as well.

How do these external economies and diseconomies alter the optimality of the allocation of resources under perfect competition? If a firm or individual takes an action that contributes to society's welfare but which results in no payment for him, he is certainly likely to take this action less frequently than would be socially optimal. Thus, if the production of a certain good, say beryllium, is responsible for external economies, less than the socially optimum amount of beryllium is likely to be produced under perfect competition, since the producers are unlikely to increase output simply because it reduces the costs of other companies. By the same token if a firm or individual takes an action that results in costs to others that he is not forced to pay, he is likely to take this action more frequently than is socially desirable. Thus, if the production of a certain good is responsible for external diseconomies, more of this good is likely to be produced under perfect competition than is socially optimal.[10]

10. Public Policy toward Basic Research: An Application

To illustrate how the theory of external economies and diseconomies, together with the other principles discussed in this chapter, can be used to throw light on problems of public policy, consider the nature of social policy toward basic research. One of the most fundamental questions in this area is: Why should the government support basic research? Why not rely on private enterprise to support sufficient basic research? In late 1963, the Committee on Science and Astronautics of the House of Representatives asked the National Academy of Sciences to prepare a report answering this, and other questions.

---

[10]It should be noted that private costs and benefits can in many instances be made to equal social costs and benefits by legal requirements that assign liabilities for damages and compensates for benefits. However, such systems often are impractical or too costly to be useful. See G. Stigler, *The Theory of Price*, New York: Macmillan, 1966, pp. 110–14; and R. Coase, "The Problem of Social Cost," *Journal of Law and Economics*, 1961. This section and Section 13 are based partly on the treatment in W. Baumol, *Economic Theory and Operations Analysis*, Englewood Cliffs, N.J.: Prentice-Hall, 1965, pp. 368–71 and 375–80.

The Academy's report, prepared in part by Carl Kaysen of the Institute of Advanced Study and Harry Johnson of the University of Chicago, emphasizes the fact that basic scientific research is likely to generate substantial external economies. Important additions to fundamental knowledge often have an impact on a great many fields. If a firm produces an important scientific breakthrough, it generally cannot hope to capture the full value of the new knowledge it creates. It cannot go into the full range of activities in which the knowledge has use, and it is seldom able to capture through patent rights the full social value of the new knowledge. Indeed, fundamental discoveries, such as natural "laws," are not patentable at all.

Because of these external economies, there is likely to be a divergence between the private and social benefits from basic research, the result being that a perfectly competitive economy would be expected to devote less resources to basic research than is socially optimal. Consequently, there seems to be a good case on purely economic grounds for the government (or some other agency not motivated by profit) to support basic research. As stated in the Academy's report.

> there is good theoretical reason for expecting that, left to itself, the market would not only tend to allocate too few resources to research in general, but would also tend to bias the allocation against basic scientific research .... These defects of the market mechanism with respect to the allocation of resources toward and among investments in research imply that the market needs to be supplemented, and perhaps, with respect to basic scientific research, entirely replaced by social provision and allocation of resources for the support of scientific research.[11]

This is an illustration of how these simple principles of welfare economics have been used to help illuminate important issues of public policy.

11.   Urban Renewal: A Further Application[12]

Another area in which the theory of external economies and diseconomies is useful is urban economics. Urban renewal is based on the idea that the market mechanism does not work properly in this area. Why is this idea

---

[11]National Academy of Sciences, *Basic Research and National Goals*, Report to the Committee on Science and Astronautics of the United States House of Representatives, 1965, p. 136.

[12]This example is based on O. Davis and A. Whinston, "The Economics of Urban Renewal," *Law and Contemporary Problems*, Winter, 1961.

reasonable? Why do profit-maximizing individuals not find it worthwhile to keep up their property? The answer lies in the fact that the value of a piece of property depends on the neighborhood in which it is situated as well as on its own design and state of repair. This is because externalities are present in people's utility functions, the enjoyment they derive from a piece of property being dependent on its surroundings.

To see why this fact can cause urban blight, consider two adjacent properties. Suppose that the two owners, A and B, are each trying to determine whether to invest some money to redevelop their properties. Suppose that the rate of return on the investment by each owner is shown in Table 15.1, this rate of return being dependent on whether or not the other owner redevelops his property as well. If both redevelop, they will each make 7 percent on their investment. If neither redevelops, each can obtain 4 percent by investing the money in some other type of investment. If one redevelops but the other does not, the owner that redevelops makes only 3 percent since little is accomplished as long as the other owner does not redevelop; the owner that does not redevelop earns 10 percent on his investment because his property benefits (at no cost) from the improvements in the other property.

Table 15.1.   Returns from Investment,
Two Property Owners.

		OWNER B	
		INVEST	NOT INVEST
		OWNER A'S RATE OF RETURN	
Owner A	Invest	.07	.03
	Not Invest	.10	.04
		OWNER B'S RATE OF RETURN	
Owner A	Invest	.07	.10
	Not Invest	.03	.04

Source: O. Davis and A. Whinston, "The Economics of Urban Renewal," *Law and Contemporary Problems*, Winter 1961.

Under these circumstances, neither owner will redevelop his property. For example, take owner A. If owner B redevelops, owner A receives a higher return if he does not redevelop than if he redevelops. If owner B does not redevelop, owner A also receives a higher return if he does not redevelop than if he redevelops. In either case, owner A believes that he is better off not to redevelop. The situation is similar for owner B. Nevertheless, from society's point of view or from the point of view of the two owners' acting together as a unit, redevelopment may be desirable. Needless to say, this example is highly simplified and rather extreme, but it does illustrate the basic point that, because of externalities of this sort, urban renewal may not be undertaken although it is socially desirable.

12.   Increasing Returns and Public Goods

If there are external economies or diseconomies, the simple conditions for optimal resource allocation in Section 3 are not valid. Other cases in which these conditions are not valid occur when some industries operate under increasing returns or when a good is a public good. First, consider the case of a good that is produced under increasing returns. In such a case the product transformation curve may look like that in panel A of Figure 15.5, rather than like that in panel B of Figure 15.5. Let curves 1 and 2 be the indifference

Figure 15.5
Product Transformation
Curve with
Increasing Returns.

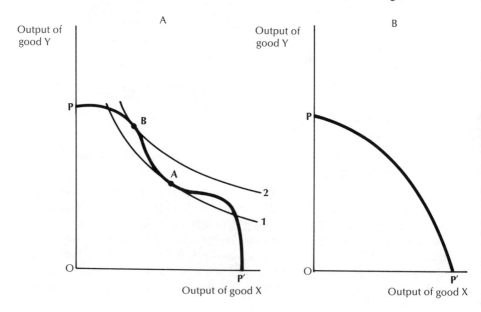

curves of the sole consumer in our simple society. Then, if the marginal rate of product transformation is set equal to the marginal rate of substitution, in accord with the third condition in Section 3, the optimal allocation of resources may not be achieved, since this condition is fulfilled at point A, which is not the optimal point, as well as at point B, which is the optimal point. In cases like this, the price system, as well as the conditions in Section 3, can give faulty signals to producers and consumers.

Turning to public goods, a consumer cannot be made to pay a price for some commodities, either because he cannot be barred from using them whether or not he pays or because it is obligatory for everyone to use them. Examples of such goods, called *public* or *collective goods*, are national defense and lighthouses. Perfect competition will not result in an optimal allocation of resources to such goods. Instead, the government or private charities generally provide goods of this type. Indeed, much of government activity consists of the provision of public goods like national defense, fire and police protection, and the services of the courts.

13.   When Is a Change an Improvement?[13]

There has been considerable controversy among economists over the circumstances under which economists, in their role as social scientists, can say that one policy is better for the welfare of society than another policy. This, of course, is an extremely fundamental question. Unless economists can tell whether one state of the world is better than another state of the world, they cannot legitimately make recommendations concerning public policy. In this section, we discuss various criteria that have been proposed as solutions of this problem. The following section discusses the relationships between individual and group decision-making.

Four criteria have been proposed to test whether a proposed change in policy is an improvement. According to the first criterion, put forth by Vilfredo Pareto at about the turn of the century,[14] a change that harms no one and improves the lot of some people (in their own eyes) is an improvement. This criterion is accepted by nearly everyone and is the basis for the rules in Section 3. However, there are many policy proposals that cannot be evaluated on the basis of this criterion. For example, a proposal that taxes

---

[13]See the last sentence of Footnote 10.
[14]V. Pareto, *Manuel D'Economie Politique*, 1909.

be levied on the rich to help the poor cannot be judged on the basis of this criterion. Indeed any change that benefits some people and harms others falls outside the scope of the Pareto criterion. In other words, the Pareto criterion evades the question of income distribution. This, of course, is a serious limitation, since most proposed changes in the real world hurt at least one person.

The second criterion, proposed by Nicholas Kaldor,[15] is meant to surmount this limitation. According to Kaldor, a change is an improvement if the people who gain from the change evaluate their gains at a higher dollar figure than the dollar figure that the losers attach to their losses. For example, if a proposed change benefits Tom and harms Harry, and if Tom would be willing to pay up to $100 to see the change occur, while Harry would pay up to $50 to avoid the change, the change, according to the Kaldor criterion, is an improvement (even though no money is paid by Tom to Harry). However, an important problem in the criterion is that $50 may mean more to Harry than $100 does to Tom. This criterion makes money, together with the existing distribution of income, a measure of the relative strength of feeling of the individuals.

The third criterion, suggested by Tibor Scitovsky,[16] is intended to meet another weakness in the Kaldor criterion. Under certain circumstances the Kaldor criterion will indicate that a change is an improvement, but it will also indicate after the change that a change back to the original state of affairs is also an improvement. For example, it might happen that the Kaldor criterion would indicate that a tax increase was a good thing, but after the tax increase, the Kaldor criterion might also indicate that a reduction of taxes to their original level was a good thing. To avoid this possibility, Scitovsky proposed that a change is an improvement only if the move from the original point to the new point is an improvement (according to the Kaldor criterion) and if the move from the new point to the old point is not an improvement (according to the Kaldor criterion). Of course, this criterion, like Kaldor's, suffers from the fact that monetary units are used as a measure of pleasure or pain.

The fourth criterion, put forth by Abram Bergson of Harvard University,[17] is based on an explicit social welfare function. Bergson argues that the problem can be solved only by formulating a set of explicit value judgments and incorporating them into a social welfare function of the sort discussed

---

[15]N. Kaldor, "Welfare Propositions in Economics and Interpersonal Comparisons of Utility," *Economic Journal*, 1939.

[16]T. Scitovsky, "A Note on Welfare Propositions in Economics," *Review of Economic Studies*, Nov. 1941.

[17]A. Bergson (Burk), "A Reformation of Certain Aspects of Welfare Economics," *Quarterly Journal of Economics*, 1937–1938.

in Section 5. This social welfare function may represent the value judgments of the legislature, a dictator, the economist himself, or the general populace (as reflected by popular vote); regardless of which it is, an explicit social welfare function is required. Once such a social welfare function is formulated, a policy change can be judged an improvement or not on the basis of whether or not it moves the society to a higher point on the social welfare function. For example, a change that moves society from point R' to R'' in Figure 15.4 is an improvement, since R'' is on the higher social indifference curve.[18] Needless to say, the difficulty with this criterion is that social welfare functions are difficult to come by in the real world. Moreover, as we shall see in the following section, social welfare functions based on democratic decision-making do not always exist.

Finally, it is important to note that, while these controversies have been going on at the level of pure theory, economists operating at a practical level have had no choice but to make recommendations to policy-makers. Perhaps a good many of these recommendations really could not pass muster if the criteria of this section had been applied. However, in many cases, the desires of the community may have been so obvious that much of the discussion of this section may have been unnecessary. For example, in the Great Depression, it must have been pretty obvious that the community wanted to reduce unemployment. Of course, there could have been some disagreement about the extent of the sacrifices that should be made by various segments of the population in order to achieve this goal, but the disagreement may have been confined to a relatively narrow range.

14. Arrow's Impossibility Theorem

Can social choices be made in such a way as to reflect individual preferences? This question clearly bears on the existence and construction of social welfare functions. The seminal work in this area was done by Kenneth

---

[18]Note that this social welfare function is of a special type: It assumes that the social welfare depends on the utility levels of the consumers. This implies the acceptance of an ethical norm regarding consumer sovereignty. Another approach might be to assume that the "government" (or some individual) can assert that "society" is better off in one situation than in another. This is a "paternalistic" or "dictatorial" approach. It is relatively straightforward, in contrast to the case in which social welfare depends on the utility levels of the consumers, but its limitations are obvious. See J. Rothenberg, *The Measurement of Social Welfare*, Englewood Cliffs, N.J.: Prentice-Hall, 1961.

Arrow,[19] who proposed the following four conditions that social choices must satisfy to reflect the preferences of the individuals comprising the society. First, social choices must be transitive. (If X is preferred to Y and Y is preferred to Z, Z cannot be preferred to X.) Second, social choices must not respond in an opposite direction to changes in individual choice. That is, an alternative that society would otherwise have picked must not be turned down because some individuals come to like it more. Third, social choices must not be dictated by any one inside or outside the society. Fourth, the social preference between two alternatives must depend only on people's feelings regarding those two alternatives and not on their opinion of other alternatives.

Arrow showed that, although these conditions may seem to be a sensible basis for democratic community decision-making, it is impossible to make a choice among all sets of alternatives without violating some of these conditions. This is a very disturbing conclusion, since it seems that, if social choice is to be consistent, it cannot be democratic. However, the moral to be drawn may not be quite as disturbing as at first it appears to be, since the fourth condition (in the preceding paragraph) is really more restrictive than it seems.

For example, suppose that opinion is split equally between citizens who believe that a billion dollars should be spent on space exploration rather than on aid to the poor and citizens who believe the opposite. According to the fourth condition, the government's choice must not be affected by the fact that the people who favor aid to the poor regard this as being the best use to which the money can be put, whereas the people who favor space exploration regard it as being less desirable than many other uses of the money. Also, the fourth condition does not allow for differences in the strength of feelings regarding various alternatives. The people who favor aid to the poor may feel that this alternative is much more desirable than space exploration, whereas the people who favor space exploration may feel that it is only slightly better than aid to the poor. Although there is no good way of measuring such differences in strength of feelings, it is hard to deny that they exist.

Arrow's work has led to a much clearer understanding of the relationship between individual preferences and social choice. There are many difficulties and traps in the analysis of decision-making by groups. Although the fourth condition may be too restrictive, it nevertheless is an eye opener to find that it is impossible to choose among all sets of alternatives without violating some of his conditions.

---

[19]K. Arrow, *Social Choice and Individual Values*, New York: John Wiley & Sons, 1951.

15. The Theory of the Second Best

Finally, we take up a very important part of welfare economics, the so-called "theory of the second best." This theory has a fairly long history, although its name and general development are due considerably to R. G. Lipsey and Kelvin Lancaster.[20] In previous sections, we have seen that the attainment of a *Pareto optimum*—a situation where no one can be made better off without making someone else worse off—requires the fulfillment of all the conditions described in Section 3. The theory of the second best is concerned with a situation in which one or more of the conditions cannot be met. It asks whether, under these circumstances, it is still desirable to fulfill the other conditions that can be met.

For example, suppose that there are a number of monopolies in a particular economy and that these monopolies are not fulfilling the conditions in Section 3. Suppose that the country's antitrust authorities are in a position to break up some, but not all, of the monopolies and force them to fulfill the conditions. The theory of the second best asks: Can we be sure that this will increase welfare?

In general the answer is no. This is the principal conclusion of the theory of the second best: Since some of the conditions for efficiency remain unfulfilled, there is no assurance that the reduction in the number of unfulfilled conditions will result in increased welfare. This has important implications for welfare economics, since it means that, if some parts of the economy are misbehaving in the sense that they are not fulfilling the conditions described in Section 3, there is no reason to believe that welfare would be greater if other parts of the economy were to be convinced (or forced) to fulfill these conditions.

To repeat, the theory of the second best states that "It is *not* true that a situation in which more, but not all, of the optimum conditions are fulfilled is necessarily, or is even likely to be, superior to a situation in which fewer are fulfilled."[21] The widespread implications of the theory of the second best should be clear. It shows that piecemeal attempts to force fulfillment of the conditions in Section 3 can easily be a mistake. Unfortunately, many practical attempts to apply the principles of welfare economics have been, and are, piecemeal attempts of this sort.

---

[20]R. Lipsey and K. Lancaster, "The General Theory of Second Best," *Review of Economic Studies*, 1956–1957.

[21]*Ibid.*, p. 12.

16. Summary

Welfare economics is concerned with the nature of the policy recommendations that economists can make. An important limitation of welfare economics is that there is no scientifically meaningful way to compare the utility levels of different individuals, the result being that we cannot tell whether one distribution of income is better than another. Putting aside the question of income distribution, there are three conditions for an optimal allocation of resources: (1) The marginal rate of substitution between any two commodities must be the same for any two consumers; (2) the marginal rate of technical substitution between any two inputs must be the same for any pair of producers; and (3) the marginal rate of substitution between any two commodities must be the same as the marginal rate of transformation between these two commodities for any producer.

One of the most fundamental findings of microeconomics is that a perfectly competitive economy satisfies these three sets of conditions for welfare maximization. To the economic theorist, this is one of the basic arguments for a perfectly competitive economy. Economists interested in the functioning of planned, or socialist, economies have pointed out that a price system could be used in a similar way to increase welfare in such economies. The prices that would be set would equal marginal cost. There have been recommendations that government-owned enterprises in basically capitalist economies also adopt marginal-cost pricing. The French electric industry has begun to do so with encouraging results.

Thus far, we have assumed that social costs do not differ from private costs and that social benefits do not differ from private benefits. In cases in which this assumption is false, perfect competition will not lead to an optimal allocation of resources. If the production of a certain good is responsible for external economies, less than the socially optimum amount of this good is likely to be produced under perfect competition. If the production of a certain good is responsible for external diseconomies, more of this good is likely to be produced under perfect competition than is socially optimal. Basic research is an example of a good that is likely to be underproduced in a perfectly competitive economy. Another area in which externalities are likely to interfere with the functioning of the price system is in urban renewal. Also, perfect competition will not result in an optimal allocation of resources in the presence of increasing returns or when a good is a public good.

There has been considerable controversy over the circumstances under which economists, in their role as social scientists, can say that one policy is better for society than another policy. At least four criteria have been proposed to test whether a proposed policy change is an improvement: Pareto's, Kaldor's, Scitovsky's, and Bergson's. Bergson's is based on an explicit social welfare function. In recent years, a considerable amount of attention has been devoted to the relationship between individual preferences and group choice, this topic being relevant to the existence and construction of a social welfare function. Finally, the theory of the second best shows that piecemeal attempts to force fulfillment of the optimality conditions can easily be a mistake. So long as some conditions remain unfulfilled, there is no assurance that a reduction in the number of unfulfilled conditions will result in increased welfare.

SELECTED REFERENCES

Arrow, Kenneth, *Social Choice and Individual Values*, New York: John Wiley, 1951. (Advanced)

Bator, Francis, "The Simple Analytics of Welfare Maximization," *American Economic Review*, March 1957.

Little, I. M. D., *A Critique of Welfare Economics*, Oxford: Clarendon Press, 1950.

Lerner, Abba, *The Economics of Control*, New York: Macmillan, 1944.

Reder, Melvin, *Studies in the Theory of Welfare Economics*, New York: Columbia University Press, 1947.

Rothenburg, Jerome, *The Measurement of Social Welfare*, Englewood Cliffs, N.J.: Prentice-Hall, 1961.

Scitovsky, Tibor, *Welfare and Competition*, Homewood, Ill.: Richard D. Irwin, 1951.

16

Technological Change and Economic Progress

1. Introduction

Chapter 15 and the latter part of Chapter 14 were concerned with the optimal allocation of resources, but they were concerned entirely with the optimal allocation of resources under static conditions. They took as given the production functions in various industries and the utility functions of consumers; they attempted to determine the allocation of resources that, given these production functions and utility functions, would be optimal. Although an analysis of this kind is interesting, it is incomplete in important respects, since one of the most important ways that economic welfare is increased is through the alteration of production functions due to technological change.

The purpose of this chapter is to discuss the microeconomics of technological change. First we take up the definition, classification, measurement, and determinants of the rate of technological change. Next we are concerned with the nature of research and development, the theory of parallel R and D efforts, and the determinants of development costs. Then we deal with

440

the innovation process and the diffusion of innovations. Finally we discuss the limitations of static efficiency, the economics of the patent system, and the effects of market structure on the rate of technological change and the rate of productivity increase.[1]

2. Technological Change

Technology is society's pool of knowledge regarding the industrial arts. The technology existing at a given point in time sets limits on how much can be produced with a given amount of inputs. Given the level of technology, there is generally a wide range of possible methods of producing a given good or service. Some require little capital and much labor, some require much capital and little labor; some are old, some are new. Given a certain amount of various inputs, it is possible to determine which method results in the maximum output and what the maximum output is. We know from Chapter 5 that the production function shows, for a given level of technology, the maximum output rate that can be achieved from a given amount of inputs.

Technological change is the advance of technology, such advance often taking the form of new methods of producing existing products and new techniques of organization, marketing, and management. Technological change results in a change in the production function. If the production function were readily observable, a comparison of the production function at two points in time would provide the economist with a simple measure of the effect of technological change during the intervening period. For example, if there were only two inputs, labor and capital, and if there were constant returns to scale, the characteristics of the production function at a given date could be captured fully by a single isoquant.[2] Under these circumstances,

---

[1]For a much more extensive and detailed discussion of technological change, see E. Mansfield, *The Economics of Technological Change*, New York: Norton, 1968. Much of this chapter is based on parts of that book; in some cases material has been reprinted.

[2]Recall from Chapter 5 that, if there are constant returns to scale, an x-percent increase in all inputs results in an x-percent increase in output. Thus, if there are constant returns to scale, there is at a given point in time a unique relationship between capital input per unit of output and labor input per unit of output. This relationship holds for any output and completely summarizes the efficient input combinations.

one could simply look at the changing position of this isoquant to see the effects of technological change.

For example, if this isoquant shifted from position 1 to position 2 in Figure 16.1 during a certain period of time, technological change had less impact during this period than if the curve shifted to position 3. As we shall see in subsequent sections, it is sometimes possible to estimate the average rate of movement of the production function by a single number, and economists often use this number to measure the rate of technological change. Of course, it is only an indirect measure but there is no way to measure the rate of technological change directly.

Technological change also results in the availability of new products. In many cases the availability of new products can be regarded as a change in the production function, since they are merely more efficient ways of meeting old wants if these wants are defined with proper breadth. This is particularly true in the case of new intermediate goods, which may result in little or no change in the final product. In other cases, however, the availability of new products cannot realistically be viewed as a change in the production function, since they entail an important difference in kind.[3]

3. Change in Technique

It is customary to distinguish between a technological change and a change in technique. Whereas technological change is an advance in knowledge, a change in technique is a change in the utilized method of production. Although technological change and a change in technique are two different things, they obviously are related to one another. Indeed, a technological change can have little economic impact unless it induces a change in techniques. The distinction between technological change and a change in technique is useful, but its sharpness should not be exaggerated. In this

---

[3]It is sometimes asserted that it is unrealistic to emphasize cost-reducing technological change, since firms report that only about 13 percent of their expenditures on research and development go for pure process improvement. But this is wrong because much of the research and development concerning new products and product improvements is devoted to new and improved intermediate goods and capital goods. In civilian industry, perhaps 80 percent of the reported research and development goes for new processes, new intermediate goods, and new capital goods.

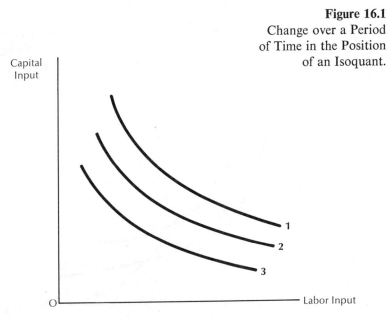

Figure 16.1
Change over a Period
of Time in the Position
of an Isoquant.

section, we show how changes in technology result in changes in techniques.

Suppose that the production function in a given industry is represented by the isoquant *PP'*, in Figure 16.2. Assuming constant returns to scale, one isoquant fully represents the production function. To determine the minimum cost technique, isocost curves (*A, B, C*) can be drawn representing the combinations of quantities of labor and capital that can be purchased for various amounts. The minimum-cost technique corresponds to the point on the isoquant that is on the lowest isocost curve. In Figure 16.2, this point is point 1.

Now suppose that there is a change in technology in this industry which shifts the production function so that *QQ'* is the new isoquant. In this case the minimum-cost technique is no longer 1, but 2 instead. Thus this change in technology will result in a change in technique. If output is held constant, the amount of labor used by the industry will decrease; so will the amount of capital used. But in actuality the industry's output will probably change because, with the change in technique, the industry's supply curve will probably shift.[4]

Although technological change can result in a change in technique, it

---

[4]Think back to the discussion in Chapter 8. What is likely to be the impact on industry output of a shift to the right of the supply curve?

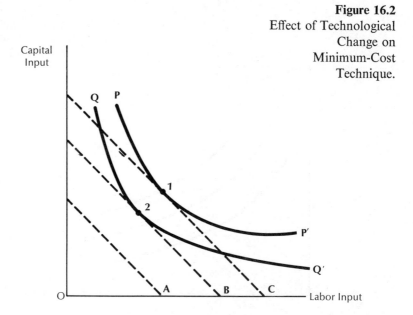

Figure 16.2
Effect of Technological
Change on
Minimum-Cost
Technique.

need not always do so. For example, consider Figure 16.3. Suppose that the original production function is represented by the *RR'* isoquant and that a change in technology results in a new isoquant, *SS'*. In this case, although there has been a change in technology, there has been no change in technique, the minimum-cost technique before and after the change in technology being represented by point 3. This is because the shape of the isoquant has been changed in such a way that point 3 remains on the lowest isocost curve.

Conversely, not all changes in technique are due to technological change. A great many occur, instead, as a consequence of changes in input prices. For example, if the production function is represented by the isoquant, *TT'*, in Figure 16.4, and if the wage rate increases and the price of capital decreases so that the isocost curves shift from *A*, *B*, *C* to *A'*, *B'*, *C'*, the minimum-cost technique changes from the one represented by point 4 to the one represented by point 5. Yet this change in technique is obviously not due to technological change, since there has been none here. According to some observers, "Detroit automation" in the auto industry has been largely of this sort. Transfer equipment to move work from one automatic machine tool to another and the interlocking of these tools to get higher utilization was first used in 1927. Like point 5, it was not economical until input prices changed.[5]

---

[5]See E. Mansfield, *The Economics of Technological Change*, New York: Norton, 1968, p. 26.

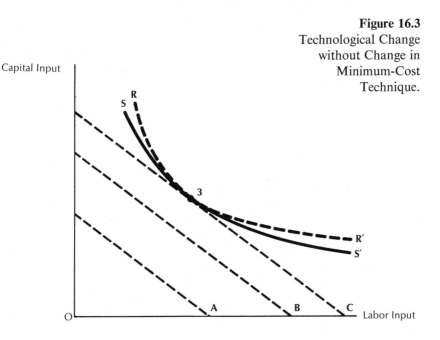

Figure 16.3
Technological Change
without Change in
Minimum-Cost
Technique.

4. Classifications of Technological Change

Technological change can take various forms: For one thing, it can be labor-saving, capital-saving, or neutral. Suppose that the output rate for a given product, as well as the relative prices of labor and capital, are held constant. If technological change results in a greater percentage reduction in capital input than labor input, it is capital-saving; if it results in a greater percentage reduction in labor input than capital input, it is labor-saving; if it results in an equal percentage reduction in capital and labor inputs, it is neutral.[6]

---

[6]This is not the only possible definition of a labor-saving or capital-saving technological change. See J. Robinson, "The Classification of Inventions," *Review of Economic Studies, 1937–1938;* R. Harrod, *Towards a Dynamic Economics,* London: 1948; and J. Hicks, *The Theory of Wages,* London: 1932. Note too that the statement in the text should not be interpreted to imply that all inputs are saved by technological change. Obviously, there may be a reduction in the use of one input and an increase in the use of another.

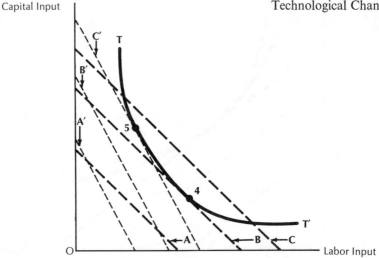

Put differently, technological change is labor-saving if the marginal rate of technical substitution of labor for capital diminishes. Under these circumstances, technological change increases the marginal product of capital more than the marginal product of labor (at a given capital-labor ratio), with the consequence that a firm is led to use more capital relative to labor. Similarly, technological change is capital-saving if the marginal rate of technical substitution of labor for capital increases. Under these circumstances, the marginal product of labor is increased more than the marginal product of capital, with the consequence that a firm is led to use more labor relative to capital. Finally, technological change is neutral if it does not alter the marginal rate of technical substitution.

Figure 16.5 shows graphically the three types of technological change. In each panel, isoquants *I* and *K* show the combinations of inputs that can produce the relevant output before and after the technological change. The ray *OL* shows input combinations with a constant capital-labor ratio. Panel A shows a case of neutral technological change. Holding the capital-labor ratio constant, the marginal rate of technical substitution is the same before and after the technological change, as evidenced by the fact that the slope of isoquant·*K* at point *B* is the same as the slope of isoquant *I* at point *A*.

On the other hand, panel B shows a case of labor-saving technological change.   Holding the capital-labor ratio constant, the marginal rate of technical substitution of labor for capital is lower after the change in technology than before.   This is shown by the fact that the slope of isoquant K at point B is flatter than the slope of isoquant I at point A.   Similarly, panel C shows a case of capital-saving technological change.   Holding the capital-labor ratio constant, the marginal rate of technical substitution of labor for capital is higher after the change in technology than before.   This is shown by the fact that the slope of isoquant K at point B is steeper than the slope of isoquant I at point A.

Technological change can also be classified as capital-embodied or dis-embodied.   Many changes in technology must be embodied in new equipment if they are to be utilized.   For example, the introduction of catalytic cracking in the petroleum industry and the diesel locomotive in railroads required new investment in plant and equipment.   On the other hand, other changes in technology consist of better methods and organization that improve the efficiency of both old capital and new.   Examples of such improvements are various advances in industrial engineering (such as the development of time and motion studies) and operations research (such as the development of linear programming).

Figure 16.5
Neutral,
Labor-Saving,
and Capital-Saving
Technological Change.

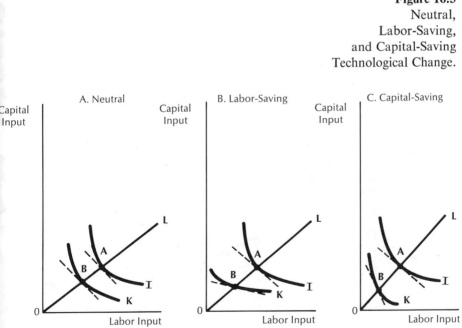

A. Neutral   B. Labor-Saving   C. Capital-Saving

5. Productivity Growth and the Measurement of Technological Change

Economists have long been interested in productivity—the ratio of output to input. The oldest and most commonly studied measure of productivity is labor productivity, output per man-hour of labor. One determinant of the rate of growth of labor productivity is the rate of technological change, a high rate of technological change being likely to result, all other things equal, in a high rate of growth of labor productivity. However, the rate of technological change is not the only determinant of the rate of growth of labor productivity, the consequence being that the latter is a very incomplete, though frequently used, measure of the rate of technological change.

To see how changes in labor productivity can produce false signals concerning the rate of technological change, consider Figure 16.6. Suppose that the relevant isoquant is II' and that input prices at the beginning of the period are such that the isocost curves are A, B, C, and so on. The least-cost combination of inputs is OL_1 of labor and OC_1 of capital. Now suppose

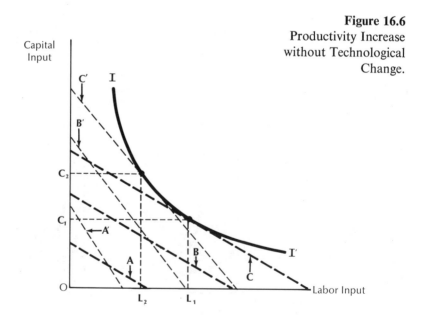

Figure 16.6
Productivity Increase
without Technological
Change.

that input prices change, labor becoming more expensive relative to capital, the result being that the isocost curves shift to A', B', C', and so on. Under these new circumstances, the least-cost combination of inputs to produce the same output is OL_2 of labor and OC_2 of capital. Since output remains constant and labor input decreases, labor productivity increases due to the change in input prices. But this productivity increase is not an indication of technological change, there being no change at all in the production function.

A more adequate measure of the rate of technological change is the total productivity index, which relates changes in output to changes in both labor and capital inputs, not changes in labor inputs alone. Suppose that the production function is of the simple form,

$$Q = \alpha(bL + cK) \tag{16.1}$$

where Q is the quantity of output, L is the quantity of labor, K is the quantity of capital, b and c are constants, and α is a number that varies over time in response to technological change. Suppose that Q_0, L_0, K_0 and α_0 are the values of Q, L, K, and α in an early period and that Q_1, L_1, K_1, and α_1 are the values of Q, L, K, and α in a later period. To determine $\alpha_1 \div \alpha_0$, which is a measure of the rate of technological change, one can compute

$$\frac{Q_1}{Q_0} \div \left(U\frac{L_1}{L_0} + V\frac{K_1}{K_0} \right) \tag{16.2}$$

where $U = bL_0/(bL_0 + cK_0)$ and $V = cK_0/(bL_0 + cK_0)$. This is the total productivity index. It is equal to the relative increase in output divided by a weighted average of the relative increase in labor input and the relative increase in capital input.[7]

Of course, the production function in Equation 16.1 is a very special case. Economists have tried to devise better measures of the rate of movement of the production function than the total productivity index. These measures rest on somewhat different assumptions about the shape of the production function, the Cobb-Douglas production function sometimes, but not always, being used. One of the pioneering studies of this type was carried out in 1957 by Robert Solow of the Massachusetts Institute of Technology.[8] The resulting estimates have proved useful in many contexts, but their limitations

---

[7]The most comprehensive study of labor productivity and total productivity in the United States is by J. Kendrick, *Productivity Trends in the United States*, National Bureau of Economic Research, 1961.

[8]R. Solow, "Technical Change and the Aggregate Production Function," *Review of Economics and Statistics*, 1957.

should be noted. In particular, since they equate the effects of technological change with whatever increase in output is unexplained by other inputs, they may not isolate the effects of technological change alone. In additon, they may contain the effects of whatever inputs may have been excluded from the analysis because of convenience, lack of data, ignorance, or some other reason.

6.   Determinants of the Rate of Technological Change

What determines the rate of technological change? Existing theory is still in a relatively primitive state, for it is only recently that economists have begun to give this question the attention it deserves. It seems obvious, however, that an industry's rate of technological change depends to a large extent on the amount of resources devoted by firms, by independent inventors, and by government to the improvement of the industry's technology. The amount of resources devoted by the government depends on how closely the industry is related to the defense, public health, and other social needs for which the government assumes major responsibility; on the extent of the external economies generated by the relevant research and development; and on more purely political factors.

The amount of resources devoted by private sources to improving an industry's technology is influenced by the anticipated profitability of the investment. From this it follows that the rate of technological change in a particular area is influenced by the same kind of factors that determine the output of any good or service.[9] On the one hand, there are demand factors that influence the rewards for particular kinds of technological change. For example, if a prospective change in technology reduces the cost of a particular product, increases in the demand for the product are likely to increase the returns from effecting this technological change. Similarly, a growing shortage and a rising price of the inputs saved by a prospective change in technology are likely to increase the returns from effecting it. For example, increases in the eighteenth century in the demand for yarn, as well as increases in spinners' wages, raised the returns to various textile inventions

---

[9]Needless to say, supply and demand are not the only factors that influence the rate of technological change. As emphasized in subsequent sections, there is considerable uncertainty in the research and inventive processes. Moreover, laboratories, scientists, and inventors are motivated by many factors other than profit. We have no intention of characterizing them as "economic men."

and directly stimulated the work leading to the invention of the spinning jenny and the spinning mule.

On the other hand, there are also supply factors that influence the cost of making particular types of technological change. Obviously, whether people try to solve a given problem depends on whether they think it can be solved, and on how costly they think it will be, as well as on the expected payoff if they are successful. The cost of making science-based technological changes depends on the number of scientists and engineers in relevant fields and on advances in basic science; for example, advances in physics clearly reduced the cost of effecting changes in technology in the field of atomic energy. In addition, the rate of technological change depends on the amount of effort devoted to making modest improvements that lean heavily on practical experience. Although there is often a tendency to focus attention on the major, spectacular inventions, it is by no means certain that technological change in many industries results chiefly from these inventions, rather than from a succession of minor improvements.

Beside being influenced by the quantity of resources an industry devotes to improving its own technology, an industry's rate of technological change depends on the quantity of resources devoted by other industries to the improvement of the capital goods and other inputs it uses. Technological change in an industry that supplies materials, components, and machinery often prompts technological change among its customers. For example, technological change in electric power generation was an important stimulus to the commercial production of aluminum and to further technological change in the aluminum industry. In addition, there is another kind of interdependence among industries. Considerable "spillover" occurs, techniques invented for one industry turning out to be useful for others as well.

Another factor that may influence an industry's rate of technological change is its market structure. Some attention will be devoted to this factor in Sections 13 to 14.

7.   Research and Development: A Learning Process

The previous section pointed out that the rate and direction of technological change depends on the extent and nature of the research and development that is carried out. Research and development encompasses work of many kinds. Basic research is aimed purely at the creation of new knowledge, applied research is expected to have a practical payoff, and development is aimed at the reduction of research findings to practice. Inventions can occur in either the research phase or the development phase of organized research and development activity. Often, the central ideas come from research, and inventions in patentable form arise in the course of development.

The organized application of science to advance technology is a relatively new thing, the first organized industrial research laboratory in the United States having been established by Thomas Edison in 1876. During the twentieth century the number of industrial laboratories has grown by leaps and bounds. Recent decades have witnessed a tremendous growth in the amount spent on research and development: for example, total research and development expenditures increased from about $1 billion in 1940 to about $24 billion in 1968; research and development performed by industry increased from about $4 billion in 1954 to about $17 billion in 1968. Much of this increase has been due to government-financed (but not necessarily government-performed) work on defense, space, and atomic energy.

Chance plays a crucial role in research and development, and a long string of failures often occurs before any kind of success is achieved. A research or development project can be regarded as a process of uncertainty reduction, or learning. Suppose, for example, that a firm that is trying to fabricate a part can use one of two alloys and that it is impossible to use standard sources to determine their characteristics. Suppose that strength is of paramount importance and that the firm's estimates of the strengths of the alloys, alloy 1 and alloy 2, are represented by the probability distributions in part A of Table 16.1. If the firm were forced to make a choice immediately, it would probably choose alloy 2, since it believes that there is better than a 50-50 chance that alloy 2 will turn out to be stronger than alloy 1.

Table 16.1. Subjective Probability Distribution of Strength of Alloys 1 and 2, before and after Test.

	A. BEFORE TEST		B. AFTER TEST	
EXTENT OF STRENGTH	ALLOY 1	ALLOY 2	ALLOY 1	ALLOY 2
	PROBABILITIES			
Exceptionally High	.20	.20	.10	.10
Very High	.40	.50	.20	.80
High	.20	.20	.60	.10
Medium	.10	.05	.10	.00
Low	.10	.05	.00	.00
Total	1.00	1.00	1.00	1.00

However, there is a good chance that this decision might turn out to be wrong, the consequence being that the part would be weaker than if alloy 1 had been used. Thus the firm may decide to perform a test prior to making the selection. On the basis of the test results, the firm will formulate new estimates, represented by the probability distributions in part B of Table 16.1. These probability distributions show less dispersion than the ones in part A; in other words, the firm believes it is able to pinpoint more closely the strength of each alloy than in part A. Because of the tests, uncertainty as to which alloy is stronger has been reduced.

8. Parallel Development Efforts

Research and development is more risky than most other economic activities. Many development projects use parallel efforts to help cope with uncertainty. For example, in the development of the atomic bomb, there were several methods of making fissionable materials, and no consensus existed among scientists as to which of these alternatives was most promising. To make sure that the best one was not discarded, all methods were pursued in parallel. The wisdom of this decision was borne out by the fact that the method that was first to produce appreciable quantities of fissionable material was one that had been considered relatively unpromising early in the development program.

Under what conditions is it optimal to run parallel research and development efforts? What factors determine the optimal number of parallel efforts? Suppose that a firm can select x approaches, spend C dollars on each one over a period of m months, choose the one that looks most promising at the end of the period, and carry it to completion, dropping the others. Suppose that the only relevant criterion is the extent of the development costs, the usefulness of the result and the development time being assumed to be the same regardless of which parallel effort is pursued. For further simplification, suppose that all approaches look equally promising. Under these circumstances, the optimal value of x—the number of parallel research and development efforts—is inversely related to C and directly related to the amount learned in the next m months. As the cost of running each effort increases, the optimal number of parallel efforts decreases. As the prospective amount of learning increases, the optimal number of parallel efforts increases.

To illustrate why it is sometimes cheaper to run parallel development efforts, consider a case in which each approach has a 50-50 chance of costing

$2 million and a 50-50 chance of costing $1 million. Since we assume that all approaches are equally promising, these probabilities are the same for all approaches. The expected total cost of development is the sum of the total costs of development if each possible outcome occurs times the probability of the occurrence of this outcome. If a single approach is used, the expected total costs of development are

$$.5(\$2 \text{ million}) + .5(\$1 \text{ million}) = \$1.5 \text{ million} \qquad (16.3)$$

since there is a .5 probability that total costs with any single approach will be $2 million and .5 probability that they will be $1 million.

If two approaches are run in parallel and if the true cost of development using each approach can be determined after C dollars are spent on each approach, the expected total costs of development are

$$.25(\$2 \text{ million}) + .75(\$1 \text{ million}) + C = \$1.25 \text{ million} + C$$
$$(16.4)$$

if each approach is carried to the point at which C dollars have been spent on it, and if the cheaper approach is chosen at that point (and the other approach is dropped). Why? Because there is a .25 probability that total costs with the better of the two approaches will be $2 million and a .75 probability that they will be $1 million. In addition, there is the certainty that a cost of C will be incurred for the approach that is dropped. The reason why there is a .25 chance that total costs with the better of the two approaches is $2 million is that this will occur only when the total cost of both approaches turns out to be $2 million—and the probability that this will occur is .5 times .5, or .25. Comparing Equation 16.3 with Equation 16.4, it is obvious that the expected total cost of development is lower with two parallel approaches than with a single approach if C is less than $250,000.

The results of this section are important because they put in perspective some of the criticisms of "duplication" and "waste" in research and development. Contrary to popular belief, parallel efforts may produce results more cheaply than attempting in advance to choose the optimal approach and concentrating all one's efforts on pursuing it. The fact that most of the parallel paths are ultimately rejected does not mean that they are a waste. On the contrary, given considerable uncertainty, this may be the cheapest way to proceed.[10]

---

[10]See R. Nelson, "Uncertainty, Learning, and the Economics of Parallel Research and Development Efforts," *Review of Economics and Statistics*, 1961. Unfortunately, difficulties seem to arise when one attempts to extend the solution to cases involving more than one review point.

9. The Costs of Development

Previous chapters have made familiar the concept of a production function for goods and services. It is convenient in some instances to think in terms of a "production function" relating the quantities of various engineering and other inputs, on the one hand, and the output of technological change, on the other. This production function helps to determine the cost of developing a new product or process. Obviously, the size of these costs will be one of the prime determinants of whether or not an attempt will be made to carry out a particular development project.

What determines how much a particular development project will cost? First, there is the size and complexity of the product being developed. It takes more resources to design a big product with a large number of components, because there are more drawings to be made, more analyses to perform, and more tests to be done. Moreover, holding the number of components constant, the cost of developing a product tends to be directly related to the interdependence among these components.

Second, there is the extent of the advance in performance that is sought. Larger advances generally mean higher costs because more components will need to be specially designed, more mistakes will be made, and more jobs will have to be redone. Third, there is the stock of basic knowledge and of components and materials. The task of developing a particular product can be made much easier and cheaper by advances in basic knowledge that allow better prediction of relevant phenomena. Moreover, the development task is obviously made easier by improvements in components and materials, improvements in materials often being particularly important.

Finally, there is development time. Some economists have postulated that there exists a function—like that in Figure 16.7—that relates expected development time to the expected total quantity of resources employed in a development effort. Their principal point is that between A and B the relationship between time and cost has a negative slope, indicating that time can be decreased only by increasing total cost. As the development schedule is shortened, more tasks must be carried out concurrently rather than sequentially, and since each task provides information that is useful in carrying out the others, there are more false starts and wasted designs. Also, diminishing returns set in as more and more technical workers are assigned simultaneously to the development effort. It is argued that these factors offset the possibility that shorter development time eliminates unnecessary work and some overhead-type costs.

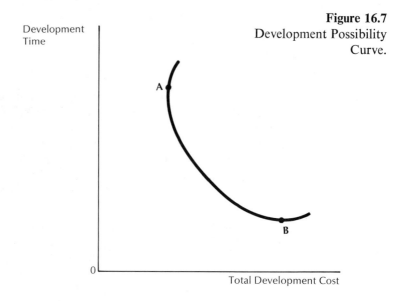

Figure 16.7
Development Possibility
Curve.

10.   Innovation

An invention, when applied for the first time, is called an innovation. Traditionally, economists have stressed the distinction between an invention and an innovation on the ground that an invention has little or no economic significance until it is applied. This distinction becomes somewhat blurred in cases like du Pont's nylon, where the inventor and the innovator are the same firm. In these circumstances the final stages of development may entail at least a partial commitment to a market test. However, in many cases, the inventor is not in a position to—and does not want to—apply his invention, because his business is invention, not production; or because he is a supplier, not a user, of the equipment embodying the innovation; or for some other reason. In these cases, the distinction remains relatively clear-cut.

Regardless of whether the break between invention and innovation is clean, innovation is a key stage in the process leading to the full evaluation and utilization of an invention. The innovator—the firm that is first to apply the invention—must be willing to take the risks involved in introducing a new and untried process, good, or service. In many cases these risks are high. Although research and development can provide a great deal of information regarding the technical characteristics and cost of production of the invention—and market research can provide considerable information regarding the demand for it—there are many areas of uncertainty that can be resolved only by actual production and marketing of the invention. By obtaining needed information regarding the actual performance of the invention, the innovator plays a vital social role.

The lag between invention and innovation seems to vary considerably, and is commonly ten years or more for major inventions. What factors does a firm consider in deciding whether or not to innovate? Clearly, the firm must begin by estimating how much profit it will realize by introducing the new product or process. If the expected profits from the introduction of the innovation do not exceed those obtainable from other investments by an amount that is large enough to justify the extra risks, the innovation will be rejected. If they do exceed those available elsewhere by this amount, the profitability and risks involved in introducing the innovation at present must be compared with the profitability and risks involved in introducing it at various future dates.

There are often considerable advantages in waiting, since improvements occur in the new product or process and more information becomes available regarding its performance and market. For example, in the case of new products, firms often employ test marketing to obtain additional information before making a full-scale commitment. However, there often are disadvantages, as well as advantages, in waiting, perhaps the most important being that a competitor may beat the firm to the punch or that the conditions favoring the innovation may become less benign. In the case of new products, there is often a considerable disadvantage in not being first; sales opportunities will be lost in the interval that competitors are in the market ahead of this firm, and part of the market may be lost for a considerable period after this firm makes its appearance.

If the expected profits exceed those obtainable from other investments by an amount that is large enough to justify the risks, and if the disadvantages of waiting seem to outweigh the advantages, the firm will introduce the innovation. Otherwise it will wait. Pioneering is a risky business: whether it pays off is often a matter of timing.

11. The Diffusion of Innovations

How rapidly an innovation spreads is obviously of great importance; for example, in the case of a process innovation, it determines how rapidly productivity increases in response to the new process. In a free enterprise economy, firms and consumers are free to use new technology as slowly or as rapidly as they please—subject, of course, to the constraints imposed by the marketplace. The diffusion process, like the earlier stages of the process of creating and assimilating new processes and products, is essentially a learning process. However, rather than being confined to a research laboratory or to a few firms, the learning takes place among a considerable number of users and producers.

When the innovation first appears, potential users are uncertain of its nature and effectiveness, and they tend to view its purchase as an experiment. Sometimes considerable additional research and development is required before the innovation is successful; sometimes, despite attempts at redesign and improvement, the innovation never is a success. Information regarding the existence, characteristics, and availability of the innovation is circulated by the producers through advertisements and salesmen; information regarding the reaction of users to the innovation tends to be circulated informally and through the trade press.

Learning takes place among the producers of the innovation, as well as the users. Early versions of an innovation often have serious technological problems, and it takes time to work out these bugs. During the early stages

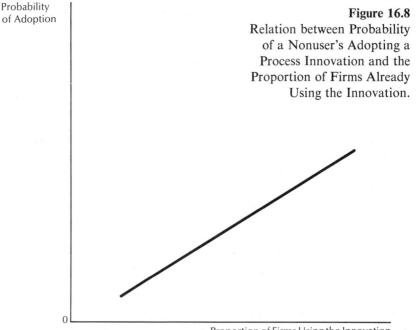

Probability of Adoption

Figure 16.8
Relation between Probability of a Nonuser's Adopting a Process Innovation and the Proportion of Firms Already Using the Innovation.

0

Proportion of Firms Using the Innovation

of the diffusion process, the improvements in the new process or product may be almost as important as the new idea itself. Moreover, when a new product's design is stabilized, costs of production generally fall in accord with the so-called "learning curve." That is, unit costs of production decrease as the producers gain experience and learn by doing. For example, in the case of new machine tools, there is some evidence that unit costs tend to be reduced by about 20 percent for each doubling of cumulated output.[11]

Figure 16.8 illustrates an important aspect of the process by which new techniques spread throughout an industry. The figure shows that the probability that a firm not using an innovation will adopt it in the next few months is influenced by the proportion of firms in the industry that already are using it. Specifically, as the number of firms adopting an innovation increases, the probability of its adoption by a nonuser increases. This is because the risks associated with its introduction grow smaller, competitive pressures mount, and bandwagon effects increase as experience and information regarding an innovation accumulate.

Other important aspects of the diffusion process are brought out by

Figure 16.9
Effect of Profitability of the
Innovation and Size of Investment
Required to Adopt the Innovation
on Probability of Adoption.

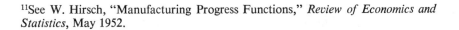

A

Probability
of Adoption

More Profitable
Innovation

Less Profitable
Innovation

0

Proportion of Firms Using the Innovation

B

Probability
of Adoption

Small Investment
Required

Large Investment
Required

0

Proportion of Firms Using the Innovation

---

[11]See W. Hirsch, "Manufacturing Progress Functions," *Review of Economics and Statistics*, May 1952.

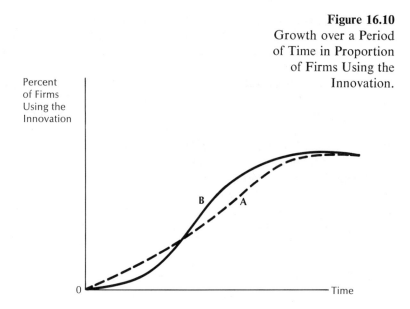

Figure 16.10
Growth over a Period
of Time in Proportion
of Firms Using the
Innovation.

Figure 16.9. Panel A shows that the probability that a nonuser will adopt
the innovation is higher for more profitable innovations than for less profitable innovations, holding constant the proportion of firms in the industry
that are already using it. The more profitable the investment in an innovation
promises to be, the greater will be the probability that a firm's estimate of its
potential profitability will compensate for the risks involved in its installation.

Panel B of Figure 16.9 shows that the probability that a nonuser will adopt
the innovation is higher for innovations requiring fairly small investments,
holding constant the proportion of firms in the industry that are already using
it (and the profitability of the innovation). This is because firms will be
more cautious before committing themselves to large, expensive projects,
and they will have more difficulty in financing them.

If the relationship in Figure 16.8 holds, it can be shown that the proportion
of firms using the innovation will increase in accord with the S-shaped growth
curve shown in Figure 16.10. Whether the diffusion process goes on slowly,
as in curve *A*, or quickly, as in curve *B*, depends on the profitability of the
innovation and the size of the investment it requires. This model has much
in common with the models used by epidemiologists to represent the spread
of contagious diseases. It has been able to explain reasonably well the
available data concerning the rate of diffusion of industrial innovations.[12]

---

[12]For details, see E. Mansfield, *Industrial Research and Technological Innovation*,
New York: W. W. Norton, 1968.

12. Static Efficiency and Economic Progress

In Chapter 15, we presented several conditions for economic efficiency: The marginal rate of substitution between any pair of commodities must be the same for all consumers, the marginal rate of technical substitution between any pair of inputs must be the same for all producers, and the marginal rate of product transformation must equal the marginal rate of substitution for each pair of goods. Given a fixed level of technology these conditions must be fulfilled (with certain qualifications discussed in Chapter 15) if consumer welfare is to be maximized.

It is important to note that these conditions result only in efficiency in a static sense. That is, they show how inputs and commodities must be allocated if welfare is to be maximized, *given a fixed level of technology.* It is possible that an allocation of inputs and commodities that violates these conditions might lead to a higher level of consumer welfare than any allocation that meets these conditions, because it might result in a faster rate of technological change and productivity increase.

Economists like Joseph Schumpeter and John Kenneth Galbraith of Harvard University[13] have argued that this is the case, and have gone on to suggest that a perfectly competitive economy is likely to be inferior in a dynamic sense to an economy including many imperfectly competitive industries (i.e., monopolies, oligopolies, etc.). In their view, although (as we showed in Chapter 15) a perfectly competitive economy will satisfy the conditions for static economic efficiency, it will not result in as high a rate of technological change and productivity increase as an imperfectly competitive economy.

To illustrate what they have in mind, suppose that we compare the performance of two economies, one perfectly competitive, the other imperfectly competitive. Suppose that they start off with comparable technology in 1970, but that the rate of technological change is higher in the imperfectly competitive economy than in the perfectly competitive economy, the result being that the annual rate of productivity change is 3 percent in the imperfectly competitive economy and 2 percent in the perfectly competitive economy. Assuming that the quantity of inputs is the same in each economy and

---

[13]J. Schumpeter, *Capitalism, Socialism, and Democracy*, New York: Harper & Row, 1947; J. K. Galbraith, *American Capitalism*, Boston: Houghton Mifflin, 1952; and H. Villard, "Competition, Oligopoly, and Research," *Journal of Political Economy*, Dec. 1958.

constant over time, it follows that

$$Q(t) = Q_0(1.02)^t \tag{16.5}$$

$$Q'(t) = Q_0'(1.03)^t \tag{16.6}$$

where $Q(t)$ is the output in year t in the perfectly competitive economy, $Q'(t)$ is the output in year t in the imperfectly competitive economy, and t is measured in years from 1970.

Suppose too that, because of the static inefficiencies due to its violation of the conditions in Chapter 15, the imperfectly competitive economy produces 98 percent as much as the perfectly competitive economy when their technology levels are the same. Thus $Q_0' = .98Q_0$, and

$$Q(t) = Q_0(1.02)^t \tag{16.7}$$

$$Q'(t) = .98Q_0(1.03)^t \tag{16.8}$$

Thus it follows that

$$Q'(t) \div Q(t) = .98(1.03 \div 1.02)^t \tag{16.9}$$

which implies that $Q'(t) \div Q(t)$ will be greater than one when t is greater than about two. Consequently, despite its being relatively inefficient in a static sense, the imperfectly competitive economy out-produces the perfectly competitive economy from about 1972 on, because it has the higher rate of technological change and productivity increase.

13. Imperfect Competition and Technological Change

This example shows that the static inefficiencies of an imperfectly competitive economy *can* be offset by its having a higher rate of technological change and productivity increase, but it does not tell us why we should expect the rate of technological change and productivity increase to be higher in an imperfectly competitive economy. This is a question that has been debated at great length. On the one hand, some economists, like Schumpeter and Galbraith, believe that there are a number of good reasons why the rate of technological change and productivity increase will be higher in an imperfectly competitive economy. On the other hand, other economists stick with the view of John Stuart Mill and J. B. Clark that this is not the case.[14]

Members of the Schumpeter-Galbraith group argue that firms under perfect competition have less resources to devote to research and experi-

---

[14]J. S. Mill, *Principles of Political Economy*, London, 1852, Book IV, Ch. VII, p. 351; and J. B. Clark, *Essentials of Economic Theory*, New York, 1907, p. 374.

mentation than do firms under imperfect competition. Because profits are at a relatively low level, it is difficult for firms under perfect competition to support large expenditures on research and development. Moreover, it is argued that, unless a firm has sufficient control over the market to reap the rewards of an innovation, the introduction of the innovation may not be worthwhile. If competitors can imitate the innovation very quickly, the innovator may be unable to make any money from the innovation.

Defenders of perfect competition retort that there is likely to be less pressure for firms in imperfect markets to introduce new techniques and products, since such firms have fewer competitors. Moreover, such firms are better able to drive out entrants who, uncommitted to present techniques, are likely to be relatively quick to adopt new ones. (Entrants, unlike established producers, have no vested interest in maintaining the demand for existing products and the profitability of existing equipment.) Also, there are advantages in having a large number of independent decision-making units, there being less chance that an important technological advance will be blocked by the faulty judgment of a few men.

It is difficult to obtain evidence to help settle this question, if it is posed in this way, since perfect competition is, of course, a hypothetical construct that does not exist in the real world. However, it does seem unlikely that a perfectly competitive industry (if such an industry could be constructed) would be able in many areas of the economy to carry out the research and development required to promote a high rate of technological change.[15] Moreover, if entry is free and rapid, firms in a perfectly competitive industry will have little motivation to innovate. Although the evidence is not at all clear-cut, this much can probably be granted the Schumpeter-Galbraith group.[16]

14. The Giant Corporation, Industrial Concentration, and Technological Change

It is one thing to grant that a certain amount of market imperfection may promote the rate of technological change, and another thing to say, as does Galbraith, that the "modern industry of a few large firms [is] an almost

---

[15]Even if supplier firms emerge that specialize in research and development, the members of the competitive industry must still carry out some technical work to be able to accept new technology rapidly. Moreover, there may have to be imperfect competition in the supplying industry if it is to be viable.

[16]Also, technological change may result in a certain amount of market imperfection, although the extent of the market imperfection is likely to vary greatly from case to case.

perfect instrument for inducing technical change."[17]   If true, this is an extremely important point. But is it true? Does the evidence indicate that an industry dominated by a few giant firms is generally more progressive than one composed of a larger number of smaller firms?

To prevent confusion, it is advisable to distinguish among several related issues. First, what is the effect of an industry's market structure on the amount it spends on research and development? Suppose that, for a market of given size, we could replace the largest firms by a larger number of somewhat smaller firms—and thus decrease concentration. If the largest firms in this industry were giants like Standard Oil of New Jersey or U. S. Steel, the available evidence, which is extremely tentative, does not suggest that total research and development expenditures are likely to decrease considerably. On the contrary, there is usually no tendency for the ratio of research and development expenditures to sales to be higher among the giants then among their somewhat smaller competitors. However, if the largest firms in the industry were considerably smaller than this or if concentration were reduced greatly, one might expect a decrease in research and development expenditures, because the size of the firm often must exceed a certain minimum for research to be profitable.

Second, to what extent would such a change in market structure be harmful because of economies of scale in research and development? Obviously, the answer to this question varies with the type of research or development being considered. In research, the optimal size of group may be fairly small in many areas; for example, the transistor, the maser, the laser, and radio command guidance were conceived by an individual or groups of not more than a dozen persons. In development, the optimal size of effort tends to be larger, particularly in the aircraft and missile industries, where tremendous sums are spent on individual projects.[18]   However, in most industries, the limited data that are available do not seem to indicate that only the largest firms can support effective research and development programs; there is generally no indication that the largest programs have any marked advantage over somewhat smaller ones.

Third, is there any evidence that research and development programs of given scale are carried out more productively in large firms than in small ones? The data are extremely limited, but they seem to indicate that, in most industries for which we have information, the answer is no. In most of these

---

[17]J. K. Galbraith, *American Capitalism*, Boston: Houghton Mifflin, 1952, p. 91.
[18]Development costs are sometimes very high in other industries, too. For example, du Pont spent $25 million to develop Corfam, and $50 million for Delrin. See J. Jewkes, R. Sawers, and R. Stillerman, *The Sources of Invention,* revised edition, Norton, 1970. This book also presents considerable evidence concerning the importance of independent inventors as sources of inventions. This is an important point.

industries, when the size of research and development expenditures is held constant, increases in the size of the firm are associated with decreases in inventive output. The reasons for this are by no means obvious. Some observers claim that it is because the average capabilities of technical people are higher in the smaller firms, research and development people in smaller firms are more cost-conscious than those in larger firms, and the problems of communication and coordination tend to be less acute in smaller firms.

Fourth, what is the effect of an industry's market structure on how rapidly new processes and products, both those developed by the industry and those developed by others, are introduced commercially? The answer seems to depend heavily on the types of innovations that happen to occur. If they require very large amounts of capital, it appears that the substitution of fewer large firms for more smaller ones may lead to more rapid introduction; if they require small amounts of capital, this may not be the case. Another important factor is the ease with which new firms can enter the industry. If increased concentration results in increased barriers to entry, it may also result in slower application of new techniques, since innovations often are made by new firms. Indeed, many new firms are started for the specific purpose of carrying out innovations.

Fifth, what is the effect of an industry's market structure on how rapidly innovations, once introduced, spread through an industry? The fact that large firms often are quicker, on the average, than small firms to use a new technique does not imply that increased concentration results in a faster rate of diffusion. On the contrary, the very small amount of evidence bearing on this question seems to suggest that greater concentration in an industry may be associated with a slower rate of diffusion. However, the observed relationship is weak and could well be due to chance.

Contrary to the allegations of Galbraith, Schumpeter, and others, there is little evidence that industrial giants are needed in all or even most industries to insure rapid technological change and rapid utilization of new techniques. Moreover, there is no statistically significant relationship between the extent of concentration in an industry and the industry's rate of technological change, as measured by the methods described in Section 5. Of course, this does not mean that industries composed only of small firms would necessarily be optimal for the promotion and diffusion of new techniques. On the contrary, there seem to be considerable advantages in a diversity of firm sizes, no single firm size being optimal in this respect. Moreover, the optimal average size is likely to be directly related to the costliness and scope of the inventions that arise. However, in general, these factors do not make giantism necessary. To repeat, there is little evidence that industrial giants are needed in all or even most industries to promote rapid technological change and rapid utilization of new techniques.

15. The Patent System

Finally, we turn to the patent system, one of the major instruments of public policy regarding technology. The United States patent laws grant the inventor exclusive control over the use of his invention for 17 years. In this section, we describe the role played by patents in a free enterprise economy and some problems involved in the patent system. Needless to say, only a few aspects of the subject can be discussed in the available space.[19]

New technological knowledge differs from most other goods in an important way: It cannot be used up. A person or firm can use an idea repeatedly without wearing it out; and the same idea can serve many users at the same time. No one need be getting less of the idea because others are using it too. This property of knowledge creates an important problem for any firm that would like to make a business of producing knowledge. For an investment in research and development to be worth considering, a firm must be able to sell its results, directly or indirectly, for a price. But who would be willing to pay for a commodity that, once produced, becomes available to all in unlimited quantity? Why not let someone else pay for it, since then it would be available for nothing?

The patent laws are a way of handling this problem. They make it possible for firms to produce new knowledge and to sell or use it profitably. However, the patent system has the disadvantage that new knowledge is not used as widely as it should be, from the viewpoint of static efficiency. This is because the patent-holder, who attempts to make a profit, will set a price sufficiently high so that some people who could make productive use of the patented item will be discouraged from doing so. From the point of view of society, all people who can use the idea should be permitted to do so at a very low cost, since the marginal cost of their doing so is often practically zero. Another way of stating this is that the price of the information should, according to Chapter 15, be set equal to its marginal cost, which is often practically zero. But this, of course, would provide no incentive for invention.

A number of proposals have been made to alter the patent system so that this problem is met, one of the best-known being Michael Polanyi's suggestion that government grants, rather than patents, be awarded to inventors.[20]

---

[19]For a very thorough discussion, see F. Machlup, *An Economic Review of the Patent System*, Study 15 of the Senate Subcommittee on Patents, Trademarks, and Copyrights, 1958.
[20]M. Polanyi, "Patent Reform," *Review of Economic Studies*, Summer 1944.

Proposals for systems of prizes and bonuses to inventors are very old: for example, Alexander Hamilton favored such a system. From the point of view of welfare economics, Polanyi's suggestion has the advantage that there would be an optimal use of new knowledge (since it would be available without charge), as well as an incentive to produce new knowledge. However, this proposal has great practical disadvantages. The problem of selecting inventors and inventions to receive grants has limited the attention accorded this kind of scheme. It seems extremely unlikely that fundamental changes of this sort will be made.

16. Summary

Technology is society's pool of knowledge concerning the industrial arts. Technological change is the advance of technology, such advance often resulting in a change in the production function for an existing product or in a new product. Technological change can be labor-saving, capital-saving, or neutral. The rate of technological change is often measured by changes in total productivity indexes. The rate of technological change in an industry depends on the amount of resources devoted to the improvement of the industry's technology, which in turn depends in part on the rewards from particular kinds of technological change and on factors that determine their costs.

Research and development can be regarded as a process of uncertainty reduction, or learning. Chance plays a large role in research and development, and many projects use parallel efforts to help cope with uncertainty. The cost of a particular development project depends on the size and complexity of the product being developed; the extent of the advance in performance that is sought; the stock of basic knowledge, materials, and components; and the development time. An invention, when applied for the first time, is called an innovation. The rate of diffusion of an innovation depends on its profitability and the size of the required investment.

Schumpeter, Galbraith, and others have argued that, although a perfectly competitive economy will satisfy the conditions for static economic efficiency, it will not result in as high a rate of technological change and productivity increase as an imperfectly competitive economy. Although a certain amount of market imperfection may help to increase the rate of technological change and productivity increase, there is little evidence that giant firms are needed in all or even most industries to insure rapid technological change and rapid utilization of new techniques. One of the major instruments of public policy regarding technology is the patent system. Unfortunately, the patent system has the disadvantage that new knowledge is not used as widely as it should be, from the viewpoint of static efficiency. But no really practical alternative to the patent system has been proposed.

SELECTED REFERENCES

Schumpeter, Joseph, *Capitalism, Socialism, and Democracy*, New York: Harper and Row, 1947.

Mansfield, Edwin, *The Economics of Technological Change*, New York: Norton, 1968.

Mansfield, Edwin, *Industrial Research and Technological Innovation*, New York: Norton for the Cowles Foundation for Research in Economics at Yale University, 1968.

Marshak, Thomas, Thomas Glennan, and Robert Summers, *Strategy for R and D*, New York: Springer-Verlag, 1967.

Nelson, Richard, Merton Peck, and Edward Kalachek, *Technology, Economic Growth, and Public Policy*, Washington, D.C.: Brookings Institution, 1967.

Schmookler, Jacob, *Invention and Economic Growth*, Cambridge, Mass.: Harvard University Press, 1966.

Solow, Robert, "Technical Change and the Aggregate Production Function," *Review of Economics and Statistics*, 1957.

Index

Adams, W., 244, 281
Addison, W., 243
Agriculture
  government subsidy programs, 248–251
  price supports, 417–419
  prices and output, 245–248
Allen, R. G. D., 388, 391
Allocation process, short and long run, 239–240
Alternative cost doctrine, 156
Altman, Stuart, 349
Aluminum Company of America (Alcoa), 254, 280–282
American Record Company, 110
Antitrust laws, 6–7
Arrow, Kenneth, 357, 358, 387, 435–436
Arrow's impossibility theorem, 435–436
Average cost curve
  long run, 172–178
Average costs, 163–171
  geometry of, 169–171
Average fixed cost, 163
Average product of an input, 119
Average product of labor, 120–122
Average total cost, 166
Average variable cost, 165–166

Bain, J., 330
Barriers to entry, 326–328
Baseball (case study), 374–375
Basic research
  development and, 451–452

costs of, 455
  learning process, 451–453
  parallel efforts, 453–454
public policy and, 429–430
Bator, F., 402, 419
Baumol, William, 105, 116, 146, 201, 213, 317, 429
Bergson, Abram, 434–435
Bertrand, Joseph, 308
Bilateral monopoly, 270–272
  collective bargaining, 377–378
Brannan Plan, 249–250
Break-even chart, 171–172
Break-even point, 172
Bronfenbrenner, M., 344
Budget line, 33–35
  effect of change in income on, 34
Burmeister, E., 72

Capitalism (U.S.), 12–14
Capron, William, 357, 358
Cardinal utilities, 30–32
Cartels
  and collusion, 318–320
  instability of, 320–321
Carter, W., 311
Cassels, J., 297
Chamberlin, Edward, 286, 295–300, 309
Chamberlin model, 309–310
Charnes, A., 217, 414
Chenery, H., 394, 397
Clark, J. B., 462
Clark, P., 394, 397

469

Clower, R., 388
Coase, R., 429
Cobb-Douglas function, 357
Cobweb theorem, 240–242
Cohen, K., 17, 244, 281, 301
Colberg, M., 323
Collective bargaining
  bilateral monopoly, 377–378
  tactical considerations in, 380–381
Collective goods, 432–433
Collusion
  cartels and, 318–320
  in electrical equipment industry, 322–323
Columbia Broadcasting Company, 110
Commodity price, effects of changes in, 56–58
Computational efficiency, 414–415
Constant cost industries, 235–238
  increasing and decreasing, 236–238
Constant returns to scale, 137–139
Constraints, 201–203
Consumers, 20–78
  behavior and demand, 50–78
  equilibrium, 35–37, 50–51
  indifference map, 24
  tastes and preferences, 20–49
    determinants of, 40–41
    exchange between, 41–43
    nature of, 21–22
    summary of, 48–49
    welfare, 73–76
Consumer's surplus
  defined, 68
  Rand study and, 67–72
  solution, 69–72
Cooper, W., 217, 414
Cost functions, 148–185
  average and marginal, 163–171
    geometry of, 169–171
    in the long run, 172–178
  break-even chart, 171–172
  comparison of alternatives, 158–159
  explicit versus implicit, 157–158
  introduction to, 148–149
  measurement of, 178–184
  optimal input combinations, 148–156
  short run, 159–163
  social versus private, 157–158
  summary of, 184–185
Cost of living, defined, 72
Cost of living indexes, 72–73
Cost-plus pricing, 325–326
Cotton textile industry, 244–245
Cournot, Augustin, 305
Cournot model, 305–307

Cross elasticities of demand, 92–94
  defined, 93
  for estimated selected commodities, 106
Cyert, R., 17, 146, 244, 281, 301

Dantzig, George, 198, 415
Davidson, Ralph, 277
Davis, O., 430, 431
Dean, G., 242
Dean, Joel, 183, 184
Debreu, Gerard, 387
Decision-making in defense, 195–197
Decreasing returns to scale, 137–139
De Haven, J., 67
Demand curves, 50–113
  consumer, 50–78
  imperfect competition, 362–367
  individual, 50–78
  industry and firm, 99–111
  kinked, 311–312
  market, 79–113
  monopolistic competition, 287–288
  oligopoly, 311–312
  perfect competition, 99–101, 337–344
  pure monopoly, 255–256
Derived demand, 343
Differentiated oligopoly, defined, 305
Diminishing marginal returns, law of, 122–126
Dirlam, J., 323
Diseconomies, external economies and, 427–429
Dorfman, R., 210, 216, 317, 397
Douglas, Paul, 357
Dual problem (linear programming), 215–216
Due, J., 388
Dunlop, J., 380
Dupuit, J., 68

Economic efficiency, perfect competition and, 422–424
Economic planning, marginal cost pricing and, 424–426
Economic profits, 232
Economic progress, technological change and, 440–468
  static efficiency, 461–462
Economic region of production, 134–135
Economic resources, types of, 9
Economic systems
  tasks performed by, 10–12
  U.S. capitalism, 12–14
Edgeworth, F. Y., 308
Edgeworth box diagrams, 41–43
  resource allocation, 398–400

Edgeworth model, 308–309
Edison, Thomas, 452
Elasticity of substitution, 356–357
Engel, Christian, 92
Engel curves
  defined, 54
  income-consumption and, 53–56
  shapes of, 55
Engel's law, 92
Entrepreneurship, 334
Equilibrium
  cobweb theorem and, 240–242
  consumer, 35–37
    behavior and demand, 50–51
  monopolistic competition
    long run, 292–294
    short run, 289–291
  perfect competition
    long run, 230–234
    short run, 229–230
  pure monopoly
    long run, 262–264, 266
    short run, 258–261
  See also General equilibrium analysis
Excess capacity, monopolistic competition, 297–299
Exchange, process of
  general equilibrium analysis, 400–402
    and production, 406–408
Exchange, theory of, 44–48
Expected profit, defined, 115
External economies, diseconomies and, 427–429

Fechter, Alan, 349
Firm
  cost functions, 156–185
    long run, 172–178
    short run, 159–163
  demand curves, 99–111
  ideal output of, 297–299
  industrial concentration and
    technological change, 463–465
  optimal input combinations, 148–156
  profit maximization, 114–116
  scale of plant, 160
  short run supply curve, 226–227
  technology, 114–147
  total costs, 162–163
  total fixed costs, 160–161, 162–163
  total variable costs, 161–162
  variable inputs, 160
First degree discrimination, 276
Fisher, F., 329
Fissionable materials, 44–48
Fixed inputs

defined, 117
firm, 160
Fixed level of technology, 461–462
Forbush, D., 323

Galbraith, John Kenneth, 461–462, 464
Game theory, 313–318
  limitations of, 317–318
  mixed strategies, 315–317
General equilibrium analysis, 384–411
  defined, 386–387
  Edgeworth box diagram, 398–400
  exchange process, 400–402
  existence of, 386–387
    condition for, 387–389
  input-output analysis, 393-397
    applicability of, 397
    extension and application, 393–394
    model, 395–396
  introduction to, 384–385
  model, 388, 395–396
    equations of, 390–391
    existence of solution, 391–393
  nature of, 386-387
  partial equilibrium analysis and, 385–386
  product transformation, 404–405
    marginal rate of substitution, 408–409
  production function, 402–409
    and exchange, 406–408
  resource allocation, 398–399
  summary of, 410–411
Gies, T., 282
Grant, E., 158
Griliches, Z., 329

Hansen, H., 111
Harrod, R., 297, 445
Heady, E., 154, 242
Henderson, A., 414
Henderson, J., 64
Hicks, J., 31, 68, 94, 344
Hirsch, W., 459
Hirshleifer, J., 67, 72
Hitch, C., 197
Hotelling, Harold, 31, 425
Houthakker, H., 92
Human wants, defined, 8–9
  wants and resources, 8–9

Ideal output of a firm, 297–299
Imperfect competition
  demand curves, 362–367
    of several inputs, 372–374
    of a single input, 370–372

Imperfect competition (*Cont.*)
  labor unions and, 375–383
    bilateral monopoly, 377–378
    collective bargaining, 377–378, 380–
      381
    economic effects, 381–382
    union objectives, 378–380
  marginal expenditure curves, 368–369
  market demand curve, 366–367
  monopsony, 367–375
  price and employment of inputs, 361–
    383
    case study, 374–375
    in product market, 362
  profit maximization, 362
  supply curve, 368–369
  technological change and, 462–463
Income distribution
  elasticity of substitution, 356–357
  inequality and, 332–333
  interpersonal comparison of utility and,
    413–414
Income elasticity of demand, 90–92
  defined, 90
  estimated, 107
Increasing returns to scale, 137–139
Indexes, consumer welfare and, 72–76
Indifference curves, 22–26, 38–40
  characteristics of, 25–26
  convexity, 28
  intersections of, 25
  marginal rate of substitution, 26–27
  measurement of, 38–40
  revealed preference, 38–40
  utility, 28–32
Indifference maps, 24
Individual demand curves
  change in commodity price, 56–58
  consumer behavior and, 50–78
  consumer welfare, 73–76
  cost of living indexes, 72–73
  equilibrium, 50–51
  inferior goods, 65–66
  introduction to, 50
  location and shape, 59
  money income, 52–56
  New York City water crisis, 66–67
  normal goods, 65–66
  price elasticity, 59–63
  RAND study, 67–72
  substitution and income effects, 63–
    64
  summary of, 76–78
Inferior goods, 65–66
Innovations, 456–460
  diffusion of, 457–460

Input-output analysis
  applicability of, 397
  extension and application of, 393–394
  simple model of, 395–396
Inputs
  defined, 9
  imperfect competition and, 361–383
    case study, 374–375
    demand curves, 363–367
    labor unions and, 375–383
    marginal expenditure curves, 368–
      369
    market demand curve, 366–367
    price and employment, 361–383
    in product market, 362
    profit maximization, 362
    of several inputs, 372–374
    of a single input, 370–372
    supply curve, 368–369
  monopsony and, 370–375
  optimal combination of, 149–156
    in corn production, 154–156
    cost functions, 156–185
    isocost curves, 151–154
  perfect competition and, 332–360
    backward-bending case (market
      supply curve), 345–347
    demand curves, 337–347
    determination of price, 347–348
    distribution of income, 332–333,
      356–357
    elasticity of demand, 343–344
    elasticity of substitution, 356–357
    firm's demand curve (one variable
      input), 337–339
    firm's demand curve (several vari-
      able inputs), 339–340
    market demand curve, 341–342
    market supply curve, 344–347
    profit maximization, 334–337
    qualitative differences, 354–355
    quasi-rents, 352–353
    rent concept, 351–353
    shortage of scientists and engineers,
      357–359
    summary of, 359–360
    volunteer army, 348–350
    wage differentials, 355–356
  price and employment of, 332–383
  substitution among, 135–137
  technology and, 116–117
Ireson, W., 158
Irwin, Richard D., 388
Isocost curves, 151–154
Isoprofit curves, 205–207
  and feasible input combinations, 207

for selected profit levels, 206
Isoquants, 132–135, 203–205
  of fixed proportions, 134
  isocost curves, 151–154
Isorevenue line, 194–195

Jewkes, J., 464
John, J., 218
Johnson, Harry, 430
Johnson, Lyndon B., 348

Kaldor, Nicholas, 434
Kaplan, A., 323
Kaysen, Carl, 329, 430
Kelley, Augustus M., 380
Kendrick, J., 449
Kinked demand curve, 311–312
Klein, L., 104
Kuenne, Robert, 387

Labor unions, 375–383
  collective bargaining and
    bilateral monopoly, 377–378
    tactical considerations, 380–381
  economic effects of, 381–382
  and imperfect competition, 375–383
  objectives of, 378–380
Lancaster, K., 437
Lanzillotti, R., 281, 323
Laspeyres index, 73–74
Leontief, W., 393, 394
Lerner, A., 425
Limit pricing, 328
Lindahl, M., 311
Linear programming, 198–220
  constraints, 200, 201
  optimal production decisions
    comparison of solutions at extreme
      points, 214–215
    computational efficiency, 214–215
    dual problem and, 215–216
    in finishing of cotton cloth, 200–203
    isoprofit curves, 205–207
    isoquants, 203–205
    minimization of costs, 208–210
    in petroleum industry, 216–219
    in production of autos and trucks,
      210–214
    linear programming as technique,
      199–200
    shadow prices, 215–216
  processes, 199–200
  simplex method, 215
Lipsey, R., 437
Long run
  average cost, 173–174

shape of, 176–178
  and barriers to entry, 326–328
  cost functions, 172–178
  defined, 117–118
  marginal cost function, 172–178
  and returns to scale, 137–139
  total cost function, 175
Long-run equilibrium
  monopolistic competition, 292–294
  multiplant monopoly, 266
  perfectly competitive industry, 230–
    234
  pure monopoly, 262–264, 266

Machlup, F., 466
McKean, R., 197
McKenzie, Lionel, 387
McNair, M., 111
Manne, A., 217
Mansfield, E., 104, 146, 158, 322, 441,
  444, 460
March, J., 146
Marginal cost functions, 148–185
  geometry of, 169–171
Marginal cost pricing
  case study, 426–427
  economic planning and, 424–426
Marginal product
  of an input, 119
  of labor, 120–122
Marginal rate of substitution, 26–27
  defined, 26
  general equilibrium analysis, 408–409
Marginal rate of technical substitution,
  136–137
Marginal revenue curves, 95–99
  defined, 96
  determination of, 97–99
  elasticity of demand, 102–103
  sellers' side of market, 95–97
  quantity demanded, total revenue, and,
    95
Market demand curves, 79–113, 337–344
  business pricing problem, 110–111
  of commodities, 79–99, 106
  cross elasticities of, 92–94, 106
  derivation and elasticity, 80–84
  imperfect competition, 366–367
  income elasticity, 90–92
  industry and firm, 99–111
  marginal revenue, 95–99
    determination of, 97–99
    elasticity of demand, 102–103
    sellers' side of market, 95–97
  measurement of, 103–107
  perfect competition, 99–101, 337–344

Market demand curves (*Cont.*)
  price elasticity, 85–90
    determinants of, 88–90
    graphical measurement of, 85–87
    linear demand curve, 86
    marginal revenue, 102–103
    pricing strategy, 110–111
    and total money expenditures, 87–88
    sellers' side of, 95–97
    summary of, 111–113
    unitary elasticity at all points, 88
    urban transportation, 107–109
Market period, price determination in, 225–226
Market structure
  classifications of, 222–252
  monopolistic competition, 285–303
  oligopoly, 222–223, 304–331
  perfect competition, 222–252
  public policy concerning, 6–7
  pure monopoly, 253–254
Marris, R., 146
Marschak, T., 427
Marshall, A., 68
Mellon, B., 217
Microeconomics
  introduction to, 1–19
  price system and, 14–15
  problem-solving and, 2–7
    science, 7–8
  summary of, 18–19
Mill, John Stuart, 462
Milliman, J., 67, 72
Models, 15–18
  evaluation of, 16–18
  role of, 15–16
Money income, consumer and, 52–56
Monopolistic competition, 285–303
  compared to perfect competition and monopoly, 299–300
  criticism of theory, 300–301
  demand curves, 287–288
  excess capacity in, 297–299
  long run equilibrium, 292–294
  price and output, 285–303
  product differentiation, 286–287
  product variation, 294–295
  selling expenses, 295–297
  short run equilibrium, 289–291
  summary of, 302–303
Monopoly, pure, *see* Pure monopoly
Monopoly (game), 253
Monopsony, 367–375
  compared to monopoly, 367–368
  defined, 367
  input supply curves, 368–369

  marginal expenditure curves, 368–369
  occurrence of, 368
  price and employment of inputs, 370–375
    baseball (case study), 374–375
    of several, 373–374
    single, 370–372
Morgenstern, Oskar, 313
Multiplant monopoly, 264–268
  changes in demand and cost, 266–267
  long run equilibrium, 266
  marginal costs, 264

Natural monopolies, defined, 255
Nelson, J., 425
Nelson, R., 454
Nerlove, M., 243
Neumann, John von, 313
New York City subway system, 107–109
  demand schedule estimate (1952), 109
New York City water crisis, 66–67
Nonprice competition, 328–329
Normal goods, 65–66

Oi, W., 349
Oligopoly, 222–223, 304–331
  barriers to entry, 326–329
  cartels, 318–321
    collusion and, 318–320
    instability of, 320–321
  causes of, 304–305
  Chamberlin model, 309–310
  classification of, 304–305
  collusion, 318–320, 322–323
    cartels and, 318–320
    in electrical equipment industry, 322–323
  cost-plus pricing, 325–326
  Cournot model, 305–307
  defined, 304–305
  effects of, 329–330
  Edgeworth model, 308–309
  game theory, 313–318
    limitations of, 317–318
    mixed strategies, 315–317
  kinked demand curve, 311–312
  long run and, 326–328
  nonprice competition, 328–329
  price leadership, 323–325
  price and output, 304–331
  summary of, 330–331
  Sweezy model, 312
Opportunity cost doctrine, 156
Optimal combinations of inputs, 149–156
  in corn production, 154–156
  cost functions, 156–185

introduction to, 148–149
isocost curves, 151–154
Optimal production decisions, 186–220
example of, 2–3
linear programming, 198–220
  comparison of solutions at extreme
    points, 214–215
  computational efficiency, 214–215
  dual problem and, 215–216
  in finishing of cotton cloth, 200–203
  isoprofit curves, 205–207
  isoquants, 203–205
  minimization of costs, 208–210
  in petroleum industry, 216–219
  in production of autos and trucks,
    210–214
  production decisions as, 199–200
  shadow prices, 215–216
output of firm, 186–197
  choice of combinations, 192–195
  decision making in defense, 195–197
  multiproduct firms, 192–195
  price equals marginal cost, 190–192
  in short run, 187–189
summary of, 216–219
Optimal resource allocation
agricultural price supports, 417–419
marginal conditions for, 414–417
rules for, 5–6
Ordinal utilities, 28–30
Output level of firm, 186–197
choice of combinations, 192–195
decision making in defense, 195–197
multiproduct firms, 192–195
price equals marginal cost, 190–192
in short run, 187–189

Paasche index, 73–74
Pareto, Vilfredo, 393, 433
Partial equilibrium analysis
defined, 386
general equilibrium analysis and, 385–
  386
Patent system, 466–467
Perfect competition
agriculture, 245–251
  government subsidy programs, 248–
    251, 417–419
  allocation process (short and long run),
    239–240
  case study, 244–245
  cobweb theorem, 240–242
  compared to monopolistic competition,
    299–300
  compared to monopoly, 268–270

constant cost industries, 235–238
  increasing and decreasing, 236–238
defined, 223–225
demand curve, 99–101, 337–344
economic efficiency and, 422–424
equilibrium, 299–234
long run
  adjustment process, 230–233
  allocation process, 239–240
  equilibrium of firm, 233–234
price determination in market period,
  225–226
price and employment of inputs, 332–
  360
  backward-bending case (market sup-
    ply curve), 345–347
  demand curves, 337–344
  determination of price, 347–348
  distribution of income, 332–333,
    356–357
  elasticity of demand, 343–344
  elasticity of substitution, 356–357
  firm's demand curve (one variable
    input), 337–339
  firm's demand curve (several varia-
    ble inputs), 339–340
  market demand curve, 341–342
  market supply curve, 344–347
  profit maximization, 334–337
  shortage of scientists and engineers,
    357–359
  qualitative differences, 354–355
  quasi-rents, 352–353
  rent concept, 351–353
  summary of, 359–360
price and output, 222–252
requirements of, 223–225
resource allocation, 239–240
short run
  allocation process, 239–240
  equilibrium price, 229–230
  firm's supply curve, 226–227
  industry supply curve, 227–229
supply curves
  backward-bending case, 345–347
  estimates of elasticity, 242–244
  market supply, 344–347
  in short run, 226–229
volunteer army, 348–350
wage differentials, 355–356
Pigou, A. C., 275
Polanyi, M., 466
Pollak, R., 72
Price-consumption curves, 57
  total expenditure, price elasticity and,
    61–63

Price, inputs and market period
employment of an input and, 347–348
in market period, 225–226
Price discrimination, monopoly, 272–278
and existence of industry, 277–278
third degree, 272–275
types of, 272–277
Price elasticity of demand, 59–64
estimated (for selected commodities),
106
for an input, 343–344
market demand
determinants of, 88–90
graphical measurement of, 85–87
linear demand curve, 86
marginal revenue, 102–103
pricing strategy, 110–111
total money expenditures, 87–88
price-consumption curve, 61–63
in pricing strategy, 110–111
total expenditure, 61–63
unitary elasticity, 60
Price and employment of inputs, 332–383
imperfect competition, 361–383
monopsony, 370–375
perfect competition, 332–360
Price equals marginal cost, 190–192
Price leadership, oligopoly, 323–325
Price and output
agriculture, 245–248
monopolistic competition, 285–303
oligopoly, 304–331
perfect competition, 222–252
pure monopoly, 253–254
Price supports (agriculture), 417–419
Price system, microeconomics and, 14–15
Pricing policy, 3–5
Problem-solving, microeconomics and, 7–
8
Processes (linear programming), 199–200
Product differentiation, 286–287
Product group, defined, 287
Product transformation curves, 193, 404–
405
defense example, 196–197
marginal rate of, 193, 408–409
Product variation, 294–295
Production function
concepts of, 118–122
general equilibrium analysis, 402–409
and exchange, 406–408
isoquants, 132–135
law of diminishing returns, 122–126
long run and returns to scale, 137–139
measurement of, 140–142
models of firm behavior, 144–147

stages of, 126–129
substitution among inputs, 135–137
summary of, 143–144
of two variable inputs, 129–132
Productivity growth, 448–450
Profit maximization
assumption of, 114–116
firm output levels, 186–197
input employment and
imperfect competition, 362
perfect competition, 334–337
Public goods, 432–433
Public policy, basic research and, 429–
430
Purdy, H., 310
Pure monopoly
bilateral, 270–272
case studies, 280–283
compared to monopolistic competition,
299–300
compared to perfect competition, 268–
270
defined, 253–254, 305
demand curve, 255–256
difference between monopsony and,
367–368
long run equilibrium, 262–264, 266
marginal costs, 257, 264
multiplant, 264–268
changes in demand and cost, 266,
268
long run equilibrium, 266
marginal costs, 264
price discrimination, 272–278
and existence of industry, 277–278
types of, 275–277
price and output, 253–284
relationship between, 261–262
public regulation of, 278–280
reason for, 254–255
short-run equilibrium, 258–261
summary of, 283–284

Quandt, R., 64
Quasi-rents, 352–353
Quirk, J., 387, 391

Rand study
consumer's surplus and, 67–72
solution, 69–72
Rational consumers, 32–33
Rent, concept of, 351–353
Resources, 8–9
Returns to scale, 137–139
Revealed preference, theory of, 38–40

Reynolds, Lloyd, 244
Robinson, J., 286, 445
Rothenberg, J., 435
Rottenberg, S., 374
Ruggles, N., 425

Samuelson, P., 31, 63, 216, 317, 340, 341
Saposnik, R., 387, 391
Sawers, R., 464
Scale of plant, 160
Schultz, H., 106
Schumpeter, Joseph, 461, 462
Scientists and engineers, shortages of, 357–359
Scitovsky, Tibor, 434
Second best, theory of, 437
Second-degree price discrimination, 276–277
Selling expenses, monopolistic competition, 295–297
Shadow prices, 215–216
Shepherd, W. G., 282
Sherman Act of 1890, 6
Short run
    cost functions, 159–163
    defined, 117–118
Short run equilibrium
    monopolistic competition, 289–291
    perfect competition, 229–230
    pure monopoly, 258–261
Shubik, M., 317
Siegelman, L., 106
Simon, Herbert, 145
Simplex method, 215
Social welfare function, 419–422
Solow, R., 216, 317, 449
Spellman, R., 218
Spencer, M., 106
Sraffa, Piero, 285–286
Static efficiency, economic progress and, 461–462
Steel Workers Union, 375
Stigler, George, 67, 157, 268, 300, 301, 312, 418, 429
Stillerman, R., 464
Substitution among inputs, 135–137
Supply curves
    backward-bending case, 345–347
    elasticity of, 242–244
    imperfect competition, 368–369
    monopsony, 368–369
    perfect competition, 226–229, 242–244, 344–347
Sweezy, P., 311
Sweezy model, 312

Teamsters Union, 375
Technological change
    classifications of, 445–447
    determinants of rate of, 450–451
    development, 451–455
        costs of, 455
        learning process, 451–453
        parallel efforts, 453–454
        research and, 451–453
    economic progress and, 440–468
        static efficiency, 461–462
    giant corporation and, 463–465
    imperfect competition and, 462–463
    industrial concentration, 463–465
    innovations, 456–460
        diffusion of, 457–460
    introduction to, 440–441
    measurement of, 448–450
    patent system, 466–467
    productivity growth, 448–450
    summary of, 467–468
    technique, 442–444
Technology
    defined, 10
    firm and, 114–147
    inputs, 116–117
Telser, L., 329
Third-degree price discrimination, 272–275
Tinbergen, Jan, 242
Total costs, 160–163
Total output, 119
Total revenue, 95
Total variable costs, 161–162
Traywick, D., 244

Unions, *see* Labor unions
Unitary elasticity, 61
    market demand curves, 88
United Automobile Workers Union, 375
U.S. Department of Defense, 195–196, 349
Urban renewal, 430–432
Utility, theory of, 28–32
Utility-possibility curve, 419–422

Value of marginal product, defined, 337
Variable inputs
    defined, 117
    firm, 160
    production function, 129–132
Verhulst, M., 143
Vickrey, William, 107–109
Villard, H., 461
Volunteer army, cost of, 348–350

Wage differentials, 355–356
Wagner Act, 375
Walras, Leon, 393
Walters, A. A., 141, 142, 181, 182, 184
Watson, D., 159, 358, 374
Wein, H., 146
Welfare economics, 412–439
  Arrow's impossibility theorem, 435–436
  change and improvement, 433–436
  economic planning, 424–425
  external economies and diseconomies, 427–429
  increasing returns and, 432–433
  interpersonal comparison of utility, 413–414
  introduction to, 412–413
  marginal cost pricing, 424–427
    case study, 426–427

  optimal resource allocation, 414–419
    agricultural price supports, 417–419
    marginal conditions for, 414–417
  perfect competition and economic efficiency, 422–424
  public goods, 432–433
  public policy toward basic research, 429–430
  social welfare function, 419–422
  summary of, 438–439
  theory of second best, 437
  urban renewal, 430–432
  utility-possibility curve, 419–422
Wheeler, J., 281
Whinston, A., 430–431
Whitaker, G., 323
Wold, H., 107